The Politics of Gay Marriage in Latin America

Addressing one of the defining social issues of our time, *The Politics of Gay Marriage in Latin America* explores how and why Latin America, a culturally Catholic and historically conservative region, has become a leader among nations of the Global South, and even the Global North, in the passage of gay marriage legislation. In the first comparative study of its kind, Jordi Díez explains cross-national variation in the enactment of gay marriage in three countries: Argentina, Chile, and Mexico. Based on extensive interviews in the three countries, Díez argues that three main key factors explain variation in policy outcomes across these cases: the strength of social movement networks forged by activists in favor of gay marriage; the access to policy making afforded by particular national political institutions; and the resonance of the frames used to demand the expansion of marriage rights to same-sex couples.

Jordi Díez is Associate Professor of Political Science at the University of Guelph. The author or editor of four previous books, he has also published numerous journal articles on social movements and public policy. A recipient of several research awards from organizations including the Social Sciences and Humanities Research Council (SSHRC) and the International Development Research Council (IDRC), both of Canada, he has taught at several universities in the Americas and Europe. He held the 2014–15 Peggy Rockefeller Visiting Scholarship at Harvard University.

To my mother

The Politics of Gay Marriage in Latin America

Argentina, Chile, and Mexico

JORDI DÍEZ

University of Guelph, Ontario

CAMBRIDGE
UNIVERSITY PRESS

CAMBRIDGE
UNIVERSITY PRESS

32 Avenue of the Americas, New York NY 10013-2473, USA

Cambridge University Press is part of the University of Cambridge.

It furthers the University's mission by disseminating knowledge in the pursuit of
education, learning and research at the highest international levels of excellence.

www.cambridge.org
Information on this title: www.cambridge.org/9781107491854

First published 2015
First paperback edition 2016

A catalogue record for this publication is available from the British Library

Library of Congress Cataloguing in Publication data
Díez, Jordi.
The politics of gay marriage in Latin America : Argentina, Chile, and
Mexico / Jordi Díez.
pages   cm
Includes bibliographical references and index.
ISBN 978-1-107-09914-2 (hardback)
1. Same-sex marriage – Latin America.   2. Gay rights – Latin America.   I. Title.
HQ1034.L29D54   2015
306.84´8098–dc23   2014043434

ISBN 978-1-107-09914-2 Hardback
ISBN 978-1-107-49185-4 Paperback

Contents

Acknowledgments

Undertaking, and completing, a project of this magnitude is a collective enterprise, and I wish to thank the numerous institutions and individuals that have been part of this great journey.

First and foremost, I thank Canada's Social Sciences and Humanities Research Council for its generous multiyear financial support. This book would quite simply not exist without it. The council's continued commitment to funding open research in the social sciences at a time of shrinking budgets is to be applauded. I am most grateful to friends and colleagues who helped at various stages of the process, from original brainstorming to its final stages. I extend a very special recognition to Janine Clark and Susan Franceschet for their indefatigable warm support throughout the entire process. I thank Javier Corrales, James Green, David Rayside, Miriam Smith, and Lavinia Stan for the generosity with which they always, and so very promptly, extended advice over the years. Julie Simmons's insights were most useful in the original stages. A note of thanks is due to Byron Sheldrick, Chair of the Political Science Department at the University of Guelph, for having been willing to rearrange my teaching schedule so that I could get away from the classroom to carry out field research. I thank the numerous people who read parts of the manuscript and who provided me with invaluable feedback: Merike Blofield, Carlos Figari, Susan Franceschet, Josh Fullan, Macarena Gómez-Barris, Katherine Isbester, Candace Johnson, Juan Pereira Marsiaj, David Paternotte, and Tony Smith. I hope that I have done fairness to their suggestions as I revised the manuscript. Several colleagues shared insight into specific aspects of sexual politics in Latin America: Pablo Ben, Guillermo de los Reyes, Joaquín Insuasti,

Daniel Jones, and Rodrigo Parrini. Three anonymous referees gave me
the most thorough external reviews I have received on my work. Pamela
Starr, at the University of Southern California, and Sergio Rivera Ayala,
at the University of Waterloo, provided me opportunities to present my
arguments at public talks at their institutions. I benefited greatly from
the truly fantastic work of several research assistants during my fieldwork: Javier Marmolejo and Andrea Meraz in Mexico City, Martín Boy
in Buenos Aires, and Ricardo Lifschitz in Santiago. Working with them
has led to prized friendships. Talented students in Guelph include: Jody
Brown, Olenka Iwanicki, and Martín Waldman, for their committed assistance. My fieldwork was made much easier by the institutional support
I received: Ana María Tepichin at the El Colegio de México's Programa
Interdisciplinario de Estudios de la Mujer, and Rossana Castiglioni at the
Universidad Diego Portales's Escuela de Estudios Políticos invited me as
visiting scholar during my time in Mexico City and Santiago, which gave
me much-needed infrastructural, administrative, and personal support.
I am eternally grateful to the numerous activists and government officials
who generously shared with me their time to help me make sense of the
rather complex world of policy making.

I have benefited enormously from the conversations I have had over
the years on Latin American politics and society, often in situ, with many
great friends: David Altman, Rachel Brickner, Ernesto Calvo, Rossana
Castiglioni, Susan Franceschet, Chile's funkiest, Robert Funk, Mario
González, Beatriz Hernández, Mala Htun, Mary Rose Kubal, James
Loxton, Alejandro Modarelli, Mario Pecheny, Jennifer Piscopo, Paulo
Ravecca, Reyes Rodríguez, Horacio Sívori, Catalina Smulovitz, Vicente
Ugalde, and Jill Wigle.

Very warm thanks must go to David Mares at the Center for Iberian
and Latin American Studies (University of California, San Diego) and
Don Ainslie at University College (University of Toronto) for the office
space to write. The Mark S. Bonham Centre for Sexual Diversity Studies
at the University of Toronto, where I am a Fellow, has offered me a space
rich in support and constant intellectual stimulation over the years. At
Cambridge University Press I thank Eric Crahan for his initial interest in
the project as well as my most esteemed editor, Deborah Gershenowitz,
for her professionalism, genuineness, personal warmth, and keen interest
in this project. It is a true delight to work with her.

My family and friends have been indispensable on numerous levels.
The support of the Díez families in Canada and the United States and
of my dear friends Ben Barkworth, Jeffrey Buttle, Janine Clark, Susan

Franceschet, Josh Fullan, Anthony Iacolucci, Delphine Lacombe, Kerry Preibisch, and Adam Sloboda, has been essential. Francisco Cos-Montiel and Antonio Torres-Ruiz encouraged me, by example, to devote energies to topics with real-life implications. Scott Rayter has constantly reminded me, rather inimitably, that the personal is political and to act accordingly.

Finally, I thank my husband, soul mate, and best friend Mathieu Maslard. This book is as much his as it is mine. He unfailingly supported me while I was away for months-on-end conducting research (at times during some very trying moments), discussed with me endless theoretical and practical issues related to the project, and read tirelessly *every* revised version of *every* chapter. Your love is what makes it possible for me to aim higher all the time.

I dedicate this book to my mother, Rosa María Méndez, for if every Latin American parent were like her, the struggles for sexual justice that I analyze in this book would likely not be necessary.

Introduction

Overturning an appellate-court decision, on May 31, 2004, Chile's Supreme Court stripped Karen Atala of the custody of her daughters. The Court argued that the daughters were in a "situation of risk" by living with their lesbian mother because it exposed them to potential social discrimination and ostracism, placing them in a "vulnerable position" in their social environment. According to the majority ruling, such a situation would affect the children's personal development. Atala, a respected jurist, availed herself of *amicus curiae* briefs, obtained support from national and international human rights organizations, and took her case to the Inter-American Human Rights Commission. In 2008 the Commission decided that the case was admissible to the Inter-American Court of Human Rights. In a historic 2010 ruling, the Court stated that the Chilean state had violated Atala's right to live free of discrimination as stipulated in the American Convention of Human Rights. It also urged the Chilean state to adopt legislation, policies, and programs to prohibit and eradicate discrimination based on sexual orientation. The ruling was a significant personal triumph for Atala's seven-year legal battle to regain custody of her daughters. It was also historic because it was the first time discrimination based on sexual orientation was considered to be a suspect classification and hence to contravene basic human rights enshrined in Inter-American treaties. But, more broadly, the recommendation amounted to an indictment of Chile's record in establishing a legal framework to prevent and eradicate discrimination based on sexual orientation. A country often used by many as the socioeconomic model of development that Latin Americans should emulate found itself exposed internationally for its failure, twenty years after the end of a brutal dictatorship that had committed gross human rights atrocities, to extend basic rights protections to one of the most vulnerable sectors of its society.

Across the Andes another important struggle for sexual rights came to an end in the same year. Following the submission of a judicial appeal by Alex Freyre and José María di Bello to the denial of their marriage license application, in November 2009 a Buenos Aires judge handed down a historic ruling arguing that the definition of marriage in Argentina's civil code was unconstitutional and ordered the city's administrators to issue the couple a marriage license. Despite the surprising decision by the city's right-wing mayor not to appeal the ruling, on the eve of their wedding scheduled for December 1, another judge issued an injunction ordering the city's administration not to issue the marriage certificate on grounds that the previous judge did not have competency to rule in that area. Their marriage was thus annulled. Flanked by gay and lesbian activists and numerous prominent politicians, the couple gave a highly emotional news conference as their right to marry had been taken away hours before the ceremony. Freyre and di Bello vowed to fight on and were seemingly destined to make history: the socially progressive governor of Tierra del Fuego Province decided to intervene and ordered her province's Civil Registry's Office to honor the first ruling. On December 28, 2009, the couple finally wed in the Western Hemisphere's southernmost city, Ushuaia, making them the first same-sex couple in Latin America to have contracted marriage. This legal victory was part of a larger struggle waged by gay and lesbian activists in Argentina to expand the traditional definition of marriage. Their struggle culminated with reforms to the civil code approved by the Argentine Congress in 2010 and promulgated into law by President Cristina Fernández de Kirchner that expanded the right to marriage nationally to same-sex couples. Argentina thus became the first country in Latin America, second in the Global South, and tenth in the world, in which this right was extended to its entire citizenry.

Mexico also witnessed a significant culmination in the struggle for the expansion of sexual minority rights in 2010. After intense collaboration between gay and lesbian activists and socially liberal city councilors, and despite stern public opposition from the Catholic Church and other conservative actors, Mexico City's Assembly approved, on December 21, 2009, reforms to the city's civil code allowing for same-sex marriage. The city's socially progressive mayor, Marcelo Ebrard, had been an open advocate of sexual minority rights and supported the reforms. He promulgated them into law and the new civil code came into effect on March 2, 2010. Gay and lesbian activists' elation for having won this battle was tempered, however: the federal government, headed by conservative president Felipe Calderón (2006–12), decided to challenge the constitutionality of the reforms before the Supreme Court. Calderón's decision was not surprising as he had taken the same course of action when legislation decriminalizing abortion was passed by the city three years earlier. The Supreme Court did not agree with Calderón's challenge and upheld the constitutionality of Mexico City's marriage laws. It subsequently ruled that marriages performed in the city are valid throughout the country. Indirectly, gay marriage was extended to all Mexicans provided that they contract marriage in the capital city.

The three developments elicit intriguing policy puzzles. Why did Argentina and Mexico adopt marriage when they did? Why did Argentina do so at the national level while Mexico first expanded such a right at the subnational level? Why does Chile appear to be a laggard in the expansion of rights to sexual minorities? The country has not adopted gay marriage, and it enacted its first antidiscrimination legislation only in 2012, pushed largely by the popular outrage caused by the death of a gay teen who was attacked and tortured by extremists in central Santiago. Why, in more general terms, do there appear to be different trajectories and outcomes in the expansion of rights to sexual minorities in the three countries? While not representative of the entire region, the three cases capture some of the variance that exists in the expansion of sexual minority rights across Latin America. Indeed, a characteristic of the region's recent "gay-rights revolution" (Encarnación 2011) is wide cross-national variance: while some countries have extended gay and lesbian rights, others have not, and yet others have in fact retrenched them.[1] The main objective of this book is to account for such variation by focusing on one policy area: gay marriage. The pursuit of this explanation fills an

---

[1] In terms of same-sex relationship recognition, by mid-2014 Argentina, Uruguay, and, in Mexico, Mexico City and Quintana Roo, were the only jurisdictions to allow gay marriage, and, through judicial rulings (detailed in Chapter 5), couples in the states of Oaxaca, Chihuahua, Guanajuato, Nayarit, and Jalisco were granted the right to marry. A ruling by a Brazilian high court in 2012 extended all the rights accorded to traditional marriages to same-sex couples, thereby allowing for gay-marriage benefits through an administrative route. In Colombia, a legal vacuum was created by the failure of Congress to abide by a Constitutional-Court ruling that challenged the definition of marriage and urged Members of Congress to legislate on the matter. Same-sex unions have been legalized in Uruguay, Colombia, and Ecuador, and in several Argentinean, Mexican, and Brazilian subnational jurisdictions, while Honduras, El Salvador, and the Dominican Republic have constitutionally banned same-sex marriage.

important gap in our knowledge of the politics of sexual minority rights in Latin America in general and of gay marriage in particular. Important work has recently been produced on this understudied topic (de la Dehesa 2010; Encarnación 2011; Marsiaj 2006; Pecheny, Figari, and Jones 2008; Torres-Ruiz 2011). Some scholars have sought to explain policy outcomes in gay rights[2] (Marsiaj 2012; Pierceson, Piatti-Crocker, and Schulenberg 2010) while others have specifically analyzed the recognition of gay marriage in Mexico and Argentina (Andía 2013; Ballina 2013; Clerico and Aldao 2010; Corrales and Pecheny 2010; Friedman 2012; Lozano 2013; Maffre 2014; Schulenberg 2012). Yet, no work has been produced that explains cross-national policy variation in gay marriage recognition in Latin America.[3] It also contributes to the debate on current explanations for the variation in same-sex marriage outside the region. Since the first country (The Netherlands) approved gay marriage (in 2001), several political scientists have attempted to identify the factors that are behind its enactment. Most of this work, however, is based on case studies (Calvo 2007; Larocque 2006; Matthews 2005; Mucciaroni 2008; Pettinicchio 2010). While they provide important insights into the legalization of gay marriage, they have limitations for they are unable to generalize beyond single cases. Some political scientists have taken an explicitly comparative approach (Kollman 2013; Paternotte 2011; Rayside 2008; Smith 2008). This work has made important contributions to the debate because they allow us to reach midrange generalizations. However, their findings can be enriched with research on countries in the Global South given that, until now, these studies have been limited to industrialized democracies.

In order to explain cross-national policy variance I have selected three cases that show variation in gay marriage recognition: Argentina, Mexico, and Chile. Gay marriage has been approved in Argentina and Mexico but not in Chile. Chile is therefore the noncase in my comparison. Using John Stuart Mill's "method of difference,"[4] the three cases allow me to explore and identify the factors that explain policy variance across countries that

---

[2] In this book I use the terms *gay* and *gay and lesbian* rights interchangeably for, among most activists and academics who work on the issue of gay marriage (the policy under study in this book), the term *gay* encompasses all homosexuals regardless of gender.

[3] Perceson, Piatti-Crocker, and Schulenberg's edited volume includes two essays on gay marriage in Argentina and Mexico, but it is not a comparative study (2012).

[4] The method consists of comparing one or more "positive" cases in which the phenomenon under study is present with another case or cases in which it is not, among cases that share important general similarities (Mill 1974).

share several important characteristics, such as levels of urbanization, education, and industrialization. I therefore control for several variables. I have selected gay marriage not only because it is understudied by political scientists, but also because it is an area of moral policy[5] reform in Latin America that has become one of the most dynamic in recent years, given the significant changes that have taken place in a very short period of time. The selection is also influenced by Theda Skocpol's view that the aim of social science research is to understand and explain real-world puzzles (2003). It is at the same time inspired by some theoretical discussions on the nature of democracy that the expansion of gay rights has inevitably ignited (Bell and Binnie 2000; Cossman 2007; Eribon 1999; Kaplan 1997; Plummer 2003). For some of these theorists, gays and lesbians attain full democratic citizenship when they are able to secure not only negative rights – such as the decriminalization of homosexual activities between consenting adults and the prohibition of discrimination based on sexual orientation – but also when they are able to wrest from the state the legal and social recognition of the ethical status of gay and lesbian relationships (Kaplan 1997). As discussions on the quality of democracy in Latin America continue, questions regarding the limits of citizenship are of increased relevance (Hagopian 2007; Yashar 2005). While there is, of course, no agreement over what democracy entails, demands for the recognition of same-sex relationships by the state, as Éric Fassin argues (2008), inevitably force a debate on what democracy and citizenship entail. The Latin American gay activists at the center of these struggles, and their allies, are pushing the boundaries of democracy and citizenship. That, on its own, warrants scholarly attention.

Explaining Policy Variance: The Argument

What accounts for policy variance in the expansion of gay marriage in the three countries? In this book I answer this question by presenting

[5] I use the terms *moral politics/policy* to refer to the political science literature that explores, broadly, sexual and reproductive rights and family law. Some scholars have argued that moral policy (gay marriage, abortion, capital punishment, prostitution, pornography, etc.) constitutes a distinctive policy type because it entails the regulation of conflicts among social values (Meier 1994, 1999; Mooney 1999). However, most of this work was theorized based on the U.S. experience where the "culture wars" have indelibly marked politics over the last three decades. Recent research suggests that such a clear distinction does not apply elsewhere. In some countries (e.g., Denmark and the United Kingdom) they are often considered nonpolitical, "ethical" issues given the composition of their party systems (Engeli, Green-Pedersen, and Larsen 2012).

research data gathered over a period of five years.[6] The research I present in this book suggests that policy variance is largely explained by a combination of three variables: 1) the ability and willingness of activists to form coalitions and networks with a variety of state and nonstate actors; 2) the type of access to the policy-making process that is conditioned by a country's institutional features; and 3) the framing of demands in a manner that resonates with larger social debates. I argue that policy change is the result of decades-long struggles to expand citizenship rights waged by numerous activists *and* allies. In the two cases in which we have seen policy change, Argentina and Mexico, activism has been characterized by higher degrees of organization, coalition building, and the development of more effective framing strategies in the pursuit of policy reform. This is then a story about the perseverance and acumen of individuals to create more equal societies by expanding rights to marginalized sectors of their societies. But agency is not enough to explain policy variance. Structures matter, and activism must be placed within its structural context. I argue that the institutional framework of each country has conditioned the type of access to the policy process that proponents and opponents of gay and lesbian rights have had. Institutions are therefore a central part of the story. Policy change has occurred in the countries in which political institutions allow meaningful access to proponents of gay and lesbian rights and over which opponents do not have formal or informal veto power to block activists' demands. However, equally important are the broader political environments in which activisms have evolved and institutions have been established, and access to the policy process is not enough to explain policy variance. Policy change has been induced when gay and lesbian activists and allies craft their demands in a manner that resonates with society at large and that convinces decision makers of the justness of their cause. Larger processes of democratization are crucial in these developments. The *type* of transition to democracy a country has undergone has conditioned the degree of political contestation that allows for

---

[6] The research data were obtained through 246 in-depth personal interviews with activists and government officials in the three countries, carried out over a period of nineteen nonconsecutive months between May 2007 and August 2012. It also comprised archival research and numerous formal and informal meetings with activists and government officials in the three countries. Funding for this research was provided by Canada's Social Sciences and Humanities Research Council. In accordance with ethics guidelines mandated by the Government of Canada, informants were given the option to remain anonymous. Accordingly, the names of participants appear only in those cases in which they formally agreed to have their names published. Descriptive, nonidentifying terms are otherwise used.

a renegotiation of the terms of citizenship rights. In the following sections I detail how these three variables – gay and lesbian mobilization, access to the policy process, and the framing of demands – play out in accounting for policy variance among the three cases.

Public Policy, Social Movements, and Networks

The vast literature on public policy offers numerous explanations for policy change. Scholars have argued that policy processes are rather complex and that policy change can come from a variety of sources (Stone 2001). One of those sources is social mobilization. Policy scholars have traditionally ignored the relationship between social movements and the policy-making process (Meyer 2005, 6–7). However, recent literature has looked at the interaction between social movements and the state (Banaszak, Beckwith, and Rucht 2003; Franceschet 2005) as well as how they are able to influence the shaping of policy beyond placing issues on public agendas (Díez 2006, 2013; Johnson, Agnone, and McCarthy 2010; Lupien 2011; Weldon 2012). In terms of moral policy reform, recent scholarship shows, rather conclusively, that social movements do indeed influence policy change. In the most comprehensive cross-national study of moral policy reform, Mala Htun and Laurel Weldon (2012) demonstrate – looking at seventy countries over a period of thirty years – that feminist mobilization in civil society accounts for variation in policy development in the area of violence against women. In the case of Latin America, scholars have become increasingly interested in the impact nonstate actors have on policy. As the posttransitional politics began to stabilize in many countries of the region – and questions of military reversals faded – some scholars began to look at the interaction between nonstate actors and governments and especially at the extent to which social mobilization was influencing policy making in the new democracies. This question assumed particular importance at the turn of the century given the highly exclusionary styles that characterized many policy-making processes during the 1990s (Centeno and Silva 1998; Teichman 2001). Because of the negative effects this was having on the vibrancy of the new democracies, such as widespread public cynicism, calls for more open and participatory policy-making practices were made in what was termed "second-generation reforms" (Molyneux 2008). There has been, as a result, increased scholarly interest in the extent to which civil society actors and organizations have been able to influence public policy within the new democratic context (Boesten 2006; Díez 2006; Garay 2007).

Results from this research point to a rather sketchy picture (Franceschet and Díez 2012). Some work suggests that there has been an increased ability of various sectors of society to gain access to decision and policy making. However, the stark socioeconomic inequalities for which the region is notorious pose veritable challenges to the ability of excluded sectors to organize and influence policy. Moreover, in many countries in the region, the close links created between the political and economic élites have continued to allow for the direct access into the policy process by the most powerful groups, access that in certain cases has become institutionalized. There has therefore been an unequal access to the process by society with an inordinate influence by economic élites. However, despite these challenges, scholarship on Latin America has also underlined the critical role social movements play in bringing about policy change in areas that tend not to be priorities for governments. Whether it is indigenous people's or women's rights, or environmental protection, political scientists have demonstrated that social movements have gone beyond the placement of demands on national agendas and that they have been able to shape policy (Díez 2006; Franceschet 2005; Lupien 2011). In the area of gay and lesbian rights, recent scholarly work has produced similar findings: gay and lesbian mobilization has been critical in bringing about policy change (Díez 2010, 2013; Encarnación 2013; Marsiaj 2012; Schulenberg 2012).

Nevertheless, the impact social movements have on policy is often difficult to determine. In Latin America, individuals who belong to social movements or nongovernmental organizations (NGOs) have increasingly been recruited into government while maintaining strong relationships with civil society organizations. This is especially the case with the region's recent shift to the left. Many of the social democratic parties that have been elected into government emerged from grassroots mobilization and have strong links with civil society actors (Díez 2010). Because in many cases they have recruited civil society individuals to government positions, the line between state and nonstate actors has consequently become blurred. Moreover, while activists belonging to social movements play pivotal roles in pursuing, and attaining, policy objectives, their efforts are very often accompanied by individuals, or "allies," who do not form part of these movements but who nonetheless play critical roles in bringing about policy change. The employment of "social movement" as a concept that refers to nonstate actors is consequently rendered of limited use. As a result, concepts used by political scientists interested in the study of public policy in Latin America such as "policy networks"

(Kubal 2012), "issue networks" (Htun 2003b), or quite simply individuals' "networks" (Hochstetler and Keck 2007) in explanations of policy outcomes seem more useful, which is demonstrated by their increased use in analyses of policy making (Torres-Ruiz 2011; Vargas Paredes 2010).

In this book, I use the broad concept of networks to account for policy change. My use of the term *network* derives from the concept of "issue network" first developed by Hugh Heclo to describe specialized subcultures of highly knowledgeable policy watchers (1978). It refers to a multiplicity of state and nonstate actors, NGOs, and professional associations that collectively pursue shared policy objectives. But my use of the term *networks* differs from Heclo's conceptualization, and its use by some scholars, in the role activists play in building, sustaining, and relying on these networks in their struggles to bring about policy change. In her groundbreaking work on gender policy reform in Latin America, Htun uses Heclo's idea of issue networks in her analysis to capture "the range of actors and interests who have contributed to gender-related reform in Latin America" (2003b, 15). However, for Htun, social movements do not play a central role in forming these networks: she argues that social movements may or may not influence them and that what links issue networks is an interest in a particular policy area and not traits such as ideological orientation or identity (2003b, 15). Such networks are decidedly different from the ones I identify in this book and that are largely behind policy change in the area of gay and lesbian rights. As we shall see, gay and lesbian mobilization has been central in the formation and sustainability of networks, and identity and ideological compatibility appear to play a central role in linking myriad state and nonstate actors. As I argue, the formation of networks is the result of the efforts made by gay and lesbian activists. They have been created over periods of time by members of gay and lesbian movements who have formed alliances with a variety of individuals with whom they share identity traits or ideological values and are characterized by a certain degree of volatility. These networks are key in explaining the expansion of rights in the countries analyzed here. Indeed, the central argument in this volume is that *policy change is induced by gay and lesbian activists who form extensive and influential networks of like-minded state and non-state actors, which in turn develop strategies and policy frames that convince policy makers and important sectors of society of their cause.* In the two countries in which there has been policy change, Argentina and Mexico, networks were determinant. The ability of gay and lesbian activists to weave alliances of state and nonstate actors to pressure governments to adopt their policy objectives has been key. The same has not taken place in Chile. Even though networks have been formed, they are weak, and their weakness is largely a function of the weakness the gay and lesbian movement in Chile has exhibited since the return of democratic rule in 1990. Indeed, the strength of networks is largely conditioned by its embeddedness within the larger gay and lesbian movement from which it is sustained, and such strength explains policy variance.

In this study I take a historical approach to the study of policy and show the importance of looking at the policy reform trajectories of each country. Because policy change in gay marriage recognition has been prompted by networks, it is important to look at their formation and evolution over periods of time. Work on gay rights points to perceived trends in their expansion, or "policy histories," where countries generally begin by decriminalizing homosexuality, followed by the adoption of human rights policy in the form of antidiscrimination provisions and culminating in gay marriage (Adam 2003). The idea of a policy history has been criticized for it is argued that policy reform in gay rights is not linear (Paternotte 2011). While that may be the case, there is no question that, as I show in the pages that follow, early experiences in policy reform influence the formation and evolution of networks that have been at the center of gay marriage recognition. The adoption of a historical approach is therefore indispensable.

State Institutions

Scholarship on Latin American politics has traditionally had an ambivalent position on the role institutions play in sociopolitical processes given their perceived weakness. Scholars have therefore tended to look at broader political processes, such as regime types and class configurations, to explain political outcomes.[7] As the politics of posttransition Latin America stabilized after military rule, however, an increasing number of political scientists have devoted their attention to the study of institutions. There is now widespread consensus that institutions matter. Indeed, scholars have increasingly debated the effect that presidentialism, constitutions, decentralization, and more recently, the judicialization of politics, have on the policy-making process (Díez and Franceschet 2012, 17–20). Institutions matter because their design delineates the distribution

---

[7] Early work on institutions was mostly preoccupied with the relationship between systems of government (presidential vs. parliamentary) and their propensity for democratic breakdown (Linz 1990).

of power among political actors and determines the mechanisms of inter-action between state and society. They are therefore central in analyses of policy making because they shape the possibilities for policy change (Pierson 1994; Thelen and Steinmo 1992). In areas that are not priori-ties for governments, the manner in which institutions distribute power establishes the type of access to the policy process proponents of change have and, consequently, their ability to place their demands on a govern-ment's agenda and to bring about reform. But institutional design also shapes the type of access to the policy process opponents have and their ability to influence and, indeed, block policy. When policy initiatives in nonpriority areas awaken opposition and run counter to the interest of some sectors of society, institutions determine the ability of opponents to have veto power over policy change.

State institutions are central in the explanation for policy change developed in this book and in accounting for policy variance in the gay marriage area across the cases it analyzes. Differences in institutional con-figurations condition the type of access gay and lesbian networks have to the policy process, and they largely determine their ability to influ-ence policy. I argue that the type of access to the policy process, which is shaped by a country's institutional features, is key in explaining policy variance among Argentina, Chile, and Mexico. The regulation of family law in a country determines the site of struggle for policy reform in gay marriage. In Argentina and Chile, the regulation of gay marriage is con-trolled by national governments whereas in Mexico it is administered by subnational governments. In the first two cases activists and their allies have consequently pushed for policy change at the national level whereas in Mexico they have had to focus their efforts at the subnational level. While both Argentina and Mexico have federal systems, family law is regulated by different levels of governments in the two countries. More than federalism, differences in policy reform in the two countries are the result of the kind of federalism they have. The type of access activists have to the policy-making process is in turn conditioned by institutional features that are largely determined by a country's party system. Policy change has occurred in countries in which the political party system allows for the penetration of networks supportive of gay marriage into the policy-making process. Smaller socially progressive political parties are an important part of the story. All three countries possess institu-tionalized party systems, but important differences exist among them. The peculiarities of the Chilean posttransition political system provides an overrepresentation of conservative parties in Congress and indirectly forces center-left parties to form coalitions to govern. Largely as a result of this institutional feature, center-left parties and smaller socially progressive parties have been forced to govern in a coalition with the centrist, but socially conservative, Christian Democrats (*Democracia Cristiana*). From 1990 until 2010, the country was governed by a coalition (*Concertación*) in which the religious Christian Democrats have been central players. Given the close links members of the Christian Democratic Party have with the Catholic Church hierarchy, and their perceived need to represent its interests, opposition to the advancement of gay and lesbian rights has had a direct entry point into the policy-making process that amounts to an institutionalized veto. Support for policy reform on gay and lesbian rights from socially liberal members from other parties within the coalition has been suppressed and attempts at advancing gay and lesbian rights blocked. Such institutional features do not exist in either Argentina or Mexico. Opposition to gay and lesbian rights is articulated through political parties, especially in Mexico through the National Action Party (*Partido Acción Nacional*, PAN). But support for policy reform has also been articulated through socially progressive legislators who belong to center-left parties and who possess an important degree of ideological autonomy over policy action.

While formal institutional arrangements are important in conditioning the type of formal access proponents and opponents have to the policy process, equally important is the role played by informal practices. Informality, I argue, counts. Scholars of public policy in Latin America have underlined the importance informal practices play in policy-making processes. In both Argentina and Mexico, gay and lesbian networks have been able to penetrate state institutions to a higher degree than in Chile. In both cases, gay and lesbian activists have been able to expand their networks, penetrate state institutions, and win over influential state allies to push for their policy objectives. Central to this phenomenon is the relatively close nature of informal relationships that exist between gay and lesbian networks and state actors, especially those belonging to socially progressive political parties that have a certain degree of policy influence. This is not the case in Chile, where institutions have been less permeable by weak social interests. Because of the marked separation that exists between the governing technocratic class and some civil society actors, a much weaker gay and lesbian network has not been able to permeate state institutions as much as those in Argentina and Mexico. On the contrary, state institutions in Chile have been permeated more directly by opponents to the expansion of gay and lesbian rights, most particularly the Catholic Church.

A fundamental difference among the three countries, which is determinant in explaining policy change, is the type of influence opponents to gay and lesbian rights have into the policy process. In Chile, the Catholic Church hierarchy has direct access in the policy process because of the country's consensual type of politics. Policy making in Chile is characterized by consensus, which, until 2010, entailed the negotiation of policy among members of the governing coalition. But consensual policy making has also included consultations with the Catholic Church hierarchy, which has direct and influential input into decisions made over divisive policy choices. As a result, state actors belonging to the Christian Democratic Party are able to represent the interests of the Catholic Church hierarchy in policy deliberations across all policy areas. It thus amounts to an informal veto point. Access to the policy process by opponents of gay and lesbian rights in Argentina and Mexico plays out differently. Argentina does not possess a significant confessional party. Access to the policy process by conservative forces must be done through individual conservative legislators. But they do not have a veto. While in Mexico the PAN acts as a direct mechanism of representation of conservative forces in the policy process, the country's federal system dilutes power and allows for the blocking of moral policy reform only when the party forms government at the subnational level.

Democratization and Framing

There exists a voluminous literature on democratization in Latin America. Since the return to civilian rule in the 1980s, political scientists have studied various aspects of the region's processes of democratization. At first, with the intention of identifying the factors that would ensure the survivability of the new democratic regimes, they focused their attention on questions regarding civilian control over the armed forces, the relationship between levels of socioeconomic development and democratization, and the internalization of "democratic values" by élites (Stepan 1988). Once it became apparent, despite some predictions to the contrary, that the new Latin American democracies had survived their rebirth, scholars turned their attention to aspects of democratic "consolidation" by looking at the extent to which the new democratic regimes had become institutionalized (Mainwaring, O'Donnell, and Valenzuela 1992). As the futility of questions regarding the stages at which democracies became consolidated set in, an entire new line of inquiry on the "quality" of Latin

American democracy emerged. Within this new wave of scholarship, and in light of numerous "fault lines" the new regimes exhibited (Agüero and Stark 1998), students of Latin America began to ponder how democratic governance could be improved (Mainwaring and Welna 2003).

Despite the various approaches to the study of democratization these waves of scholarship took, they shared an important commonality: democracy (however defined) was the unit of analysis. Whether researchers asked questions regarding the necessary conditions for democratic survivability or the mechanisms through which democratic governance could be improved, the dependent variable was the state of democracy in the region. Yet, previous experiences with democratization in Latin America had shown that the type of democratic transition can have an effect on the posttransitional politics of a country. As Terry Lynn Karl argued more than twenty years ago, the durability and the distribution of power in posttransitional polities (the rules of the game) were greatly conditioned by the type of democratic transition that took place (1990). Karl therefore suggested, based on previous experiences, that political scientists pay attention to the "modes" of transition to democracy that Latin American countries underwent, for they would likely determine the context within which posttransitional politics plays out. Adopting a path-dependent approach, Karl argued for the need to place analyses of posttransitional politics within the structural-historical constraints ("confining constraints") established when democracy is restored. According to her, these structural and institutional constraints can "restrict or enhance the options available to different political actors attempting to construct democracy" (1990, 6). For that reason, she suggested that the mode of democratization of a country would condition the type of democracy that would likely emerge and account for possible variations in policy outcomes (1990, 15–16).

The adoption of democratization as an independent variable is useful in understanding the politics of gay and lesbian rights in Latin America and in explaining policy variance in gay marriage among the three cases. In this book I suggest that the specificities of each country's type of democratic transition have conditioned the overall context of citizenship debates. In Argentina and Mexico democratization has been characterized by more political contestation than in Chile. In Chile the type of democratic transition conditioned broader political debates among state and nonstate actors. Contrary to what has happened in many other Latin American countries, including Argentina and Mexico, the return to democratic rule in Chile saw a significant decline in social mobilization. In large part as a result of the political élite's fear of a return to military rule, the preservation of the sociopolitical *status quo* was a feature of posttransition politics in Chile. Because of the nature of their democratic transitions, in both Argentina and Mexico democratization has been seen by large sectors of society and élites as ongoing processes in which the limits and contents of politics have been in constant contestation. The consequences of this type of political transition have been sustained levels of social mobilization in both countries and more encompassing social debates about political life than in Chile, up until recently.

Processes of democratization in the three countries have in turn conditioned the contexts in which attempts at expanding gay and lesbian rights have unfolded. In Argentina and Mexico, greater and sustained contestation has meant that there has been greater social and political receptiveness to demands made by gay and lesbian networks. In both countries, discussions regarding human rights have been at the core of national debates, and democratization has, at least discursively, largely been equated with greater respect for human rights. Gay and lesbian activists and their allies have thus been able to achieve what framing scholars refer to as "frame alignment." Their demands for gay marriage recognition have been framed as an issue of equality and human rights (a "collective action frame") that has resonated with larger social debates ("master frames"), which have seen human rights as central elements of democratic citizenship. The same has not been the case in Chile. In posttransitional Chile the debates over human rights were tempered by the political élites in an attempt not to destabilize the political system. While human rights made it to the agenda in national debates in Chile, the country's experience was characterized by more limited political contestation. Indeed in what Alexander Wilde termed the "conspiracy of consensus" (1999), Chilean political élites, up until recently, sought to minimize political conflict, build consensus, and limit direct interaction with the citizenry and their demands. Attempts at expanding citizenship rights on the gay and lesbian front have therefore met a less favorable political environment.

Alternative Explanations

Modernization and Political Culture

This book advances an explanation of policy variance that differs from influential theories of policy change. Some work on moral policy identifies differences in political culture as an important explanatory variable for policy variance on the expansion of gay rights (Kollman 2007). The use of political culture approaches, captured mostly by public opinion data, is not surprising given that, despite the intense criticism it has received over the past few decades, there has been a recent revival of interest in the concept. Some scholars argue that political culture, broadly understood as the cultural values, beliefs, and attitudes shared by societies (Inglehart 1988; Pye 1991), is largely responsible for driving political behavior and processes. Some of these explanations are undergirded, explicitly or implicitly, by the "modernization thesis." Grounded in the work of Karl Marx and Max Weber, who sought to predict how industrialization would shape the sociopolitical evolution of Western European societies, supporters of that thesis argue that socioeconomic development brings about important cultural change. As societies become industrialized, it is argued, their citizens become less interested in basic life necessities, such as food and shelter. They consequently adopt "postindustrialist" values, such as environmental awareness and tolerance toward difference. One of the foremost proponents of this thesis is Ronald Inglehart. In his decades-long work, Inglehart has argued, based on extensive polling data, that the adoption of postindustrial, or "self-expression values," is closely associated with levels of economic development: as societies start reaching a postindustrial phase, predictable changes away from absolute norms and values and toward increased rationality, tolerance, and trust will occur (Inglehart and Welzel 2005). In their work, Inglehart and his collaborators use tolerance of homosexuality as a clear postindustrial value.

Political culture has been identified by some authors to explain moral policy reform in gay rights. Peter Nardi, for example, argues that strong family values and the prevalence of machismo in Italy are at the core of the continued struggle for legal recognition of same-sex couples in the country (1998). Accounting for policy convergence on same-sex relationship recognition, Kelly Kollman argues that: "in western democracies, culture is a more important variable for explaining policy outcomes than the institutional variables highlighted in the literature" (2007, 333). Others have argued that, as societies become more individualistic, citizens demonstrate a growing acceptance of human rights and gender equality (Frank and McEneaney 1999).

Nevertheless, "modernization" and political culture fail to explain cross-national policy variance in gay marriage recognition. If levels of economic development were good predictors of policy change in this area, how does one explain the wide variance that exists among industrialized democracies in gay marriage recognition? Why, for example, has gay marriage been approved in Spain but not Italy, or in the United Kingdom, but not Germany – countries that have very similar levels of economic development? Given the high levels of development that characterize Western Europe, one would expect policy convergence on gay marriage in the region. That is clearly not the case. In the case of Latin America, work on moral policy reform has exposed the limitations of the modernization thesis. Htun, for example, demonstrates that a relationship between levels of economic development and gender policy reform in Argentina, Brazil, and Chile does not exist (2003b). Economic development clearly does not seem to account for policy variance across the three cases analyzed in this book. Argentina, Chile, and Mexico exhibit very similar levels of socioeconomic development, yet there is variance in policy outcomes. Based on the very crude measure of gross national income (GNI) per capita, the three countries are essentially on the same level: in 2010, Argentina's GNI per capita was U.S. $14,603, Mexico's was U.S. $13,971, and Chile's was U.S. $13,561.[8] The difference is one of approximately $1,000. The same holds true when a more refined measure of socioeconomic development is used, such as the Human Development Index (HDI) – an index developed by the United Nations that takes into account education levels and life expectancy rates. Indeed, according to regional rankings of the index, the three countries, along with Uruguay, exhibit the highest levels of human development in Latin America and the difference among them is twelve rank placements: in 2010 Argentina's HDI was 0.775, Mexico's was 0.750, and Chile's was 0.783.[9] Clearly, economic development is not an explanatory variable; something else must be at play.

Political culture does not account for policy change either. While in democratic systems policy makers can be expected to react to public opinion and formulate policies that are socially acceptable, and politically gainful, they do not always do so, especially around contentious issues. An important problem with the use of political culture as an explanatory variable is that, as Marc Ross argues, proponents adopt reductionist cultural frameworks to explain aggregate-level outcomes and differences in terms of variations across systems in the distribution of individual values (2009). Ross underlines that connections between individual-level

---

[8] Figures taken from the United Nations' 2010 *Human Development Report* (UNDP 2010).
[9] To place these numbers in perspective, Zimbabwe's GNI per capita in 2010 was $176 and Norway's was $58,810. For the same year, the highest HDI was 0.938 and the lowest was 0.140 (UNDP 2010, 143–6).

TABLE I.I. *Tolerance of Homosexuality and Support for Gay Marriage*

	Homosexuality Is Never Justifiable (2005/2006, %)[a]	Support for Gay Marriage (2010, %)[b]	Support for Gay Marriage (2012, %)[c]
Argentina	33.4	57.7	55.4
Chile	28	39.7	45.1
Mexico	34.4	37.8	45.4

Sources: [a] World Value Surveys (2006 in Argentina and Chile and 2005 in Mexico).
[b] Data obtained from the 2010 AmericasBarometer survey.
[c] 2012 AmericasBarometer.

differences and the collective behaviors of interests are often treated as self-evident rather than demonstrated. Political culture is certainly not useful in efforts to account for moral policy reform. Work on moral policy reform in Latin America demonstrates that levels of religiosity and "cultural values" do not explain policy variance (Blofield 2006; Htun 2003b). In terms of gay marriage recognition, the political culture explanation is limited, to say the least. As Peter Pettinicchio argues, public opinion does not explain variance in policy reform in industrialized countries (2012). As he underlines, European countries that show very high levels of support for gay marriage (Switzerland and Ireland) have enacted civil unions but are yet to provide full gay marriage recognition. Public opinion certainly does not explain differences in gay marriage recognition in Argentina, Mexico, and Chile (Table I.1).

At first glance it would appear that the high levels of support for gay marriage in Argentina would explain why it was the first country in Latin America to adopt such a policy. Indeed, some explanations have included the strong presence of liberal values in Argentina as one of the factors (Corrales and Pecheny 2010b). However, support for gay marriage is essentially the same in Chile and Mexico, and it does not explain why gay marriage has been approved in Mexico and not in Chile. Cultural values and public opinion, then, do not seem to be the definitive factor in accounting for policy change; one must look at alternative explanations.

International Influence on Policy

Another potential explanation for policy variance on gay marriage reform is the influence of international factors in shaping policy. Political science scholarship has suggested that international influence on domestic policy occurs primarily through two main forms. One is the impact that international agreements, treaties, and norms – known as "regimes" in the international relations field – have on the enactment of legislation and the establishment of institutions at the domestic level. Two policy areas in which such influence has been well established are environmental and gender policies. Scholarly work on environmental and gender policy making has shown that commitments made by Latin American countries during the 1990s and early 2000s were responsible for the adoption of some environmental and gender policies (Díez 2008a, 306; Htun 2003a). The most important ones have undoubtedly been the 1992 Rio Declaration and the 1993 Vienna Declaration on the Elimination of Violence against Women. Throughout the region, with admittedly varying degrees of speed, the passage of legislation and the establishment of agencies tasked with the promotion of environmental protection and protection against domestic violence were influenced by the ratification of these international agreements.

Nevertheless, pronounced differences exist between gay and lesbian rights and other policy areas, and international regimes cannot be expected to have a significant impact on the expansion of gay marriage in Latin America. International attention to environmental degradation, for example, dates back to the 1970s and a consensus emerged during the 1990s on the importance of paying increased attention to environmental protection. As a result, there exists a robust international environmental regime made up of several environmental treaties, conventions, and agreements that binds countries to foster environmental protection and that has been responsible for domestic policy change (Díez 2008b, 30–5). The same has not transpired in regard to an international regime in support of gay marriage. One can only speak of a very incipient gay and lesbian antidiscrimination regime given the transpiration of some recent international and regional initiatives that aim to foster the protection of sexual minorities. At an international level, these include the 2006 Yogyakarta Principles, the 2007 Southern Cone Common Market Declaration on Sexual Minorities, and the 2008 UN Declaration on Sexual Orientation and Gender Identity. Importantly, in 2011 the UN Human Rights Council approved a resolution, sponsored by South Africa, requesting that the UN Human Rights Commission document and report on violations that gay, lesbian, bisexual, and transgendered people have suffered around the world. Upon the publication of the report later in the year, the UN Human Rights Commissioner called for the repeal of laws criminalizing homosexuality, the adoption of equal ages of consent between homosexuals and heterosexuals, and the adoption of antidiscrimination legislation.

The discussion of gay rights at these international fora has been bolstered by some notable recent developments. In December 2011, then–U.S. Secretary of State Hillary Clinton delivered a historic speech to the UN Human Rights Commission in Vienna, in commemoration of the Universal Declaration of Human Rights, in which she urged member states to push for gay rights, arguing that they are inalienable human rights and declaring: "gay rights are human rights, and human rights are gay rights." What is more, in July 2013 the United Nations launched its first campaign to promote tolerance and greater equality for sexual minorities. More recently, the World Bank, with the personal backing of its president, Jim Yong Kim, began endorsing the fight against discrimination against sexual minorities, notoriously withholding a loan to Uganda in early 2014 after the enactment of its "antigay" bill.[10] These developments have clearly placed gay rights on the international agenda. Regional regimes on gay rights have also crystallized, and, in some cases, they have had an influence on domestic policy. In Europe, various supranational institutions and agreements have over the years played an important role in the decriminalization of same-sex activity and in the advancement of gay rights generally (Kollman 2007). In the Americas, the 2010 Inter-American Court of Human Rights, in the Atala case, included for the first time sexual orientation as a suspect classification, which will apply pressure on member states not to discriminate against sexual minorities. Nonetheless, these emerging regimes call for the decriminalization of same-sex relations and the enactment of antidiscrimination legislation, not recognition of gay marriage. Even in the case of Europe, where a regional regime has been found to have influence on domestic policy in gay rights (Kollman and Waites 2011), such influence has not applied to gay marriage, for otherwise there would be policy convergence among member states on gay marriage in the same way that occurred for the decriminalization of homosexuality. Indeed, the limits of the influence European institutions and regimes can have on legislation pertaining to gay marriage were clearly established by the European Court of Human Rights, which, in a 2010 ruling on an Austrian case,

---

[10] Yong Kim's leadership appears to be key to the bank's new position. In early 2014 he penned a personalized op-ed in *The Washington Post* calling for the derogation of antigay legislation in member countries. He did so by referring to his own personal experience of discrimination growing up Asian in Iowa (*The Washington Post*, February 27, 2014). He subsequently convened public discussions on gay rights with activists and academics at the 2014 World Bank's Spring Meetings (*The Economist*, April 12, 2014).

declared that states are not obliged to allow gay marriage (*The Guardian*, June 24, 2010).

International influence on domestic policy making can also take place through transnational activism. The deepening of connections among nonstate actors that has occurred over the last twenty years, largely the result of significant changes in information technologies, has spun webs of international networks made up of NGOs and social movements that are at times able to induce domestic policy change in areas such as human rights and environmental issues (Della Porta and Tarrow 2005; Keck and Sikkink 1998). Such phenomenon can occur through the ability of network activists to place issues on the international agenda or the application of pressure on national governments to effect policy change by resorting to international bodies. Transnational activism has influenced policy in Latin America. Gender and environmental policies are also good examples. In both areas, well-organized and, in many cases, well-financed networks of nonstate actors have been able to exert pressure successfully on national governments to achieve policy objectives (Díez 2008a; Friedman 2009a). Recent work on public policy making in Latin America has underlined the importance these networks play in the transfer of foreign policy ideas and models, or policy diffusion, and their adoption at the national level (Kubal 2012).

In terms of gay rights, research on the European experience shows that a strong and effective transnational network of gay and lesbian activists and allies has had an effect on same-sex relationship recognition (Paternotte and Kollman 2013). Such influence, however, has met several other factors. Kelly Kollman (2007) shows, for example, that the effects of these networks have been conditioned by variables such as élite preferences, public opinion, and religious countermovements. In Latin America, the fight to contain the HIV/AIDS epidemic has contributed to the development of international networks of gay activists and health practitioners, which have been able to influence health policy (Torres-Ruiz 2011). But it is less clear that gay and lesbian activism has acquired similar degrees of international connectedness and strength around the pursuit of gay marriage. To be sure, Latin American gay and lesbian activism historically has been influenced by foreign ideas and developments. Since the emergence of the first liberation movements in the late 1960s and early 1970s, gays and lesbians in Latin America have adopted concepts, discourses, and strategies developed and deployed by activists in Europe and the United States (de la Dehesa 2010). Globalization processes have during the last two decades accelerated the transfer of ideas across borders, and gay and lesbian activists have certainly not been immune to this phenomenon. Indeed, the identities and aspirations of some sectors of gay and lesbian populations in Latin America – mostly the urban, middle-class ones – have increasingly resembled those of their northern counterparts and a clear cultural collective homogeneity across borders has begun to emerge. However, policy diffusion is not a unidirectional phenomenon in an increasingly globalized world. Some scholars underestimate the agency individuals in the Global South have in developing ideas, articulating demands, and bringing about political change. They convey the idea that people in the developing world are simply receptive to forces from industrialized countries, an appreciation well captured by the idea of "progressive colonialism" used by Elisabeth Friedman to describe foreign influence on gay mobilization in Latin America (2009b). Some have actually gone so far as to claim that "like McDonald's and Disney, global queering began in the United States and has transformed the planet's queer cultures by cultural borrowing and cultural imperialism as a result of American hegemony" (Jackson 2009, 358). A careful reading of history, alas, suggests otherwise. For example, gay mobilization began in Argentina in 1967, two years before the New York Stonewall Riots, the mythical beginning of the U.S. gay liberation movement. Moreover, as Diego Sempol argues, Argentine gay activists were pioneers in articulating a discourse that connected human rights and sexuality, confirming the power of the notion of human rights to politicize social action and enabling the emergence of new subjects of rights (2013, 101–8). More concretely, the adoption of foreign ideas does not appear to have translated mechanically into the development of strong transnational activisms with international organizations in the pursuit of gay marriage. Recent research on the enactment of gay marriage in both Mexico and Argentina indeed points to the domestic origins of policy change (Andía 2013; Ballina 2013; Hiller 2010; Lozano 2013; Schulenberg 2012). A process of policy diffusion has certainly occurred and gay activists in Latin America have been inspired by developments elsewhere, but international activism does not appear to be key in effecting policy change in gay marriage.

Structure of the Book

The volume is structured around two main parts. The three chapters in the first part of the book set the stage for the comparative analysis I develop in the second part. Chapter 1 provides the general context within which the struggles for the recognition of gay marriage have unfolded by detailing the broader politics of sexual politics in Latin America. It looks at the factors and forces that have been at play over the last three decades in the push by Latin American gays and lesbians for the advancement of sexual rights. As I argue in the chapter, policy change in gay marriage entails more than simply legislative reform: gay marriage fundamentally alters foundational elements of Latin American societies by recognizing nonheteronormative sexualities and providing same-sex relations equal status with traditional relationships. Chapter 2 contextualizes the stories the book offers in the subsequent chapters by providing a brief overview of the broader political histories of each country and the evolution of state-society relations. Such context is indispensable to gain a fuller understanding of gay marriage reform. In the three countries under study, state-society relations have been influenced by historical legacies, political traditions, and larger processes of political change. Chapter 3 advances a historical overview of the evolution of the gay and lesbian mobilization in the three countries. It is simply impossible to understand the enactment of gay marriage without contextualizing the early battles waged by activists. Chapter 4 focuses on Argentina. The country's enactment of gay marriage in 2010 placed it at the forefront of gay and lesbian rights, for it is among a handful of countries, and the first in Latin America, that has passed legislation at the national level extending such a right. This chapter looks at the process and identifies the main factors behind this policy change. The analysis in this chapter suggests that the sources of policy change in Argentina are found with the country's gay and lesbian movement. I argue in that chapter that policy change in the gay marriage front is the result of the ability of gay and lesbian activists to weave extensive and effective networks in their push for policy reform and to convince policy makers of the merits of their policy objective in a manner that resonates with larger social debates. Key to policy reform was the permeability of the political system by networks in support of gay marriage and the lack of veto points by opponents. In the case of Argentina, such permeability was significantly facilitated by the existence of socially progressive state allies belonging to left-leaning parties, especially smaller ones.

Chapter 5 presents the Mexican experience. Gay marriage was approved by Mexico City's Legislative Assembly in late 2009 and it came into force in 2010, the same year it did in Argentina. This chapter explores the Mexican experience of policy reform in gay marriage. My analysis shows that the main factors behind policy reform in the

Argentine case can be identified in the fight for gay marriage in Mexico, which originated in Mexico City. As in Argentina, the sources of policy change are found with the gay and lesbian movement: the networks formed by gay and lesbian activists proved critical in convincing policy makers to support their policy objective and drove the process that led to the approval of gay marriage by Mexico City's Legislative Assembly in 2009. In both cases, the persuasion of state actors to support policy reform was done in a way that resonated with larger national debates surrounding the country's process of democratization. Successful framing, then, was also at play. Strikingly, in the case of Mexico, a smaller socially progressive political party played a key role in placing the issue on the agenda and in pressing for policy change. Chapter 6 looks at the Chilean experience, which represents the noncase in the cross-national comparison. The chapter shows that, contrary to Argentina and Mexico, Chile has not enacted gay marriage because of important differences that it exhibits in the three main independent variables. First, historically its gay and lesbian movement has been weak and, during the last ten years, unable to build strong networks capable of pursuing policy change. Second, formal and informal features of its institutional framework allow for a more inordinate access to the policy process by opponents to the expansion of sexual citizenship. Third, its democratization process has been characterized by broad social consensus: there is broad agreement on the rules of the game and low levels of political contestation that provide limited opportunities for significant changes in the terms of citizenship.

PART I

SETTING THE STAGE

I

Citizenship, Sexuality, and Gay Marriage

Introduction

Ideas are fundamental in understanding policy processes and outcomes. Public policy making involves the contestation of different conceptions of what constitute social problems and how they should be addressed and solved by governments (Pal 2006). These conceptions are in turned filtered through normative and ideological positions of what societies should look like held by policy actors. Analyses of policy making are consequently strengthened by explorations of how actors come to understand and develop their policy interests and goals. In effect, recent scholarship on public policy has underlined the important role ideas play in the conception, formulation, and implementation of policy in industrialized countries (Béland 2005; Béland and Cox 2010) as well as in Latin America (Díez and Franceschet 2012). A study of cross-national variance in the expansion of gay marriage in Latin America can therefore benefit from analyzing the conception and evolution of competing visions and positions held by policy actors on the regulation of sex and intimacy. As feminist scholarship has shown, the role of ideas is particularly important in studies of policy areas that regulate the social order for they have historically served as bases for the establishment of legal codes and political institutions that organize most aspects of societies (Kenny 2007; Okin 1989). However, while ideas are important in identifying the factors behind policy change, we still need to understand why certain ideas and ideological positions gain prominence and prevail over competing ones. The historical and social context within which ideas emerge and evolve is therefore key. In the case of Latin America, political science scholarship has demonstrated the need to take into account broader power relations and struggles among social forces in gaining deeper understandings of policy-making processes as well as the historical processes that allow certain ideas to become dominant over time (Htun 2003b, 29–57; Teichman 2012).

The regulation of sexuality is highly contested among social and political actors who hold different views on a democratic state's role in determining which sexualities and intimate associations are legitimate. These views are in turn filtered through broader worldviews. Indeed, the expansion or retrenchment of a sexual right is embedded within broader historical and societal conceptions of the relationship among intimacy, gender, citizenship, equality, and democracy. For some who adhere to the historically dominant position, heterosexuality is the only legitimate sexuality and the heterosexual family the basic, and only, organizational unit of contemporary societies. This position is best captured by the concept of "heteronormativity," which refers to a "set of institutionalized norms and practices that supports and compels private heterosexuality, marriage, family, monogamous dyadic commitment and traditional gender roles" (Green 2002, 542n4). As Adam Green notes, in Western societies heteronormativity has been a fundamental organizing principle throughout the social order (2002) and has imposed on individuals the expectation of establishing affective sexual relations with persons of the opposite sex, raising children and conforming to gender roles based on ideas of masculinity and femininity. Some authors have thought of this notion as a "sense of rightness and normalcy" that is embedded in things beyond sex and reproduced in almost every aspect of the forms and arrangements of social life (Berlant and Warner 1998, 554). Indeed, reproductive sexuality is often seen as a marker for judging a person's worth and social acceptance. Importantly, heteronormativity has not only shaped social relationships but also those between individuals and the state, and it has conditioned the distribution of basic citizenship rights. Gay marriage necessarily challenges historically dominant heteronorms for it represents a challenge to heteronormative understandings of the relationships among sex, gender, and sexual desire. Proponents of gay marriage have argued that nonheterosexual sexualities should not only be sanctioned by the state, but that they are legitimate bases upon which to demand state protection as well as the recognition of nontraditional family units. In Latin America these opposing views have been at the core of struggles over same-sex relationship recognition in recent years and have generally been adopted by the most visible and active opponents to, and proponents of, gay marriage. Gay marriage recognition necessarily provokes a clash between two very different worldviews, and that is why it has ignited intense social and political confrontations.

This chapter provides the general context for the struggles for the enactment of gay marriage in Argentina, Chile, and Mexico that I analyze in this book by detailing the broader politics of sexuality in Latin America. It provides a brief historical overview of sexual regulation in the region and engages the theoretical debates on the relationships among sexuality, citizenship, and democracy more broadly. In Latin America, the enactment of gay marriage entails more than simply legislative reform: it fundamentally alters foundational and historically dominant heteronormative elements of Latin American societies by recognizing nonheteronormative sexualities as bases for a redefinition of the family, which has been a central unit for citizenship. Some critical scholars see gay marriage as having a normalizing effect and argue that it does not represent an important change to the social order. However, for those who adhere strictly to the organization of society along heteronorms, it does, and that is why it ignites fierce opposition, posing formidable challenges to activists in their attempts to redefine historically dominant definitions of marriage.

The Regulation of Sexuality in Latin America

Attempts to redefine traditional definitions of marriage clash with the historically dominant position on sexuality that is undergirded by Natural Law ideas elaborated by Saint Thomas Aquinas that equate sex with reproduction. Writing in the thirteen century, Aquinas made marriage and procreation central "human goods" and argued that in order for a sexual act to be moral it has to be of a generative kind and performed within the bounds of a married life. As such, any type of sexual activity performed outside marriage and that cannot result in reproduction is considered immoral. According to this reasoning, homosexual acts are therefore inherently immoral. Thomist ideas have formed the bases for the positioning of the main Christian religions on issues related to the function of marriage and the family, the significance of reproduction, and the morality of sexuality, and have therefore been very influential in shaping social perceptions on homosexuality.

As the influence of Christian theology declined in the latter part of the nineteenth century with the ascent of positivist thinking, discussions on homosexuality became dominated by the medical sciences, particularly psychology. While liberalism has been an influential force in Latin America, imbuing debates on democracy, citizenship, and equality, social relations and citizen rights have been organized along Thomist ideas since the founding of the republics in the nineteenth century. Challenges to heteronormativity in Latin American have therefore invariably met fierce opposition from the Catholic Church, and other Christian religions, which have followed Natural Law principles. Opposition to the expansion of gay and lesbian rights has been formidable because policy reform in this area amounts to more than changes in legal provisions: it alters fundamentally foundational notions of the ethics of sexuality in Latin America that have remained virtually unchanged since colonial times. In this section, I outline (briefly) the historical regulation of sexuality since colonialism in an attempt to highlight why gay marriage recognition alters foundational elements of Latin American societies.

Colonial Origins

Given the limited scholarship that exists on the sexual lives of indigenous peoples in Pre-Columbian Latin America, it is difficult to obtain a clear picture of their sexual practices and norms. The task is further complicated by the fact that contemporary interpretations must rely for the most part on accounts chronicled by colonizers that were filtered through their own worldviews on sexuality.[1] Evidence suggests that some Pre-Columbian societies did not adhere to uniform norms regulating sex that followed dichotomized male-female gender roles based on sexual activity focused on reproduction. In some societies, such as the Mexica, the Zapotec, and the Nahua, hereditary lineage among the political élite was an important mechanism for the maintenance of power and opposite-sex marriage performed a central role in its sustenance (Buckhart 1997; Sousa 1997). Two-gender systems built around procreation therefore appear to have been important for the élites within these systems. However, in what were highly stratified societies, evidence also suggests that, outside the ruling classes, the existence of nondichotomized gender systems among indigenous peoples was common. In effect, scholars have pointed to the existence of a variety of gender, sexual, and social roles that did not conform to Western understandings of male/female-gender systems and to varied

---

[1] Early chronicles of conquistadors depict societies in which same-sex relations were rather common. However, as has been argued, exaggerations of the prevalence of nonheterosexual sexual behavior contributed to colonizers' justification to civilize "barbarians" and such accounts must therefore be treated with caution (Cardín 1989, 33).

ideas of what constituted appropriate sexual behavior (Stephen 2002; Williams 1986).

Nevertheless, any fluidity that existed in accepted sexual behavior prior to colonialism in Latin America was suppressed by the imposition of a very rigid and totalizing set of norms surrounding sex, gender, and marriage with European colonization. The colonization of Latin America occurred within a context of hardened intolerance of homosexuality in the Iberian Peninsula, alongside the persecution of Jews, Muslims, and other groups, which followed the incorporation of Natural Law ideas into the official doctrine of the Catholic Church. In what is known as the "second Spanish scholasticism," Saint Thomas Aquinas's argumentation that same-sex relations violated natural law contributed to the crystallization of the notion that sodomy constituted the worst type of sin and the proscription of homosexuality became Church policy (Jordan 1997). Given the dominance of the Church in medieval Spain, Church policy translated into official state policy and same-sex relations became punishable by death. Spain's early medieval law code, the *Fuero real*, promulgated by King Alfonso X in the latter part of the thirteen century, ordered that all "sins against nature" be punished by death (Tomás y Valiente 1990). The code remained valid well into the Conquest. In terms of homosexuality, in 1497, five years after Christopher Columbus's arrival to the Americas, the Spanish kings, Ferdinand and Isabella, reaffirmed provisions of the *Fuero real* by upholding the death penalty for the commission of the "heinous crime against nature" (*pecado nefando contra natura*) and made it punishable by burning at the stake (Cardín 1989).

The Crown's official position on homosexuality became colonial policy and set the stage for its regulation during the colonial period. In 1543, the first bishop of Mexico, Juan de Zumárraga, authored a document on Catholic orthodoxy, *Doctrina breve muy provechosa*, which became the official guiding manual for priests and colonists. In it, following Thomist philosophy and the Crown's policy, Zumárraga declared same-sex relations a sin against nature and the most heinous of sins. During Latin America's colonial period, what would commonly be referred to as the *pecado nefando* (the heinous sin), became thus a crime against nature, God, and the Crown and was persecuted by civil authorities and the Inquisition (Garza Carvajal 2000). Starting with the prosecution of the first "sodomite" by Mexico's Inquisition in 1524, same-sex relations, along with heresy and other crimes against the Crown, were systematically and severely persecuted by civilian and Church authorities during the first two centuries of the colonial period. A policy of extermination of those who did not adhere to medieval understandings of sexuality was thus set in motion.

The condemnation of homosexuality in colonial Latin America was linked to the main pillar of sexual regulation, also derived from Natural Law ideas: the notion that a patriarchal heterosexual family is the basic unit of social organization. Reacting to Europe's Reformation, which challenged the Catholic Church's centuries-old monopoly over religious doctrine in Christendom, in the mid-sixteenth century the Church undertook a series of reforms, through what is known as the Council of Trent. The reforms revised teachings in a variety of areas and, among other things, produced a series of decrees that made heterosexual marriage the most important of its sacraments, declaring it to be a perpetual and indissoluble union that has as its primary purpose the procreation and education of offspring. The heterosexual family thus became central to a Catholic life and, following Thomist philosophy that regarded women as being less rational and competent than men, made women subordinate to male authority in the family as husbands had exclusive authority over household decision making. Making any other type of sexual activity outside marriage unethical and punishable, the heterosexual family became the only sanctioned formal unit of social organization in colonial Latin America.

The scant scholarship that exists on the regulation of sexuality during Latin America's colonial period, partly as a result of a lack of documentation, makes it difficult to obtain a clear picture of how it played out in practice. Particularly, we know little regarding the implementation of Catholic teachings and colonial policy regarding sexual practices. We know that civil courts and the Inquisition fiercely persecuted same-sex relations during the first two hundred years of colonial rule,[2] and that, despite the fact that there is very little scholarship on homosexuality in Latin American during the 1700–1800 period, as late as 1800 descriptions of homosexuality as the sin against nature and as a violation of the Sixth Commandment were still in place (Nesvig 2001).[3] We also know

---

[2] The prosecution of sodomites by both the Mexican and Spanish Inquisitions is well documented (Bennassar 1979; Carrasco 1985; Monter 1990; Sebreli 1997). In terms of civilian courts, the dualism that characterized legal formulation and compliance with the law in the colonies in most areas of life could have translated into a less fierce persecution of same-sex relations by local civil authorities. However, the identification of sodomy as a crime continued in jurisprudence during colonial times, and some work does suggest that civil authorities did prosecute homosexual activity (Garza Carvajal 2000; Gruzinski, 1993).

[3] However, while homosexuality was still considered the most heinous of sins, Jorge Bracamonte Allaín has argued that, as a result of a reduction of Church influence, the official discourse had started to shift from referring to it as a sin to referring to it as a

that, despite the rigidity of colonial sexual codes, sexual behavior that did not conform to Catholic teachings was common and, in certain cases, went unpunished (Alberro 1992; Boyer 1995; Johnson and Lipsett-Rivera 1998; Villafuerte 2005). Importantly, some research points to the development of hybrid notions of gender and sexual relations among some colonized societies. For example, work on the Yucatecan Maya of the sixteenth and seventeenth centuries points to a hybrid model of sexual desire that shaped understandings of all inhabitants of the Peninsula. According to Pete Sigal, the colonized Maya did not abandon completely their preconquest views on sexuality and adapted to life under colonial rule by developing hybrid notions of sexual practices that allowed for varied gender and sexual expressions (1997).[4] Such research suggests that colonialism suppressed precolonial understandings of sexuality but did not completely eliminate them, allowing for the continuation of a certain degree of fluidity in understandings of sex and gender. This is not a minor point because contemporary conceptions of gender and sexual practices in Latin America, despite official discourses, do not always conform in practice to a strict binary view on sex and gender, and this phenomenon may well be rooted in the region's colonial past. As the work of Lynn Stephen suggests, colonialism did not completely eradicate diverse understandings of gender and sexuality of precolonial Latin America and they continue to manifest themselves to the present day (2002). What we know for certain is that, since the beginning of the conquest, and up until 1800, the ethics of sexuality during the Latin America's colonial period was rooted in Thomist philosophy that excluded any sexual expression other than heterosexuality and made the patriarchal family the organizing unit of the social order.

Family, Sexuality, and Nation Building

Latin America's "one hundred years of solitude," the bloody and unstable years of the nineteenth century, saw significant sociopolitical change as the colonies gained independence and attempted to form liberal republics. Yet, independence did not fundamentally alter important elements of the social organization of the new republics as several features of colonial societies remained virtually intact, such as stark class stratification and the continued dominant position of powerful social actors such as

crime and that there was a reduction in both the number of criminal offences reported and penalties applied (1998).

4 Sigal's work suggests that homosexuality for Yucatecan Maya was more or less acceptable as long as it held a ritualistic meaning.

the landed élite and the military. In terms of the regulation of sexuality, the years that followed independence witnessed the perpetuation of the patriarchal family as the main formal unit of social organization, which gave men socioeconomic and political privileges that were legally protected and socially sanctioned. Despite the Liberal bent of the early Latin American leaders, the legal systems adopted by the newly independent states, particularly civil codes, were influenced by Catholic ideas that outlined the roles men and women were to play in society and politics: women were prohibited from participating in the public realm, were subordinated to men, and their access to legal and social rights, such as property and inheritance, were severely curtailed. Independence did not therefore change the legal subordination of women. As part of this patriarchal family model, nonheterosexual sexual expressions were not tolerated and the first postcolonial legal frameworks contained provisions criminalizing homosexuality.

As Liberal forces gained force in the mid-nineteenth century, leaders attempted to secularize the regimes and pursued the separation of church and state. They forced the Catholic Church to transfer many important prerogatives it had retained since independence, such as the administration of school systems, cemeteries, hospitals, and jails. A central element of this process was the secularization of legal systems through the creation of the legal entity of civil marriage, which took away from the Church one of its most important social roles: the administration of marriages. Nevertheless, and very significantly, the new legal systems reproduced Thomist ideas of family by upholding the monogamous and indissoluble nature of marriage, reaffirming the patriarchal and procreative nature of the family, and giving men authority over women and children. The legal subordination of women thus continued and the patriarchal family carried on being the locus of social activity and the entity through which society interacted with the state.[5] As Mario Pecheny and Rafael de la Dehesa have argued, despite the weakening of the Church, the heteronormative model of social organization was consolidated by the new secular-liberal regimes of the latter part of the nineteenth century in Latin America (2010).

The consolidation of heteronormativity during this time occurred alongside two important developments regarding the regulation of homosexuality. First, Latin American countries were importantly influenced by

---

[5] In most Liberal constitutions of nineteenth-century Latin America the concept of the family was enshrined and declared to be the founding block of the new regimes.

French political developments and ideas. The constitutions and subsequent legal frameworks drafted by Liberal leaders in their push to secularize states were imbued by French Liberalism, which reproduced Napoleonic codes of law. Because the French civil code of 1804 did not criminalize homosexuality, the adoption of Napoleonic codes in most of continental Latin America resulted in the decriminalization of same-sex relations. However, while intimate sexual relations between adults were decriminalized, provisions criminalizing "indecency" and "scandal" in the public sphere were included in penal codes. Homosexuality may have been decriminalized but it continued to be socially unacceptable, and any public expression of scandalous homosexual activity was punishable. Second, the latter part of the nineteenth century in Latin America, its period of "order and progress," was deeply influenced by Europe's ideas of positivism and modernity. The region thus saw the proliferation of medical and psychological explanations for homosexuality. Scholarship on homosexuality for this period shows a similar process of medicalization to that which occurred in North America and Europe as medical and positivist explanations for homosexuality emerged and began to consider it a disease, a physiological defect, and a social threat.[6] While homosexuality may have been decriminalized, its treatment as a medical condition, as a pathological abnormality, contributed to the sustenance of the heteronormative model of social organization well into the twentieth century. Nation building in Latin America was then characterized by the consolidation of heteronormativity as the primary mechanism to regulate gender relations and sexuality.

Populism and Corporate Citizenship

One of the most important developments in Latin American politics during the first half of the twentieth century was the establishment of nationalist-populist regimes built on corporatist systems of state-society mediation. As the Great Depression of the 1930s hit the commodity-dependent Latin American economies, leaders throughout

---

[6] As Ken Plummer details (1981), during the late 1800s medical establishments in Western Europe appropriated the study of nonheterosexual sexual activities and began to portray them as being deviant pathological expressions. It is through the process of a "medicalization of sexuality" that homosexuality was ascribed a pathological category and the term *homosexual* coined (Plummer 1981). Social and political discussions on the status of homosexuals were as a result framed as medical issues, and arguments against homosexuality were subsequently based primarily on grounds related to mental health and illness. For accounts of the medicalization of homosexuality in Latin America, see Salessi 1995 and Bao 1993.

the region adopted import-substituting policies in an effort to delink their economies from the international trading system. Backed by the armed forces, the new economic models were managed by a new configuration of political forces that established new forms of mediation with society along corporatist lines. Organic-statist models of state-led corporatism, in both military and democratic regimes, incorporated the newly emerging working classes and other sectors of society through corporatist modes of intermediation as they began to demand for inclusion, resources and political representation. Establishing new forms of state-society relations, leaders attempted to capture the support of institutionalized corporate groups through the extension of social rights including education, health, credit, and subsidies. This new arrangement, which Deborah Yashar has labeled a "corporatist citizenship regime" (2005, 47–9), saw the extension of social rights to privileged units in exchange for support.

The expansion of rights to previously marginalized groups included – unevenly and with intense opposition from the Catholic Church – the expansion of rights to women. Starting in the 1930s, women were granted the right to vote as well as several other civil and legal rights that decreased the historical subjugation of women to men and granted them greater legal equality. Legal changes still denied married women full legal agency in principle (Htun 2003b, 49), but changes to the patriarchal basis of law altered the idea that the patriarchal family was the sole mechanism of interaction between state and society.

While corporatist regimes in Latin America reformed the main pillar that had up until then regulated gender and sexual relations, they sustained heteronormativity as the organizing principle of the social order. The expansion of some women's rights decreased their *de jure* subjugation to men, but heteronorms continued to be upheld by the new regimes as sexual expressions that did not conform to normative heterosexuality were systematically repressed. Indeed, heteronormativity was not altered despite the significant sociopolitical changes Latin American countries underwent during populist rule. Women may have increased their legal agency, but the idea that the heterosexual family was the ideal, and only, type of social organization supported by gender roles and with procreative ends did not end. The medicalization of homosexuality during the late nineteenth and early twentieth century formed the basis for government policies that regarded homosexuality as a deviance and a social crime that needed to be suppressed. In some instances, the nationalistic overtones that many Latin American regimes adopted portrayed homosexuality as a threat to national security that needed to be fought. As

Osvaldo Bazán (2010) details in one of the most complete histories of homosexuality in Latin America, during this time Argentine homosexuals were considered *apátridas* (unpatriotic) by governments because they challenged the social order and were publicly ridiculed and summarily punished. Across Latin America, and despite the fact that, in most countries, homosexuality had been decriminalized in the nineteenth century, the systematic repression did not cease as populist-nationalist regimes continued to see it as a social threat.

Contemporary Challenges to Heteronormativity

Students of Latin American politics commonly remark that some of the region's social features have endured various historical phases since colonialism. Whether they be ethnic stratification, land concentration, or gender inequality, it is often noted that sociopolitical change has not brought about significant change to these important social features. Much less attention has been paid to the endurance of heteronormativity. As I have tried to show, sexual regulation in Latin America has been shaped by colonial legacies, the predominant role of the Catholic Church in organizing the social order, and the particularities of the process of separation between church and state as a result of the infusion of liberal ideas during the nineteenth century. These factors have contributed to the entrenchment of heteronormativity as an organizing principle of the social order in Latin America. Heteronormativity continues to be a guiding idea for accepted social behavior, perhaps best captured by the commonly used remark "*Es un hombre de familia*" (he is a family man). As Javier Corrales and Mario Pecheny (2010b, 3) argue, it guides the distribution of rights and interactions between state and society given that leaders and opinion makers "often apply the standard of reproductive heterosexuality in judging a person's worth and eligibility for rewards such as acceptance, inheritance, pensions, social status, welfare benefits and job promotions."

The expansion of rights to gay and lesbians is therefore at its core about challenging heteronormativity. Arguments for the equal recognition of gays and lesbians as equal citizens under the law, which includes marriage rights, inherently pose a challenge to the historically dominant idea of obligatory reproductive heterosexuality. In Latin America, activists and allies have articulated arguments for the expansion of citizenship rights that are based on the idea of equal treatment under the law for gay and lesbian citizens within more robust conceptions of democracy. These arguments collide with historically dominant Natural Law conceptions of family and sexuality. Because they continue to be central to formal and informal mechanisms of regulating sexuality, they awaken uncompromising opposition from sectors of society, especially the Catholic Church, which continue to adhere to Thomist ideas on sexuality and reproduction. Unlike other policy areas, policy change in the gay and lesbian rights area necessarily means a confrontation of intrinsically different ways of conceiving the social order. In the next section I outline some of the theoretical debates regarding democracy, citizenship, and sexuality.

Ideas on Democracy, Citizenship, and Sexuality

Democracy and Citizenship

The study of democratization in Latin America has mainly focused on the conditions that allowed for democratic transition and consolidation (Mainwaring, O'Donnell, and Valenzuela 1992), on the institutional performance of new democracies (Linz and Valenzuela 1994; Mainwaring and Scully 1995; Mainwating and Shugart 1997; Morgenstern and Nacif 2002), and, more recently, on the quality of democracy in the region (Mainwaring and Welna 2003). With some exceptions (Fox 1994; Jelin 2003; Jelin and Hershberg 1996; Yashar 2005), political scientists have generally ignored the relationship between democratization and citizenship. Yet, as Frances Hagopian (2007) has reminded us, citizenship is central to democracy. While definitions of democracy vary, all include a combination of basic civil and political rights, and these make up a fundamental dimension of citizenship. Citizenship, at its most basic level, refers to an individual's polity membership and, specifically, to the rights and the responsibilities that such membership confers and demands. It is about belonging. In democratic systems, citizenship membership necessarily entails the possession of civil and political rights. Because an equal distribution of power among citizens is central to all conceptualizations of democracy, the extent to which individuals possess the legal entitlements to interact with the state and one another on an equal basis is therefore central to the democratic process. The study of democratization is consequently incomplete without the incorporation of citizenship given that it involves the acquisition and exercise of rights needed to enjoy equality. Some scholars have in fact argued that democratization amounts to the constant expansion of rights (Friedman 1999).

Nevertheless, while there may be a consensus that democracy entails rights, there is a great deal of debate in regard to which rights it ought to include. According to Liberal democratic theory, democracy requires the enshrinement of civic and political rights as a means to protect individual freedoms from interference by other individuals or the encroachment of the state (Walzer 1989). For liberal democrats, citizenship is essentially about political freedom and democracy is equated with the civil and political rights required to protect such freedom. For others, who belong to what can be termed a social democratic tradition, citizenship rights encompass more than social and civil rights and should include social rights. The most influential contemporary conceptualization of citizenship that goes beyond Liberal understandings is T. H. Marshall's *Citizenship and Social Class* (1950). Marshall saw that, in England, rights evolved in successive stages and, accordingly, divided citizenship rights into three categories: civil rights, political rights, and social rights. For him, a full expression of citizenship requires a liberal democratic welfare state that, in addition to civil and political rights, must guarantee social rights, such as, public education, health care, and unemployment insurance.

The view that social rights are integral components of democracy became accepted by many theorists and policy makers during the postwar period, especially in Western Europe. However, the equation of citizenship to these three "levels" of rights is contested. Some, who see democracy in minimalist terms and who adopt a Liberal position, argue that the welfare state creates a culture of passivity among citizens and a dependence on the state. For them, the full integration of the citizenry, particularly the poor, depends upon going beyond the "entitlement" of rights and, instead, on the poor's responsibility to make a living (Mead 1986). According to this view, social rights are in fact an impediment to the attainment of citizenship. Others have argued that the enshrinement of social rights by a polity is not sufficient for the expansion of citizenship membership to all groups. Marshall believed that the expansion of social rights in England would foster a shared identity, a "common culture," that would integrate previously excluded groups, especially the working classes. Citizenship for him was also about an expression of one's membership in a community.

Nevertheless, Marshall's prediction did not materialize. In the United States, for example, some groups, such as Aboriginal peoples and peoples of African descent, felt excluded from common group membership, despite their legal entitlement to the possession of the three levels of rights Marshall had identified. These groups' difference from the majority in fact became a source of exclusion. As a result, some theorists argued – all while accepting that social rights are indeed part of citizenship – that citizenship membership must account for these differences in order for individuals to be able to exercise the various levels of rights. According to what Iris Marion Young has called "differentiated citizenship," members of certain groups can only be fully incorporated into a society if these differences are taken into account (1990). For Young, the establishment of genuine citizenship equality can only be guaranteed through the affirmation of group differences because culturally excluded groups are at a disadvantage in the political process and have distinctive needs. According to her, the state ought to encourage mechanisms of group representation and adopt group-differentiated policies. The concept of differentiated citizenship has expectedly been criticized. Critics have argued that differentiated-group rights violate the principle of equality, making some citizens "more equal" than others; that they are arbitrary because there is no "objective" way to determine which groups are deserving of differentiated rights; and that they fracture a sense of community and common purpose that can lead to mistrust and even conflict (Cairns 1993; Offe 1998; Waldron 2002).

These debates unfolded within a renewed interest in the meaning of citizenship in the last decade of the twentieth century among political theorists, an interest that transpired partly as a result of the challenges that the increased mobility across borders induced by globalization posed to territorial conceptions of citizenship, as well as a variety of new demands advanced by new subjects of rights (Beiner 1995). Young's work on differentiated citizenship, for example, was produced alongside that of theorists who have been interested in questions regarding citizenship and difference, or what has come to be known as "identity politics": theorists such as Charles Taylor (1992), Seyla Benhabib (1996), and Will Kymlicka (1995).

Citizenship and Sexuality

It is within these larger debates over the content of citizenship that some theorists and activists have also questioned Liberal conceptions of citizenship that view individuals as sexless (Nussbaum 2002; Plummer 2003). For some, all citizenship is sexual because all citizens are sexed through political discourses of the family as heteronormative (Bell and Binnie 2000). New understandings of citizenship are therefore required to account for nontraditional sexualities given that notions of rights as a set of civil, political, and social rights, as well as common membership in a shared community, are closely associated with the institutionalization of heterosexuality (Richardson 1998). Because the institutionalization of heteronormativity has excluded those who engage or exhibit nontraditional sexual practices and behaviors, calls for the notion of "sexual citizenship" have emerged. However, there is little agreement on what sexual citizenship entails. As Diane Richardson has noted, "the idea of sexual citizenship is a work in progress" (2000, 86). For many theorists it encompasses claims for "sexual rights," and the expansion of these rights is seen as necessary for the attainment of full citizenship in contemporary democratic societies (Calhoun 2000; Evans 1993; Heaphy and Donovan 2001; Kaplan 1997; Plummer 2003; Richardson 2000; Waites 1996; Weeks 1998). Sexual rights build on a long tradition of feminist scholarship that sees the private sphere as being political (Pateman 1988). In what he calls "intimate citizenship," Ken Plummer (2001, 238), for example, reframes liberal democratic conceptions of citizenship based on public-private divisions to argue for a new definition of "rights, obligations, recognitions and respect around those most intimate spheres of life – who to live with, how to raise a child, how to handle one's body, how to relate as a gendered being, how to be an erotic person." For these authors, democratic citizenship requires a robust conception of rights, which includes gay and lesbian rights.

Also establishing a strong connection between the personal and the political, Morris Kaplan (1997, 3–4) argues that sexual desire is central to individual self-making and a fulfilled life, and, as such, the right to privacy is crucial in the development of the citizen: "the importance of personal liberty in shaping one's desires to determine the course of a life must be articulated in relation to the political freedom of citizens collectively to decide the forms of their common life." For Kaplan, equal citizenship requires individual freedom to shape oneself through a variety of intimate associations. However, because our intimate associations extend to the social realm and shape our social identities, he argues that sexual justice and full democratic citizenship require more than simply the repeal of sodomy laws and the inclusion of sexual orientation in civil-rights legislation; it requires the provision of social support and political possibilities through the extension of marital status to same-sex couples. Discussions of gay rights are thus necessarily embedded within larger ideas about morality. As Kaplan argues, contrary to the rights of other minority groups, the advancement of gay rights has been subjected to the moral principles of societies: "lesbian and gays alone have been told that their freedom must be limited to accord with the moral standards of the community" (1997, 2). The acceptance of gay rights – and their relationship to larger notions of citizenship and democracy – inevitably depends on the extent to which nonheterosexual sexual expressions are viewed as ethical.

While agreement exists among some authors and activists on the idea of sexual rights, what these exactly entail is not always clear (Richardson 2000). Sexual rights, a category under which gay rights are generally placed, encompass a variety of demands and their conceptualization has been influenced by claims advanced by gay and lesbian activists since the 1960s, jurisprudence, and political theorization. Several main claims can be grouped into the two broad categories of "negative" and "positive" rights, a division easily derived from the work of Isaiah Berlin (1969). Berlin divided democratic liberties between positive and negative. Negative liberties, according to Berlin, are based on the notion of negative freedom which "is simply the area within which a man can act unobstructed by others" (1969, 3). Negative rights can be understood as the entitlement of the right of non-interference by the state or other individuals: the "right to be left alone." Berlin's positive liberty refers to "the wish on the part of the individual to be his own master" (1969, 8). Positive rights can be understood as entitlements to the provision of a good or a service.[7]

The conceptualization of (negative and positive) gay rights has evolved alongside the advancement of claims made by activists which has generally moved from demands for negative to demands for positive rights. Within the negative-rights category, the two main claims involve the decriminalization of homosexual activities between two consenting adults and the prohibition of discrimination against gays and lesbians. Arguments for the decriminalization of homosexual activities have primarily been advanced by liberal civil libertarians, who, influenced by classic Liberal theory underpinned by the writings of John Stuart Mill, have argued against the intrusion of the state into one's private life (Nussbaum 1999; Wintermute 1995).[8] The right-to-privacy argument advanced here is that the individual has the right to do what she likes with her body so long as she does not harm others. Such reasoning has been foundational to the argumentation of cases aimed at striking down antisodomy laws in several countries.[9] Arguments for the prohibition of discrimination based on sexual orientation have for the most part been

---

[7] For an excellent, and succinct, overview of Berlin's ideas on liberty, see Naverson 2001, 22–31.

[8] Primarily because libertarians on the right have at times supported the same argument. See, e.g., Posner 1992.

[9] Generally, countries that have been influenced by the Napoleonic Code have not enacted such measures given that in its original drafting of 1791 the Code did not include

based on the notion that gays and lesbians have historically suffered persecution and discrimination in similar ways other groups have. Because they are considered to be an oppressed class due to social stigmatization, it is argued, gays and lesbians need the protection of the state (Bamforth 1997; Halley 1989; Koppleman 1996; Mohr 1990). The logic here is very similar to the one used regarding racial minorities, women, and the disabled: discrimination can result in the denial of basic civil and political rights and such situations can only be alleviated through an active role of the state. Discrimination is then seen as inherently unjust as it can result in the abridgement of the civil rights of an individual in a context in which others enjoy a full set of rights.[10] It therefore violates the principle of equal citizenship because it denies the rights to which people are entitled. Gays and lesbians are thus reduced to second-class citizens because of their group membership. Accordingly, the introduction of antidiscrimination legislation is therefore not only justified, but needed (Karst 1989). Richard Mohr has argued that such legislation is required to guarantee fundamental rights and describes the role of the state as a "civil shield" (1990). In the United States, demands for state protection have been made under civil-rights legislation, such as the Civil Rights Acts of 1964 and 1965, invoking the Equal Protection Clause of the Fourteenth Amendment. While courts in the United States have generally rejected the claim that classifications based on sexual orientation should be treated similarly to race, in 1995 the Canadian Supreme Court, in *Egan v. Canada*, ruled that discrimination against gays and lesbians is analogous to racial discrimination.

Citizenship and Gay Marriage

Within the positive-right category of sexual rights, the main claim has been for the equal treatment for same-sex and heterosexual couples and particularly gay marriage. The main argument advanced in support of gay marriage is based on the equality principle of democratic theory: equal treatment necessarily requires that same-sex marriages be

---

them. One of the first articulations of the right-to-privacy argument was a recommendation made by England's 1957 Wolfenden Commission, which called for the decriminalization of private, same-sex acts. Since then, the argument has been deployed in numerous court cases, including several of the most influential ones, such as *Griswold v. Connecticut* in 1965, *Bowers v. Hardwick* in 1986, and *Lawrence v. Texas* in 2003 in the United States; *Dudgeon v. United Kingdom* in 1981, *Norris v. Ireland* in 1988 in Europe; and *National Coalition of Gay and Lesbian Equality v. Minister of Justice* in 1998 in South Africa.

10 This is also referred to as a "double wrong": not only are individuals denied civil rights but they are also victims of unjustified mistreatment.

legalized (Eskridge 1996; Wardle 1996). The argument is that equal treatment under the law requires the removal of unjustifiable obstacles faced by same-sex couples to achieve the "same good" available to heterosexual couples (Corvino 2005; Macedo 1996). Andrew Koppleman has also argued that the denial of marriage to same-sex couples does not only constitute discrimination based on sexual orientation, but that it amounts to sex discrimination: if it is legally permissible for an individual to marry someone of the opposite sex, not being able to do so with someone of the same sex amounts to discrimination based on sex (1994). Echoing Hannah Arendt's argument for the need to establish a private home in order to participate in political life (1998), arguing for plural forms of associational life, and seeing social diversity as a consequence of political equality, Kaplan argues that gay marriage extends needed protections and possibilities for organizing lives that are necessary for full political participation and citizenship. For him, civil equality for gays and lesbians is a crucial component of modern democratic states and the achievement of gay and lesbian rights, including gay marriage, is "part of the unfinished business of modern democracy" (1997, 3). Indeed, for some authors, such as Cheshire Calhoun, the right to marry is a fundamental prerequisite of citizenship, for, without it, there is a "systematic displacement of gay men and lesbians outside of civil society so that gay men and lesbians have no legitimate place, not even a disadvantaged one" (2000, 76). Marriage, for her, is the primary issue underlying the exclusion of lesbians and gay men from full participation in the democratic process and the failure to extend its privileges to gays and lesbians means that they are denied a social location in both private and public that results in continual marginalization and resubordination. Gay marriage, according to this position, is essential to the achievement of full citizenship.

Gay marriage has become the central site of struggles for the expansion of sexual rights in several industrialized democracies, especially the United States (Rayside 2010). Such centrality can mask the deep divisions that exist among theorists and activists regarding the desirability of gay marriage as a policy objective. Numerous, and, at times, fierce, are the criticisms that have been leveled against gay marriage, from academics and activists alike. A detailed review of them need not detain us here. However, some of these criticisms have been part of discussions among Latin American activists, and their identification is warranted. One of the arguments is that, unlike early struggles for sexual liberation, gay marriage amounts to a reregulation of sexual relations and their assimilation into structures that have served as mechanisms of domination. This perspective, which is imbued by feminist thought, sees gay marriage as an inherently conservative institution that attempts to normalize homosexuality by embedding it into deeply traditional and patriarchal understandings of the family (Pascoe 2000; Polikoff 2000). As we will see, some Latin American activists that take this position have instead pushed for other forms of same-sex relationship recognition, such as civil unions, because they offer the same benefits as gay marriage, yet they do not reproduce historic forms of domination. Some of the criticism takes on a class perspective. The argument is that gay marriage as a policy objective has been pursued by wealthy and middle-class activists, thereby ignoring the fact that many other sexual and gender minorities, because of their marginalized positions, are not yet able to exercise a variety of basic civil and socioeconomic rights (Conrad 2014; Warner 2000). It thus ignores a variety of rights that would benefit the entire community. It is also argued that, by fighting for one family model, and making it normal, it stigmatizes sexual minorities who choose to form other types of relationships (Ettlebrick 1993; Warner 2000).

Several points are worth making. First, while some may lament the centrality gay marriage has assumed in recent years, which, it is true, can force other important issues off the agenda, many activists and theorists would not dismiss the importance of its pursuit. That is certainly the case of the activists that are at the center of the struggles this book covers. As David Rayside sensibly suggests, gays, lesbians, bisexual and transgendered people would not argue that same-sex recognition should supplant all other issues, but "they would see such rights as having substantive and symbolic relevance to the overall agenda – part of the fabric of policies and practices that define who is counted as a citizen and who is not" (2008, 16). For many it is part of a larger set of policies that is inherently about citizenship. Second, regardless of the various positions on gay marriage among activists and theorists, calls to have the state recognize same-sex relationships often stem from very concrete needs to access socioeconomic benefits. Because in numerous societies, including in Latin America, the family has been the mechanism through which the state has distributed numerous benefits, limiting marriage to heterosexual couples is, by definition and in practical terms, exclusionary. In Latin America, as we shall see ahead, the push for same-sex relationship recognition has often stemmed from the very practical consequences of such exclusion, which some activists have actively experienced when their life partners have been deprived of benefits, whether they be pensions or health coverage. This is especially relevant in countries in which welfare regimes have been expanded through corporate citizenship. In some cases these are not merely socioeconomic: numerous are the stories of gay and lesbian activists having been inspired to push for gay marriage recognition as a consequence of their inability to have had visitation access to their partners at their deathbeds.

Third, and related to the first point, gay marriage has a powerful symbolic dimension. Precisely because marriage has historically been the structure used to determine ethical sexual behavior and to exclude, and oppress, individuals who do not conform to heteronorms, challenging its assumed natural character is, in and of itself, important symbolically. For many activists in Latin America, as we will see, part of the desirability to push for gay marriage lies in that it helps to force a debate on basic assumptions of sexual behavior, challenging thereby the ethics of sexuality more broadly. Fourth, while for some gay marriage may not represent significant social change, for others it is in fact considered an alteration to the basic unit of social organization. Opponents present marriage as being apolitical, natural, and foundational. It is precisely because supporters of traditional marriage describe it as foundational to society that attempts to change its definition have met uncompromising opposition by socially conservative actors. In other words, if gay marriage did not change much: Why the unyielding opposition to its recognition by some sectors of society? Because in Latin America the patriarchal heterosexual family has been foundational in the organization of the social order since colonial times, changes to its conception necessarily mean changes to foundational notions of these societies. Gay marriage therefore represents a challenge to the heteronormative worldview that has guided the social and political organization of Latin American polities.

In Latin America these discussions have not remained at the theoretical level. As we shall see, there has been a historic and sustained dialogue among academics, intellectuals, and gay and lesbian activists, and discussions regarding the ethics of sexuality have permeated claims for the expansion of gay rights, including gay marriage. These discussions have unfolded within the larger context of democratization, which has provided opportunities to a variety of social movements to push for broader conceptualizations of citizenship as social and political actors engage in debates over what democracy is. For many, the deepening of democratic governance necessarily means a redefinition of the terms of citizenship. Indeed, over the last three decades, social movements have challenged definitions of citizenship that are restricted to the legal acquisition of civil and political rights and have pushed for the attainment of a variety of new rights. As Evelina Dagnino has noted: "adopting as its point of departure the conception of *a right to have rights*, this new re-definition has supported the emergence of new social movement subjects actively identifying what they consider their rights and struggling for their recognition" (2003, 5). The most salient examples of struggles to redefine citizenship have undoubtedly been the numerous Latin American indigenous movements that have demanded the extension of cultural rights (Lupien 2011; Van Cott 2007; Yashar 2005). It is within this context of challenges to Liberal conceptions of citizenship that gay and lesbian activists in Latin America have also pushed for a rethinking of what citizenship is through their demands for gay marriage recognition. Their efforts at challenging the terms of citizenship by demanding equality of access to marriage necessarily clashes with historically dominant heteronorms. It thus explains the uncompromising opposition to gay marriage mounted by socially con-servative actors that continue to adhere to a Thomist worldview on the ethics of sexual behavior.

2

State-Society Relations in the Twentieth Century

Introduction

Gay and lesbian mobilization is at the core of gay marriage recognition in Argentina and Mexico. Policy change in the two countries has been largely the result of the ability of gay and lesbian activists to build networks with a variety of state and nonstate actors over time and to press for their demands effectively on the state. The same has not occurred in Chile. State-society relations are therefore central to the analysis of this book. Yet, these relations vary importantly across the three cases. A journey through the evolution of state-society relations in Argentina, Mexico, and Chile can therefore afford considerable insight on the specificities of each case. In this chapter, I contextualize the analysis I offer in the subsequent chapters by providing a brief overview of the broader political histories of each country with a special focus on the evolution of state-society relations. Such context is indispensable to gaining a fuller understanding of gay politics in general and gay marriage specifically. While all three have undergone processes of democratization over the last three decades, patterns in state-society interactions vary considerably. In the case of Argentina and Mexico, posttransitional politics have been characterized by much higher levels of social contestation and mass mobilization than in Chile. This has allowed a variety of social movements to advance policy demands outside formal mechanisms of interaction with the state.

Argentina: A Political History of Instability
and Mass Mobilization

Argentina's contemporary political history is one of instability. Its politics
has conformed to Latin America's notorious pattern of swings between
authoritarian and democratic rule. Since 1930, six constitutionally elected
governments have been overthrown by military coups, there have been
six countercoups and, between 1952 and 1994, no democratically elected
president had served out his full term in office. Scholarship on Argentina's
political development has advanced numerous explanations for the country's tumultuous past, including a political culture unable to internal-
ize liberal democratic values (Calvert and Calvert 1990); the inability of
civilian authorities to bring the armed forces under control (Potash 1969,
1980); the distortion of capitalist development through the creation of
corporatism (Lewis 1990); and the weakness of an Argentine state unable
to reconcile a perceived incompatibility between liberal democracy and
capitalist development (Smith 1990). While explanations vary, what is
certainly true is that political volatility is partly due to the propensity of
Argentina's political process to resolve conflict outside political institutions as a result of the limited formal institutional representation societal
interests have had. For most of the twentieth century, Argentine politics
was characterized by the inability of its political system to mediate conflict internally. Social demands on the state generally have been applied
from the outside and have been mostly expressed through mass social
mobilization, and regime changes have for the most part occurred when
élites have been unable to contain mobilized social discontent. Intense
political contestation and mass mobilization have been a defining feature
of Argentina's political tradition.

Argentina's political instability during the twentieth century is traced
back to 1930. Following the institution of political reforms in 1912,
which, among other things, instituted obligatory compulsory male suffrage, the Radical Party (*Unión Cívica Radical*, UCR) managed to attract
the support of a growing urban population and was able to win the 1916
national elections, displacing the historically dominant landholding élite.
The assumption of power by the UCR, under the leadership of Hipólito
Yrigoyen, began a period of relative political tranquility as the demands
of important sectors of the population were met through their inclusion in the political process and the provision of some social benefits.
This early experiment in mass democracy and institutional politics came
to an abrupt end with the onset of the Great Depression of 1929. The

precipitous fall in the demand for Argentina's commodities that followed the global crisis resulted in a steep decline in export revenues, collapsing the economy. Yrigoyen's seeming ineptitude at dealing with the economic crisis encouraged the landed and commercial élites to wrest back control of the political system and to orchestrate a successful military coup in 1930. What followed was a thirteen-year period of turmoil, known as the "infamous decade" (*década infame*), which set off more than five decades of continuous political volatility and a pattern of social contestation outside political institutions.

During the infamous decade, subsequent conservative leaderships reversed Yrigoyen's efforts to establish inclusionary politics through the institution of limited democratic representation that banned political parties, engaged in political repression, and carried out fraudulent elections. The establishment of this system occurred during a period of important socioeconomic changes in Argentina that made it inherently unstable. During the 1930s, the adoption of an industrial policy based on the substitution of imports expanded manufacturing activity that produced an important increase in the size of industrial workers mostly through the migration to cities from rural areas. Labor organizations, and the generally weak Communist Party (*Partido Comunista*), began attempts to organize and articulate the growing socioeconomic demands of the new working class, such as housing and urban services (James 1988). However, these demands were unmet by the conservative élites, and given that the political system did not allow for meaningful representation, social discontent grew significantly. At the same time, the beginning of World War II saw the strengthening of the nationalist movement that called for change in the social order and the establishment of a new political order with features resembling Southern European regimes (Rock 1987). These developments provoked volatile conditions that the conservative élites were simply unable to contain. Given the increased role of the military in politics, in 1943 a group of authoritarian and nationalist military officers staged a coup and overthrew the conservative administration.

The 1943 coup marked an important change in state-society relations in contemporary Argentina but continued a pattern of political contestation outside formal democratic institutions. Juan Domingo Perón, perhaps the country's most famous politician, belonged to the group of military officers that carried out the coup. With great political skill, Perón managed to obtain the support of Argentina's sizeable working class by offering it a voice in the political process and the delivery of immediate social benefits, starting thus one of the most powerful political movements in the country: Peronism. With the rapid solidification of his power within the military leadership, and the support of workers and labor unions, Perón, after being imprisoned by the military and eventually released, easily won the 1946 elections that brought him to the presidency. Peronism changed the way in which important sectors of the population interacted with the state as it opened mechanisms of representation through the establishment of corporatist structures of interaction. Chief among these was labor. Perón maintained democratic practices, such as regularly scheduled elections, the division of power among the various branches of government, and certain political party competition, but at the same time engaged in antidemocratic ones, such as censorship, the persecution and harassment of political opponents, and the restriction of certain basic freedoms like assembly, expression, and organization (Rock 1987). While corporatism opened up channels of representation to the political process to some groups, it also closed others as opponents were unable to compete freely for power. It thus continued exclusionary politics, contributing to the persistence of social discontent among some sectors and their inability to channel it through political institutions. Importantly, Argentina's working class, the largest in Latin America at the time, gained political voice with the strengthening of the labor movement and the inclusion of its leadership into key policy decisions. However, the accumulation of significant resources by labor leaders, through the imposition of compulsory membership dues and social-benefit contributions, were used to reward the loyalty of followers, and representation within the movement became based on patronage. The leadership slowly became disconnected from the rank and file as corruption set in. Perón was able to attain a certain degree of control over the labor movement through the Ministry of Labor, but given the strength of its leadership, he was never fully able to assert complete control (James 1988).

Given the populist logic behind Perón's political project, the labor movement's support was conditioned on the provision of socioeconomic benefits that ultimately proved fickle. Indeed, Labor's support for Peron's government was strong during its early years as the socioeconomic conditions of wage earners increased significantly within a postwar economic boom, but as the economic model experienced difficulties by the start of his second inauguration in 1952, support waned. With the worsening of economic conditions and the ensuing loss of support from his political base, Perón decided to affirm control through the reinforcement of antidemocratic practices by declaring a state of siege, taking over the main newspapers, stiffening censorship, and forcing membership into the Peronist Party. Such policies not only alienated further his support base but also they encouraged the coalescence of his opponents who supported a faction of the military that ultimately overthrew him in a coup in 1955. The experience of limited corporatist representation came to an end.

The 1955 coup signaled the end of attempts by Conservatives during the infamous decade and Perón's administrations to govern with the support of some sectors of society while excluding others. In both cases, the decision not to allow the channeling of opposition through the party system resulted in the collapse of the existing political order. Despite the consequences that political exclusion had brought in both instances, subsequent antipopulist civilian and military administrations that followed Perón's overthrow decided not to expand political representation, an approach that only deepened political instability. Key to this development was the division of Argentine society between Peronists and anti-Peronists. As Peronism became the most important political force in Argentine politics, its exclusion from politics turned into a top objective for the conservative and economic élites. In effect, between 1955 and 1973, Peronists were partially or completely banned from participating in electoral politics. Exclusionary, and, during military regimes, repressive, politics was practiced within a context of deteriorating economic conditions largely brought about by mismanagement, thereby intensifying social tensions. While Peronists were not allowed to compete electorally, they engaged in active political opposition: encouraged by an exiled Perón, they held constant strikes and demonstrations opposing the regime in turn, actions that intensified over time. Political instability reached a new pitch in 1969 as discontent became violent.

Beginning with an uprising in Córdoba in May of that year (the *Cordobazo*), social confrontation gathered momentum as opponents engaged in guerrilla activity, including the armed wing of the Peronists, the *Montoneros*, and assassinations and bombings were carried out by paramilitary groups linked to both Peronists and nationalists within the army. In an attempt to restore some order in the face of urban insurrection and guerrilla activity, the military allowed the Peronists a return to electoral politics. Perón was elected in 1973 and his wife, María Estela Isabel Martínez de Perón (Isabel Perón), succeeded him upon his death in 1974. However, the return of Peronists to power did not quell social unrest but rather exacerbated it given Isabel Perón's decision to resort to authoritarian practices, her general mismanagement of the economy, and her support for paramilitary activity to suppress opposition. By 1976, Argentina had descended into complete political crisis prompting the military to intervene and establish the most brutal dictatorship the country had ever seen.

The military dictatorship, which ended with the restoration of civilian rule in 1983, has indelibly shaped the country's democratic politics. The brutality people suffered during such a veritable nightmare, in which an approximate thirty thousand Argentines were killed and thousands more tortured, convinced most Argentineans that military intervention was no longer an option in solving the country's problems. The country's historic swings between military and civilian regimes have finally halted as a broad social consensus around the need for democratic government has crystallized. Political and economic crises have certainly continued since 1983, but they have been addressed with an adherence to constitutional democratic principles.

The emergence of such democratic consensus in a country with a long-standing tradition of social mobilization has shaped state-society relations in posttransitional Argentina. In what Enrique Peruzzoti calls "the new politics of social accountability" (2005), Argentine society has experienced a continuation of strong mass mobilization with the emergence of numerous civic campaigns demanding more transparent and accountable government. According to Peruzzoti, Argentina has undergone a social and cultural transformation in which wide public concern for civil rights and the rule of law has deepened and a more sophisticated citizenry has internalized the need to demand actively accountability from governments. The leading actors in this social change have been myriad active and visible nongovernmental organizations (NGOs), social movements, and advocacy groups (Peruzzoti 2005, 236–7). This is the context within which the gay and lesbian movement has evolved over the last three decades, as we shall see in Chapter 3. Key to Argentina's cultural transformation was the role the human rights movement played in the democratic transition as it managed to generate widespread popular support for its cause as they became a pivotal concern to the main political actors. State-society relations in posttransitional Argentina have been thus characterized by strong and constant pressure applied on the state by civil society through social mobilization[1] and by the placement

---

[1] Argentina's continued mobilization is commonly associated with the Madres of the Plaza de Mayo (Arditti 1999; Guzmán Bouvard 1994). But mobilization has been strong by other sectors, such as labor, women, and, more recently, youth, with the *Cámpora*

of human rights atop national debates. The enforcement of rights has admittedly been weak and some have been applied differentially (Bonner 2007), but the defense of human rights has been, at least discursively, central to national debates on democratization. The association of human rights with democratic consolidation has contributed to the emergence of a "master frame" in Argentina that has facilitated the advancement of gay and lesbian rights. Sustained social mobilization and the emergence of a national discourse associating democratic consolidation with human rights marked the resurgence of Argentina's gay and lesbian movement and enabled it to attract social attention to its cause, as we will see in Chapter 3.

An overview of state-society relations in Argentina in the twentieth century would be incomplete without a discussion of the role of the Catholic Church in politics given that it has been the standard bearer and primary defender of Thomist ideas on sexuality, which gay marriage challenges. As in the rest of Latin America, the Catholic Church has historically played a dominant role in Argentine politics. It derived much of its power from the privileged position it has enjoyed controlling vast swaths of land and part of the educational system. Despite the success of Liberal leaderships in taking away control from the Church in the nineteenth century, it retained several *de jure* prerogatives. It, for example, continues to benefit from some advantages, such as the subsidization of its educational system. However, the Church is considered to have had less influence in politics than in other Latin American countries. This is partly a result of the generally lower levels of religiosity in the country as well as the visible and important presence of other religions, such as Protestantism and Judaism. The Church's social presence and influence also weakened during the last military dictatorship given its ambiguous position in terms of human rights violations and the perceived closeness its leadership maintained with the members of the military junta. Upon the return of democratic rule, the Catholic Church suffered significant damage to its public image and entered the new democratic context from a weakened position.

This largely explains why some highly conservative organizations, such as Opus Dei and the Legionaries, have not been successful in garnering

movement (Briones and Mendoza 2003; Ranis 2006; Sutton 2007). The best illustration of such mobilization is perhaps the *piquetero* movement, a movement that began in the mid-1990s in resistance to the introduction of market-friendly economic policies but that has maintained important visibility (Borland and Sutton 2007; Eltantawy 2008; Epstein 2003).

much support from society. Moreover, because Argentina does not possess a confessional party (Chapter 4), conservative social forces do not have effective political representation, particularly in national discussions held in Congress. As a result, the Church's hierarchy has attempted to influence the Executive directly (Blofield 2006). Its influence therefore depends upon the sympathy of the sitting president, and such sympathy has varied over time: while it found a very receptive ear during the 1990s as Carlos Menem (1989–99) veered social policy to the right, access was closed off during the administration of Néstor Kirchner (2003–7) who took a confrontational approach. The extent to which the Church is able to influence moral policy depends thus on the president in turn (Htun 2003b).

Mexico: The Slow Demise of the "Perfect Dictatorship" and Increased Social Mobilization

In stark contrast with Argentina's contemporary political development, Mexico's politics for most of the twentieth century was characterized by remarkable political stability. Whereas prior to the 1976 coup Argentina's political system was unable to mediate social conflict internally, Mexico established a complex authoritarian political system – which Peruvian novelist Mario Vargas Llosa once called the "perfect dictatorship" (1991) – that managed to resolve social and political differences with limited coercion. Indeed, Mexico is the only country in Latin America not to have experienced a military coup since 1930. By establishing a delicate balance among loyalty, co-optation, and repression, Mexico's variant of authoritarianism ensured political stability as it met societal interests within corporatist structures without threatening the regime. However, the deterioration of socioeconomic conditions during the 1980s gave rise to unprecedented social mobilization as sectors of society pulled out of corporatist structures to place demands directly on the state. Social mobilization continued as the country moved toward political liberalization in the early 1990s and corporatism weakened, giving way to more direct forms of interaction between state and society amid pronounced social mobilization.

The contemporary Mexican state drew its legitimacy from a "political pact" that was reached among the victors of the Mexican Revolution at the beginning of the twentieth century. Following the rather highly violent and bloody period that lasted from 1910 until 1917, the political élite that emerged became in charge of achieving the three ideological goals of the revolution: constitutionalism, social justice, and economic development (Purcell 1975). Responding to the country's desire to restore political order, in 1929 President Plutarco Elías Calles founded a national political party, the National Revolutionary Party (*Partido Nacional Revolucionario*, PNR), with the intention of assuaging political rivalries that remained during the 1920s among various military *caudillos*. Controlled by the president (*jefe máximo*), the PNR became a centralized institution that forced military rivals to resolve their conflicts within the party in exchange for control over their regional areas and material benefits. The establishment of the PNR coincided with the Great Depression of the 1930s. Similar to Argentina, and, indeed, most of Latin America, the global economic downturn severely affected Mexico's commodity-dependent economy and it adopted inward-oriented measures, such as high tariff barriers, in an attempt to protect their markets from foreign competition and spur both internal production and consumption. The implementation of these policies began a process of state-led industrialization that led to urbanization and a significant increase in the size of labor and popular organizations.

It was during this period of economic crisis (a third of the workforce had been laid off by 1933) and enormous social change that a well-respected and socially progressive general, Lázaro Cárdenas, became president. Cárdenas (1934–40) introduced far-ranging changes to the political system that resulted in the consolidation of the national party and the establishment of corporatism with a populist veneer. Cárdenas reorganized the official party and integrated the labor movement, the peasantry, and popular organizations vertically into the party's leadership. By this means, leaders representing the various corporate groups (e.g., labor unions and the peasantry) exchanged party loyalty for material benefits. With remarkable political skill, Cárdenas, similar to Argentina's Perón, managed to consolidate power in the office of the presidency through the new corporatist system. This was done through populist reforms that included land redistribution, the protection of labor, and the nationalization of the petroleum industry. The new political pact guaranteed that the official party could rely on the various corporate groups to win elections in exchange for the provision of economic and political benefits, all while controlling popular mobilization.

Cárdenas established the foundations of Mexico's dominant rule under the Revolutionary Institutional Party (*Partido Revolucionario Institucional*, PRI) that enjoyed legitimacy for several decades. By the end of his administration, the basic characteristics of the new regime were in place. The authoritarian-corporatist system that emerged was able to contain opposition through an elaborate process of clientelistic co-optation, electoral fraud, and selective repression. As the state broadened its role in an expanding economy and increased revenues, opportunities arose for party loyalists while political rivalries were mitigated within the party. While the president assumed untrammelled power, non-re-election guaranteed élite turnover allowing those who adhered to the party the potential for a lucrative career and the various groups and factions within the regime an opportunity to reach the top (Lawson 2002). The president assumed the unwritten "right" to choose the party's presidential candidate in the next election, adding to his presidential power and strengthening presidentialism.

From 1940 until the early 1980s, the PRI dominated all aspects of national life. Its authoritarian-corporatist structure allowed for the resolution of conflict within the party, maintaining political stability. Thirty years (1940–70) of high and sustained economic growth, the so-called Mexican Miracle, provided the regime with resources necessary to distribute within its corporatist structure and along a very well-developed system based on clientelistic networks. The PRI's traditional rule has been described as a "gigantic, pork-barrelling political machine, soaking the bulk of the population and selectively rewarding its leaders and adherents" (Lawson 2002, 16).

Nevertheless, cracks in the system began to show by the late 1960s and the beginning of the 1970s. On the economic front, the corporatist-populist economic model began to show signs of exhaustion. State-owned enterprises and tariff-protected private firms became highly uncompetitive, subsidies followed political direction rather than economic rationale, the balance-of-payments deficit grew as agricultural production declined, and macroeconomic policy became highly politicized. On the political front, as part of more generalized patterns of social mobilization in Latin America, some sectors of society, especially students, began to demand an opening of the political system and started to mobilize. The regime responded with a violent crackdown in 1968, the Tlatelolco Massacre, in which more than two hundred student demonstrators were killed by government troops. The regime consequently lost a great deal of legitimacy and the authoritarian structure came under strain. President Luis Echeverría (1970–6) attempted to regain support for the regime by allowing for greater political expression through an electoral reform that made it easier for small opposition parties to gain seats in the lower house of Congress. He loosened government censorship over some media outlets and co-opted some leaders of mobilized groups. He also expanded significantly the size of the government bureaucracy and increased social infrastructure in an attempt to use the state's largesse to foster economic growth, thereby greasing the gigantic political-corporatist machine with state resources.

With the help of high petroleum prices and heavy borrowing from international financial markets awash in "petrodollars," Mexico enjoyed a brief period of economic boom from 1976 until 1981, when the economy grew at an average of 8.5 percent per annum. The PRI was therefore able to contain social discontent. But the boom busted soon. When international petroleum prices fell in 1981–2, and the price of borrowing from international lenders increased, Mexico was unable either to service its foreign debt or secure the foreign exchange necessary to pay for essential imports, thus forcing a steep devaluation. The Mexican economy consequently crashed and what remained of the old economic model crumbled. In 1982 alone gross domestic product (GDP) dropped by 1.5 percent; inflation reached 100 percent; unemployment doubled to 8 percent; and the public deficit soared to 18 percent of GDP. This economic meltdown – the worst since the Great Depression – marked the onset of a new era of economic reform, the beginning of the demise of the PRI's hegemony, and the rise of social mobilization.

The 1980s witnessed a profound change in Mexico as it adopted a new economic model based on neoliberal tenets and began a process of political transition. The administrations of Miguel de la Madrid (1982–8) and Carlos Salinas de Gortari (1988–94) implemented structural adjustment policies and a fairly sweeping series of market reforms. The crash of 1982 and the ensuing economic deterioration, together with the economic reforms, had a severe impact on social conditions: unemployment increased, real wages dropped steadily, and standards of living generally declined. This economic downturn had serious repercussions for the regime. Within the PRI, the economic meltdown strained the party's heterogeneous coalition, as it could no longer afford to provide resources to its various allies – peasants, organized labor, the federal bureaucracy, and employees of state-owned enterprises. It also gave rise to mass social mobilization. In what an author has called Mexico's "political awakening" (Chand 2001), the economic crisis had a lasting effect on state-society relations: social discontent contributed to the emergence of significant social mobilization as new social groups began to bypass the corporatist structure in an attempt to place demands directly upon the state. While some social mobilization had taken place earlier, the mid-1980s in comparison saw the mobilization of urban middle classes, whose privileged economic and social status became affected (Chand 2001; Tamayo 1990), a process accelerated by the 1985 earthquake. This powerful earthquake (7.6 on the Richter scale) hit Mexico City on September 13, 1985 and claimed the lives of approximately twenty thousand residents.

The Mexican government proved highly inadequate in providing relief and assistance to the hundreds of thousands of victims and homeless people. Due to delayed government action and sheer incompetence, residents of Mexico City began to organize swiftly and in large numbers to provide food, water, shelter, and medical supplies to the victims. Social mobilization witnessed the formation of a significant number of social organizations, a phenomenon that is regarded as a catalyst in the crystallization of large-scale social movements in contemporary Mexico (Foweraker 1990). It culminated when Cuauhtémoc Cárdenas (son of former president Lázaro Cárdenas) defected from the PRI and was able to amalgamate widespread social discontent, attracting the support of a significant number of both popular and middle-class movements for his independent presidential candidacy in 1988. Although Cárdenas *officially* lost to Salinas de Gortari in the election marred by allegations of fraud, it is widely believed that he was the first opposition leader to have obtained a higher percentage of votes than the official candidate, further eroding the PRI's legitimacy. The unprecedented upsurge in social mobilization applied increasing pressure to Mexico's corporatist structures. Even though there was little agreement by the early and mid-1990s on whether corporatism was in crisis or even if social movements were having an effect on the democratization of Mexico, Mexican civil society thickened during the 1980s as citizens began to withdraw from the corporatist structure of the party to channel their demands directly upon the state.

Like Argentina, mass social mobilization has been a constant feature of its transitional politics. The upsurge of mass mobilization that occurred during the mid-1980s continued well into the 1990s, a process best captured by the 1994 Zapatista uprising. But the indigenous uprising was but one of many movements that strengthened during this time and that actively demanded a variety of concessions from the state (Mattiace 2012). Moreover, social mobilization has continued even after the defeat of the PRI in 2000 as numerous sectors of society have continued to place demands directly on the state despite the emergence of more representative democratic institutions (Bizberg 2010). Like Argentina, state-society relations in Mexico have thus been characterized by continued social mobilization within an overall context of democratization.

Also like Argentina, a discourse around the respect for human rights became part of debates on democratization. Under the banner of change, Vicente Fox (2000–6), who defeated the PRI for the first time in 2000, campaigned with a platform based on the need to break away from the PRI's regime and argued that a transition into democratic rule required higher respect for human rights. The Social Democracy Party (*Partido Democracia Social*, PDS) contributed to the emergence of the debate. Among the various political parties that presented candidates for the elections (nationally and in several subnational races, including Mexico City), this newly formed party, led by its presidential candidate Gilberto Rincón Gallardo (the first physically disabled presidential candidate), was the only party that built its entire campaign around the need to increase the respect for the rights of vulnerable groups, including women, the disabled, and sexual minorities. Although Rincón Gallardo's party was unable to obtain 2 percent of the votes needed to maintain its official party status and receive government funding, the party's platform had an important effect on the campaign as the issue of discrimination made it to the public debate.[2]

The issue of human rights did not stay as a campaign promise and continued to be part of national debates: once elected, Fox's administration assumed unprecedented activism in the promotion of human rights, both domestically and internationally (Anaya Muñoz 2009). The extent to which Fox successfully tackled human rights violations, evidenced by his lukewarm efforts at investigating the ones perpetrated during PRI rule, has been extensively debated and his genuine commitment naturally questioned (Aguayo 2010). In effect, the discourse to place greater emphasis on human rights protection was largely the result of a desire to project a positive image internationally.[3] Regardless of the degree of genuine commitment, there is no question that human rights remained, at least discursively, a central component of Mexico's political transition after the 2000 elections. In the case of discrimination, for example, soon after his election, and as I detail in Chapter 5, Fox sent to Congress the country's first national antidiscrimination bill, which was unanimously approved in both houses in 2003.

---

[2] That the issue made it to the campaign is well illustrated by Fox's decision to hold a meeting with NGOs advocating for lesbian, gay, bisexual, and transgender and women's rights less than a month before the election, at which he pledged to listen to their demands (*Reforma*, June 3, 2000).

[3] Personal interview, Adolfo Aguilar Zinser (National Security Advisor 2000–2, and Mexican Ambassador to the United Nations, 2002–3), Mexico City, July 30, 2004.

Mexico's transition, then, has been characterized by sustained mass social mobilization and the emergence of a master frame around human rights, and this is the context within which a variety of social movements, including those representing sexual minorities, have pushed for the extension of rights.

In terms of religion and politics, the role of the Catholic Church in Mexican politics is rather complex as it is played among high levels of religiosity in a strong secular state. Similar to the rest of the region, the Church has historically played a significant role in politics and society. It was particularly strong during colonial times given the centrality New Spain had in the colonial project. Unlike Argentina, however, and the rest of Latin America, the *de jure* separation of church and state went much further in the nineteenth century, making Mexico one of the most *de jure* secular countries in the world. The Church's position was therefore weakened much more than in most of Latin America before the twentieth century. That process was not a smooth one, however: it was the result of violent conflicts that unfolded during the first half of the nineteenth century, and which culminated with the adoption of a secular constitution in 1857 and reform laws introduced the following two years (1858–9). Nor has it been universally accepted. Conservative forces in Mexico have resisted the country's secularization, and at times this tension has erupted in violence: toward the end of the Revolution, conservative elements violently pushed back the perceived anticlericalism of the ascendant Revolutionary Family in what has come to be known as the *Cristero* War (1926–9).

While the uprising was solved through diplomatic means, and the postrevolutionary political regime that emerged reinstated secularism, the 1930s saw the political organization of Catholicism through the establishment of several religious organizations and of a confessional party: Mexico's Christian Democratic party, the National Action Party (*Partido Acción Nacional*, PAN). While weak during Mexico's perfect dictatorship, the party emerged as a clear player in the country's democratization. Given Mexico's official secularism, which successive PRI administrations dutifully respected, the Catholic Church has been forced to attempt to influence politics indirectly. It has done so through the PAN and other politically engaged religious organizations, such as Opus Dei. Such political representation has also been financially supported by some of Mexico's wealthiest entrepreneurs (Chapter 5). The case of Mexico is one in which high levels of religiosity exist within a strong secular state. According to some observers, this has resulted in a deeply entrenched view in the population that the Church should not meddle in politics (Blancarte 2001). However, despite that secularism, the Catholic Church, unlike in Argentina, has had important political representation through the PAN. The ability of the Church and other religious organizations to influence policy is therefore dependent on the political and electoral success of the party. Moreover, the Church's social presence is also felt in national conversations through the political pronouncements some of its leaders volunteer on a regular basis, especially in matters of sexuality and morality. Since his appointment in 1985 by Pope John Paul II (1978–2005), the highly conservative Archbishop of Mexico, Norberto Rivera, has continually advanced comments on all areas of politics during the main mass celebrated at noon in Mexico City's cathedral, breaking the law (which bars religious leaders from doing so). His comments are amply and *de rigeur* covered by the main Mexican dailies on Monday morning.

Chile: Consensual Politics and Limited Social Mobilization

Like Mexico, Chile's political development prior to the 1973 military coup was characterized by notable political stability. However, unlike Mexico and Argentina, and, indeed, most of Latin America, Chile had a liberal and competitive pluralist democratic system. Up until 1973, the country's democratic system proved remarkably adept at mitigating differences among the country's three main ideological political forces. Key to this mitigation was a political tradition of policy negotiation. Nevertheless, over time, the incorporation of growing demands, especially from a growing working class and the peasantry, progressively strained the political system as they threatened the interests of the oligarchy, which eventually lost a desire to allow for policy concessions. Unlike Argentina and Mexico, which integrated sectoral interests into the policy process through corporatist mediation, in Chile they did not have direct input into the policy process but rather depended on political parties for political representation (Stallings 1978). By the late 1960s, as the oligarchy refused to compromise on policy, the political system lost its historic flexibility, setting the stage for the 1973 coup and the subsequent military dictatorship. The coup and the dictatorship profoundly shaped Chile's contemporary politics: the resumption of civilian rule in 1990 saw the emergence of a particular type of politics in which the political élites sought policy consensus and the demobilization of society in order to prevent a reversal to authoritarianism.

Like Argentina and Mexico, the origins of Chile's twentieth-century politics can be traced back to the 1930s. The Great Depression convulsed the country's historically stable politics as the economy, which was primarily dependent on copper and nitrate exports, was thrown into disarray. After a series of short-lived military coups, in 1932 Arturo Alessandri Palma was sworn in as new president and he reestablished democratic politics in the country. The return to electoral politics was possible because of the emergence of a consensus among the economic and landowning élites to allow for the integration of social demands through the electoral process. Chile began thus a period of relative economic prosperity and political stability, generally referred to as the "classic democratic" period. Adhering to the regional trend of the time, post–Great Depression Chile saw the steady expansion of the state in economic activity as it adopted import-substitution policies aimed at industrialization, a process that assumed vigor in 1938 during the Popular Front government. The new model was supported by the industrial and financial sectors, which were active in shaping economic and industrial policy through a highly presidentialist and centralized political system. However, bucking another regional trend, Chile did not establish a corporatist system of state-society mediation built on personalistic bonds around charismatic leadership. For both peasants and the working sectors influence on policy was channeled through the electoral arena and by the solicitation of support of left parties. Given that electoral politics mediated state-society relations in this system, the twenty years that followed the economic crisis of the 1930s saw the consolidation of the country's main political parties. The Conservative and National parties (which would subsequently merge into the National Party) emerged as the parties representing the right. The Radical Party, and later the Christian Democrats, began to dominate the center, and the Socialist and Communist parties occupied the left side of the political spectrum. Chile's three main ideological poles coalesced around these political parties, which competed for votes advancing distinct policy proposals for economic development and social change.

The political system proved stable until it began to lose its flexibility in the early 1960s as the Christian Democrats and Radicals began to move to the left of the political spectrum seeking to represent growing working-class and peasant demands. Electoral representation allowed organized labor to make some gains: an increase in employment opportunities provided wide sectors with an income and the state expanded social security protection to members of the working and middle classes. However, poverty and inequality did not improve significantly during this period and, as a result, and despite legal and institutional obstacles for collective action, workers and peasants began to mobilize steadily. Facing such mobilization, the administration of Carlos Ibañez (1952–8) reacted by instituting repressive measures to contain their demands (Mamalakis 1976). The result was the galvanization of workers who decided to form a nationwide organization in 1953, the CUT (Single Workers Central, *Central Única de Trabajadores de Chile*), to press for their demands. The creation of this organization encouraged a closer relationship between workers and left parties, which, by the end of the Ibañez administration, decided to form an alliance, the Popular Action Front, and to present a single candidate, Salvador Allende, for the 1958 elections. In order to expand their electoral base, the Radicals and Christian Democrats began to veer left to appeal for support. The Christian Democrats made significant inroads in 1958 and began to replace the Radicals as the main centrist party. However, the conservative Jorge Alessandri (1958–64) won those elections and adopted further antilabor policies that alienated the center and center-left parties, which were well on their way in their move leftward.

Alessandri's administration accelerated such a move, which contributed to the polarization of society as the political center began to vanish. In 1964, having recruited support from the urban poor, peasants, and the working class, Eduardo Frei (1964–70) won the elections for the Christian Democrats. Reflecting the country's leftward shift, his candidacy was backed by the Conservatives and Liberals who feared the more radical Popular Action Front. Under the banner of Revolution in Liberty, Frei promised a socioeconomic reform agenda that included land reform and an expansion of workers' rights. Despite opposition from the Right and sectors of his own party, he carried out key elements of its agenda undertaking wealth redistribution as he increased social spending (Sigmund 1977). The Frei administration began thus to set the stage for the 1973 coup as divisive policies increasingly polarized the country. The implementation of certain elements of his agenda, such as agrarian reform, alienated his right-wing allies and some of his party's members, whose interests became directly threatened (Kaufman 1972). It also encouraged the mobilization of groups, such as peasants, women, and students, through the financing of their activities, and facilitated unionization with a reform to the labor code in 1967 that allowed for rural unions (Angell 1972). These actions fueled a general mobilization of society. Newly empowered workers began to strike to demand further concessions and the number of land invasions increased. Similar to what occurred in Argentina and Mexico, mass mobilization surged at this time, and some sectors became aggressively militant with a more general context of radicalization in the region. In Chile, the Movement of the Revolutionary Left (*Movimiento de Izquierda Revolucionaria,* MIR) went underground and began calling for insurrection. By the end of Frei's administration, the political Right had withdrawn support from the Christian Democrats.

Social mobilization at both ends of the political spectrum and the polarization of society reached a crescendo after 1970 with the election of Salvador Allende (1970–3). As candidate of a coalition between Socialists and Communists, named Popular Unity (*Unidad Popular*), Allende gained the presidency with only 36.2 percent of the popular vote. Soon after taking office, he launched an ambitious reform program that included the large-scale nationalization of firms, wide-ranging agrarian reform, and a significant extension of social programs. Within a context of a steep deterioration of economic conditions, Allende's policies deepened class conflict and polarized society further. On the one hand, in a country with a tradition of policy compromise, he decided to bypass Congress to expropriate assets from the private sector (Teichman 2011, 28), essentially signaling an end to policy negotiation. The private sector, the upper classes, and sectors of the middle class were thus shut out of the policy process and moved in direct opposition to the government. As economic conditions deteriorated, previously disengaged sectors, such as professional associations, joined mobilizations and began to challenge the government. On the other hand, as economic hardship deepened, with food shortages intensifying and the economy reaching hyperinflation, the working classes and the rural laborers became more militant. Confrontation escalated as some groups began calling for the end of capitalism and for armed insurrection (de Vylder 1976). An increasingly obstructionist Congress forced Allende to bypass the legislature to implement policy, and Chilean politics assumed a zero-sum-game logic. With the full support of the United States, which did all it could to destabilize the economy and that supported putschist military officials, Chile's élites and important sectors of the middle classes called for a military coup. As it is well known, on September 11, 1973, the military overthrew Allende's government through a military coup, with a ferocity that surprised most Chileans. Chile's "classic democratic" period, and Latin America's longest-living democracy, came to an abrupt end as state institutions became unable to integrate increasing demands from previously underrepresented sectors of society within a context of mass mobilization and radicalization.

Upon seizing power, the military, led by General Augusto Pinochet (1973–90), undertook a series of dramatic reforms. Within a year of the coup, the new regime introduced a radical market-reform program, known as a "shock treatment," which saw the liberalization of trade and finance, the privatization of state-owned enterprises, and a steep reduction in government spending. In 1979 additional reforms that privatized the social security system – pensions and the education systems (based on vouchers) – and created a two-tiered health care system were adopted. (Silva 1996). The military regime also reformed the labor code to weaken organized labor, shutting it out completely from the policy process. On the political front, it established a highly centralized authoritarian system as it closed Congress indefinitely, proscribed political parties, and banned all form of political activity. It also implemented a policy of repression to eliminate any perceived threats to national security. In the months that followed the coup it repressed anyone who the regime thought sympathized with the Left, such as political activists, union leaders, and local urban organizers. A campaign of state terror was thus unleashed as thousands of people were arrested and executed and hundreds of trials held by war councils (Verdugo 2001). In 1974, Pinochet established the Directorate of National Intelligence (*Dirección de Inteligencia Nacional*, DINA) to carry out a nationwide campaign targeting possible "subversives." It arrested thousands of people suspected to be involved in political activity and deemed to be a threat to national security, and placed them in detention centers where they were tortured to death or simply executed. The regime relied on the extensive use of disappearances to exterminate political opponents. DINA was dissolved in 1977 and replaced with another security institution, the National Information Center (*Central Nacional de Informaciones*, CNI). While repression lessened after 1977, a more targeted campaign continued.

Unlike Argentina, Chile's authoritarian regime was highly institutionalized and thus able to structure politics significantly. It therefore allowed the military to manage the transition to democracy, having an indelible effect on contemporary politics. In 1980 Pinochet introduced a new constitution that was approved by a majority of Chileans in a plebiscite of questionable fairness. The constitution gave the military a variety of prerogatives intended to prevent any significant alteration of the economic model as well as to guide not only political transition, but also to manage the political system after democratization in the form of a "protected democracy." It also established a timetable for a transition: it set for the holding of a binding referendum to ask Chileans whether Pinochet could continue to rule by taking on an eight-year term as president or allow for elections, to be held in October 5, 1989. A "yes" vote would leave Pinochet as president and allow for congressional elections, and a "no" vote would allow for both presidential and congressional elections to be held. Adhering to the constitution, the regime respected the timetable and the plebiscite was held as scheduled. To the surprise of the regime's leadership, 54.7 percent of Chileans rejected the proposal, paving the way for democratic elections in December 1989 and the return to electoral politics.

A direct consequence of such structuring of politics was the revival of political parties and their organization into two main political poles. Although legally proscribed until 1987, leaders of the Christian Democrats, the Radicals, Socialists, and some center-right dissidents, created the Democratic Alliance (*Alianza Democrática*) in 1983. The Alliance allowed for a rapprochement of center-left political forces that had fractured in the conflictual years that preceded the 1973 coup. Party leaders came to the conclusion that the breakdown of democratic politics in the early 1970s had been largely the result of their inability to reach political compromises (Cavarozzi 1992). They consequently agreed to form a common front to fight together for the restoration of democratic rule. When the legal proscription of political parties ended in 1987, two main parties emerged from Chile's historic right-wing pole: the National Union, later named, National Renovation (*Renovación Nacional*), led by a younger generation of free-market and democratic, right-wing individuals who supported a return to democracy; and a hard-line proregime party, the Independent Democratic Union (*Unión Democrática Independiente*, UDI) that pledged unconditional support for Pinochet and the neoliberal economic model.

After Pinochet's loss of the 1988 plebiscite, the center-left opposition, now called the *Concertación de Partidos por la Democracia* (Coalition for Parties for Democracy), agreed to present a single candidate for the 1989 elections, the conservative Christian Democrat, Patricio Aylwin (1990–4). On the center-right, National Renovation and the Democratic Union agreed in turn to present themselves a single candidate, Finance Minister Hernán Büchi. The elections were also held as scheduled on December 14, 1989. *Concertación's* Aylwin won 55.2 percent of the votes against 44.8 percent for the conservatives, although those were split between Büchi and another right-wing candidate. The political forces that contested the 1989 elections shaped transitional politics in Chile. The various political parties entered into sustained coalitions formed around the 1988 plebiscite and the 1989 elections. From 1990, when Aylwin took over as president, until the 2013 elections,[4] Chile's main center-left parties have run all campaigns as a unified bloc under *Concertación* with the center-right as an opposing bloc.

The return to electoral politics was managed by the military in a way that profoundly shaped posttransitional political life. From the time the plebiscite was held until Aylwin's assumption of power, the military negotiated with the *Concertación* numerous changes to the Chilean constitution that shaped the institutional design upon the return to democracy. The negotiation of the transition, known as the *proceso de amarre* (mooring process) forced *Concertación* to accept numerous provisions that guaranteed the control of the military over the transition process, the so-called authoritarian enclaves.[5] An important and long-lasting effect was the adoption of a binomial electoral system to ensure an overrepresentation of political parties from the right in the legislature and the creation of an institutionalized mechanism that would foster less political-party fragmentation and, consequently, less polarization.[6] This important institutional feature provided Chile's political system a new point of equilibrium by encouraging coalitions to form around two opposing poles with an overrepresentation from the right. As a result, elections held since 1990 have forced the historically fragmented Chilean multiparty system to converge around two main, broad-based coalitions. Because of the modalities of Chile's transition to democracy, these two poles have roughly been configured by the two camps that supported the "no" (*Concertación*) and the "yes" (UDI-RN) sides of the 1988 plebiscite.

---

[4] The coalition of parties changed its name to New Majority (*Nueva Mayoría*) for the 2013 elections.

[5] These included the retention of the nine appointed senators from military ranks as well as loyal members of the state bureaucracy by providing them with tenure, guarantees against investigation and retribution regarding past violations of human rights, and the appointment of new members of the Supreme Court. Others had been enshrined in the 1980 Constitution and *Concertación* was unable to remove them.

[6] According to this model, which allocates two congressional seats per district, in order for a party or a coalition to win the two seats from a district, it has to double the vote of the closest opponent, otherwise the party or coalition that comes in second place receives the other seat. Given Chile's electoral history of high competition and low margins of difference, the likelihood of a party or coalition obtaining double the amount of votes from an opponent is low. As a result, the system provides the runner-up, that is, the right, with overrepresentation.

These political dynamics have encouraged consensual politics in Chile. In the years leading up to the 1989 plebiscite, *Concertación*'s leaders engaged in a series of discussions regarding the most suitable type of posttransitional politics in Chile in light of what they perceived to have been failed transitions in some Latin American countries. A group of approximately twenty highly educated social scientists, twelve of whom were appointed as cabinet ministers or deputy ministers by Aylwin in 1990, believed that the 1973 coup had been brought about by the polarization of Chilean society and that the country required a system of politics based on consensus and negotiation. They thus articulated a political strategy for Chile's return to democracy that was deeply influenced by Arend Lijphart's model of "consociational democracy" in pluralist societies (1968). Indeed, in a series of working papers authored by these individuals in the late 1980s they used Lijphart's intellectual paradigm as the model to adopt in Chile (Joignant 2012, 112). It was no coincidence that Lijphart spent time in Chile in the 1980s and met with the group of social scientists on several occasions. After Aylwin's assumption of power in 1990, a model of consensual politics was thus implemented in Chile.

Alfredo Joignant, in a fascinating study, analyzes 113 previously undisclosed policy briefings authored by the twelve *technopols* from 1990 to 1994 that served as policy road maps for the new administration (2012). The documents reveal that *Concertación*'s leadership possessed a deep sense of fear of a democratic reversal should the new government be unable to provide stability in the country, and that a rational, tranquil, gradual, and negotiated democracy was to be the government's *raison d'état*: change should only be brought about through consensus and gradualness. In order to achieve this, the policy briefings suggest, it was necessary to neutralize political divisions, attain absolute majorities and negotiate with the opposition through the adoption of a consociational style characterized by the coresponsibility of political and social actors in collective decisions (Joignant 2012). The documents also show the intention to avoid polarization by ensuring that social groups also enter negotiations with the government. In terms of human rights, they called for a realistic, prudent, and conservative approach that would seek justice "within reason," even if that resulted in certain forms of impunity.

The desire to establish a consensual style of politics transcended the Aylwin administration as several informal features adopted by 1994 became entrenched and endured the four *Concertación* governments as part of a "democracy by agreement" (*democracia de los acuerdos*), in what Siavelis calls the "transitional enclaves": the *cuoteo* (quota distribution);

the *partido transversal* (an informal group of coalition leaders that hold key jobs in the powerful, "political," ministries that have strong influence over policy); and the *democracia de los acuerdos* (informal negotiations with opposition leaders in Congress and powerful nonstate actors in order to assuage fears of a potentially reactionary Right) (Siavelis 2006, 2014). These mechanisms were informal in nature, but they acquired a degree of institutionalization over the *Concertación* years. For example, while the *partido transversal* was an informal group, its members met once a week at an office in *La Moneda* (presidential palace) to set the agenda and to negotiate and decide on policy. The group, informally known as the *grupo político* (political group) by government insiders, distributed its decisions on policy agendas after its weekly meetings among cabinet ministers, deputy ministers, and staff at *La Moneda*.[7] These mechanisms rendered the Executive – and more importantly, the informal negotiations that take place in the floors of *La Moneda* among *Concertación* leaders, senior cabinet officials, and nonstate actors – the main site of policy making. To influence policy, state and nonstate actors had to have access to the negotiations that took place in *La Moneda* and convince members of the *grupo transversal* to pursue their policy objectives. For *Concertación* Members of Congress this meant that influence over setting the agenda had to be advanced up the ranks and through their party leaders all the way to the *grupo transversal*. While parliamentary groups and individual legislators could advance bills in either chamber of Congress, the decisions over what legislative items were put to a vote rested with the Executive for that is where *Concertación* party leaders decided the agenda. Specifically, this was done through the prerogative the Chilean Executive has to manage the discussion of bills in Congress by designating them as more or less worthy of discussion (*urgencia*).[8]

Another effect of the grand political strategy adopted during the Aylwin administration regards state-society relations. The 1983–5 economic crises triggered mass social mobilization as various sectors of society protested deteriorating conditions. Indeed, some groups, such as MIR, resurfaced in 1983 and took up arms calling for the toppling of the military regime through insurrection. Social mobilization was short lived, but the regime reacted with force to quell it, and important allies, such as the middle classes, withdrew support out of fear (González 2008,

[7] Interview, Deputy Minister, Santiago, November 27, 2009.
[8] It has the prerogative to accord all nonbudgetary bills with three levels of urgency: *simple*, *suma*, and *inmediata*.

92). Moreover, the 1988 plebiscite imposed on the opposition forces the requirement to focus efforts on winning the vote, which meant challenging demands institutionally through the "no" camp. The search for élite consensus resulted in the dismantling of organizational structures of social movements, which consequently weakened (Oxhorn 1994). However, the demobilization of civil society continued after the resumption of electoral politics. The brutality with which the dictatorship repressed the population discouraged people to mobilize, engage in politics, and demand political change after the return to civilian rule in 1990. In what Patricia Politzer has termed a "culture of fear" (2001), important sectors of Chilean society, especially those associated with mass mobilization, such as members of unions and left parties, were discouraged from organizing for years after democratization. Moreover, because the fear that the political actors, which had historically been aligned with social movements (now belonging to *Concertación*), could provoke instability and prompt a possible return to military rule, they actively sought the demobilization of civil society upon the resumption of electoral politics. Being fully aware of the effects mass mobilization had on the country's polarization in the early 1970s, political élites were simply afraid of provoking the Right. As a result, within the new politics of consensus *Concertación* not only sought to suppress divisive issues in order to avoid confrontation, but also it purposefully pursued the institutionalization of political activity and the deactivation of social mobilization (Hipsher 1996; Oxhorn 1995; Roberts 1998, 128–61).

Posttransitional politics in Chile was therefore characterized during the *Concertación* years by what Alexander Wilde termed a "conspiracy of consensus" that originated among the political classes but that spread to the entire society. Such politics refers to a widespread aversion by the citizenry to open conflict and a tendency among political élites to avoid public debate and direct contact with civil society and to engage in a cautious politics of élite consensus building with few channels for civil society to express discontent (Wilde 1999).

It is therefore not surprising that, within this context, human rights and accountability for violations committed during the dictatorship did not become a feature of Chile's transition to democracy. Aylwin's campaign platform explicitly promised to repeal the 1978 amnesty law introduced by Pinochet, but he failed to do so while in power. Within two months of assuming office, he established the National Truth and Reconciliation Commission (*Comisión Nacional de Verdad*), known as the Rettig Commission, in order to document and clarify atrocities committed

during the Pinochet years. The Commission released its report the following year, in which it documented 2,729 cases of execution. However,
the commission was not allowed to name perpetrators. Aylwin transmit-
ted the report to the judiciary to take "proper measures," but not much
progress was made. Some cases were opened, but amnesty was usually
invoked. As Cath Collins states: "the accountability scenario continued
to consist of a reduced and scattered case universe, overseen by a handful
of committed but poorly resourced human rights lawyers" (2009, 73).

The release of the Rettig Report expectedly provoked the military,
which responded by protesting what they perceived to be a campaign to
dampen the prestige of the military. It thus engaged in a public display
of force to intimidate Aylwin's government. Aylwin was unable to settle
the issue of human rights as legislation he sent to Congress to accelerate investigations and proceedings for pending cases of human rights
abuses was rejected by Congress. The administration of Eduardo Frei
(1994–2000) initially attempted to depoliticize the issue of human rights
by delegating it to the judiciary, but, conforming to the new politics of
consensus, he opted for a compromise: he introduced a constitutional
reform intended to accelerate legal proceedings in exchange for prosecu-
tions being limited to atrocities committed during the 1973–8 period.
But even such compromise was not possible: the bill was defeated in
the Senate given the overrepresentation of the Right. The "conspiracy of
consensus" therefore prevented the emergence of a large social debate on
human rights in the years following the return to democratic rule.

In terms of religion and politics, the Catholic Church has been historically strong in Chile. Unlike the clear separation between church and state
that took place in Mexico in the mid-nineteenth century, Catholicism was
the state religion until the introduction of the 1925 constitution. While the
new constitution weakened the Church, *de jure*, it continued to be a powerful force throughout the twentieth century. Similar to Argentina, the Church
has derived much of its power and political presence from landownership
(it is the largest landowner in Chile) and the control of very important sectors of the private education system. Prior to the 1973 coup, it exercised
political influence through the country's Christian Democratic Party. The
Church assumed significant social and political esteem during the military
dictatorship given its overt criticism of human rights abuses by a number
of bishops (influenced by Liberation Theology). It also established an organization in the early years of the dictatorship, the Vicariate of Solidarity
(*Vicaría de la Solidaridad*) intended to stop the abduction, torture, and kill-
ing of Chileans, and it also established centers of aid for victims.

In stark contrast to Argentina, the Church's active involvement in the protection of human rights during the dictatorship meant that it enjoyed a great deal of social legitimacy upon the return of democracy. With the return to civilian rule, it managed to translate such moral authority into political influence (Haas 1999). The Christian Democratic Party has been a direct conduit to the policy process, but not the only one: the Church has maintained close relationships with several parties across the spectrum. In addition to political party representation, the Church's presence and influence are undergirded by a vast network of socially conservative associations. Chile's Opus Dei is one of the strongest and largest in Latin America. Moreover, it has continued to influence politics through the education system: a large part of Chile's social and political élite is educated and trained in private Catholic schools and universities.

3

Early Mobilization: The Long Road to Gay Marriage

Introduction

Variance in policy trajectories and outcomes in the expansion of gay and lesbian rights across the three cases analyzed in this book is largely explained by the type of mobilization that has taken place in each country. A central claim of this book is that policy change has occurred in those cases in which gay activism has shown higher levels of organizational strength, pursued more effective political strategies, and woven stronger networks with state and nonstate actors in the pursuit of policy reform. The characteristics of activism in Argentina, Mexico, and Chile have been largely shaped by early challenges to the heteronormative order waged by gays and lesbians. An appreciation of early struggles is therefore necessary to understand contemporary gay activism in the three countries and the struggles around the pursuit of gay marriage.

In this chapter, I sketch the emergence and early evolution of gay and lesbian liberation movements in Argentina, Mexico, and Chile. This exercise sets the stage for the analyses of policy reform in gay marriage presented in subsequent chapters. In the two countries in which gay marriage has been enacted, Argentina and Mexico, gays and lesbian have a much longer history of mobilization, which has allowed them to build coalitions over time and to begin a policy reform trajectory much earlier than in Chile. In both countries mobilization can be traced back to the late 1960s and early 1970s when gays and lesbians began to organize, mobilize, and challenge heteronormative social views on sexuality. In both cases the movements suffered a weakening after a first burst of mobilization: in Argentina as a result of the repression carried out by the 1976–82

74

military dictatorship and in Mexico because of internal divisions and the effects of the economic crisis. However, democratization provided propitious conditions for gays and lesbians to engage in collective action to demand the halt of state repression and to start framing their demands as part of democratization processes. By the mid-1990s, both movements possessed an important degree of organizational strength and had placed their demands on national agendas. Chile's experience has been markedly different. While gays and lesbians also began to organize in the early 1970s, the establishment of a military dictatorship by Augusto Pinochet in 1973 eliminated any possibility for collective action, thwarting the emergence of a gay and lesbian movement. Chile's democratic transition witnessed some gay and lesbian mobilization, but largely due to internal divisions, it proved short lived. In stark contrast with Argentina and Mexico, Chile's gay and lesbian movement remained weak until the early 2000s.

Argentina: The Precursor in Gay Mobilization

The Emergence of Latin America's First Gay and Lesbian Movement
As we saw in Chapter 2, by the mid-1970s, Argentina's long tradition of political instability reached a new level as its politics descended into significant turmoil. It is against this backdrop of chronic political instability and mass mobilization in the country that Latin America's first gay liberation movement emerged, a movement to be the first to challenge the region's heteronormative order.

The formation of Latin American states during the nineteenth and early twentieth centuries saw the consolidation of heteronormativity as the primary mechanism of sexual regulation despite the influence of Liberalism. Argentina fit the general regional mold. Influenced by the French civil code, sodomy was decriminalized with the drafting of the country's first penal code at the beginning of the nineteenth century and has never since been considered a criminal activity. Moreover, Liberal élites enacted a Liberal constitution in 1853 that limited the ability of the state to intrude into people's private spheres, including sexual relations. Reforms to the penal code in 1888 eliminated completely the legal punishment of all forms of consensual sexual activity between adults, and the latter part of the nineteenth century was characterized by a general relaxation of legal persecution of homosexuals (Ben 2010). However, legal changes did not change social attitudes toward homosexuality and, as part of the medicalization of sexuality that occurred toward the end of the nineteenth century (Chapter 1), homosexuals were seen as abnormal. Such attitudes hardened in the 1930s within a context of growing nationalism in Argentina, and the systematic harassment of homosexuals began with the introduction of legal regulations by several police forces known as "police edicts" (*edictos policiales*), which were aimed at controlling urban unrest.[1] These legal regulations introduced penalties for same-sex sexual relations and for actions that would offend proper public behavior and good morality. In Buenos Aires, police edicts were introduced in 1932 and remained in place until the mid-1990s. These legal provisions were systematically used by the police to repress, and to extort money from, homosexuals.[2] Social intolerance of homosexuality was thus supported by a legal framework that allowed for the repression of nonnormative sexual behavior, a framework that was upheld by various political regimes until the late 1960s.[3]

Social intolerance and police repression motivated Argentine homosexuals to organize and mobilize in the late 1960s.[4] Within the broader general context of political instability and mass mobilization, in October 1967, predating the 1969 Stonewall riots in New York, a group of homosexuals, led by Héctor Anabitarte, founded the first gay group in Latin America: *Nuesto Mundo* (Our World). Having as guiding objective to "work against heterosexist repression," these individuals came together to stop continuous police detentions. At the time police frequently arrested homosexuals and sent them to a secluded building of Villa Devoto prison

[1] As explained in Chapter 1, the regulation of sexuality was an integral part of nation building in Latin America and nationalism was associated with notions of virility, masculinity, and heterosexuality. In Argentina, with the strengthening of nationalism in the 1940s, homosexuals were increasingly considered unpatriotic and, as a threat to national security, consequently repressed. The electoral law of 1943 banned homosexuals from voting or running for office or holding public-sector jobs, and a reform to the military code of 1951 banned the enlisting of homosexuals in the armed forces.

[2] While police edicts were introduced in Buenos Aires in 1880, they did not include references to sexual activities between men. The wording of these regulations changed during the sixty-six years they were in force, but even when same-sex relations were not specifically mentioned, police regularly detained homosexuals based on references to the interdiction to wear clothes of the opposite sex as they violated public order and good morality.

[3] The repression of homosexuals after the 1930s was not limited to these legal regulations. In 1946, the electoral code of Buenos Aires Province specifically prohibited homosexuals from voting and in 1951 the new military code was introduced (referred to in the preceding note). Moreover, throughout the country, provinces and local governments began introducing *códigos de faltas* (offence codes), intended to regulate "proper morality" and "public decency." In many of these codes, the prohibition of cross-dressing in public was introduced and these stipulations were readily used by police to detain homosexuals.

[4] This section draws from correspondence with Héctor Anabitarte in January 2012.

for three to four weeks. As was the case with gay and lesbian mobilization in Latin America, the Argentine movement emerged from within a mobilized revolutionary Left that sought to bring about substantial political change. As such, Our World was mostly formed by left-leaning individuals. Anabitarte had in fact belonged to the youth wing of the banned Communist Party (*Partido Comunista*), from which he was expelled for his "condition." Our World's activities at the time consisted primarily in printing and distributing flyers in which they denounced the detention of homosexuals.

In August 1971, members of the group joined forces with social-science students and faculty from Buenos Aires University and intellectuals to form the network *Frente de Liberación Homosexual* (Homosexual Liberation Front, FLH). Similar to liberationist groups that emerged at the time in Europe and North America, the group began to articulate a discourse based on the need to liberate homosexuals from police repression but also social stigmatization. However, because of the political situation in Argentina, the discourse was framed around the need to liberate homosexuals from repressive structures that included the authoritarian regime as well as imperialism (Díez 2011a). The FLH thus called for an end to the current "exclusive and compulsive heterosexual" means of sexual oppression and for an alliance with the "national and social liberation movements" to make visible and natural homosexuality (Perlongher 1985, 273). Influenced by theorists such as Michel Foucault, and engaging larger Marxist debates led by authors such as Gilles Deleuze, Félix Guattari, Herbet Marcusse, and Charles Reich, they argued for the need to challenge the "family ideology" that sustained the state. The articulation of their liberationist discourse was the product of the influence intellectuals had on the formation of FLH. While Our World was an organization made up of working-class individuals, the FLH's foundation saw the inclusion of intellectuals and academics that shaped the group's discussions based on theoretical debates that challenged social assumptions regarding sexuality and politics.[5] This marked the beginning of an enduring relationship between the Argentine gay and lesbian movement and intellectuals. It also saw the start of a close relationship with feminists. Influenced by second-wave feminism, they forged a close

[5] Some of these individuals included intellectuals and writers who subsequently gained important social recognition in Argentina and Latin America, such as Pepe Bianco, Néstor Perlongher, Blas Matamoros, Juan José Sebreli, Manuel Puig, and Juan José Hernández, some of whom belonged to the literary group *Sur*.

relationship with women's organizations, such as the Argentine Feminist Union, the Women's Liberation Movement, and the Union of Socialist Women, that would strengthen over time and prove critical in the formation of coalitions in subsequent years. In effect, while leftist parties and organizations refused to join their cause, feminist groups lent them support and, indeed, two heterosexual women belonged to FLH.[6]

By 1973, activists had begun to attract some public attention to their plight to end police repression through the publication of a newspaper, *Homosexuales*, distributed in some newsstands of Buenos Aires, in which they called attention to their cause, and the appearance of articles in prominent publications, such as the magazine *Así*. They had also been able to gain some public presence through their participation in some social protests carrying banners calling for homosexual liberation, not a small feat given that the oppression of homosexuals continued to suffer even after the election of the Peronists in 1973.[7]

The movement's early activity reduced significantly when state repression hardened under Isabel Perón's government as she began to rely on paramilitary groups to suppress social unrest. It was forced to go underground in 1975 and its activities came to an abrupt end with her overthrow in 1976 by the armed forces.[8] Her inability to contain mass mobilization and solve the political crisis resulted in the establishment of the dictatorship that began the so-called process of national reorganization. The military regime unleashed an unprecedented wave of repression that prohibited all forms of collective action as it set out to "cleanse" society through the elimination of "subversive" left-wing opposition. State terror became state policy as the military sought to annihilate any form of dissent. A fierce oppression campaign was launched in

---

[6] These relationships were fortified through discussions held by feminists and gay activists through the group Sexual Politics Group (*Grupo Política Sexual*), which had as an objective the articulation of arguments in favor of sexual liberation. Women and gay members of this group participated in some marches in favor of reproductive rights in 1974 (Bellucci 2010, 112–13).

[7] Given that Peronism, as a political movement, agglutinated multiple forces with varied ideological perspectives, sectors within it were as repressive of homosexuality as authoritarian regimes prior to 1973. Indeed, Jorge Osinde, leader of the right-wing faction within Peronism, initiated a campaign in which he associated the *Montonero* movement with homosexuality.

[8] On February 12, 1975, in a weekly publication supported by the founder of the paramilitary group Argentine Anti-Communist Alliance (*Alizanza Anticomunista Argentina*, AAA), and chief advisor to President Isabel Perón, Carlos López Rega, published an article calling for the lynching of homosexuals and specifically mentioned FLH (Green 1994, 9).

March 1978, as part of the preparatory "cleansing" for the soccer World Cup, carried out by the "moral brigade." The harassment, imprisonment, torture, and murder of "subversives," some of whom were homosexual, intensified during this darkest period of Argentine history. The movement completely disappeared. It became simply impossible for homosexuals, most of whom belonged to leftist organizations, to socialize, let alone organize, and the priority became mere survival. Activists could not organize for fear of losing their lives and several chose to exile themselves internationally.

The repression perpetrated by the military dictatorship left an important imprint on Argentina's gay and lesbian movement. While the state did not have a specific policy that targeted homosexuals, leaders later claimed that four hundred homosexuals had disappeared, and would use such alleged targeted repression to build a discourse around human rights, as we will see next.[9]

Democratic Transition and the Resurgence of Gay and Lesbian Mobilization

The advent of democratic politics in 1983 appeared to have opened a new era for gays and lesbians in Argentina. As part of the social effusiveness that democratic liberalization provoked among the population at large, known by Argentines as the "democratic spring," gays and lesbians began to socialize publicly and several bars and clubs opened in Buenos Aires and Rosario in the months following the October 1983 elections.[10]

---

[9] Carlos Jáugueri was the first to come up with the four-hundred figure in a book published several years after the return to democracy (1987, 171). There are no hard data on "disappeared" homosexuals and academics have only recently begun to explore this particular aspect of Argentine history (Insausti 2014). Jáugueri appears to have arrived at that number through informal conversations he is believed to have held with one of the authors of the famous *Nunca Más* (Never Again) report (which was tasked with documenting the disappeared during the dictatorship). That the regime's moralizing campaign targeted homosexuals is highly debated among Argentine activists and academics. On the one hand, it is likely that homosexuals died at the hands of the regime, but many of them belonged to identified "subversive" organizations and political parties. On the other hand, some of the pioneer activists, such as Anabitarte and Perlongher, were never arrested even though the Buenos Aires police found FLH literature in their apartments. Systematic repression is suggested by work published years later (see, e.g., Rapisardi and Modarelli 2001), but the issue appears to have ignited some retrospection in recent years among activists and academics (Insausti 2014).

[10] Following the fiasco of the Falklands conflict, by the end of 1982 it was apparent that the military dictatorship was not going to last and several groups emerged, creating the Gay Coordinating Committee (*Coordinadora de Grupos Gay*). However, repression

However, the return to civilian rule did not bring about palpable change in social attitudes toward homosexuality nor did it mean an end to state repression. Scarcely four months after Raúl Alfonsín (1983–9) was sworn in as the newly elected president, on March 22, 1984, members of the Police Morality Division detained approximately fifty activists in the gay club *Balvanera* in Buenos Aires, invoking the decades-old police edicts that were not reformed during the democratic transition (Díez 2011a). Democratization may have restored social and political freedoms, but a legal pillar of the sustenance of heteronormativity in Argentina, the police edicts, remained in place. Their use to repress homosexuals represented a continuation of intolerance toward nonnormative sexual behavior, which was fully supported by the state. Between December 20, 1983 and March 1984, 343 individuals were detained by police (Jáuregui 1987, 187). Indeed, the official position of the new democratic government on homosexuality was that it was abnormal. The Interior Minister during the first four years after the return to democracy, Antonio Tróccoli, declared, when asked about constant police raids against gays and lesbians: "Homosexuality is a disease and we plan to deal with it as such. If police have acted it is because there were exhibitions or actions that compromise what can be called the rules of the game of a society that wants to be spared that type of behavior. There is no persecution; on the contrary, I think that it has to be dealt with as a disease" (Bazán 2010, 395–6).

For Argentine homosexuals, then, it soon became evident that electoral politics did not equate sexual justice and that, along with other sectors of society, there was a need to mobilize and demand the end of state repression. As a result, a month after the Balvanera raid, a group of approximately one hundred gays and lesbians decided to hold a meeting and establish what would become the most visible gay organization in contemporary Argentina: the Homosexual Community (*Comunidad Homosexual Argentina*, CHA). Energized by mass mobilization within the larger context of democratization and the national importance human rights had acquired, these individuals sought to create public awareness of their continued repression. Soon after the formation of the CHA, two prominent members of the organization agreed to be photographed, embracing, on the cover of a national magazine, *Siete Días*, for an article titled "The Risks of Being a Homosexual in Argentina." The article galvanized gays and lesbians, many of whom decided to express publicly,

continued and, according to Stephen Brown, between January 1982 and November 1983, a former member of FLH and at least seventeen other gay men were killed (2002, 121).

through a series of interviews with national media, cases of abuse. The publicity gained through these public interviews further encouraged other Argentine homosexuals to join the movement, which grew steadily in size during the 1980s.

The generation of publicity was part of a larger objective to induce change in social perceptions of homosexuality by forcing a public debate on the ethics of sexuality through increased visibility. The elaboration of this strategy was partly due to the influence larger theoretical debates around sexuality were having on gay activism at the time. Of particular relevance was the work of French philosopher Michel Foucault, who, in his *The History of Sexuality* published in the late 1970s, argued that homosexuality is a relatively recent invention, distinct from earlier forms of same-sex relationships, which was largely brought about by its medicalization in the latter part of the nineteenth century. According to Foucault's reading of the historical regulation of homosexuality, the emergence of European scientific knowledge turned a physiological sexual practice into a psychological category, one that is socially constructed and that was made a pathology (1978). These arguments influenced a generation of Argentine gay activists, among whom was Carlos Jáuregui, one of the movement's most important public figures in the 1980s. In one of the first nonliterary academic works on homosexuality in Latin America, Jáuregui, a history professor trained in France, relied on Foucault to argue that views on homosexuality are culturally dependent, and for the need to accept homosexuality as a legitimate form of sexual expression and as a variant of human sexuality (1987).

Jáuregui and other activists, rejecting the movement's previous revolutionary approach to social change, and adopting a "reformist" approach based on human rights and civil liberties, thought that social visibility was an important tool to bring about change to social perceptions on sexuality by questioning heteronormativity publicly (Belucci 2010, 51–3; Rapisardi and Modarelli 2001, 207–8).[11] Academic arguments and ideas influenced the elaboration of gay activism in Argentina in the 1980s, continuing its relationship with academia that had started in the 1970s,

---

[11] The concept of heteronormativity was not coined by sociologists until the early 1990s. However, without explicitly using the term, Jáuregui refers to "reproductive heterosexuality." In his book, he writes: "there exists, then, an official sexuality, one which, as we have said, attempts to colonize every sexual minority. This is none other than heterosexuality. But it is not every heterosexuality, it is that which is devoted to reproduction and that, moreover, has to be civilly and/or religiously legalized" (1987, 24–5).

and that has become an important feature of the gay and lesbian movement in the country.[12]

In addition to challenging social perceptions of homosexuality through the attraction of public attention, activists decided to frame their public demands to end repression within larger national debates on democracy and human rights. For them, an effective way to change social perceptions and gain sympathy was through the establishment of a clear link between human rights and the consolidation of democracy. They thus adopted the motto "Freedom to express one's sexuality is a human right" with the intention of inserting their demands within a popular national discourse of the time. The pursuit of this strategy early on is well illustrated by the decision of CHA members to run advertisements in the daily *Clarín* (the most widely read daily in the country), in May 1984 and April 1985 that read: "with discrimination and repression there is no democracy" (Jáuregui 1987, 225–7). By appealing to a common cause, they attempted to gain the support of people who would back their struggle for a democracy without repression. To accomplish this, activists adopted, from the very beginning, a strategy to collaborate with other social movements on a variety of issues, such as human rights and violence: groups and people that had also been repressed by the dictatorship (Brown 2002, 124–5). As a result, gays and lesbians began to cooperate with numerous organizations and activists in several campaigns, and to forge important alliances with activists belonging to other social movements.[13] Of particular importance were women's groups: close, personal relationships were formed among gay, lesbian, and women activists during this time. Perhaps the most visible was the one with Laura Bonaparte, a prominent figure of the organization Mothers of the Plaza de Mayo, the most iconic human rights group in Argentina, who publicly supported CHA's activities.

---

[12] The influence of intellectuals on the movement's activities was not limited to Jáuregui: academics Perlongher, Sebreli, and Atilio Borón, and writer Alejandro Modarelli would also have an important theoretical influence on the movement in the 1980s and early 1990s.

[13] E.g., gay activists collaborated in marches and other activities organized by human rights organizations, such as the Jewish Movement for Human Rights (*Movimiento Judío por los Derechos Humanos*), headed by the renowned journalist Herman Schiller, who publicly supported gay rights; the Permanent Assembly for Human Rights (*Asamblea Permanente de Derechos Humanos*); the Centre for Social and Legal Studies (*Centro de Estudios Legales y Culturales*), headed by Emilio Mignone; and unions, through the umbrella organization Human Rights Union Committee (*Comisiones Sindicales de Derechos Humanos*) (Bellucci 2010, 55–6, 62).

The reformist approach adopted by gays and activists in posttransition Argentina meant that they sought collaboration with state actors and political parties. Their previous negative experience with the Peronists forced activists to interact with other parties, and the movement began to work closely with smaller, progressive political parties, such as the Workers Party (*Partido Obrero*), the Humanist Party (*Partido Humanista*), and the Movement for Socialism (*Movimiento al Socialismo, MAS*). While open to dialogue, MAS was the only party that included in its platform a reference to the human rights of sexual minorities (Bellucci 2010, 48). An important tactic used by activists to force a public debate, and which would be systematically used in subsequent struggles, was the solicitation of positions on homosexuality from candidates across political parties during elections. In effect, one of the very first activities militants undertook during the transition to democracy was the administration of questionnaires to several candidates for the 1983 elections, a practice that has continued to this day. They also approached state actors in the Deputy-Ministry for Human Rights and Members of Congress advancing their demands and, importantly, establishing relationships that subsequently allowed for coalition building in subsequent struggles. This was facilitated by the fact that many newly elected politicians had been activists in human rights organizations with which gays and lesbians had collaborated.[14]

The movement's framing of its struggles around the need to deepen democracy through the respect and expansion of human rights shaped the articulation of its demands, strategies, and activities during the latter part of the 1980s and early 1990s as it grew in strength and visibility. Their intention to gain attention proved successful and their demands were placed on the public agenda. Starting with the advertisements in *Clarín*, activists engaged in highly publicized events that attracted significant social attention.[15] Undoubtedly one of the most visible ones was their public struggle to gain legal recognition for CHA in the early 1990s.

---

[14] Such as Augusto Conte, Néstor Vicente, Alfredo Bravo, Graciela Fernández Mejide, and Simón Lázara.

[15] Because reliance on mass media was part of their strategy to gain publicity, gay and lesbian activists systematically appeared on television shows and did radio interviews. The best example is the appearance of writer and lesbian activist Ilse Fuskova in the most watched show in 1991 (*Almorzando con Mirtha Legrand*), in which she openly discusses her homosexuality. The public reaction was such that the show was rerun several times (Bellucci 2010, 150). That homosexuality had been placed in national debates was well demonstrated by the upsurge in films and soap operas that had gay and lesbian characters (see Bazán 2010, 425–32).

Having been denied the issuance of a permit to register the organization as a legal entity by the government in 1990 on the grounds that it was "a deviation from normal sexual instinct," its members appealed the decision to the National Appellate Court. That Court subsequently upheld the decision and the case moved up to the Supreme Court, which ultimately also upheld it on the grounds that the family had to be protected. While their demand was turned down, the case attracted considerable attention. In a highly publicized event, then-president Carlos Menem (1989–99) was confronted by a student after a speech he delivered at Columbia University, in New York. The student challenged his country's record on human rights and made specific reference to the inability of gays and lesbians to register a nongovernmental organization (NGO). Pressure resulting from the publicity was such that the president authorized the organization's legal registration a few months later. Securing legal recognition for one of its organizations was the first concrete policy achievement of Argentina's gay and lesbian movement. Importantly, the policy triumph amounted to an explicit validation by the state of the link that exists between human rights and the right to express a nonnormative sexuality, the movement's objective. Indeed, according to some observers (Sempol 2013), the Argentine gay movement was the first to advance their demands through an explicit link among sexuality, human rights, and democracy.

By the early 1990s, then, Argentina's gay and lesbian movement had grown in strength and visibility. Hundreds of activists had joined several organizations.[16] While divisions existed, in 1992 they joined forces to organize the first gay pride parade in Buenos Aires, which represented an important achievement for it meant the gaining of public space without state repression. They had managed to gain important visibility and to place their demands in national debates. Their actions had not resulted in the derogation of the police edicts, and police harassment would continue, although with significantly less intensity, but their objective to associate human rights with the right to express one's sexuality freely began to prove successful, as demonstrated by Menem's decision to grant the CHA the right to register as a legal entity. Moreover, it also meant the establishment of important professional and personal relationships with activists

---

[16] In addition to the CHA, these organizations included Gay for Civil Rights (*Gays por los Derechos Civiles*), Society for Gay-Lesbian Integration of Argentina (*Socieda de Integración Gay-Lésbica Argentina*), Research Group on Sexuality and Social Integration (*Grupo de Investigación en Sexualidad e Interacción Social*), The Ones and the Others (*Las Unas y las Otras*), and Eros, among others.

and prominent political actors that, as we shall see in Chapter 4, would be crucial in the weaving of networks needed to pursue policy change. The growth in strength and visibility of the gay and lesbian movement in Argentina was, by the early 1990s, clearly shaped by a process of democratic transition that saw the placement of human rights atop the agenda, a process characterized by a "new politics of accountability" in a country with a long history of intense social mobilization.

Mexico: Uneven Gay Mobilization

The Rise of Mexico's Gay and Lesbian Movement

Like Argentina, the emergence of Mexico's gay movement took place within a context of social mobilization in the late 1960s and early 1970s. Higher levels of urbanization and literacy, brought about by the postwar Mexican Miracle, produced important changes in social attitudes toward established norms. Some groups, led primarily by university students, began to challenge conceptions of morality, question ideas, such as the patriarchal family, and demand access to contraceptives. Encouraged by the social mobilization that took place during this time in the United States and Europe, and gaining consciousness of the limited social and political freedom that existed in the country, heightened by the Tlatelolco Massacre, numerous countercultural and antiestablishment groups emerged demanding sociopolitical change. Such an environment motivated Mexican homosexuals to organize. Inspired by the New York Stonewall Riots of 1969, and encouraged by a highly visible case in 1971 in which an employee at Sears Roebuck was fired for exhibiting "homosexual demeanour," a handful of homosexuals, led by Nancy Cárdenas and Luis González de Alba, decided to get together to analyze the oppression and the stigmatization of homosexuality in the country. In 1971, they thus formed Mexico's first homosexual group: the Homosexual Liberation Movement (*Movimiento de Liberación Homosexual*). They held meetings in which they shared experiences of discrimination and analyzed what they meant in terms of broader social debates about sexuality (Díez 2011b).

The group was forced to operate underground given the political repression of the time. As a response to increased mobilization, and the radicalization of some groups in southern Mexico, Luis Echeverría (1970–6) implemented a policy of repression toward social dissidence that came to be known as a "dirty war." Best illustrated by a second student massacre in June 1971, the regime sought to contain social mobilization and began to target and "eliminate" activists belonging to various social groups, most notably students and independent union leaders. Similar to the Argentine case, state repression was justified on the grounds that mobilization represented a threat to national security and it was framed as a conflict against terrorism. For homosexuals, the risks to mobilize were high as several of them belonged to student groups and unions, and homosexuality was seen as a form of subversion. The regime's position on homosexuals at the time was captured by a declaration Echeverría made during his fourth State of the Union address, when he stated: "among other things that characterized the background of the terrorists operating in Mexico was a high incidence of masculine and feminine homosexuality" (Lumsden 1991, 55).

Echeverría's declaration was unprecedented given that in Mexico homosexuality was not criminalized and was generally tolerated by the state. Similar to Argentina, Mexico's founding constitution of 1857 limited the state's ability to intrude into people's private lives and did not criminalize homosexuality.[17] The country's first penal code, enacted in 1871, made no reference at all to same-sex relations, but it introduced the vague notion of "attacks against morality and good customs." The clause would be interpreted openly by police to harass and detain homosexuals. Moreover, despite the generally liberal legal framework, the social stigmatization of homosexuality was strong. The medicalization of sexual regulation took place in Mexico at the turn of the century and homosexuality was socially maligned given that it was constructed as a deviance (Lizárraga 2003).

Public intolerance toward homosexuality by the turn of the twentieth century in Mexico is well depicted by the legendary raid of 1901: "the dance of the forty-one" (*el baile de los cuarenta y uno*). In November of that year, Mexico City police raided a private ball in which nineteen out of forty-one men present were found cross-dressed. Police arrested all nineteen of them declaring that the party was an attack on good morals. The event attracted a great deal of attention given that some of the revellers belonged to the political and economic élite, and, according to some accounts, the nephew of the country's president was present (Mosiváis 2001). Newspapers covered the episode extensively. The established daily *El Universal*, for example, declared in a front-page editorial that the shameless ball amounted

---

[17] The 1857 constitution replaced Mexico's first constitution of 1824 and has served as the basis for Mexico's contemporary political life. The 1917 constitution, valid until this day, was modeled after the 1857 one.

to an affront to "public decency and public morals." The dance of the forty-one became part of Mexico's popular consciousness and formed the basis for numerous cultural portrayals of homosexuality during the first half of the twentieth century.[18] To this day, the number forty-one is still used as innuendo to suggest that someone is homosexual.

In a way, the raid became a harbinger of how social attitudes on homosexuality would develop in twentieth-century Mexico and of its regulation by the state. While publicly decried, and often ridiculed, homosexuality was generally accepted among certain sectors of society, such as intellectuals and sectors of the working class, so long as it did not become publicly acknowledged. Homosexuals were thus able to find spaces for recreation in the main cities, and, a vibrant, though under-ground, culture developed from 1920 onward (Monsiváis 2001). This is partly the result of the fluidity that exists in Mexico regarding the for-mation of identities based on sexual practices. Indeed, contrary to what became common elsewhere, in Mexico dichotomized gay versus straight cultures did not develop (Gallegos Montes 2007; González Pérez 2001; Laguarda 2009; Núñez Noriega 2000, 2007), and it is estimated that approximately 30 percent of Mexican males between the ages of fifteen and twenty-five engage in same-sex sexual activities (Carrier 1995). The result of the historical legacies of relatively fluid understandings of sex-ual relations that survived colonization, views on sexuality are captured by the well-known adage *obedezco pero no cumplo* (I obey but I do not comply with). Frequently used to refer to attitudes toward the law, it more generally refers to individuals' propensity to acquiesce publicly to social norms while rejecting them in private. In Mexico this applies to attitudes to morality issues, including homosexuality: there may have been public disapproval of homosexuality, but some fluidity existed in the private sphere.

Yet, the centrality of family in Mexico has upheld heteronormativity as the organizing principle of the social order and, despite a certain degree of tolerance toward homosexuality in the private sphere, it has not meant public acceptance. Similar to Argentina, masculinity has been intrinsic to nation building in Mexico and homosexuality has often been depicted as a betrayal of the nation. The story of Manuel Palafox illustrates this well. In 1918, Palafox, secretary general to revolutionary Emiliano Zapata, was

---

[18] Among the most popular was a novel by Eduardo A. Castrejón and a well-known depic-tion of the event illustrated by the famous political cartoonist José Guadalupe Posada.

accused of having divulged secrets through his homosexual encounters to political enemies. He was publicly humiliated and forced to leave the revolutionary cause. In this case, masculinity represented loyalty and his supposed rejection of it was thought to be politically seditious and a threat to social stability (Kaplan 2006, 264). In the decades following the consolidation of the Revolutionary Institutional Party's (*Partido Revolucionario Institucional*, PRI) rule, the harassment and detention of homosexuals was common practice through the invocation of provisions of the criminal code on morality and good customs (de la Dehesa 2010, 31–2). The PRI may not have had an explicit policy of repression of homosexuals, but constant police harassment and abuse were common.

Such harassment, which hardened during the early repressive years of Echeverría's administration, motivated Mexican homosexuals to pursue collective action beyond the private sphere and begin to seek public attention to their cause. In 1975, González de Alba and intellectual Carlos Monsiváis drafted and distributed the first gay manifesto in Mexico, titled "Against the Use of the Citizen as Police Booty." In it, they denounced constant police persecution and called for its halt (Díez 2011b). Like the Argentine experience in the early 1970s, the discussions these early activists held were influenced by developments outside Latin America. In the Mexican case, activists were directly inspired by the liberationist discourse that their U.S. counterparts adopted and framed their demands around the need to liberate themselves from social stigma and oppression.[19] Also like their Argentine counterparts, writers and intellectuals played an important role in the development of the liberationist discourse. Individuals such as Monsiváis, José Joaquín Blanco, and González de Alba were well versed in broader theoretical debates on sexuality and began to argue for the acceptance of homosexuality as a diverse and legitimate form of sexual expression.[20] These discussions incentivized gays and lesbians to organize and, by 1978, three main gay groups had been formed: the Revolutionary Homosexual Front (*Frente Homosexual de Acción Revolucionaria*, FHAR), Lambda (*Grupo Lambda de Liberación Homosexual*), and Okiabeth.[21]

---

[19] Crucial to this was the influence activists such as Juan Jacobo Hernández had. Hernández lived in New York City during the Stonewall riots and was personally influenced by them. Hernández, as well as Monsiváis, obtained literature produced by U.S. gay groups and were key in the adoption of liberationist arguments. Interview, Juan Jacobo Hernández, Mexico City, August 2, 2007.

[20] E.g., Blanco relied on the work about sexuality by the German sexologist Magnus Hirshfeld in early discussions (Blanco 1979).

[21] Okiabeth derives from the Mayan phrase *lling Iskan Katuntat Bebeth Thot*, which in Spanish means: "warrior women that make way spreading flowers."

The relaxation of political repression by the regime in the latter part of the 1970s, which was accompanied by moderate political reforms, allowed activists to take to the streets to advance their demands and claim public space. On July 26, 1978, members of FHAR participated in a march commemorating the Cuban revolution, and on October 2, 1978, members of the other two groups joined another demonstration to commemorate the tenth anniversary of the Tlatelolco Massacre. These were the first in a series of actions that would allow the movement to attain important visibility in subsequent years. Armed with slogans such as "there is no political freedom without sexual freedom" and "the personal is political," and taking advantage of the political opening of the time, gay activists were successful relatively quickly in achieving the right of assembly as they convinced the Mexico City government to allow them to hold a gay pride parade in 1979, the first in Latin America. During the same time, they held protests in front of the office of Mexico City's Chief of Police, Arturo Durazo, demanding a halt to police raids that were systematically carried out in gay bars in the city (Lumsden 1991). The movement gained further visibility with the publication of several novels with a gay theme, the opening of acclaimed gay plays, and the establishment of Gay Cultural Week, a week of cultural events that has been held yearly ever since.

Nevertheless, the decision of activists to pursue elected office in 1982 was undoubtedly the most influential in gaining national attention. As a result of the 1977 reforms introduced by Echeverría, as a means to allow for the expression of social discontent through elections, small parties were given the opportunity to run for seats in an enlarged Congress. A newly created committee representing gays and lesbians was established by several activists who decided to support the presidential candidacy of Rosario Ibarra for the 1982 general elections, and two openly gay individuals ran for seats in the lower house.[22] Their candidacies were ultimately unsuccessful, but the unprecedented decision of a political party to field openly gay candidates for a general election forced a national debate on homosexuality given the extensive attention it attracted. In a country where homosexuality was generally not discussed in the public sphere, national coverage in radio and television contributed to the placement of homosexuality, and of the movement's demands, on the national

---

[22] She ran for the Revolutionary Workers Party (*Partido Revolucionario de los Trabajadores*). The other leftist political party that presented a presidential candidate in these elections was the United Socialist Party of Mexico (*Partido Socialista Unificado de México*).

agenda (Díez 2011b). Importantly, the pursuit of elected office would become a preferred medium to advance demands of some gay activists in Mexico in the mid-1990s, as we shall later see.

During its emergent years, a period to which some activists refer as the "golden years," Mexico's gay movement shared important characteristics with its Argentine counterpart. In Mexico, the development of the movement's discourse and strategies was influenced by theoretical debates on sexuality in sociology and philosophy as it was in Argentina. For Mexican activists at the time, the main strategy was the attainment of visibility to demand basic negative liberties, such as the right of assembly without repression, to force broader debates on sexuality. Key to this process was the influence intellectuals and writers had on the movement since the very beginning and that would become an enduring characteristic. In addition to well-known intellectuals such as Monsiváis, activists Xavier Lizárraga and Claudia Hinojosa were central in the development of a discourse that questioned established norms of sexual behavior. For both of these activists, the writings of philosophers such as Foucault were fundamental in their understandings of sexuality and the elaboration of discourse that challenged the prevailing ethics of sexuality.[23] According to Lizárraga, the replacement of the term *homosexual* with the postliberationist term *gay*, for example, was influenced by his reading of Foucault's deconstruction of contemporary ideas of sexuality and was seen as an attempt to demonstrate that same-sex relations were natural forms of sexual expression and natural bases upon which to build legitimate identities.[24] Also like Argentina, some Mexican activists embraced struggles against patriarchy as a central component of their militancy and women played a central role in activism. Groups such as Lambda were made up of both gays and lesbians and adopted women's rights as part of its policy objectives. However, in the Mexican case, there was a much wider range of perspectives among gay activists on the role feminism should play. While members of Lambda fully embraced a feminist discourse, the more radical FHAR rejected it completely: it was in effect made up of only men. However, for members of the lesbian group Okiabeth, influenced by radical lesbian writers such as Monique Wittig, feminism took precedence over gay liberation.[25] Nevertheless, moderate members of Mexico's gay movement, the so-called reformists, adopted women's rights as part

[23] Interviews, Xavier Lizárraga, Mexico City, July 3, 2008, and Claudia Hinojosa, Mexico City, June 25, 2008.
[24] Interview, Lizárraga, Mexico City, July 3, 2008.
[25] Interview, Yan María Castro, Okiabeth founding member, Mexico City, August 2, 2007.

of their struggle and developed important relationships with women's groups, relationships that would strengthen over time and became critical in the building of coalitions in future years.

The Effects of the HIV/AIDS Epidemic

By the early 1980s, Mexico's gay movement had been successful in achieving its main objectives: national visibility and public space. Even though police raids on gay restaurants and bars continued, the movement had forced a national debate on homosexuality. However, unlike the Argentine gay movement, which saw a steady strengthening during the 1980s within the general context of democratization, Mexico's movement experienced a certain loss of visibility in the mid-1980s (de la Dehesa 2010, 18–19; Díez 2011b, 699–703; 2013; Salinas Henrández 2010, 83–5). Once the movement had attained its main objectives, visibility and some public space, deep disagreements emerged within the leadership. While the more radical groups, such as FHAR, advocated social revolutionary change, others, such as Lambda, endorsed gradual social change through political institutions. Divergent opinions over whether to support political parties were central to these divisions. Activists were therefore unable to agree on the next course of action.[26] The economic crises of the 1980s also had an effect. Financial difficulties meant a reduction in resources available to continue mobilization. In practical terms, it meant that many activists were forced to move back to their parents' homes where they were unable to express their sexualities freely.[27] Activists failed to frame their demands in a way that resonated with the deep economic crisis that affected large sectors of the population. As the pioneer activist Claudia Hinojosa stated:

> We were unable to deploy a language to engage the horrible crisis. We did not see the relationship between our cause and broader changes. We should have hooked our demands on economic realities, but we could not. The liberationist language was not enough. Here we are, liberated, and then?[28]

Another, and certainly the most important, reason was the effects the onset of the HIV/AIDS had on Mexican activism. The appearance of the disease cost the lives of many activists, devastating the movement's leadership. It also reoriented efforts among gay men to provide community services to

---

[26] Interview, Hernández, Mexico City, August 2, 2007.
[27] Interview, Lizárraga, Lambda founding member, Mexico City, July 3, 2008.
[28] Interview, Mexico City, June 25, 2008.

victims. Several organizations, such as Colectivo Sol and Cálamo, were established to generate funds to provide information sessions and social services. While in previous years the objective was to gain visibility, from 1985 onward it became mere survival. Gay activism took an inward turn and abandoned the pursuit of public debates on homosexuality. Activists were also forced to abandon public debates largely because of the fierce reaction to the virus unleashed by conservative forces in the country. For example, the Apostolic Nunciature to Mexico declared: "AIDS is the punishment that God sends to those who ignore his laws . . . homosexualism is one of the worst vices condemned by the Church" (*Excélsior*, August 31, 1985). Such accusatory language was not limited to the Catholic Church. In the same year, the head of the Gastroenterology Department of Mexico's National University (*Universidad Nacional Autónoma de México*, UNAM) in Mexico City stated: "92% of sufferers from this disease are promiscuous homosexuals and drug addicts . . . homosexuality and drug addiction are interrelated. . . . Why does that disease only affect homosexuals? It could be the result of divine punishment" (*El Sol de México*, August 24, 1985). The victims thus became culpable for the disease, which was called the "gay plague" or "pink cancer." The persecutory discourse destabilized activists given the paucity of knowledge about the disease. They were consequently forced to focus efforts on self-help activities (Galván Díaz 1988).

However, while activism lost some visibility during this time, it also underwent important changes: the onset of the AIDS crisis forced activists to establish links with a variety of other organizations, including feminists, and to begin collaborating with the state. Following several regional meetings of women's groups held during the early 1980s, at which the topic of lesbianism was discussed extensively, several lesbians established important personal relationships and subsequently founded in 1987 the National Coordinating Group of Lesbian Women (*Coordinadora Nacional de Mujeres Lesbianas*). Made up of eleven organizations from several regions of the country, the group devoted itself to activities ranging from general consciousness-raising activities to the inclusion of discussions of sexuality in labor unions (Mogrovejo 1999). Gays and lesbians continued to work on certain issues with feminist groups building coalitions to press for change. Discussions on sexuality and gender earlier in the decade had brought together a variety of activists from leftist movements that saw the development of important relationships. These relationships proved fundamental in the first policy triumphs the movement achieved. For example, after a series of massive police raids in the early 1990s in Mexico City, the chairwoman of Mexico City's Public Safety Commission, Amalia García, pushed for reforms in 1992 to replace the Police and Good Governance bylaws, which were used to justify raids, and to create a city-level Human Rights Commission. The bylaws were changed in 1993 and included, for the first time in Mexico's history, a stipulation stating that no one could be persecuted on the basis of sexual orientation (de la Dehesa 2010, 152). This was the first provision covering sexual minorities introduced in Latin America. García was a member of the Campaign for Women's Access to Justice (referred to in the preceding text). Collaboration with feminists and other groups that had started earlier continued and strengthened even during a period of low visibility for the gay movement. In effect, in 1996, collaboration among these various groups resulted in the formation of a cross-sectoral network, the Democracy and Sexuality Network (*Red de Democracia y Sexualidad*, DEMYSEX) which brought together some 250 groups dedicated to sexual and reproductive rights as well as human rights more generally (de la Dehesa 2010, 155). The network's objective was to pool resources and to press for policy change across a variety of areas in sexuality and women's rights, ranging from abortion to sexual education.[29] This network deepened the relationships among activists working on sexual and reproductive rights. Importantly, they managed to establish working relationships with state actors across several ministries, including education and health. While gay and lesbian mobilization in Mexico lost some visibility in the early 1990s, activists began to develop networks around sexual and reproductive rights and to deepen relationships with women's groups in the shadow of the hegemonic PRI (de le Dehesa 2010).

As the AIDS crisis deepened some activists began to advance their demands for social and medical services to government agencies and to establish important relationships with state actors. Indeed, gay men organized themselves into numerous organizations and began to hold national meetings to gather and share information in the mid-1980s. In 1987, a Guadalajara-based gay NGO, Homosexual Pride Liberation Group (*Grupo Orgullo Homosexual de Liberación*, GOHL) organized a conference to discuss the pandemic, and, for the first time, officials from the state of Jalisco participated in the discussions. Later in the year, the PRI organized a panel discussion to which activists were invited. At the federal level, activists in Mexico City were invited to consultations to

---

[29] Interview, José Ángel Aguilar Gil, National Coordinator Mexico City, July 21, 2008.

reform the Health Law, which established the National AIDS Council (*Consejo Nacional para Prevención y Control del SIDA*, CONASIDA) (de la Dehesa 2010, 154). By 1989, some activists, led by prominent activist Arturo Díaz, formed the NGO *Ave de México* and established a nationwide umbrella organization, Mexicans against AIDS, to lobby government agencies to provide medical assistance to patients, support the provision of free testing and promote HIV education programs (Torres-Ruiz 2011, 41).

These activities were mostly supported by financing provided by international institutions. At first, the relationship activists had with state institutions was one of confrontation, consisting mainly of denunciations of government inaction. It was also marred by internal conflicts among groups for international funding and disagreement over priorities. However, over time, confrontation led to collaboration and, by the mid-1990s, effective working relations were established. Activists were invited to participate in the formulation of HIV-prevention programs and were very influential in shaping the state's response to the crisis (Salinas Hernández 2010, 85). Close collaboration between state and nonstate actors resulted in the enactment of an Executive Directive (*Norma Oficial*) by President Ernesto Zedillo (1994–2000) on January 17, 1995, which tasked government institutions to confront the pandemic in a concerted manner (Magis 2000). Research on the making of the adoption of this policy shows that gay activists played a definitive role in shaping it (Torres-Ruiz 2011, 43). Importantly, this type of interaction with government officials, medical experts, and international agencies would allow members of Mexico's gay movement to develop close relationships with a variety of individuals that would later be very important in the formation of coalitions and networks, as we shall see in Chapter 5.

These efforts were made by framing the issue of access to health as one of human rights: like their Argentine counterparts did years earlier, activists began to articulate a discourse that connected sexuality with human rights. For some activists, access to health care could only be brought about through legislative change and the most powerful way to achieve it was by articulating their demands through a human rights discourse, which had become part of national discussions on democratization. According to Díaz, struggles for sexual justice had to be carried out "through [changes to] the law."[30]

---

[30] Interview, Mexico City, June 25, 2008.

Close collaboration with government in the elaboration of health policy and increased financing from abroad resulted in the professionalization and institutionalization of the movement by the mid-1990s. In 1995, Letter S: HIV/AIDS, Sexuality and Health (*Letra S: VIH/SIDA, Sexualidad y Salud, Letra S*), was established, an organization in charge of coordinating and implementing HIV prevention programs. Mexico's gay activism coalesced around this NGO as it attracted significant funds for HIV-prevention campaigns and began to recruit professional staff. *Letra S*'s director, Alejandro Brito, became one of the most prominent gay activists in Mexico and continued the movement's tradition of having close relations with intellectuals and feminists. While HIV prevention was the central focus of the NGO's work at its foundation, over the next several years it began expanding its agenda to include other issues, such as collecting data on hate crimes based on homophobia and the expansion of civil rights. The organization gained a great deal of visibility as it developed a monthly supplement devoted to sexuality issues in the Mexican daily *La Jornada*, one of the most widely distributed newspapers in the country. Similar to what occurred during the decade with other social movements in Mexico, such as the environmental one (Díez 2006), activism underwent a process of "NGOization" as gays and lesbians joined NGOs to advance a variety of policy objectives (Díez 2011b; Torres-Ruiz 2011).[31] The movement's adoption of a collaborative approach with the state, as it professionalized, occurred at a time when Mexico's democratization accelerated, presaging its reawakening.

Democratization and Resurgence
Mexico's democratization process accelerated in the latter part of the 1990s. The implementation of political reforms fueled the country's protracted transition to democracy as the regime lost its majority in the lower house of Congress for the first time and the mayoralty of Mexico City in 1997. Those elections changed state-society relations in important ways. The left-leaning Party of Democratic Revolution (*Partido de la Revolución Democrática*, PRD), which had strong connections with grassroots movements, won the mayoralty of Mexico City, the majority of the seats of its first-elected assembly, and 25 percent of the seats in the divided lower house of Congress. Smaller, socially progressive candidates were also successful in gaining seats. For many social movements, the

---

[31] The term *NGOization* was coined by Sonia Álvarez (1999) to refer to the proliferation of feminist NGOs in Latin America during the 1990s.

arrival of Mexico's main leftist party to the Mexico City government and its increased presence in Congress represented a significant opening of opportunities to push for policy reform.

For the gay and lesbian movement, these political developments marked a definitive turning point. Not only did they help revive the movement by giving it a visibility it had not enjoyed since the early 1980s, but they opened the door to press for policy change. At the federal level, Patria Jiménez, a lesbian feminist, became the first openly lesbian Member of Congress in Latin America, after having formed an electoral alliance between her own party and the PRD. As the first lesbian elected to national office, her campaign and inauguration attracted a great deal of attention in national media. At the local level, Mexico City's new council held a Legislative Forum on Sexual Diversity and Human Rights in 1998 organized by newly elected PRD councilor David Sánchez with the objective of discussing the movement's demands and priorities. The forum brought together more than seventy organizations that included gay and lesbian groups, feminists, human rights organizations, and AIDS NGOs.

The event was significant on many fronts. After Jiménez's election to Congress, the forum gave the movement additional visibility as it was the first time a state institution had organized an event specifically attending to sexual-diversity issues. As such, it essentially meant the placement of the movement's demands on the legislative agenda and it amounted to a structuring of relations between the state and the movement. For the first time, discussions between state and nonstate actors on issues relating to sexual diversity were carried out in an institutionalized way. Moreover, by inviting numerous organizations, the forum brought together the main activists in Mexico, many of whom had not come in contact since the movement had weakened in the 1980s. While there was no agreement on several issues among activists, they came together for the first time in more than a decade and some among them began to set policy objectives. For many activists, the forum represented a new beginning in the movement's evolution and in relations with state institutions. As Díaz, a key figure in the organization of the event, put it: "the forum was a long-overdue family reunification that forced us to decide what the next steps of our struggle were . . . it opened a new phase of our history, giving us hope."[32]

As the movement became professionalized and gained visibility, activists began to articulate a discourse to press for demands framed around the concept of "sexual diversity" in an attempt to connect it strategically

[32] Interview, Mexico City, July 24, 2007.

with larger national debates regarding human rights and democratization. The adoption of the notion of sexual diversity was to a great extent influenced by theoretical debates about sexuality, particularly a body of literature known as Queer Theory, as well as the increasing importance of cultural diversity at the international level (which translated into a push for the adoption of policies intended to protect cultural, indigenous, and ethnic minorities in numerous countries around the world).[33] Like Argentina, intellectuals and academics played an important role in the development of the new discourse.[34] For activists, framing their demands around "rights to sexual diversity" was seen as an opportunity to appeal for support given the salience debates surrounding social diversity had acquired in Mexico's process of democratization. In what Deborah Yashar has called the "post-liberal challenge" (2005), the Zapatista rebellion of 1994 had a significant effect on national discussions about democracy and human rights as it challenged the country's national narrative of a *mestizo* nation. Zapatista demands called for greater respect for human rights and democracy and included a recognition of the country's cultural, linguistic, and social diversity (Monsiváis 2004; Stavenhagen 2002; Yashar 2005). The strategy to build a discourse that would resonate with larger sociopolitical debates was well summarized by Antonio Medina, Director of Communications at *Letra S*:

> The idea was to insert into the social consciousness the idea that it was about rights, to pair the concepts (*crear un binomio de los conceptos*) of human rights and sexual diversity. At the time, you could not talk about democracy without talking about human rights . . . and the notion of sexual diversity was being used by movements in the United States, in Canada. For us, it was a strategic decision to start calling for the rights of sexual minorities.[35]

As Mexico's democratization gained speed, its gay movement assumed renewed visibility and strength and began to articulate a discourse in a manner in which activists thought would resonate with larger debates. Given the specific characteristics of Mexico's protracted process of democratization, it would take Mexican activists longer to achieve the level of strength and visibility that their Argentine counterparts had by the early 1990s. Nevertheless, once the struggle against the HIV/AIDS pandemic eased as antiretroviral drugs and medical treatment became

---

[33] For a detailed account, see Díez 2011b, 704–8.
[34] Individuals such as Gloria Careaga, Ana Amuchástegui, Marta Lamas, Hinojosa, Xavier Lizárraga, and Norma Mogrovejo played important roles.
[35] Interview, Mexico City, June 18, 2008.

available, Mexico's gay movement emerged from its period of relative obscurity with new discursive tools and a set of demands to begin a new phase in its fight for the expansion of rights.

Chile: Weak Mobilization

A History of Repressive Sexual Regulation

In Chile, gays and lesbians have confronted a historically more repressive regulation of homosexuality than in Argentina or Mexico. Unlike most of the region, Chile did not undergo a clear break from its colonial past in the criminalization of homosexuality. In 1823 it declared valid the Spanish body of laws, *Las Siete Partidas*, and established a series of special committees in charge of determining the constitution of criminal offences in court. Carrying on the Natural Law tradition, homosexuality continued thus to be regarded as a "heinous crime." While not systematically applied, there are documented cases of judges calling for burning homosexuals at the stake during the subsequent decades and, up until 1873, records show that homosexuals were either sent to prison or received corporal punishment (Contrado 2011, 105–6). After several failed attempts, in 1874 Chile enacted its first penal code. The influence of the French civil code in the region notwithstanding, Chile's first penal code established sodomy as a crime, making it one of the few exceptions in Latin America.[36] Alongside a variety of other sexual crimes, such as adultery and incest, its Article 365 made same-sex relations punishable by up to three years in prison (Rodríguez Collao 2004, 17–19). Similar to Argentina and Mexico, Chile's first penal code also included offences against immoral public behavior: along the other sexual crimes, Article

---

[36] The decision of Chilean élites to continue penalizing sodomy in the civil code seems to be related to the continued influence of Conservative forces. Unlike other countries in the region, Chile modeled its code after Belgium's 1867 code, and not the Napoleonic Code. The Belgian code did not contain antisodomy provisions, but it was more conservative than the Napoleonic Code as it contained the idea of collective crimes derived from individual action, which included sexual crimes (Rodríguez Collao 2004). The retention of sodomy as a crime in the code was therefore in keeping with a more restrictive approach to individual freedom. It was also enacted during Chile's Liberal-Conservative Alliance (*Fusión Liberal-Conservadora*) that ruled from 1858 until 1873. Unlike other Latin American countries, which were undergoing a strong anticlerical wave at the time as Liberal forces governed (Mallimaci 2000), religious Conservatives in Chile were still in power. As such, the first serious attempt at reducing the influence of the Catholic Church in politics did not occur until reforms were undertaken in 1883 (*leyes de reformas teológicas*) and Catholicism continued to be the state religion until a new constitution was enacted in 1925 (Schwaller 2011, 184–5, 200–1).

363 enacted the criminal offence against "public morality and good customs." The penal code hardened the persecution of homosexuals: from 1875 until 1900, thirty-three court cases involving the heinous crime are recorded in official documents (Contardo 2011, 111).

As in Argentina and Mexico, in nineteenth-century Chile social attitudes toward homosexuality were intertwined with processes of state formation that were associated with ideas of gender and masculinity. Within a general context of enhanced nationalism following the War of the Pacific (1879–83) against Peru and Bolivia, after which Chile annexed the provinces of Tacna and Arica, a new discourse on Chilean national identity emerged, an identity centered on an idealized strong and masculine warrior. Representative of the Chilean race, a decidedly working-class (*roto*) masculine mestizo soldier was depicted by the new national narrative as the only one able to repel the enemy, often portrayed as effeminate men (*maricuelas*).[37] Some of these ideas would prove enduring and the depiction of political enemies as weak with references to homosexuality have been used as recently as the early 1970s. As occurred elsewhere in the Americas and Western Europe, the public discourse on homosexuality was influenced by the medicalization of sexuality that took place around the turn of the century. As Óscar Contardo details, from the 1890s onward, the medical community in Chile began to portray homosexuality as a deviant form of behavior that had to be diagnosed and controlled as it was considered, along with other diseases, a threat to public health (2011, 147–98).

The criminalization and medicalization of homosexuality in Chile during the nineteenth century contributed to strong social intolerance that lasted well into the late twentieth century. While a gay subculture developed in the cities of Santiago and Valparaiso in the first half of the twentieth century, tolerance of homosexuality by the state was minimal and harassment and persecution strong. Attitudes toward homosexuals in Chile hardened with the enactment of a security law in 1954 during the administration of Carlos Ibañez (1952–8) who, as we saw in Chapter 2, instituted repressive measures to suppress social mobilization. The law (*Ley de Estados Anti-Sociales*) introduced the concept of "dangerous state," which allowed security forces to detain individuals suspected of becoming a threat to national security. Under its legal provisions, a collection of suspect individuals, including beggars, drunks, and

---

[37] This is well captured by the writings of Juan Rafael Allende, founder of the Democratic Party (*Partido Democrático*) in 1887.

drug addicts could be detained. Homosexuals were, of course, included. The law went so far as to stipulate the establishment of agricultural farms in which all these dangerous beings would be held. The law was not implemented given that its regulation (*reglamento*) was never enacted and homosexuals were therefore not sent to these farms. However, the existence of all these various legal provisions contributed to the public portrayal of homosexuals as delinquents and fostered a police culture that resulted in the systematic detention of homosexuals up until the early 1970s (Contrado 2011, 186–98).[38]

As we have seen, Chile, like Argentina and Mexico, experienced intense social mobilization by the late 1960s, a process that reached a new pitch with the election of Salvador Allende in 1970. However, while in Argentina and Mexico gays and lesbians began to organize and mobilize to challenge heteronormativity during this time of social upheaval, in Chile they did not. In a well-documented case, a group of approximately twenty-five working-class gay men held a brief demonstration in Santiago's main square (*plaza de armas*) on April 22, 1973 demanding a halt to police repression. These individuals cited systematic harassment and repression by police who regularly invoked offences against public morality and good customs when detained (Robles 2008, 11–18). The protest dispersed quickly, however, and while it attracted some media attention, its coverage was invariably highly derogatory. Other than this incident, Chilean gays and lesbians did not join forces to advance political demands. In Argentina and Mexico homosexuals began to organize to engage larger debates on the politics of sexuality and to articulate a liberationist discourse. This did not happen in Chile. Paradoxically, at a time when the country was undergoing unprecedented mass mobilization, no gay organization formed and a homosexual liberationist movement did not emerge.

That paradox is partly explained by historical legacies of stern sexual repression. As Contrado argues, the historic repression of homosexuality in Chile contributed to the emergence of a highly discriminatory political discourse against homosexuals among the political class, which included the Left (2011, 253–304). In effect, the 1970s elections were characterized by a campaign in which parties on the Left, including Allende's Popular Unity, questioned the integrity of the candidate on the

---

[38] However, the detention of homosexuals was regularly carried out on charges of offences against public morality and good customs (Article 363), and not the antisodomy clause of the penal code. In effect, Article 365 was widely regarded as dead letter as cases were not brought to court.

Right, Jorge Alessandri, given his nonconformity to heteronorms: they suggested that Alessandri was unfit for office because, given that he was not married, he had to be homosexual (Contrado 2011, 267–74). In such context, the possibility that Chilean homosexuals could find allies within parties of the Left was essentially nonexistent. This was specially the case with the Communist Party, which had close ties with the Cuban regime, a regime that, at the time, placed homosexuals in concentration camps.

But that paradox is undoubtedly also explained by the failure of homosexuals in Chile to reach across social divides and coalesce around the pursuit of political goals. The failure of intellectuals and academics to get engaged to raise consciousness and articulate demands appears to be of particular importance. In both Argentina and Mexico intellectuals came together in the early 1970s with homosexuals and feminists from various backgrounds, such as the labor movement, to discuss the politics of sexuality, gender, and feminism. Through their discussions they engaged larger debates around homosexuality that were being held at the time across the Americas and Western Europe. In Chile this did not occur. A good illustration is the evident disconnect that existed between the demands advanced by the individuals who held the protest in the *plaza de armas* and the liberationist discourse advanced by gay activists in the Americas at the time: while in the United States the American Psychiatric Association declassified homosexuality as a mental disorder in 1973 largely as a result of mobilization by the gay liberationist movement, the Chilean protesters called for the stop of police repression arguing that homosexuality was a disease and not a crime.

Arresting Development: Gay (Im)Mobilization under Pinochet

If any opportunity existed for gays and lesbians to mobilize within a context of mass social upheaval in the early 1970s in Chile, it disappeared considerably after the seizure of power by Augusto Pinochet in 1973. During the dictatorship's most generalized phase of repression (1974–7), gays and lesbians, especially the poor and those belonging to the working classes, were systematically detained by the police forces as the regime launched its terror campaign (Robles 1998). However, Chile's military regime did not have an explicit policy regarding homosexuality, and, once repression became more targeted in 1977, some gay organization did occur. In 1977, a group of approximately fourteen gay men at the Catholic University formed a discussion group, first called Betanía and subsequently referred to as the Integration Movement (*Movimiento de Integración*), which was led by a progressive priest influenced by Liberation Theology. Ostensibly inspired by the U.S. group Gay Power, group members discussed the personal implications of being homosexual. The group was formed for mostly therapeutic and not political reasons and dissolved in the mid-1980s. In 1979 another group, Movement for the Liberation of the Third Sex (*Mivimiento para la liberación del tercer sexo*), made a public appearance through the publication of an open letter in the daily "*Últimas Noticias*" on October 13 in which they called for an end to discrimination and the repeal of Article 365 of the penal code. While they appear to have had concrete political objectives, their actions were limited to the publication of that one letter. Except for these limited activities, gays and lesbians did not mobilize to advance political demands given the stifling environment of generalized repression. From 1980 onward, the regime allowed gays and lesbians to socialize in commercial establishments. As Pinochet's neoliberal economic model took hold, several gay bars and clubs were allowed to open in Santiago and Valparaiso. The liberalization of market forces included thus the satisfaction of the demand for recreational spaces by gays and lesbians. But tolerance was limited to social interaction in commercial establishments and constant police harassment did not abate. While an open policy of repression toward homosexuals may not have existed, repression was exercised in an indirect manner as it discouraged any type of dissenting form of political organization.

Such generalized repression during the Pinochet years prevented the public emergence of a gay and lesbian movement even when political conditions changed in the mid-1980s. Social mobilization resurged as a result of the economic crises that rocked the country in the early 1980s, but gays and lesbians did not take to the street and organization continued to occur in the private sphere. In 1984, as a reaction to the murder of a lesbian, Mónica Briones, in what appeared to be a crime committed because of her sexual orientation, a group of lesbians, led by Cecilia Riquelme, Susana Piñera, and Carmen Ulloa, formed the first overtly political lesbian organization in Chile: *Ayuquelén*. Motivated by the interaction Riquelme had with other lesbians in a regional forum held in 1983,[39] *Ayuquelén* was founded to challenge the social order through a questioning of heteronorms, calling it "compulsory heterosexuality" – likely borrowing from Adrienne Rich's early work in which she coined the term (1980) – and to integrate feminist ideas into debates on sexuality (Robles 2008, 21). Over the following several years the group grew in

[39] This refers to the Second Latin American Caribbean Feminist Conference held in Lima, Peru. According to Riquelme, the meeting was key in encouraging her to form the group (de la Dehesa 2010, 18).

size and reached a membership of thirty lesbians. But the group remained confined to the private sphere. In 1987, as the advent of democratization became palpable, group members decided to go public through an interview they gave to a magazine that opposed the military regime, *APSI*, but they did so under condition that their names not be published and that there not be any photographs.

The AIDS epidemic had some effect on gay mobilization during Chile's military dictatorship. The first case of infection was reported in May 1984 and the first death in August of the same year. Media coverage of these cases was generally negative and alarmist, referring to it as the "pink plague" and a "gay cancer" (Contrado 2011). Such coverage contributed to the setting in of panic among the general population, similar to what happened in Mexico. Pinochet's regime reacted by treating it as a problem that affected a limited number of people and by attempting to contain it through the surveillance and control of gay men: raids on gay bars and clubs intensified with the apparent intention of stopping the spread of the disease through the identification and isolation of carriers of the virus. The regime did not formulate a health policy intended to provide services to the affected population. In the face of government inaction, affected gay men were forced to organize and, in 1987, they formed an organization, Corporation for AIDS Prevention (*Corporación de Prevención de SIDA*), to carry out prevention campaigns and to provide basic services to infected individuals. The Corporation became one of the main gay organizations in Chile in the years following the transition to democracy. However, up until 1990, it focused on grassroots work and kept a low profile without attaining much public visibility. By 1988, when Pinochet held the plebiscite, a gay and lesbian movement had therefore failed to emerge in Chile.

Democratization and Weak Mobilization

Chile's transition to democracy provided opportunities for gay mobilization. On June 28, 1991, a year after the inauguration of Patricio Aylwin (1991–4) as the newly democratic president, the Corporation for AIDS Prevention held a meeting to discuss a possible workshop on civil rights. The meeting was attended by a variety of individuals, most of whom belonged to the Communist Party or trade unions and who had been actively involved in the struggles against the Pinochet dictatorship (Robles 1998). Foreshadowing the evolution of Chile's gay movement during the 1990s, and beyond, congress participants could not agree on much and a number of them were expelled from the Corporation. A few days later, on July 1, seven of these expelled individuals formed a new organization: the Movement for Homosexual Liberation (*Movimiento de Liberación Homosexual*, MOVILH). Over the next several months, members held discussions on the various objectives the nascent movement should pursue in the new democratic context, and they agreed to work toward increased visibility and to fight discrimination based on sexual orientation. However, the legacies of their isolation during the long military dictatorship soon became obvious as they lacked the theoretical and discursive tools to advance their demands. For example, Rolando Jiménez, cofounder of the movement and one of the most visible activists in the country, was tasked during these early meetings with the organization of the first pride parade. Despite the fact that pride parades in the early 1990s were fairly common in several cities in the Americas, he had no knowledge of what these were. As he declared: "we had to start from scratch" (*empezar de cero*).[40]

In terms of discrimination, a member of the organization who was then a law student, Juan Cabrera, was in turn tasked to review any discriminatory provisions in Chilean legislation. Cabrera appears to have "stumbled upon" Article 365 of the Penal Code as he did not know it existed (Contardo 2011, 380). In effect, MOVILH's founding members had only a vague idea of the existence and implications of the antisodomy provision of the code,[41] highlighting the lack of contact they had with gay men during the dictatorship. Neither had they had contact with lesbian activists, academics, or intellectuals and, as result, contrary to what had occurred in Argentina and Mexico a decade earlier, the new activists were not immersed in broader theoretical debates on sexuality and gender. While lesbian feminists had engaged these debates in the 1980s, gay activists had not had contact with them during the Pinochet years and would not be able to cooperate jointly to advance their demands for years to come. The dictatorship not only stalled the emergence of the movement, but it had also prevented the establishment of relationships with individuals from other sectors of society, relationships that, as we have seen, were essential to the articulation of demands in Argentina and Mexico.

Despite these limitations, activists began to fight for public space and to advance a series of demands over the next several years. Having obtained

---

[40] Interview, Santiago, October 8, 2009.
[41] Interviews, MOVILH founders, Marco Ruiz, Santiago, November 25, 2009, and Carlos Sánchez, Santiago, November 23, 2009.

some international funding,[42] in early 1992 they joined a march to com-memorate the first anniversary of the Rettig Report's release (Chapter 2) holding a banner that read: "For our fallen brothers. Movement for Homosexual Liberation." While an important event given that this was the movement's first public appearance, activists marched covering their faces and did not disclose their names, underscoring the fear they still held in becoming public. However, for the second anniversary of the report's release, and encouraged by the political environment, they joined the march without covering their faces with the slogan "For the right to be different." They also held a press conference on the same day at which they denounced discrimination based on sexual orientation. This event, as well as the first gay prides that activists held for the first time during this time, even while sparsely attended, generated some publicity in the media.[43] Some media coverage referred to the emergence of the movement as a sign of the country's new democratic opening (*La Tercera*, June 11, 1993).

As activists conquered these public spaces, an important accomplish-ment given that sodomy was still a criminal activity, they attempted to decide on the main goals to pursue. Strong divisions, however, prevented agreement and the incipient movement soon fractured. Because the return to democratic rule had not marked a change in public policy to deal with the HIV/AIDS epidemic, several activists believed that the priority should be placed on prevention campaigns, providing support for infected indi-viduals and demanding the adoption of a health policy that directly dealt with the disease. Other activists believed that it was a mistake to place the fight against HIV/AIDS as the movement's main objective given that, among other things, it would give the movement a negative public image and prevent it from pursuing other goals.[44] These differences appear to have been irreconcilable. Some activists were consequently expelled from MOVILH and new organizations emerged, such as Lambda (which would concentrate efforts on HIV prevention activities) and the Center for the Study of Sexuality (*Centro de Estudios de la Sexualidad*). The movement generally divided into two main groups based on the goals they decided to pursue: those who worked on HIV prevention and those who advocated themselves to civil rights.

---

[42] MOVILH was able to obtain funding from the Dutch congregation of nuns *Zusters van Liefde*.

[43] The press conference was covered by the daily *La Época* the day after (March 4, 1993).

[44] Interviews, Leonardo Fernández (cofounder of MOVILH), Santiago, November 20, 2009, and Rolando Jiménez, Santiago, October, 9, 2009.

Early discussions held by activists that belonged to the second group
revolved around the need to frame their demands as an issue of human
rights, an idea partly influenced by the Argentine experience. However,
for these activists, it soon became clear that this would not be possible
in transitional Chile. Because Chile's dictatorship did not have a clear
position on homosexuality, it made it difficult to articulate a discourse
demanding the expansion of new rights in reference to atrocities perpetrated against them during the Pinochet years, contrary to what their
Argentine counterparts had done in the 1980s. As an activist put it,
"we did not have a martyr shot by the dictatorship"[45] around whom
to mobilize. Moreover, while the release of the Rettig Report had been
an important event, public debate on human rights in Chile did not
reach the same level of intensity as it had in Argentina a decade earlier (Chapter 2). Chile's transition to democracy forced those who had
opposed the military dictatorship to temper their discourse for fear of a
democratic reversal. The *Concertación* administrations during the 1990s
thus made conscientious efforts to limit divisive political debates and to
demobilize civil society. Within this context, placing sexual rights in the
national debates, through their connection with human rights, proved
extremely difficult.

As a result, and unlike their Argentine and Mexican counterparts,
Chilean activists did not attain the public visibility required to force a
social discussion on homosexuality until the early 2000s. Despite having
obtained some media attention in the years following the transition, the
loss of strength, mainly through a significant reduction in the number of
activists as they abandoned the cause,[46] meant that such attention proved
ephemeral. During the early 1990s activists held marches, provided several interviews to media outlets, and held weekly shows on national
radio, but these activities were not sustained. Indeed, after a march held in
1992, they did not hold the first Gay Pride parade until 1999. In a rather
short period of time gay activism in Chile lost public visibility. According
to one activist: "by 1997 the movement reached a profound crisis . . . we
lost all the media attention we had obtained earlier . . . it was as if we
had gone back into the closet."[47] Chile's situation contrasts significantly

[45] Interview, Marco Ruiz, Santiago, November 27, 2009.
[46] According to calculations by Carlos Sánchez (one of the pioneering activists), by 1997
there remained only ten activists out of the five hundred that were affiliated with
MOVILH in 1993. Interview, Santiago, November 23, 2009.
[47] Interview, Leonardo Fernández, activist and movement historian, Santiago, July
24, 2012.

with Argentina's and Mexico's where activists managed to attract, and sustain, national attention to their struggle and, by the late 1990s, public debates on homosexuality had been placed on the agenda. In Chile, by contrast, homosexuality did not make it to national debates and activists failed to begin challenging social attitudes and heteronorms. Discussions of sexual rights had to be therefore limited to the decriminalization of same-sex relations as it was the only area in which activists sensed change would be possible given that Chile stood out within a regional context on this front. As Marco Ruíz Delgado, one of the main activists of the time, said: "The repeal of 365 became our main fight (*caballo de batalla*). It was our struggle's banner. We knew that there was no space for other struggles. It was all closed."[48] These realities forced activists to limit their demands for civil rights to the repeal of Article 365 of the Penal Code.[49] Over the next several years activists in Chile mounted a campaign to repeal that provision of the code, as we shall see in Chapter 6.

Gay activists in Chile were unable to build coalitions with other groups and movements, forge relationships with state and nonstate actors, and establish networks. According to a key activist of the time, activists did not build a movement based on broad-based alliances (*movimiento de alianzas*).[50] Leonardo Fernández, a pioneering activist, asserted: "While we were ideologically prepared to collaborate with other groups given our leftist origins and the common fight we had waged against the dictatorship, we had to overcome the distrust that existed vis-à-vis our population."[51] Relationships with other actors were for the most part limited to the arts community (Sutherland 2001). Some activists believe that this development stemmed partly from the legal status of homosexuality in Chile: until same-sex behavior was decriminalized in 1999, it was difficult to cooperate with other groups because gays were *de jure* criminals.[52] While this appears to be a factor, it certainly is true that activists' failure to establish relationships with other actors was to a large extent due to internal movement dynamics and the rather exclusionary approach some of its members adopted, which were at the core of its divisions. Jiménez adopted a masculinist position in the definition of the movement's identity. Such a position contributed to the movement's exclusion of transgendered people,

---

[48] Interview, Santiago, November 27, 2009.

[49] As part of posttransitional discussions, the Aylwin administration repealed the 1954 security law, referred to in the preceding text, which was never implemented.

[50] Interview, Carlos Sánchez, Santiago, November 23, 2009.

[51] Interview, Santiago, July 24, 2012.

[52] Ibid.

lesbians, and effeminate men. But it also prevented the establishment of relationships with women's groups. Jiménez rejected – and, indeed, continues to do so[53] – the embrace of feminism in his approach to the challenge of heteronorms. According to Jiménez, women's issues and priorities differ from those of gay men and the movement's energy had therefore to be directed to the issues that specifically afflicted gay men. In the early 1990s it meant concentrating efforts on the derogation of clauses in the criminal code that prohibited same-sex behavior. This approach contrasts, rather sharply, with the Argentine and Mexican experiences that were characterized by the formation of networks around the advocacy of sexual and reproductive rights that emerged through the close collaboration between gay and women's activists.

The early weakening of the gay movement in Chile, a movement that emerged relatively late when compared to the Argentine and Mexican cases, meant that, by the late 1990s, it had not attained national visibility. Unlike their Mexican and Argentine counterparts, Chilean activists were unable to force a national debate on homosexuality. Because Chile's transition to democracy severely constrained national discussions as posttransitional *Concertación* governments suppressed debates in their pursuit of social consensus, the discussion of divisive issues was discouraged.

---

[53] As articulated as recently as 2012. Interview, Santiago, July 19, 2012.

PART II

EXPLAINING POLICY STASIS AND CHANGE IN GAY MARRIAGE

4

Argentina: The Precursor in Policy Reform

Introduction

Argentina's enactment of gay marriage in 2010 placed the country at the forefront of gay and lesbian rights. This chapter looks at the process that led to the adoption of gay marriage in the country and identifies the main factors behind policy change. Such an exercise requires a careful analysis of the interaction between state and nonstate actors, the type of access to the policy process proponents and opponents to gay marriage enjoyed, and the effectiveness of supportive and opposing arguments regarding sexual justice. The analysis in this chapter suggests that the sources of policy change in Argentina are found with the country's gay and lesbian movement. I argue that policy change on the gay marriage front is the result of the ability of gay and lesbian activists to weave extensive and effective networks in their push for policy reform and to convince policy makers of the merits of their policy objective in a manner that resonated with larger social debates. Key to policy reform was the permeability of the political system by networks in support of gay marriage and the lack of veto points by opponents. In the case of Argentina, such permeability was significantly facilitated by the existence of socially progressive state allies belonging to left-leaning parties, especially smaller ones.

A fuller understanding of the process that led to gay marriage in Argentina must, I argue, take a broader, historical dimension. In the case of Argentina, the adoption of gay marriage is part of a larger trajectory in the country's reform path in the gay and lesbian rights area. Indeed, the enactment of gay marriage can only be explained by looking at the role the gay and lesbian movement played in previous policy reforms. These experiences contributed to the expansion of activists' networks, which they had begun to form decades earlier, and the acquisition of effective discursive tools, strategies, and lobbying tactics, all of which played an important role in pushing the state to expand the right to marry to same-sex couples. While the adoption of gay marriage in Argentina surprised many a foreign casual observer, it is but part of a much larger policy history that has been characterized by sustained efforts by gay and lesbian activists to wrest rights from the state.

Getting Started: Early Successes in Policy Reform

Fulfilling Negative Liberties: Antidiscrimination Policy Reform

The early 1990s marked an important change in the politics of gay and lesbian rights in Argentina. Having achieved the legal recognition of Argentine Homosexual Community (*Comunidad Homosexual Argentina*, CHA), and having pressured successfully the federal government into passing a national law to fight the AIDS epidemic, some gay and lesbian activists turned their attention to the articulation of demands for civil rights. The most prominent of these organizations, Gays and Lesbians Civil Rights (*Gays y Lesbianas por los Derechos Civiles*, Gays DC), sought to normalize homosexuality through the pursuit of equal treatment before the law. As such, upon its formation its founders established three main policy priorities: the enactment of legislation to prevent discrimination based on sexual orientation, the extension of socioeconomic benefits to same-sex couples, and the repeal of the police edicts in Buenos Aires. Part of their strategy to achieve these policy goals was to sustain public visibility in order to place the idea of nondiscrimination based on sexual orientation on the public agenda. According to Marcelo Ferreyra, cofounder of Gays DC, sustained visibility was critical because their intention was "to advance their new demands as legitimate subjects of rights."[1] For activists there was a need to go beyond demanding the end of repression and claim equality as subjects of rights. The new rights-claim phase marked the beginning of what has become central to the interaction between the movement and the state in Argentina: the identification of state allies that would be sympathetic to their demands. In their pursuit of antidiscrimination protection, one of their first state allies was Buenos Aires city councilor

---

[1] Interview, Buenos Aires, June 22, 2009. Gays DC was founded on October 1, 1991 by Carlos Jáuregui, Marcelo Ferreyra, César Cigliutti, and writer Alejandro Modarelli.

Inés Pérez Suárez. Pérez Suárez belonged to the progressive wing of the (Peronist) *Partido Justicialista* (PJ), whose then-leader, Carlos Grosso, had established a close relationship with CHA activists during the 1980s. As an activist in the women's movement during the country's transition to democracy, Pérez Suárez had a special interest in promoting issues related to discrimination of various groups including sexual minorities (Bellucci 2010, 72). As a councilor, she began to engage representatives of several movements, such as women and youth, in an effort to integrate their priorities into the council's agenda. In September 1993 Pérez Suárez invited the leaders of the various gay organizations and asked them, pretending to be councilors in a mock-up session, to present their demands articulated in the form of actual bills. Activists presented ten specific demands that Pérez Suárez promised to promote in city council. The event served to place activists' demands formally on the agenda at the city level and to establish relationships with state actors. This activity marked the beginning of a strategy for Argentine activists to pursue their objective by interacting directly with lawmakers while mobilizing broader social support through public demonstrations and activities. In effect, it was during the same time that the Gay Pride marches began to be organized in Buenos Aires.

Having articulated and placed their demands on the political agenda, a significant opportunity to push for them opened up with the devolution of power to the city of Buenos Aires following the 1994 constitutional reforms. The reforms were the result of a negotiation between President Carlos Menem (1989–99) and leaders of the Radical Party (*Unión Cívica Radical*, UCR), generally known as the Olivos Pact (*Pacto de los Olivos*). In the agreement the UCR leadership agreed to allow for presidential reelection, which Menem sought in earnest, in exchange for the autonomy of the city of Buenos Aires (Negretto 2001). Following the signing of the agreement, the Argentine Congress passed a law in late 1993 calling for the establishment of a constitutional convention to draft constitutional reforms in line with the contents of the Olivos Pact.[2] On April 10, 1994, the provinces and the city of Buenos Aires elected constitutional conventionalists. The election of constitutionalists represented an important opportunity for gay and lesbian activists to ensure that their demands remained atop the agenda and to insert them into the debates surrounding the enactment of the new constitution.

[2] For the best discussion of this process, see Falleti 2010, 112–19.

Supported by several gay groups, CHA cofounder Carlos Jáuregui was invited to become a candidate for conventionalists for a coalition of smaller socialist parties, called Socialist Union (*Unión Socialista*), which adopted a progressive platform that included the decriminalization of abortion (Belluci 2010, 80–5). Following examples of Scandinavian countries,[3] Jáuregui proposed the inclusion of nondiscrimination provisions based on sexual orientation into its coalition's platform, which was accepted. While he was ultimately unable to obtain enough votes to get elected as a constitutionalist, Jáuregui's candidacy, as an openly gay man, attracted important public attention as national dailies reported it, allowing the movement to keep homosexuality in political debates. The constitutional reforms were approved by the constitutional conventionalists in August 1994. They granted the City of Buenos Aires autonomy in various areas of policy making, allowed for the election of a mayor through direct popular suffrage, and awarded the city the prerogative to draft its own constitution. On June 30, 1996, the city's first elected mayor and sixty city constitutional drafters (*estatuyentes*) were elected to design the new constitution.

For gay and lesbian activists, the drafting of the constitution for the newly decentralized city of Buenos Aires represented a golden opportunity to demand the inclusion of equal rights for gays and lesbians. Once the drafting assembly was formed, and as the content of the constitution came up for negotiation, gays and lesbians mobilized to push for antidiscrimination provisions. For Gays DC the strategy consisted in forming coalitions with other social groups that also pursued the inclusion of civil rights and to frame a new discourse (*imponer un discurso*) that presented nondiscrimination on the basis of sexual orientation as a fundamental right.[4] Key to the framing of this discourse was close collaboration with journalists. Alliances with several human rights organizations and women's groups, as well as collaboration with progressive journalists, were established as activists began a very public campaign to demand the inclusion of sexual-orientation provisions. For activists, gaining social support for their cause was both critical and possible given the importance human rights played in national debates around the need to deepen democratization.[5] At the same time, they began identifying constitutional drafters that had been involved in women's and human rights groups in

---

[3] By 1992, Norway and Denmark had included antidiscrimination provisions based on sexual orientation in their constitutional frameworks.

[4] Interview, Ferreyra, Buenos Aires, June 22, 2009.

[5] Interview, Cigliutti, CHA President, Buenos Aires, June 3, 2009.

the past and with whom they had collaborated in activities during the country's transition to democracy in the 1980s. These "latent contacts," as Ferreyra describes them,[6] included people such as Raúl Zafaroni and María José Lubertino, individuals who fully supported their cause and who became important supporters of subsequent policy changes. These allies in turn worked in convincing other drafters of the cause.

Having secured allies within the constitutional assembly,[7] activists began "harvesting votes" in support of their demand through the application of pressure on conservative drafters who were ambivalent or opposed to the inclusion of sexual-orientation provisions in the new city's constitution. They exercised pressure through forcing individual drafters to take a public position on the issue. Activists believed that it would be difficult for these individuals to oppose publicly their demand given the saliency of human rights in posttransitional Argentina,[8] and they seem to have read things correctly: according to constitutional drafter Diana Bisuti, "the issue of non-discrimination was so well placed (*instalado*) in public debates that no one . . . opposed to it would dare express it publicly."[9]

The issue of discrimination was indeed part of national discussions given the introduction in 1988 of the first antidiscrimination law and the establishment of the National Institute against Discrimination (*Instituto Nacional contra la Discriminación, La Xenofobia y el Racismo,* INADI) in 1995 following the 1994 attack on a Jewish community center. Given the prominence the issue of discrimination had assumed, for gays and lesbians it was a matter of convincing constitutional drafters that antidiscrimination provisions should not be limited to race or religion but should also include sexual orientation. Their strategy proved fruitful: on August 30, 1996 the drafting assembly approved the inclusion of sexual orientation into the city's constitutional nondiscriminatory provisions. The vote marked the first time sexual orientation was included in the constitution of a Latin American jurisdiction. According to several drafters, the lobbying strategy pursued by gay and lesbian activists was

---

[6] Interview, Ferreyra, Buenos Aires, June 22, 2009.
[7] In some instances, activists had established good working relationships with some of the drafters that were important in obtaining support. For example, Enrique Rodríguez had previously worked with César Cigliutti in the Labor Ministry (personal interview, Enrique Rodríguez, Buenos Aires, June 1, 2009).
[8] Interview, Cigliutti, Buenos Aires, June 3, 2009.
[9] Interview, Buenos Aires, June 1, 2009.

fundamental in obtaining a majority of votes.[10] The attainment of this policy goal provided activists with an important lesson on how to lobby a legislature and how to navigate various progressive and conservative forces. Indeed, in this first lobbying exercise activists learned of the importance of finding fissures within the established political parties to locate supporters and garner support.[11] This would become central in the pursuit of gay marriage at the national level in subsequent years.

Their first policy triumph had an important symbolic dimension for many activists. As María Luisa Peralta, prominent lesbian activist of the time, indicated, the inclusion of a sexual right in the city's constitutional framework "gave us a great deal of visibility and made us new subjects of rights."[12] Given that Buenos Aires, as the financial, political, and cultural center of the country, carries important weight in national life, the social repercussions of this policy change could be potentially significant. However, its practical potential was soon evident. Once the constitutional assembly approved the new constitution, the contradiction between the new antidiscrimination provisions and the decades-old police edicts became clear. As we saw in Chapter 3, the edicts had been in place since 1932 and had historically been used by police to repress homosexuals. With the inclusion of the right not to be discriminated into the constitution, the powers given to the police force to detain homosexuals and the newly enshrined right became legally contradictory. As a result, the assembly decided to repeal the edicts when the city enacted a new code (*Clarín*, September 11, 1996). Soon after this decision, activists, led by CHA, and in close collaboration with the Center for Legal and Social Studies (*Centro de Estudios Legales y Sociales*), mounted a campaign to eliminate references to homosexuality in the new code. The campaign was markedly influenced by their previous experience and activists pursued a very similar lobbying strategy: finding allies within the legislature, applying pressure from the outside through the ignition of a public debate and forcing legislators to take a public position. Their approach was, again, successful: on March 4, 1998, the city's first legislature voted to replace the edicts with the enactment of a new Contravention Code (*Código Contravencional*), which deleted homosexuality as cause for detention.

Pressure from the gay and lesbian movement to bring about policy change during this time was mostly limited to Buenos Aires. The only

---

[10] Interviews, Rodríguez and Alicia Perrini, Buenos Aires, June 22, 2009; Bisutti, June 1, 2009; and Aníbal Ibarra, July 22, 2009.
[11] Interview, Cigliutti, Buenos Aires, June 3, 2009.
[12] Interview, Buenos Aires, August 21, 2011.

exception is the city of Rosario, the third largest in Argentina, in which some gay activism built up by the mid-1990s. Inspired by the debate over the Buenos Aires constitution, activists successfully convinced city councilors to enact legislation protecting sexual minorities against discrimination. Following the submission by activist Guillermo Lovagnini of a draft proposal based on the Buenos Aires experience, on December 20, 1996, the city's council adopted an antidiscrimination clause. This policy success was largely the result of a close collaboration between gay activists in this city and members of the progressive Socialist Party (*Partido Socialista*, PS). Since the return to democratic rule the PS has had as its stronghold the province of Santa Fe, of which Rosario is the capital. This relationship would play an important role in the adoption of gay marriage in subsequent years, as we will see in the following text.[13] While important, the passage of this bylaw did not have the same significance as the inclusion of antidiscrimination into the Buenos Aires constitution given the influence the capital has in national discussions. With this exception, though, gay activism, by the late 1990s, was mainly located in Buenos Aires and most activists believed that they did not have the capacity "to generate opportunities for policy change outside the city."[14]

Civil Unions

The attainment of the right not to be discriminated on the basis of sexual orientation in the city of Buenos Aires forced an internal discussion within the movement to establish its next policy objectives, and the legal recognition of same-sex relationships and the extension of partnership rights emerged as one of priority. The need for such recognition became evident with implications following the painful loss of partners, many of whom died of AIDS-related causes. For many gay men the AIDS crisis had multiple traumatic effects. The pandemic not only took away their beloved ones: several activists recount stories of numerous gay men, themselves included, not being able to access medical services because their partners' social benefits did not include them; being denied access to seeing their lifelong partners at their deathbeds one last time because they were not considered to be family members; or having their possessions taken away by their partners' families. Such experiences convinced many activists of the need to fight for positive rights and demand the

---

[13] Rosario has long been considered the second most liberal city in Argentina after Buenos Aires and, since the return to democracy in 1983, fairly tolerant of gays and lesbians. For the best account of gay life in the city, see Sívori 2004.

[14] Interview, Ferreyra, Buenos Aires, June 22, 2009.

recognition of their same-sex relations. Interviews with activists reveal a deep sense of injustice. They therefore began to seek the extension of socioeconomic benefits to same-sex partners in the late 1990s.

One of the first actions was to seek the extension of medical benefits for public employees. Some activists engaged the leadership of the social security system for teachers (*Obra Social para la Actividad Docente*, OSPLAD) and demanded the expansion of medical coverage (*La Nación*, May 17, 1997). The couple, leaders of a gay organization (*Sociedad de Integración Gay Lésbica Argentina*), argued that it met the requirements for coverage as they had lived together for ten years. OSPLAD administrators agreed to extend these benefits. The legislation established that coverage included "individuals that live with the insured employee and who receive an ostensibly similar family treatment," without specifying gender. Following that decision, several individuals submitted applications for pension benefits to the national social security system (*Administración Nacional de Seguridad Social*, ANSES). However, despite the fact that the law was gender neutral in its reference to pension beneficiaries, on December 29, 1997, the ANSES administration issued a decree denying benefits based on the argument that the concept of "apparent marriage" stipulated by the pension law had to be interpreted with reference to the definition of marriage as established by Argentina's civil code. The code specified that marriage was between a man and a woman. The decree specifically mentioned that while the notion of apparent marriage refers to the link between two individuals not legally certified (*vínculo de cónyuges no celebrado legalmente*), same-sex relations were not recognized publicly in practice (Díez 2012). In this instance the extension of a benefit to an individual's partner was denied based on the traditional conception of marriage even though the law under question did not specifically establish that partnerships were between a man and a woman.[15]

This case, in which the extension of socioeconomic rights was denied because of heteronorms, solidified for many activists the need to pursue the legal recognition of same-sex relationships by pushing for civil unions. Encouraged by the ability of Spanish activists to press successfully for the recognition of same-sex civil unions in several of Spain's

---

[15] Following that case, gay and lesbian activists in Argentina pursued the judicial route to demand the expansion of benefits, but their attempts suffered reversals. Following a long and tortuous judicial road, the ANSES director, Amado Boudou, issued a decree in which same-sex couples became entitled to pension benefits a decade later (*Clarín*, August 20, 2008). For a detailed account, see Díez 2012.

autonomous regions during the 1990s, as well as the introduction of the French civil union (PACS) in 1999, CHA leaders, Cigliutti and Marcelo Suntheim, along with author Alejandro Modarelli, held discussions in early 2000 and decided to begin the process to push for the adoption of same-sex unions in the city of Buenos Aires.[16] For these activists the possibility to achieve this policy was strong given the city's recently acquired policy-making autonomy and, importantly, the inclusion of the antidiscrimination provision in the city's constitution.[17] To be sure, the decision to push for civil unions created divisions within the movement. For some activists the quest for civil unions restricted the struggle for gay rights to the assimilation into mainstream social life and prevented them from waging a larger battle of sexual liberation.[18] For proponents of civil unions, however, it was an important struggle to wage because, they argued, it could play a role in changing basic social assumptions about homosexuality. Cigliutti, who became the most visible face behind the civil-union campaign, argued that the debates over civil unions could have powerful social repercussions, beyond the practical socioeconomic benefits they would extend, as it would dispel misinformation in society regarding homosexuality. Cigliutti's reasoning was directly influenced by the theoretical formulations elaborated by Jáuregui fifteen years earlier (see Chapter 3): he believed that the struggle for such a right, given its contentious nature, would in itself increase social consciousness of citizenship rights. Moreover, he argued, it was critical to move the demand for rights from tolerance to equality. Cigliutti and other activists, who had been immersed in feminist thought, rejected the assimilationist argument regarding civil unions for they thought that this arrangement superseded the patriarchal foundations of traditional marriage. This position is important in understanding the debates over gay marriage that ignited in 2007.

Once CHA members established civil unions as a policy priority they developed a strategy that had been behind their recent policy victories: securing support from other social organizations, identifying actors

---

[16] This paragraph draws heavily from interviews held with Cigliutti, Buenos Aires, June 3, 2009 and December 8, 2010; and Suntheim, Buenos Aires, June 29, 2009 and August 24, 2011.

[17] However, it is important to note that while the pursuit of this policy objective became an area of priority, gay and lesbian activists continued to work in a wide variety of areas, such as the public denunciation of discriminatory acts, the reporting and collection of data on hate crimes, and casework. See CHA 2002.

[18] Interview, Peralta, Buenos Aires, August 21, 2011.

within government supportive of their proposal, forcing a social debate all while collaborating with the media, and lobbying each and every legislator by compelling them to take a public position. As a first step they solicited the endorsement of a renowned jurist and magistrate, Graciela Medina. Medina had been the first judge in Argentina to have ruled in favor of a case involving the extension of benefits to a same-sex couple. She agreed to support them and drafted the bill proposal.[19] They then secured the support of various institutions and organizations in which individuals who had been involved in the fight for human rights had worked and with whom they had developed close relationships over the years since the return to democracy, such as INADI, the Deputy-Ministry of Human Rights, the Buenos Aires Human Rights Commission, and Human Rights Ombudsperson's Office.[20] These institutions drafted letters of support arguing that it was an issue of human rights. They also received support and advice from legal experts and academics from established academic institutions, such as the faculties of law from Palermo University and the University of Buenos Aires, to develop lines of argumentation in support of civil unions. Through their collaboration with these individuals, activists began to form personal relationships that over time have been the basis for the development of personal networks.

Subsequently, through canvassing the legislators, they identified those who would be natural supporters of their proposal given their known liberal positions and commitment to human rights, individuals such as María Elena Naddeo, Daniel Bravo, and Roque Bellomo.[21] The identification of other supportive state actors was facilitated by the processes that had led to the inclusion of antidiscrimination provisions and the repeal of the police edicts. Some of the constitutional drafters whom

---

[19] Interview, Graciela Medina, Buenos Aires, June 22, 2009.

[20] These refer to individuals such as Diana Maffia, an academic, feminist, and human rights activist who had worked with gay and lesbian activists during and since the return to democratic rule. In 2000 she was the Deputy Ombudswoman (*Defensora Adjunta*) of Buenos Aires and a key player in gathering support from various institutions (interview, Buenos Aires, June 18, 2009).

[21] Nadeo is one of the most prominent human rights activists in Argentina and had been a city councilor when gay activists were first approached to present their proposal in the early 1990s (see preceding text). Daniel Bravo is the son of a prominent human rights figure in Argentina, Alfredo Bravo, an activist who was kidnapped and tortured by the military dictatorship. Daniel Bravo had been city councilor during the repeal of the police edicts three years earlier and lent his immediate support (personal interview, Buenos Aires, June 1, 2009). Bellomo made his position clear early on and was the councilor who decided to push the bill inside the legislature (personal interview, Buenos Aires, June 18, 2009).

activists had engaged during the adoption of these policies were elected to office in the Buenos Aires elections of 2000. Individuals such as Alicia Perrini, Enrique Rodríguez, and Anibal Ibarra (who was elected mayor) had worked with activists during the drafting of the Buenos Aires constitution and were supportive of their cause. Two days after the proposal was submitted to the legislature, twenty-three (out of sixty) councilors had signed in support of the bill (Bazán 2010, 445). Public debate ignited after the submission of the acceptance of the proposal by the council's human rights committee. Similar to what occurred during the debate over the Buenos Aires constitution and the repeal of the police edicts, activists sought to obtain the remainder of the necessary votes to pass the bill by forcing city councilors to adopt a public position on the issue and framing the debate around an issue of the equality of human rights. For activists it was necessary not to engage arguments framed upon moral principles. They believed that, by framing it as a human rights issue, they would be able to force hesitant and opposing councilors to vote in favor, given the salience debates over human rights had in posttransition Argentina.[22]

The framing strategy elaborated by activists in support of civil unions proved successful, as I detail elsewhere (Díez 2013). The close collaboration they established with journalists who were sympathetic to their cause helped to present the issues as one of basic rights. Editorials from important newspapers, such as *Página 12* and *Clarín*, supported the initiative and did so based on a rights argumentation.[23] Moreover, opposing arguments from socially conservative actors, such as academics from the Catholic Argentine University, religious organizations, and conservative councilors from the two main parties, opted, in what Juan Marco Vaggione has called "strategic secularism" (2005), not to advance moral arguments but rather to oppose the bill on technical and legal grounds. One of the strongest arguments opponents to civil unions advanced was that the city of Buenos Aires did not have the constitutional prerogative to legislate on family matters because the civil code is regulated by the national government (Hiller 2008).

Developing a line of argumentation based on human rights proved ultimately critical in obtaining the necessary votes to pass the legislation. Policy makers involved in the process, including the then-mayor Aníbal Ibarra, admitted in interviews that presenting the proposals as

---

[22] Interviews, Cigliutti, Buenos Aires, June 3, 2009 and December 8, 2010.
[23] Journalist and historian Osvaldo Bazán played an important role in helping frame the debate by writing pieces that linked gay marriage with human rights and democracy.

a human rights issue was fundamental in convincing legislators who had not originally supported the bill. According to councilors belonging to left-leaning parties, this was crucial in convincing legislators who belonged to more conservative wings of their parties. Given the way the public debate unfolded, legislators had a sense that the debates had been won in the court of public opinion by the time the vote was held, making it easier for reluctant councilors to vote in favor (Díez 2013). After a fourteen-hour debating session, on December 12, 2001 the Buenos Aires legislature voted in favor of the proposal. Ibarra, the city's mayor, subsequently signed it into law and it came into effect in March 2002.

The devolution of power to the city of Buenos Aires after the 1994 reforms opened up a policy avenue for the advancement of gay rights in Argentina, an opening gay and lesbian activists dexterously seized by successfully pushing for antidiscrimination provisions and, subsequently, civil unions. The two policy processes shaped the politics of gay and lesbian rights in important ways, and they are vital in understanding the adoption of gay marriage in 2010. The opening allowed activists to maintain the visibility they had acquired in previous years and to keep the debate over sexual rights on the national agenda. While these policy changes took place at the subnational level, the politics of the city of Buenos Aires carries important weight in national conversations. Discussions on sexual rights continued thus to be atop national debates. The two reforms also underlined for activists the effectiveness of advancing demands framed around a discourse that equated sexual rights with human rights and which went beyond state repression, a discourse that began to permeate discussions on sexuality in Argentina (Pecheny 2005). The importance of acquiring powerful discursive tools became therefore evident. For some activists it had been clear for some time that raising social consciousness on the relationship between sexuality and citizenship rights was crucial.

These policy reforms demonstrated the potency of such discourse in the pursuit of concrete policy changes. They also provided activists with important lessons on how to lobby effectively. In both cases, activists learned the significance of identifying state allies that helped them push for policy reform within state institutions. The availability of allies was possible given that, in many cases, they had been involved in other forms of social activism, particularly in the areas of human and women's rights. As we have seen, many state actors that supported the adoption of antidiscrimination provisions in the city's constitutions were subsequently elected as city councilors, and they supported civil unions. The collaboration they undertook with many of these state actors contributed to the formation of relationships that played an important role in the push for gay marriage later on. The same was true for the formation of relationships with other groups and social movements. Indeed, it is from such cooperation with state and nonstate actors that Argentine gay and lesbian activists have managed to weave extensive networks that have been decisive in more recent policy changes. Finally, for activists it became clear that access to the policy process and the formation of alliances with state and nonstate allies was not enough, and that forcing the debate on moral policies was definitive. Because of the controversial nature of these policies, they learned the importance of forcing policy makers to take a clear and public position on policy. Given the country's long tradition of social mobilization and the emergence of the new politics of accountability since the return of democratic rule, as detailed in Chapter 3, forcing state actors to engage in public debates proved effective.

The Adoption of Gay Marriage

Tracing the Origins of Policy

The introduction of civil unions in Buenos Aires in 2002 had limited ripple effects in the diffusion of policy at the subnational level in Argentina. Attempts were made at introducing similar legislation in several jurisdictions across the country: in the provinces of Río Negro, Santa Fe, and Entre Ríos as well as the cities of Villa Carlos Paz and Río Cuarto in Córdoba Province. However, most of them failed. In the case of Río Negro, a civil-union bill was passed in both provincial and congressional chambers in early 2003, but its implementing regulation (*reglamento*) was not issued. In Santa Fe two bills were approved in 2008 and 2009 in the province's lower chamber, but they were not subsequently discussed in the upper chamber; and in Entre Ríos an initiative to include the right to civil unions in the province's constitution did not obtain enough votes in the constitutional assembly. Out of all of these efforts, only in the city of Villa Carlos Paz – with a population of less than sixty thousand – were civil unions approved.[24] The main reason behind failure at policy reform is the general weakness of the gay and lesbian movement outside Buenos Aires. According to the activist behind the Santa Fe project, for example, the situation in that province is very different from Buenos Aires given

---

[24] In 2009, the city of Río Cuarto, also in Córdoba, enacted a local ordinance that established a registry for same-sex couples. However, it extends limited social benefits.

that weak organization and mobilization had failed to bring visibility to sexual rights.[25]

With the passage of civil unions in the cities of Buenos Aires and Villa Carlos Paz, the sexual rights landscape in Argentina looked rather patchy by the mid-2000s. By 2005, ten provinces still had the decades-old police edicts, which had historically been used by police forces to detain and harass sexual minorities, and only the cities of Buenos Aires and Rosario had introduced legal provisions that prohibited discrimination on the grounds of sexual orientation.[26] Such unevenness meant that, for the gay and lesbian movement, the push for the expansion of additional rights had to be pursued on several fronts. While the adoption of civil unions attracted the most public attention, activists pressed for change on various levels. Continuing a practice begun in 1993, CHA activists documented cases of homophobic hate crimes through the release of annual reports. They also pressed for the derogation of police edicts. In May 2008, CHA members, in collaboration with the civil rights organization Association for Civil Rights (*Asociación por los Derechos Civiles*), launched a campaign to convince the nine remaining provinces to repeal these legal provisions (*Página 12*, May 9, 2008). The campaign consisted of urging provincial governors and several federal ministers (Human Rights, Interior, and Justice) to introduce reforms. It was also joined by a recently created organization, the Argentine Federation of Lesbians, Bisexuals and Transgendered People (*Federación Argentina de Lesbianas, Gays, Bisexuals and Trans*, FALGBT).[27] Their demands were taken up by the Minister of Justice, Aníbal Fernández, who, after consultations with CHA and FALGBT activists, declared his commitment to pressure provincial governments to repeal the police edicts, thereby conforming with a 2003 ruling handed down by the Inter-American Human Rights Court that had urged the Argentine state to do so (*Página 12*, September 20, 2008).[28] The campaign was successful: over the following four years the nine remaining Argentine provinces agreed to repeal them and did so. With the derogation of the edicts in the province of Formosa in May 2012, the last one to have them on the books, the decades-old struggle

[25] As expressed by Mirta Pederi (*Página 12*, December 19, 2002).

[26] In 2009, the city of Puerto Madryn – in the province of Chubut and with a population of forty-seven thousand – included in its local charter provisions of discrimination against sexual orientation. However, the charter has been challenged in the courts, making it inoperable.

[27] The FALGBT was founded in June 28, 2006 by five smaller organizations.

[28] The ruling related to the death of Walter Bulacio in 1991 after a raid perpetrated by the Buenos Aires police in April 19 of that year.

to take away the main tool at the state's disposal to repress gays and lesbians came to an end and a negative right had finally been conquered in Argentina.

In terms of antidiscrimination legislation, once activists secured the passage of civil unions in Buenos Aires, they began to press to reform the national antidiscrimination law to include sexual-orientation provisions. A series of efforts were made to introduce bills to reform the antidiscrimination law with the support of Member of Congress Marcela Rodríguez (from the dissident Peronist party Egalitarian and Participatory Democracy, *Democracia Igualitaria y Participativa*).[29] However, they were eclipsed by the launch of a national antidiscrimination plan by the administration of Néstor Kirchner (2003–7) in 2005. The antidiscrimination plan originated during the presidency of Fernando de la Rúa (1999–2001). De la Rúa, who was the main actor behind the adoption of Argentina's antidiscrimination law in 1988, committed his administration, following a visit by the UN High Commissioner of Human Rights in 2001, to the development of a plan to fight discrimination. He did so with the intention of adhering to the recommendations set out by the Durban Declaration of 2001.[30] Under the auspices of the Ministry of Foreign Affairs and INADI, a series of consultations were held with various civil-society organizations representing historically discriminated groups – among which were gays and lesbians – to draft a national plan to fight discrimination.[31] The plan was completed by the end of 2004 and, in September of the following year, Kirchner signed a decree to implement it.

The plan contains numerous provisions to fight discrimination in Argentina, including the reform of an enactment of thirty-one pieces of legislation, the strengthening of INADI, the pursuit of national awareness campaigns, and the launch of training programs for the civil service. In regard to sexual orientation, the plan called for the adoption of a national civil union, the derogation of police edicts and the extension of visiting rights to prisoners' same-sex partners and several awareness programs (Villalpando, Feierstein, and Cassino 2006, 315–59). The inclusion

---

[29] In Argentina "dissident Peronist" parties are those that belong to the broader Peronist movement but that take different positions from the PJ leadership.

[30] This refers to the declaration drafted after the UN 2001 World Conference against Racism held in Durban, at which country delegates committed to fight racism and discrimination.

[31] Interview, Waldo Villalpando, Plan Development Coordinator, Buenos Aires, August 23, 2011.

in the plan of provisions intended to eradicate discrimination based on sexual orientation was an important achievement for gay and lesbian activists, who were actively engaged in drafting the plan.[32] While INADI progressively expanded its operations from strictly fighting racism when it was first established to cover other areas, including sexual orientation, the plan institutionalized the fight against discrimination based on sexual orientation and gave INADI a strong directive to do so. Since then it has become a very important player in the advancement of sexual rights in Argentina and played an important role in the passage of gay marriage, as we will see in the following text. But the adoption of the plan also meant that, for many activists, the need to pursue a reform of the national antidiscrimination law seemed less urgent. Attempts at reforming the national antidiscrimination law continued, mostly led by Deputy Rodríguez, and, indeed, in 2010 a reform to include penalties for discrimination based on sexual orientation was passed in the Chamber of Deputies.[33]

All while working on these various areas, activists pressed for the expansion of benefits to same-sex couples. The idea to change the definition of marriage to include same-sex couples was influenced by international debates and events, particularly the passage of gay marriage in Spain in 2005. But it emanates from the Argentine gay and lesbian movement, and it is part of its larger trajectory to have the state recognize same-sex relationships. Indeed, as early as 1992 Jáuregui advanced a proposal for gay civil marriage, and activists continued to press for the expansion of same-sex benefits, as the teachers' pensions/ANSES case shows. These efforts were accompanied by casework that produced important, if less visible, court rulings at the subnational level.[34]

This trajectory assumed a new thrust with the decision to demand civil-union recognition and subsequently gay marriage at the national level. Once the passage of civil unions in Buenos Aires had been secured, activists decided to push for same-sex recognition nationally with the advancement of a civil-union proposal that would encompass rights not

---

[32] Interview, Cigliutti, Buenos Aires, June 3, 2009.

[33] According to Rodríguez, there was limited pressure from gay and lesbian activists in the passage of the bill, and it was only possible because of the limited public attention it received. By 2008, gay and lesbian organizations essentially stopped pushing for a reform of the law (interview, Buenos Aires, August 19, 2011).

[34] For example, in 2003 a provincial court in Santa Fe Province granted legal recognition to a same-sex couple (*La Nación*, September 21, 2003), and in 2005, after a long legal battle, medical coverage was extended to same-sex couples in Córdoba Province (*Clarín*, September 3, 2006).

included in subnational legislation, such as adoption, areas that were regulated by Argentina's national civil code. Replicating their earlier successful strategies, CHA activists found an ally in Congress, Senator Diana Conti from the Victory Front (*Frente para la Victoria*, FVP),[35] who agreed to submit a national bill to the Senate in 2005.[36] However, the idea of gay marriage resurfaced as some activists believed that they should rather push for complete equality. Activists such as María Rachid and Claudia Castro, who had been actively involved in the passage of civil unions in Buenos Aires, and also supported civil unions nationally, were inspired by the approval of gay marriage by the Socialist Party in Spain in 2005 and began to advocate for gay marriage. They believed that if gay marriage had been approved in Spain it could be done in Argentina, and that the debate should at least begin.[37] Rachid and Castro held a meeting with other activists, who formed the FALGBT the following year, some of whom, such as Lovagnini and Esteban Paulón, had worked closely with the Socialist Party or were active party members in the city of Rosario.[38] These discussions, held in September 2005, convinced participants that they should attempt to place the debate of gay marriage on the national agenda. As a result, with the support of Deputy Eduardo di Pollina (PS), with whom Paulón had worked very closely in the Socialist Party, a bill was submitted to the Chamber of Deputies in December of the same year. The bill obtained the support of eleven deputies from left and left-of-center political parties.

Neither of the two initiatives got far for they lost parliamentary status, not making it to the legislative agenda. But they marked an ideological schism within the movement around the appropriate type of same-sex union that should be given priority. For activists such as Rachid and Paulón, the idea of complete equality was central to the struggle for sexual rights and the recognition of any form of unions other than gay marriage would not produce equality but rather "second-class citizenship." Influenced by the debate around gay marriage in Spain, but also by the emerging discourse in favor of complete equality for gays and lesbians

---

[35] FPV was formed by Kirchner in 2003; it is formally a group within the PJ and belongs to the larger Peronist movement.

[36] Bills that would establish "civil partnerships" were introduced to Congress in 1998, 2000, and 2002 were pushed by activists (belonging to SIGLA) and supported by two Members of Congress (Laura Musa and Margarita Stolbizer) but were never placed on the legislative agenda.

[37] Interviews, Claudia Castro and María Rachid, Buenos Aires, July 20 and 22, 2009.

[38] Paulón was an active Socialist Party member before he joined gay activism (interview, Buenos Aires, September 9, 2009).

in several other countries, such as Canada and the United States, they decided that gay marriage was the best way to ensure total equality.[39] They consequently decided to propose a reform to the Argentine civil code, which regulates marriages, and to change the definition of marriage from one between a "man and a woman" to "two individuals."

For Paulón the enactment of gay marriage could have a powerful symbolic effect as it would bring radical social change challenging established ideas regarding gender, sexual equality, and citizenship. Indeed, the potential effect of having gay marriage approved was such that it became FALGBT's number one priority.[40] For CHA activists, however, civil unions and gay marriage were both legitimate models for same-sex recognition, but they believed civil unions should be given priority given that they could offer the same rights marriage extended, such as socio-economic benefits and inheritance and adoption rights, without some limitations, such as the perpetuation of a religious concept in civic life. Cigliutti and Marcelo Suntheim, CHA leaders, were deeply steeped in feminist thought and marriage for them had profound patriarchal roots; they therefore considered civil unions a superior relationship given their liberating component. They, accordingly, formulated a strategy to give civil unions priority and pursue them through the legislative route while using the courts for gay marriage.[41] These differences proved temporary, however, as, by 2009, the movement coalesced around gay marriage and made it a policy priority.

Coalescing around Policy and Placing It on the National Agenda

The makeup and dynamics of Argentina's political party system are central in understanding the placement of gay marriage on the national agenda and its subsequent passage. As detailed in Chapter 2, since the return to democracy in 1983 Argentine politics has been dominated by the two main traditional parties, the PJ and the UCR. The PJ has traditionally been associated with Argentina's working classes and the UCR has been identified as a secular and liberal center-left party. Neither party has served as an exclusive mechanism of representation for social

---

[39] While Argentine activists were certainly influenced by the Spanish experience, they were well immersed in the theoretical and legal debates in support of gay marriage in several countries. Key to this has been the work of activist and journalist Bruno Bimbi, who carried out extensive work collecting and circulating among activists arguments in favor of gay marriage derived from numerous legal cases in several countries. For a very detailed overview, see Bimbi 2010.

[40] Interview, Buenos Aires, September 9, 2009.

[41] Interview, Suntheim, Buenos Aires, August 24, 2011.

conservative forces. Peronism is a political movement that developed through the inclusion of various social expressions. Conservative voices have certainly been incorporated, and at times they have influenced the movement's decisions, but have not been dominant (McGuire 1997). Social conservatives influenced the UCR during its formation at the turn of the twentieth century (Alonso 2000), but since the 1930s they carried little weight (Rock 1975).

Unlike other Latin America countries, then, Argentina has not seen the emergence of a sizeable Christian Democratic party able to agglutinate and represent socially conservative interests.[42] Smaller right-of-center parties are represented in the Chamber of Deputies, but they tend to compete at the subnational level. Conservative societal interests have therefore not found meaningful legislative representation and instead try to influence policy through the Executive (Johnson 2001). As Merike Blofield details, their ability to influence policy in areas of moral policy is largely conditioned by the type of relationship that they manage to establish with the president in turn (2006, 137–55). It also means that progressive nonstate actors that seek reform in this policy area can find allies within the two main political forces in Congress. They also find allies in several smaller left and left-of-center parties that are represented in both chambers, among which is the Socialist Party. While Argentina has a strong presidentialist system, on which Guillermo O'Donnell based his now-famous concept of "delegative democracy" (1993), and exhibits high levels of party discipline (Jones 2002), Congress plays an important role in the policy process and presidents rely heavily on its support to get their policy programs enacted (Jones and Hwang 2005, 116), contrary to what is generally assumed. Indeed, in the most comprehensive study of executive-legislative relations in Argentina since the return to democracy, Ernesto Calvo debunks the long-established myth that Argentina's Congress is weak by showing that, from 1983 to 2007, it rejected 41 percent of bills submitted by the Executive; it modified a third of all bills submitted; and 58 percent of the bills it approved emanated from the legislature (2014). Importantly, supporters of moral policy reform have used the legislature to force issues on the national agenda and have at times been able to achieve reform through this route. The legalization of

---

[42] The small Christian Democratic Party (*Partido Demócrata Cristiano*) does exist, but it has played a minor role in national politics, and it is decidedly on the left of the political spectrum. It emerged in 1954 from religious forces within Peronism and has, since the return to democracy, backed PJ candidates in presidential elections.

divorce in the 1980s is a good case in point: the push for reform came from Argentine's Congress and Raúl Alfonsín (1983–9) decided to abide by what Congress decided (Blofield 2006, 130–2). This policy change has profoundly shaped perceptions among advocates for the expansion of sexual rights (Pecheny 2010), who have since then regarded the legislature as a good channel through which to push for reform.

The introduction of the di Pollina's bill to allow for gay marriage may have lost parliamentary status but it began to place the issue on the legislative agenda. After that first attempt a very similar bill was reintroduced to Congress in May 2007, this time supported by a larger number of Members of Congress, including some belonging to Kirchner's ruling party's political *bloque* (parliamentary group), the FPV, the UCR, and other smaller parties. In October of the same year, Peronist Senator Vilma Ibarra (member of the "critical Peronist" party *Nuevo Encuentro*, New Encounter) submitted a similar version, which she reintroduced the following year to the lower house after she got elected as deputy, a bill pushed by FALGTB and CHA. In a highly publicized formal event in the Senate, the president of INADI, Lubertino, a longtime ally of the gay and lesbian movement introduced another bill to the Senate the same year.[43] A year later, Silvia Augsburger, Socialist Deputy from Rosario, presented another bill in very close collaboration with FALGBT Paulón. These bills began to place the issue of gay marriage on the national agenda as they gathered media attention. However, activists did not limit their efforts to attain policy change to the parliamentary route: their strategy also involved pressing for reform through the other two branches of government.

In terms of the Executive, President Cristina Fernández de Kirchner (2007–15) had declared her support for civil unions in 2005 at a meeting she held with some activists as senator,[44] but her position on gay marriage was less forthcoming. In August 2007, during her election campaign, she declared, when pressed by the media, that she was committed to working with gays and lesbians on "second-generation" rights, given the importance her administration accorded human rights, and that, in regard to marriage, "Parliament would debate it" (*Perfil*, October 21, 2007). Néstor Kirchner, then-president, and Fernández de Kirchner were in fact surprised

---

[43] As explained, Lubertino was a close ally of the gay and lesbian movement and played an important role in the drafting of the Buenos Aires constitution. By 2008 she had made gay marriage and abortion her institute's top priorities.

[44] Interview, Suntheim, Buenos Aires, June 29, 2009. Before being elected president, she was senator from 2005 until 2007.

that legislators belonging to their parliamentary group had presented bills
to Congress without having consulted them.[45] During the same election,
activists met with the then–Minister of Justice, Aníbal Fernández, who
expressed that the government had not taken a position on the issue and
asked them to "create the necessary conditions" so that the government
would be able to support the enactment of gay marriage, and that they
could count on his support to press for the cause within the cabinet. For
Fernández, the creation of those conditions meant "convincing society"
and the other "political forces" of the merits of such a policy.[46] Finding
an ally in cabinet opened an important door. Fernández became Head
of Cabinet after Fernández de Kirchner's election in October 2007 and
activists continued to pressure him to have the government support their
policy. In several meetings they held with him following the election,
Fernández let it be known that the president had not taken a position and
that he needed time to convince his cabinet colleagues. He therefore asked
activists to provide him with documentation and in fact commissioned
a poll to gauge public opinion. Despite the relatively strong support for
gay marriage the poll showed,[47] the results of which were handed to the
president, she remained noncommittal well into 2009, when the public
debate over gay marriage started to heat up. But the fact that she did not
rule it out, and that activists counted on the support of the most important
cabinet member, meant that they were given the green light to "create the
conditions" to obtain the president's support.

The push for policy change also unfolded through the judiciary.
Continuing a tradition of casework, activists decided to press for gay
marriage through the courts and to deploy what they commonly refer to
as "strategic litigation." That is, the active pursuit of *writs of amapro*,[48]
after the denial of marriage certificates to same-sex couples by *registros
civiles* (marriage-granting authorities in Latin America), to push the
issue up the judicial hierarchy through appeals. Because the Argentine
Supreme Court sits atop the judiciary and serves as the country's highest
appellate court, the strategy was to pursue *writs of amparo* by claiming

---

[45] Interview, Deputy Vilma Ibarra, Buenos Aires, December 2, 2010.
[46] Interview, Rachid, FALGTB President, Buenos Aires, November 28, 2010 and Bimbi,
FALGTB member, Rio de Janeiro, June 15, 2009.
[47] The poll showed that 68 percent of Argentines supported gay marriage. But it also
showed that a slight majority were opposed to adoption. The sample size was small
(eight hundred), however, and only included the six largest urban areas.
[48] These refer to judicial remedies available in civil-law systems that give citizens the opportunity to redress violations to constitutional rights.

the unconstitutionality of the civil code's provisions that established marriage to be between a man and a woman with the aim of reaching the highest court. According to Argentina's civil-law system court rulings only affect the parties involved (*inter partes*) and, unlike common-law systems, they do not set precedent (*stare decisis*). The Court has the power of judicial review and can rule on the unconstitutionality of legislation, but it does not have the prerogative to change statutory law and its rulings on unconstitutionality only apply to the parties involved. Nevertheless, they are binding to all lower-level courts: if the Court rules that a legal provision is unconstitutional, all of the courts are forced to rule the same, a process which in essence indirectly amounts to *stare decisis*. While the final aim of the strategy varies depending on the activist or lawyer interviewed, some activists were encouraged by the appointment of a more progressive bench in 2003 by Kirchner, among whom included Zafaroni (a longtime ally of the movement, as mentioned, who maintained personal relationships with some activists), and believed that, once their cases reached the Supreme Court, it would rule for the unconstitutionality of the civil code on the grounds of an unequal treatment of citizens. Such ruling could potentially force Congress to legislate on the matter. The Court could also hand down a ruling specifically urging the legislature to do so, as was the case with the 1986 ruling regarding divorce. While the final outcome of the strategy was not certain, activists and their legal advisors believed that litigation would, at the very least, place the issue on the agenda in a forceful way, as was the case.

The litigation strategy was carefully developed and launched in early 2007. The idea was to have numerous same-sex couples request marriage certificates and, once denied, file *amparos* to appellate courts. To achieve this, activists worked closely with numerous lawyers and legal scholars who joined the cause.[49] They provided critical input to strategize the best course of action. These involved several prominent lawyers, legal academics, and law students, both national and international. Many of these individuals had been involved in the passage of civil unions in the city of Buenos Aires six years earlier. This network of individuals, mostly directed by Rachid, was critical in determining which judges were likely to rule in a way that would make it more effective to have their cases work their way up to the Supreme Court. The first several cases attracted significant media attention. In February 2007, Rachid and her partner Castro, another activist, requested a marriage license from a Buenos Aires

---

[49] Interviews suggest that at least twenty lawyers were involved in the various cases.

Civil Registry. The request was denied and they immediately filed for an *amparo* based on an infringement to their constitutional right to equality. A judge subsequently ruled against them, arguing that marriage between homosexuals would undermine an institution intended for procreation.

The case was then submitted to the Supreme Court, accompanied by the submission of *amicus curiae* from numerous national and international individuals and organizations. It was followed, in June 2007, by the submission of a marriage certificate by Alejandro Vanelli and a famous soap-opera actor, Ernesto Larrese, to another Civil Registry. In order to attract the most attention possible, the event was attended by other famous personalities, such actors as Boy Olmi and Mercedes Morán, as well as Lubertino, INADI's president (*Página 12*, June 28, 2007). Once the Registry denied their request, they filed another *amparo* and later on appealed to the Supreme Court. Shortly after this, CHA's Cigliutti and Suntheim, having got married in Spain months earlier, deployed the same tactic requesting the recognition of their marriage in Argentina. Their case also worked its way to the Supreme Court.[50] These cases were only the first in a long list: by late 2009, approximately sixty cases were in the processes of following the same path toward the Supreme Court.[51] Their litigation campaign was largely intended to obtain wide media coverage and to make it a media topic (*instalar el debate en los medios*).[52] In addition to organizing highly visible events around the submission of marriage certificates for same-sex couples, the expanding network of allies and supporters began to incorporate journalists with whom activists had close relationships and who work in established newspapers.[53] The court rulings were given extensive media coverage and activists were interviewed systematically on television, radio, and newspapers.

The pursuit of policy change through the judiciary and the legislature placed the issue on the public agenda by late 2009. The mid-term national elections and a court victory in November of the same year marked critical turning points. Elections for half of the legislators in the Chamber of Deputies and a third of senators were held in June 2009. In that election, in which Kirchner was elected deputy, the FVP's parliamentary alliance lost a majority in the lower house as its representation dropped to 39 percent of the seats. The loss of a majority meant that the government

---

[50] For an excellent, detailed account, see Schulenberg 2012.
[51] Interview, Carolina von Opiela, lawyer, Buenos Aires, November 30, 2010.
[52] Interview, Paulón, Buenos Aires, November 11, 2010.
[53] These included individuals such as Soledad Vallejos, who writes for *Página 12*.

had to rely on opposition parties to get its agenda through and that legislative politics would become more fluid. For supporters of gay marriage it meant uncertainty because changes were expected. Augsburger, the Socialist deputy who introduced one of the gay-marriage bills, was a member of the Standing Committee on the Family (*Comisión de Familia, Mujer, Niñez y Adolescencia*), one of the committees to which the various bills had been submitted. Augsburger, who had the support of the committee's president (Juliana Di Tullio, FVP), had not stood for reelection and her term came to an end in December of that year (when the legislative session concluded). Ibarra, who introduced another of the bills, was Chair of the Standing Committee on Legislation (*Comisión General de Legislación*), the other committee to which the bills had been submitted. Ibarra's term was not up in December, but, because the government's parliamentary group had lost a majority in the lower house, her position as chair was not guaranteed come December. Committees play a key role in the legislative process in Argentina and their chairs function as gatekeepers of bills when they do not emanate from the Executive or do not have its support, as was the case for gay marriage. The possibility of getting any of these bills on the committee's agenda would therefore decrease at the end of the legislative session.

Given such uncertainly, proponents of gay marriage decided to act. Following the elections, Ibarra and Augsburger held meetings with the two most visible activists, Rachid and Cigliutti, and decided that the time had come to begin the debate by introducing the issue to the legislative agenda.[54] All agreed and decided to develop common strategies. Even though Cigliutti, as many other CHA members, believed gay marriage was not the ideal type of same-sex relationship recognition, he decided to join forces and deploy CHA resources and its extensive network of allies to push for gay marriage. For him opening the definition of marriage to include gays and lesbians carried powerful symbolism as marriage had been the cornerstone of sexual regulation in Argentina. After these meetings, Argentina's gay and lesbian movement coalesced around gay marriage, making it a priority. The meetings were followed by intense collaboration among activists and an agreement on a common strategy, which involved the application of pressure on legislators through direct, individual lobbying as well as winning the debate in the court of public opinion. Their strategy was very much influenced by their success in

---

[54] Interviews with Ibarra, Rachid, and Cigliutti, Buenos Aires, November 28, December 2, and December 8, 2010.

the passage of civil unions in Buenos Aires. In interviews activists and
allied legislators constantly referred to the notion that in Argentina *las
leyes se ganan en la calle* (laws are won in the street). To win the debate,
their push for marriage had to be framed around an issue of equality,
human rights, and democracy, given how these issues figured prominently
in national discourses and underpinned the "new model" the Kirchners
promoted during their administrations. Influenced by the Spanish experience, their campaign slogan became "the same rights with the same
names" (*los mismos nombres con los mismos derechos*). As with civil
unions, the first step was to begin the debate in Congress and thereby
placing the issue on the legislative agenda.

Such a step was taken on October 29, when Ibarra's and Augsburger's
bills were debated in the two committees at a joint session for the first
time. Two additional sessions were held to discuss the bills, but quorums
could not be reached because the government instructed its legislators not
to proceed.[55] The bills thus stalled. The discussions were widely covered
by national media and sparked an intense national debate, a debate that
was further fueled by the movement's first legal victory: days after the
last committee meeting was held, a judge in the city of Buenos Aires ruled
that the articles of the civil code that established marriage to be between
a man and woman, which prevented Alejandro Freyre and José María
di Bello from marrying, violated equal protection by the state, as well as
the Buenos Aires constitution that prohibits discrimination on the basis
of sexual orientation (*Clarín*, November 12, 2009). The judge ordered
the Buenos Aires Civil Registry to issue the couple a marriage license.
In a surprise move, the right-wing mayor of Buenos Aires, Mauricio
Macri, declared that he would not appeal the ruling, paving the way for
the first gay marriage to become a reality in Argentina. The couple made
an appointment to marry on December 1. On the eve of their wedding
another judge issued an injunction ordering the city's administration not
to issue the marriage certificate on grounds that the previous judge did
not have competency to rule on that area. The marriage was therefore
suspended. Flanked by gay and lesbian activists and numerous prominent politicians, and in front of dozens of national and international news
media reporters, the couple gave a news conference and vowed to fight on.
Days later the socially progressive governor of Tierra del Fuego decided

---

[55] Fernández de Kirchner was scheduled to pay an official visit to the Vatican at the end of
November, and instructed legislators from her party not to give quorum for fear that it
would create frictions with the Pope (interview, Ibarra, November 28, 2010).

to intervene and ordered her province's Civil Registry to honor the first ruling despite the fact that it had been made in a different jurisdiction. On December 28, 2009, Freyre and di Bello finally wed in the Western Hemisphere's southernmost city, Ushuaia, making them the first same-sex couple in Latin America to have contracted marriage. Their marriage was subsequently declared void by an Ushuaia judge in April 2010 because the couple did not meet residency requirements. It was followed by similar cases in which courts ruled favorably on the grounds of unconstitutional-ity, many of which were overturned by other judges. These cases expect-edly attracted substantial public attention and fueled an intense national debate. Gay and lesbian activists had been successful in placing the issue on the national agenda and now had to apply pressure to have gay mar-riage enacted.

The Enactment of Gay Marriage

The national discussion around gay marriage that activists ignited con-tinued well into 2010.[56] As the debate continued, conditions looked increasingly favorable given a seeming solidification of support for policy reform from the Executive. In early 2010, Kirchner, who had been elected deputy in the 2009 mid-term elections, made public his personal support for gay marriage in an interview with a reporter, all while stating that it was a decision for parliament to make (*Página 12*, January 10, 2010). As former president and the president's husband, Kirchner was a key actor in the government's decisions.[57] His support for the policy was partly based on the perceived need to strengthen the government's "political model" following their underperformance in the elections. Human rights were central to the Kirchners' new "model" and, for them, the drop in support for the government's coalition in the elections, particularly in urban areas in Buenos Aires Province, had to be met with a reinforcement of attention to human rights.[58] However, the government did not take an official position for fear that opposition parties, which held a majority in the lower house, would instinctually oppose the Executive's position. Activists were thus told that the Executive would not make any public

---

[56] This section draws largely from data obtained through interviews carried out with six-teen deputies and six senators from five different political groups during November and December 2010.

[57] His influence is well documented in a biography of Fernández de Kirchner published in 2011 (Russo 2011).

[58] According to interviews held with two Members of Congress close to Kirchner, Buenos Aires, November 28, and November 30, 2010.

pronouncements but would support policy change should the reform pass Congress. They were also told that the government would take a public position once the Catholic Church began to oppose policy change, as it was expected to do. Fernández committed himself to applying pressure on legislators and asked activists to work on getting enough votes from opposition parties as well as from conservative deputies allied with the government.[59] Soon after Kirchner's interview, the FPV's party leader in the Chamber of Deputies, Agustín Rossi, declared that they would support the bill approved at the committee level (*La Nación*, March 19, 2010). Given the Executive's tacit support, the government's party whip (*Secretaria Parlamentaria*) in the chamber, María Teresa García, in turn committed herself to working with activists inside and outside Congress to garner the necessary votes.[60] Rachid, Cigliutti, and García held conversations during which they agreed to move forward and, as a first step, to get quorum at the committee level to force a discussion.

Continuing a tradition dating back to the drafting of the Buenos Aires constitution, activists knew of the effectiveness in forcing hesitant legislators to take a public position on human rights issues to obtain their support for policy reform. They were confident that they would be able to win a debate on the issue given the currency human rights had in posttransition Argentina. They strategically framed their demand as an issue of equality, human rights, and democracy, captured by the slogans they used: "equal rights," "equal marriage," and "the same rights with the same names." They knew they needed to force legislators to take a public position, applying thus pressure on them to vote favorably. What was required was to ensure the initiation of a parliamentary debate. As Paulón, one of the leading activists, stated: "many deputies had not thought about the issue and had no position. We had to force them to think, to take a position, to force a discussion . . . we had to get it on the parliamentary agenda."[61] As a road map to policy change transpired through the discussions activists held with their allies in parliament, the debate over gay marriage intensified as the judicialization of the issue gathered pace. Rulings in favor and against gay marriage cases continued, and, by the end of February 2010, some sixty couples had filed for *amparos*. Importantly, in mid-February a Supreme Court judge indicated, through an interview conceded to the daily *Página 12*, that the court was

[59] Interview, Rachid, Buenos Aires, December 2, 2010.
[60] Interview, Buenos Aires, December 7, 2010.
[61] Interview, Buenos Aires, November 11, 2010.

ready to rule on the issue and, in a rather cryptic way, that it would do so favorably because the prohibition of gay marriage did not pass constitutional muster (*Página 12*, February 15, 2010). The judge also indicated that the debate on the bench was whether they should wait until parliament debated the issue.

It is within this context that activists decided to act and to push again for a debate of the bills at the committee level and an extensive network of state and nonstate actors thickened. Inside Congress, a parliamentary alliance (*Frente Parlamentario por la Diversidad Sexual*) made up of thirty supporters of policy reform was assembled. The alliance was made up of socially progressive, mostly female, Members of Congress who had worked together in debates over sexual and reproductive rights over several years.[62] Legislators belonging to this alliance came mostly from smaller leftist parties, namely the Socialist Party, *Libres del Sur*, *Coalición Cívica ARI*, *Nuevo Encuentro*, *Encuentro Popular y Social*, *SI*, and *Forja*, but also included individuals from the governing FPV coalition and the UCR. Continued close collaboration among actors involved in the advancement of sexual and women's rights facilitated the formation of this group. Alliance members held a press conference in late February declaring its support for policy reform and their commitment to place gay marriage as a priority in the new legislative session. Convincing hesitant peers to support the bill became part of their plan.[63] During this time activists managed to convince the leaders of the bigger congressional groups to allow their members to vote freely.

Drawing on the numerous relationships activists built over the years, they began to solicit the support from, and to strategize with, numerous nonstate actors belonging to various sectors that included lawyers, academics, intellectuals, prominent personalities, and union leaders. Critical among them were journalists such as Soledad Vallejos, Andrés Osojnik, and Osvaldo Bazán who published frequently in several of Argentina's main dailies and who, as the debate began, systematically published articles with arguments, directly or indirectly, in favor of gay marriage.

The placement of the marriage reform bills on the legislative agenda was facilitated by the reappointment of Ibarra as chair of the Legislation Committee and of Di Tullio as member of the Family Committee in the new legislature. They placed them on their committees' agendas among

---

[62] Most of the legislators belonging to this group had worked closely in setting up a national sexual education program in 2006 and worked on the decriminalization of abortion.

[63] Personal interviews with seven deputies belonging to this alliance.

the first order of business. The date for the first debate was set for March 18 with a vote for April 14. As a timetable was established, activists and their congressional allies engaged in an intense lobbying effort to ensure that quorum was reached in joint sessions of the two committees. While there was opposition among some committee members, and getting enough support was not easy, the issue had gained so much public prominence that, according to several legislators interviewed, legislators could simply not be seen as blocking the process.

The committee discussions included public hearings at which, in addition to activists and their congressional allies, individuals from the public were invited to argue for and against what became a joint reform bill. Drawing from their networks of allies, numerous prominent lawyers, legal experts, and academics attended the hearings to argue in favor of the reform. Their arguments were framed as an issue of equality and human rights (*Página 12*, March 18, 2010). These included individuals such as renowned constitutional experts Roberto Gargarella and José Miguel Onaindia, jurists Gil Domínguez and Gabriela Seijas, as well as deans of the Law Faculties from the Universities of Palermo and Buenos Aires, who had declared their support for civil unions a decade earlier. Speakers who opposed the bill were individuals affiliated with religious institutions, such as Nicolás Laferriere, from the Catholic University of Argentina, and Eduardo Sambrizzi, from the Corporation of Catholic Lawyers. These discussions were followed by a vote on April 15, at which quorum was reached and a majority secured. With a favorable vote, activists and their allies managed to surmount the first obstacle, and the bill moved on to a debate on the floor of the chamber two weeks later.

Opposition to the bill at this stage of the process came primarily from evangelical groups. Two main organizations, the Christian Alliance of Evangelical Organizations (*Alianza Cristiana de Iglesias Evangélicas de la República Argentina*, ACIERA) and the Evangelical Pentecostal Confraternity Federation (*Federación Cofraternidad Evangélica Pentecostal*, FECEP), met with various committee members to express their opposition on religious grounds, deploying the argument that marriage, as a sacrament, could not be changed from that of a man and a woman (*Parlamentario*, April 9, 2011). While some representatives from the Catholic Church also met with committee members, their opposition was expressed mostly through public declarations caught by the media.

The limited direct access to the process religious groups had is of particular note. In terms of evangelical groups, only one deputy, Cynthia

Hotton, identified herself as a professing evangelical, and was, according to every deputy interviewed, the only legislator that served as an access point into the discussions and deliberations. None of the political party leaderships in the lower chamber served as mechanisms of representation for evangelical groups. Indeed, the main opposition to the bill inside the two committees came mostly as a result of political calculations made by deputies who opposed what they perceived to be a policy pursued by the government (Bimbi 2010, 325–34). The little direct pressure exerted by the Catholic Church, which was felt primarily through the Catholic lawyers who spoke during the hearings, surprised many deputies. According to some of them, weak pressure was the result of their misreading of the support the initiative had. Di Tullio, for example, stated: "The [Catholic] Church thought we did not have the votes and lobbied very little . . . their opposition began to be felt right after that vote."[64] The low profile the Church's leadership kept could be explained by the wide media attention a sex-abuse scandal involving a former bishop was attracting at the time,[65] as well as the concrete steps it was taking to lessen the strong tensions that had characterized its relationship with the Kirchner administrations since 2003.[66]

Having won the vote at the committee level, the bill moved onto the floor of the Chamber of Deputies with a vote scheduled for May 4. The vote's imminence ratcheted up the debate significantly both socially and in the halls of Congress. Activists continued their traditional strategy of winning the debate with society to apply indirect pressure on legislators and to force them to take a position to vote favorably. They mobilized thus every ally to make public pronouncements in favor of gay marriage. The relationships that activists had built over the years with a variety of individuals, organizations, and other movements became critical in building an alliance in support of the bill, and the network of supporters thickened. Contributing to framing the issue as one of human rights, some of the most prominent defenders of human rights in Argentina, such as Estela Carloto, Hebe de Bonafini, Nora Cortiñas, Tati Almeyda, Rosita

---

[64] Interview, Buenos Aires, November 30, 2010.

[65] On December 29, 2009, the ex-archbishop of Santa Fe, Edgardo Stroni, was sentenced to eight years in prison for having abused sexually a seminarian in the early 1990s. The sentencing reverberated across Argentina.

[66] A month before the vote, Jorge Bergoglio, the country's cardinal, met with the president, supreme court judges, and the Senate president to communicate his desire to end the "state of permanent confrontation" (*Crítica*, March 17, 2010). For good descriptions of such confrontation, see *Clarín*, July 29, 2009 and http://www.perfil.com/, accessed April 1, 2009.

Callado, and Adriana Calvo, declared their public support for the bill. Legal scholars, jurists, and deans of several law faculties from several universities, such as Sofía Hariri, Alberto Bovino, Martín Böhmer, Roberto Sabsay, Roberto Gargarella, Gustavo Arballo, and Mónica Pinto, among others, also came out supporting the bill publicly. Several of these individuals had worked closely with activists during the passage of civil unions in Buenos Aires.

Labor unions also added their support: Hugo Moyano, leader of Argentina's powerful union federation, the General Labor Confederation (*Confederación General del Trabajo*), and Hugo Yasky, leader of the Congress of Argentine Workers (*Confederación de Trabajadores Argentinos*), made public pronouncements in favor of gay marriage. Activists had maintained close, personal working relationships with many of these individuals. As CHA's Suntheim indicated: "not everyone has Moyano's cellular [telephone] number."[67] Beyond public declarations, many of these individuals contacted party leaders in the lower house asking them to approve the bill. Social media played an important role in promoting the cause. A Facebook page titled "I Am in Favor of the Legalization of Gay Marriage," which had been established earlier in the year, had more than sixty-two thousand members by the end of April.[68] The page was used to circulate information, articles, and news on the debate; announce when a prominent social personality joined the campaign; and asked members to write directly to deputies asking them to support the bill. The number of journalists who supported the bill and who covered the debate in a supportive way increased and included, in addition to the ones already mentioned, Eduardo Aliverti, Luis Majul, Víctor Hugo Morales, Adrián Paenza, and Roberto Petinatto. Except for the editorial line of the right-wing newspaper *La Nación*, coverage was for the most part positive. *Clarín*, the most widely circulated newspaper in the Spanish-speaking world, published sympathetic articles at this point and would eventually publish an editorial explicitly defending gay marriage.

Opposition intensified immediately after the vote at the committee level took place. From having kept a low profile, the Catholic Church leadership articulated vociferous public opposition. Six days after the committee vote, the Plenary Assembly of the Argentine Bishops' Commission revealed its official opposition, through the publication of a

---

[67] Interview, Buenos Aires, August 24, 2011.
[68] Number recorded by the author.

document, titled *On the Unalterable Good of Marriage and the Family*, in which they opposed gay marriage based on Natural Law principles (Vaggione 2011, 941). Soon after, and reaffirming a heteronormative view, Bergoglio, then-cardinal and elected Pope in March 2013, declared that marriage between a man and a woman was the "foundation of the family and society" (*Crítica*, April 23, 2010). Demonstrating the extent to which proponents of gay marriage had been able to frame the debate as an issue of human rights, the Church's official opposition was framed as an issue of children's rights and discrimination. The cardinal declared that "children have the inalienable right to develop in the bosom of their mothers . . . it would be an unjust discrimination against marriage and the family" to approve gay marriage (*Crítica*, April 23, 2010).

Opposition was not limited to public declarations and soon turned into the direct lobbying of legislators. A few days before the vote in the lower chamber, a bishop in the city of La Plata, Antonio Marino, met with several deputies and senators from various political groups to demand that they not vote in favor of gay marriage. Marino argued that heterosexual marriage is neither "negotiable nor comparable" to gay marriage and that, based on Natural Law, heterosexual marriage is a natural right: "human rights are not given nor extended, but we are born with them" (*Clarín*, April 29, 2010). Direct lobbying of deputies intensified in the days prior to the vote and was characterized by personal visits to the deputy offices by religious representatives and the sending of e-mails. All of the eighteen deputies interviewed stated that they were highly pressured to vote against, one referring to it as being "infernal, even personal." These interviews revealed that pressure was particularly intense on deputies whose jurisdictions were in the provinces. Within the government's parliamentary group, a deputy from Mendoza Province, Patricia Fedel, in collaboration with conservative provincial governors with close ties with the Church, lobbied deputies to vote against.

Activists, for their part, relied on the network of allies to generate a favorable vote. Having secured a commitment from all the parliamentary group leaders to allow for a free vote, they embarked upon the task of convincing legislators to vote in favor, one by one. Using the Socialist Party's congressional office as a "bunker" of activities, some activists held constant discussions with their allies in Congress to determine which legislators they needed to convince. Original counts pointed to having from 100 to 119, with the rest either undecided or against. True to their lobbying tradition, they undertook the painstaking and time-consuming effort to speak with each and every single legislator forcing them to take a public position on the issue. An important element of this tactic was to have their allied journalists report on the various positions taken. While the Executive fulfilled its commitment to apply pressure on deputies, the fact that they had allowed for a free vote meant that there was some fluidity in support within the governing party's parliamentary group and that votes were not guaranteed. At this crucial point their allies inside and outside Parliament worked tirelessly to gain votes. Inside Congress, members of the Parliamentary Alliance played particular key roles. Female deputies, who had been strong advocates of reproductive and women's rights and longtime allies of gay and lesbian rights – such as Di Tullio, María Luisa Storani, and Cecilia Merchán – met constantly with their counterparts to make a case. Also active were several congressional staffers, such as Juan Manazzoni, Maximiliano Zwenger, and Natalia Gradaschi, some of whom were also activists.

Nonstate actors also played active roles. Academics, intellectuals, and legal scholars provided important documentation ranging from peer-reviewed material with evidence showing that children adopted by gay parents achieved normal development, material with reminders that homosexuality had been delisted as a medical condition, summaries of arguments in favor of gay marriage from judicial cases in several European countries and North America, and reviewed work by theorists, such as Michel Foucault's, who argued for the social construction of sexuality. The lead figure in the collection of this material from academics and its distribution among legislators was Bruno Bimbi, one of the main strategists from the FALGBT and, at the time, a reporter for the daily *Crítica*. Allied union members also lobbied. Once the leaders of the two main unions declared their public statements in favor, allies within these unions contacted members of Congress asking them for their support. Finally, the use of social media to lobby increased. The Facebook page, mentioned previously, had been joined by seventy thousand members on the eve of the vote. The page was used to inform friends of the Members of Congress who had not taken a position and to ask them to write to them directly asking them to vote in favor.

While the arguments used to convince legislators to vote in favor varied, the guiding one was, according to activists and legislators interviewed, that expanding the definition of marriage was an issue of equal rights and a fundamental part of the new Argentine democracy. With legislators who identified with Peronism, supporters of the bill made reference to historic contribution the movement had made in the expansion of rights, citing the enfranchisement of women under Perón, and the suffering undergone by Peronists under the various dictatorships. For example, García, the government's party whip, stated:

I used Peronist doctrine, and my condition as woman, to get votes. I reminded them that Peronists had been behind the expansion of rights to minorities . . . and to correct situations of injustice . . . you are in a position of power and cannot deny these rights. I am a practicing Catholic, but this is a question of rights. I told them that I would listen to priests the day they stop abusing children.[69]

With legislators that identified with the Radicals, a common reference used was the 1980s reform that allowed for divorce, reforms signed into law by President Alfonsín. The advancement of arguments framed around equality and human rights appears to have been effective: all of the eighteen Members of Congress interviewed stated that they were crucial in getting votes.

These arguments also appear to have resonated with larger national debates. A review of the debate that took place among deputies on the floor of the plenary the night of the vote certainly suggests it: the word "rights" was uttered 629 times by legislators, "equality" 200 times, "citizenship" 60 times, and "democracy" 65 times. It was also captured by declarations made by deputies from various political groups. To wit:

We want full citizenship for all Argentines. We want to eradicate homophobia and to end all forms of discrimination by respecting the rights of minorities to enjoy a full life and the freedom to chose with whom they want to share their life . . . that is what we are here today for: to legislate in favor of equality of rights as guaranteed by the constitution, in favor of the inclusion of minorities and for human rights. UCR Deputy Silvia Storni

It is not then about extending a benefit to a minority. What this bill proposes, and what we come here to endorse with our opinion and our vote, is to move forward so that all of us who make up this immense and diverse social collectivity have the same rights and the same responsibilities in this democracy. EDE Deputy Martín Sabbatella

Democracy as a system is not only about guaranteeing the efficient making of collective decisions, but to allow every individual to carry out his own way of life . . . to make his own decisions on an equal basis with the rest. FPV Deputy Hugo Prieto

The lobbying strategies pursued by activists and their allies inside and outside Congress ultimately proved successful. The vote took place on May 4, as

---

[69] Interview, Buenos Aires, December 7, 2010.

scheduled. After a twelve-hour debate, the progay marriage forces won the debate with 126 votes cast in favor, 110 against, and 4 abstentions. The vote's final numbers reflect the dynamic of how support and opposition forces played out within the political party system. There were divisions within the two main historical political parties: forty-six deputies from FVP voted in favor, thirty-one against, and ten were not present; and seventeen from UCR voted in favor, twenty-four against, and one was not present. Opposition and support for policy change therefore cut across the two main parties, showing internal ideological divisions, rather than along party ones. The same applied to most other parliamentary groups in which there was internal opposition: there were votes in favor in all parliamentary groups. This included the right-of-center Republican Proposal (*Propuesta Republicana*, PRO) which cast four votes in favor out of ten. While the opposition to gay marriage managed to secure negative votes in several parliamentary groups, it did not count with direct political representation through one political group as a whole. All the seven smaller left-of-center parties voted unanimously in favor. Rather tellingly, support for the bill from women was disproportionately higher: 65 percent of female legislators voted in favor, while 46 percent of men did so, reflecting the close collaboration that existed between gay and lesbian activists and their female allies.

The approval of the gay marriage bill in the Chamber of Deputies moved the debate onto the Senate. Argentina's upper chamber exhibits different characteristics from the lower house. One is the overrepresentation of conservative forces. The majority of Argentines live in cities and almost half of the population lives in the city of Buenos Aires and the Province of Buenos Aires (which surrounds the capital); the Chamber of Deputies tends therefore to be proportionally more represented by less conservative Members of Congress because these jurisdictions generally have a more liberal electorate. This is not the case for the Senate as, proportionally, rural and more conservative areas have greater representation. After constitutional reforms, implemented in 2001, every province in Argentina elects directly three senators (there is a total of seventy-two). The result is that social conservatives from rural Argentina tend to have a disproportionately higher representation, and hence influence policy more inordinately, than liberal forces. Moreover, senators generally have very close relationships with provincial governors. They tend to have a great deal of sway over how senators vote. Because the presence of the Catholic Church is felt more strongly in rural areas, and some governors tend to have close relationships with provincial religious leaders, the ability of religious groups to influence votes is stronger. Senators in Argentina also tend to be widely known political figures who occupy a larger presence in national debates and the media. This is not only because of their fewer numbers, but also because the upper chamber carries a great deal more prestige in national politics. Senators tend to be, therefore, more account-able for their actions to local constituents as well as society more broadly. These features mean that the debate over gay marriage took on a larger national dimension and that the outcome was less certain. Indeed, the higher representation of conservative forces meant that the first activist and media surveys of intentions predicted voting ties. In interviews activ-ists admit that they did not believe they would win the vote, but that they strategically had to convey the public impression that they would so as to rally support among movement members and allies. Voting intentions fluctuated until the night of the vote.

Proponents of gay marriage replicated the strategies pursued dur-ing the previous stage to win the public debate prior to the Senate vote. However, they intensified their efforts and made an important adjust-ment. Despite their attempt at framing their arguments as one of equality and rights, the media systematically referred to the bill as one that would approve gay marriage. They therefore launched a campaign calling their demand as one for "egalitarian marriage" to ensure that the bill would become synonymic to equality. The campaign consisted in recruiting numerous famous artists, actors, and musicians, many of whom had per-sonal relationships with activists and allies, to support the cause.[70] A key part of their renewed campaign was the recording of video clips in which these personalities declared their support for egalitarian marriage and for the "same love, with the same rights." The videos were widely circulated through the Facebook page and presented at Senate committee hearings. Facebook membership reached 270,000 adherents by the time the vote took place. They also organized a rally in late June in front of Congress at which they presented a list of organizations, public figures, and personali-ties that had declared their support for gay marriage (*Página 12*, June 29, 2010). The list was published free of charge by the newspaper *Tiempo Argentino*, whose editor-in-chief was a close ally.

Opponents also intensified their efforts and made some adjustments. Having suffered an unexpected loss in the lower chamber, religious groups began to lend support to civil unions clearly in order to avoid a change to

---

[70] These included individuals such as Cecilia Roth, Alfredo Alarcón, Ricardo Darín, and Natalia Otero.

their heteronormative understanding of marriage (*Clarín*, June 1, 2010). They also called for a referendum on gay marriage, convinced that a majority of Argentines were not in favor. In addition, street mobilization became part of their renewed efforts to forestall the passage of the bill. Soon after the vote in the Chamber of Deputies, evangelical groups organized a variety of rallies in front of Congress demanding that the bill not be approved (*Clarín*, June 1 and *La Nación*, June 4, 2010). The Catholic Church leadership in turn ramped up its attack substantially. In what became a key moment in the debate, a letter that the cardinal sent to a congregation of Carmelite nuns in Buenos Aires leaked and became widely covered by the media. In it, Bergoglio used very strong language declaring that the proposal to approve gay marriage was a product of the "devil's envy" that intended to destroy "God's image . . . this is not merely a legislative project, but a machination by the Father of Lies who pretends to confuse and mislead God's children. This is not your war, but God's. Join it" (*Tiempo Argentino*, July 7, 2010). Bergoglio also ordered priests throughout the country to read a declaration against gay marriage during mass the Sunday before the scheduled vote. The Church's hardening of its position seems to have provoked a backlash and is likely to have detracted from its ability to influence public opinion. Several senators came out publicly condemning the attacks and, according to senators interviewed, provoked repudiation. As Senator Mercedes Corregido indicated: "[the Church's] onslaught (*embestida*) served to remind some of my peers of Argentina's authoritarian past, when the Church collaborated with [former dictator Jorge Rafael] Videla . . . that image is still present in the country's popular consciousness (*imaginario colectivo*)."[71]

Importantly, the letter incentivized the Executive to take a public position, which it had not yet done. Once it became public, President Fernández de Kirchner declared that "we have the responsibility to build a more equal society, in which minorities have the same rights as the majorities" (*Clarín*, July 9, 2010). Several senators interviewed stated that the letter marked a turning point as Kirchner began to apply strong pressure to ensure the bill got passed. By the time the vote on the Senate floor was held, on July 14, the opposition appeared to have lost the debate in the court of public opinion. For one thing, and unlike supporters of gay marriage, they were unable to expand their constituency and obtain sympathy from a broader sector of society. Except for the support they obtained from lawyers and academics from denominational universities

---

[71] Interview, Buenos Aires, November 26, 2010.

and law firms, they were unable to establish alliances with unions, cultural groups, or other sectors of society (Hiller 2012, 146). Moreover, unlike proponents of gay marriage, religious organizations and churches did not advance a unified front. Several Protestant churches, known in Argentina as the "historic" ones, which included Lutherans, Anglicans, and Methodists, as well as Jewish leaders, such as Rabbi Daniel Goldman and Guido Cohen, declared their support for the reform and subsequently submitted a letter, cosigned by several other rabbis, to senators urging them to vote in favor (*La Nación*, June 10, 2010). Finally, while they may have attempted to frame their arguments as an issue of rights, their legal arguments were not as well crafted as the ones advanced by proponents of gay marriage, which had equality as a guiding rationale (Garcia Andía 2013). The extent to which supporters were able to win arguments in social debates is reflected by the generally positive media coverage their cause obtained. On July 11, three days before the vote, Ricardo Kirschbaum, editor-in-chief of the daily *Clarín*, wrote an open editorial supporting gay marriage (*Clarín*, July 11, 2010). The piece, coming from someone who had been in constant confrontation with the Kirchners' successive administrations, meant that, except for *La Nación*, every major news media in the country had joined the cause.

The push for gay marriage in the Senate replicated the strategies activists had pursued in the lower house: to harvest votes, one by one, by forcing senators to take a public position and justify it, to rely on allied senators to lobby from within, and have their now extensive network of allies and supporters convince senators to vote in favor. Original counts made by activists and allies showed a voting tie around the figure of twenty-nine senators on each side and fourteen undecided. They concentrated their efforts on the undecided ones and attempted to persuade the ones who had declared to vote against to abstain. Unlike how the process unfolded in the Chamber of Deputies, the Chair of the Senate Standing Committee (*Comisión de Legislación General*), Liliana Negre de Alonso, decided to hold public hearings across six provinces, some of which are known in Argentina to be conservative, to collect opinions from regions that are usually ignored by *porteños* (residents of Buenos Aires) (*Clarín*, May 31, 2010; *La Nación*, June 10, 2010). Negre de Alonso, a member of the highly conservative Catholic organization Opus Dei, was widely believed to have organized the hearings to ensure that more opposing voices from provincial Argentina were heard. For activists this meant that they had to take their arguments to their provinces. INADI played an important role at this stage, for it underwrote most of the expenses to have activists, some of whom, such as Rachid and Rapisardi, held positions in the institution, be present at these hearings. The numerous contacts activists had with universities, local activists, human rights organizations, and unions also proved key in having them attend these hearings and present arguments in favor (Hiller 2011, 159). During the last in this series of hearings, held in Buenos Aires and widely covered in the media, activists and their allies presented their arguments and evidence in support of gay marriage, all framed as an issue of human rights in the same way they did during previous stages.

In addition to well-known public personalities, such as theater director and playwright Pepé Cibrián Campoy, deputations at the hearings were made by some of their allied jurists, legal scholars, and academics. Their extensive personal and professional connections were critical in collecting and presenting convincing information. Both CHA and FALGBT elaborated a series of reports citing scientific evidence that pointed to the normal development of children adopted by gay parents, knowing quite well that adoption was one of the most sensitive issues for a number of senators. They were also able to secure the support of more than six hundred scientists and academics registered under the country's main research organization, the National Council for Scientific and Technical Research (*Consejo Nacional de Investigaciones Científicas y Técnicas*). In a public hearing held by the Senate at the beginning of July, called "Science says yes to equality," the signatures of these academics and scientists were presented along with a monograph titled *Per scientiam as justitiam*. The monograph, elaborated by Catamaraca University Professor Carlos Figari, a close ally, reviewed academic work on sexuality from various fields (Figari 2010). Deeply influenced by the work of Foucault, Figari clearly made the case for an understanding of sexuality as a social construction and argued that the debate over gay marriage was political, not moral. The vote at the committee level took place on July 6, and while a majority voted against gay marriage in principle, they voted to allow for a vote on the Senate floor.

From the time the committee held its vote until the Senate did so on July 14, 2010, both sides intensified their lobbying efforts significantly pursuing the same strategies they had during the vote in the lower house. While the Catholic Church had retained a relatively low profile during the vote in the lower house, they ramped up their efforts substantially and began to apply enormous pressure on senators to vote against, threatening to campaign against them at the next election. Various senators interviewed stated that they received threatening telephone calls from bishops asking them to vote against.

It is within this context that pressure from the Executive congealed. Interviews with the same senators reveal that the pressure on hesitant senators and on those who were opposed to the bill increased dramatically. Because of the influence provincial governors and party bosses have on senators, Fernández de Kirchner's officials appear to have lobbied them hard to get the bill passed. Moreover, in what legislators close to Kirchner believe was a deliberate move to guarantee its passage, the president invited several senators who were opposed to the bill to join her on an official visit to China that coincided with the vote in the Senate. Such pressure and tactics seem to have been crucial: the Senate vote, held at 4:30 a.m. on July 15 after a fourteen-hour-long debate, was close, with thirty votes in favor and twenty-seven against. Every legislator interviewed declared that the pressure exerted from the president, Kirchner, and his officials was critical in getting the bill voted favorably.

Similarly to what occurred during the debate in the lower house, the framing of gay marriage as an issue of human rights, equality, citizenship, and democracy resonated. This appears to have occurred at a larger societal level: as we have seen, arguments in favor of gay marriage were supported by a wide variety of individuals and organizations as well as most established media outlets. But they were also instrumental in obtaining votes from senators. Interviews with senators certainly reveal this. For example, Senator Norma Morandini, a prominent human rights advocate and feminist whose two brothers disappeared during the dictatorship, indicated: "when we [activists and allied senators] sat down with my colleagues, many of whom had been involved in struggles for human rights, it was just simply not possible for them to argue against this initiative when we presented it as an issue of equality and human rights."[72] Such resonance is also captured by the debate that took place on the Senate floor prior to the vote:

I want to say that my mind opened when I listened to socialist deputy Cuccovillo . . . and many other testimonies: from Cibrián . . . Rachid, Rabbi Goldman, the priest from Serna, and journalist Bazán. These were testimonies that opened my mind. I did not know how to express it, really, the only answer is equality. Senator Daniel Filmus

---

[72] Interview, Buenos Aires, December 1, 2010.

We are talking about rights, about the responsibility the democratic system has with these discriminated minorities. Senator Blanca Osuna

We have to march toward equality, but that does not mean erasing differences, because, paradoxically, it would be contradictory to erase them for the path to democracy and its deepening is tolerance of difference. Senator Rubén Giustiniani

It also resonated with the Executive. Two days before the vote was held, the president declared:

I think this is fair. It is fair to expand this right to minorities. And I think that it would be a terrible distortion of democracy when majorities, exercising those majorities, would deny rights to the minorities. . . . We are talking about whether we are going to be a society that recognizes the rights of those minorities. That is the issue. Télam 2010

In a carefully choreographed ceremony held at the Casa Rosada (presidential palace) on July 21, 2010, surrounded by numerous gay and lesbian activists, legislators, provincial governors, judges, mothers and grandmothers of the Plaza de Mayo, and artists, President Fernández de Kirchner promulgated the law. She delivered a speech that made references to previous expansions of rights and to the importance of building a more equal society:

We have not only promulgated a law, we have promulgated a social construction, and like all social constructions, it is transverse, diverse, plural and wide, and it does not belong to anyone but to those who built it: society.

Acknowledging that the push for gay marriage had emanated from civil society and that she was only responding to its demands, her signature brought to an end the efforts Argentine gay and lesbian activists had begun years earlier, and a positive right was finally conquered.

5

Mexico: A Case of Fragmented Reform

Introduction

Gay marriage was approved by Mexico City's Legislative Assembly in late 2009 and it came into force in 2010, the same year it did in Argentina. Mexico and Argentina thus became the first two countries in the region in which gay marriage was legalized. While in Mexico it was approved at the subnational level, a Supreme Court ruling on August 10, 2010 mandated every one of the thirty-one states in Mexico to recognize gay marriages contracted in the capital city. The right of marriage was therefore also extended, albeit indirectly, to same-sex couples throughout the country. This chapter explores the Mexican experience of policy reform in gay marriage. My analysis shows that the main factors behind policy reform in the Argentine case can be identified in the fight for gay marriage in Mexico, which originated in Mexico City. As in Argentina, the sources of policy change are found with the gay and lesbian movement: the networks formed by gay and lesbian activists proved critical in convincing policy makers to support their policy objective and drove the process that led to the approval of gay marriage by Mexico City's Legislative Assembly in 2009. In both cases, the persuasion of state actors to support policy reform was done in a way that resonated with larger national debates surrounding the country's process of democratization. Successful framing, then, was also at play.

The Mexican experience in policy reform in gay marriage has to be understood within its type of federalism. Unlike Argentina, where family law falls under the jurisdiction of the national civil code, in Mexico it is administered by the civil codes of the thirty-two "federative entities" (thirty-one states plus Mexico City). As in the United States, activists in Mexico have therefore had to pursue policy change on gay marriage at the subnational level. The politics of gay marriage in Mexico has consequently played out differently than in Argentina. The decentralized regulation of marriage offers multiple entry points into the policy process to proponents of and opponents to gay marriage. However, opportunities to push for policy reform have been mostly limited to Mexico City, where gay and lesbian activism has been strongest. An ideal opportunity to pursue policy change opened, and was seized, when a progressive faction of Mexico's main leftist party, the Party of Democratic Revolution (*Partido Revolucionario Democrático*, PRD), gained power in the city's 2006 elections.

The Mexican experience is one of fragmentation: policy change has occurred in Mexico City, and policy reform has been blocked in other policy venues by the representation of socially conservative forces through political parties, especially the Christian Democratic National Action Party (*Partido Acción Nacional*, PAN). Similar to my analysis of the Argentine experience, this chapter reveals the importance of adopting a historical approach to policy change. A careful look at the evolution of Mexico's gay and lesbian movement shows that the ability of activists to build networks of allies and supporters to push for gay marriage can only be appreciated by looking at past experiences in the pursuit of rights. These experiences were formative in acquiring effective lobbying strategies and discursive skills to push for reform successfully.

Early Successes in Policy Reform

Fulfilling Negative Liberties: Antidiscrimination Policy Reform
Similar to Argentina, the mid-1990s saw an important change in gay and lesbian politics in Mexico. Having achieved access to antiretroviral medication, Mexican gay activism assumed a new impetus in the pursuit of the expansion of sexual rights in 1997. The election of the PRD to the mayoralty of Mexico City that year opened up an important avenue for reform. A key development was the organization and hosting of the first Forum on Sexual Diversity and Human Rights in 1998 by the city, coordinated by legislator David Sánchez Camacho (Chapter 3). The forum brought together more than seventy organizations and individuals that included gay and lesbian groups, feminists, and human rights organizations. Its main objective was to gather what had been a

somewhat-fractured movement to discuss policy priorities.[1] The importance of this forum cannot be understated: it marked a new era in the politics of sexual rights in Mexico and a turn toward the struggle for civil rights by the movement. Historic ideological disagreements within the movement resurfaced through the discussions over policy priorities among activists, but several prominent activists – those who believed in reform through legislative change and who had begun articulating a rights-based discourse – agreed on the need to pursue several concrete policy objectives, along with their allies.

Discussions during and after the forum among activists crystallized the identification of three main policy priorities: legislation protecting gays and lesbians against discrimination; the extension of social benefits to same-sex couples; and gay marriage. While for most activists it was clear that pushing for gay marriage was premature, the idea was to at least begin the debate.[2] Gay marriage as a policy goal was thus articulated in Mexico by activists some twelve years before its eventual enactment. The event was also successful in attracting significant public attention as it was widely covered by the media, thereby helping to place the issue of sexual rights on the public agenda after a period of relative absence. According to the then-city's Director of Health and Social Development, Clara Jusidman, an ally who would subsequently join the push for gay marriage, the forum was critical in distilling for the new government what the priorities of the movement were and it placed them on the new government's legislative agenda.[3]

The forum also contributed to the thickening networks that had been developing for several years among gay activists, feminists, academics, lawyers, and state actors. While activists had been collaborating with women's and human rights organizations for some time, and a network of individuals advocating for sexual and reproductive rights had begun to form for at least a decade, the forum strengthened those relationships.

It also marked a shift of approach for many activists as they decided to focus their attention on bringing about legislative change and adopted a strategy that has become a central feature of Mexican gay activism since then: the formation of broad-based coalitions made up of socially progressive individuals and organizations to push for policy reform. Soon after the forum was held, several gay and lesbian activists joined forces

[1] Interview, David Sánchez Camacho, Mexico City, July 2, 2008.
[2] Interview, Rodolfo Millán, lawyer and activist, Mexico City, July 17, 2007.
[3] Interview, Mexico City, August 25, 2008.

with some of the most prominent women's organizations, such as Integral
Women's Health (*Salud Integral para la Mujer, A.C.,* SIPAM) and the
Information Group for Elective Reproduction (*Grupo de Información en
Reproducción Elegida,* GIRE), to launch a campaign for sexual and reproductive rights: The Campaign for Women's Access to Justice (*Campaña
de Acceso a la Justicia para las Mujeres*). The campaign, which was joined
by approximately forty different groups, articulated several policy goals,
among which included the right to abortion, legislation intended to eliminate domestic violence, and victims' rights. Collaboration between gay
activists and women's groups intensified with the launch of the campaign and continued in subsequent years. It was facilitated by a change
of strategy in Mexico's women's movement toward the latter part of
the 1990s: numerous Mexican feminists adopted a less confrontational
approach to their interaction with the state and decided to advance their
demands by advocating the engagement of partisan politics (Lamas
2001). Having set their main policy objectives, activists began to push for
legislative change on several fronts.

Similar to their Argentine counterparts, Mexican activists decided to
devote efforts to the documentation of acts of discrimination against
sexual minorities, especially those that resulted in death. They did so in
order to ensure that crimes perpetrated against homosexuals did not go
unresolved and to generate evidence to convince policy makers of the
need to enact nondiscrimination legislation.[4] Relying on the relationships
they had built with feminists and other prominent figures, and benefit-
ing from some funding made available to the main nongovernmental
organization (NGO), *Letra S* (see Chapter 3), several activists formed
the Citizens Commission against Homophobic Hate Crimes (*Comisión
Ciudadana Contra los Crimenes de Odio por Homofobia*) in the weeks
following the forum. The Commission was joined by high-profile intellectuals and feminists, such as Carlos Monsiváis, Elena Poniatowska,
and Marta Lamas, thus gathering media attention. Since its formation,
the commission has been very successful at drawing attention to violence perpetrated on sexual minorities through the publication of reports
documenting hate crimes. Over the years the reports have been used by
activists and state actors to argue for the need to pass antidiscrimination
legislation. In effect, the data generated by the Commission were used as
bases to justify a reform of Mexico City's Penal Code in 2009. The bill,
passed unanimously by the city's Legislative Assembly in August of that

---

[4] Interview, Alejandro Brito, Director, *Letra S*, Mexico City, July 23, 2007.

year, introduced severe penalties for hate crimes perpetrated against a variety of historically discriminated groups, including sexual minorities.

In addition to the documentation of hate crimes, activists began to push for the derogation of antidiscriminatory provisions in Mexico City's legislation and for the enactment of antidiscrimination legislation. Soon after the forum was held, they began to pressure the new administration to adopt their policy proposals in close cooperation with feminists and human rights organizations. Taking advantage of the opening provided by the election of the PRD to the city, they worked with city legislators that agreed to take up the cause and who had been active participants in the forum: Sánchez Camacho and María de los Angeles Correo de Lucio. Collaboration between these legislators and some gay and feminist activists led to the establishment within the city's Legislative Assembly of a Working Group on the Penal Code, which included legislators with senior positions. In what since then has become a feature of lobbying Mexico City's Legislative Assembly, proponents of changes to the penal code focused their attention on convincing PRD legislators, who have held a majority since 1997. This has meant learning how to navigate the various factions within the party. As the main party representing the Mexican Left, the PRD, since its formation in 1989, has amalgamated a widely diverse group of individuals and organizations that have developed into several factions (colloquially known as *tribus*, tribes) that are identified with particular politicians (Mossige 2013). The position of the various factions on moral policies has not been uniform and, while those that developed close relationships with women's organizations have supported moral policy reform, this has not been the case for others that have adopted more traditional positions.

In terms of sexual rights, the various factions within the PRD have also taken different positions, and it was not until 2005 that the party established a Sexual Diversity Commission. After sustained pressure, activists were able to obtain the support of the most prominent legislator at the time and a key national figure within the PRD: Martí Batres. During a series of meetings held in late 1998 and late 1999, Batres agreed to their main demands. Reforms were thus enacted in 1999 to the city's penal code that involved: first, the derogation of a clause that considered homosexuality to be child molestation, and thus a crime, and; second, the introduction of a penalty, of up to three years in jail and one hundred days of community service, for discrimination against vulnerable groups, including sexual minorities. The reforms were passed unanimously by all parties represented in the Legislative Assembly, making Mexico City the first jurisdiction in the country to enact antidiscrimination legislation protecting sexual minorities.

These reforms showed activists and their allies the importance of deploying a rights-based discourse while making a connection to democratization in pushing for sexual rights. The acceleration of Mexico's transition to democracy, and the saliency human rights took in the process, facilitated the advancement of their demands. Within the PRD, agreement to support sexual rights was not reached automatically by city deputies. Activists thus had to convince them of the importance to do so: they argued that, as members of a party that had placed human rights as a pillar of its overall *raison d'être*, they could not deny the expansion of these rights.[5] The acquisition of a rights-based discourse in the fight for antiretroviral drugs was therefore crucial. The saliency of human rights by the late 1990s was such that PAN deputies were unable to oppose the reforms.[6]

The acceleration of Mexico's democratization by the end of the 1990s propelled the issue of discrimination to the national level, and it became part of debates in the lead-up to the 2000 election, as detailed in Chapter 2. During this time, some feminist organizations moved away from a confrontational approach with the state and decided to enter legislative politics. The prominent feminists Patricia Mercado and Elena Tapia registered the NGO, Diversa, as a political association in 1999 with the intention of subsequently turning it into a political party. With the idea of launching a new political project based on pluralism and inclusion, Diversa formed a broad-based coalition that agglutinated a variety of NGOs, members of unions and political parties, and feminist men with sights on influencing the 2000 elections.[7] For those elections Diversa approached political parties across the political spectrum and requested the inclusion of its policy objectives into their electoral platforms as well as the selection of some of its members as candidates at the national and subnational levels. It also established an alliance with the Social Democracy Party (*Partido Democracia Social*, PDS) that allowed it to introduce into the debate demands that had hitherto been avoided by other political parties, such as the decriminalization of abortion and civil

---

[5] Interview, Arturo Díaz, activist, Mexico City, July 24, 2007.

[6] Tellingly, Patricia Espinoza Torres, a PAN national deputy (subsequently appointed as director of the National Institute for Women by President Vicente Fox in 2000), attended the Forum and argued that a full democracy included the right not to be discriminated on sexual-orientation grounds.

[7] For a good discussion of Diversa's formation and evolution see Sutter 2008.

unions for same-sex couples. Diversa was able to place twenty-two of its members as candidates in several different parties at the national and subnational levels. While only three were elected, the debate had intensified and, as activist Arturo Díaz put it: "we had to take advantage of the democratic opening."[8]

The rights of sexual minorities did not stay at the level of discourse during the election campaign, however; they transcended it and made it to the new government's agenda. Such was largely the result of their incidence with broader issues of human rights that were central to that election and the emergence of a master frame around them. Among numerous reforms, Vicente Fox (2000–6) pushed for a constitutional reform to prohibit all forms of discrimination, a reform that came into effect in 2001. The reform banned discrimination against an individual's preferences.[9] In terms of sexual rights, Fox became the first Mexican president to have referred to the importance of protecting sexual minorities from discrimination in his first speech as president-elect. Soon after taking office, he appointed Rincón Gallardo as chair of a citizens' commission in charge of studying ways to tackle discrimination. Specifically, Fox tasked the new commission with producing legal and institutional proposals that would help in the fight against deeply entrenched forms of discrimination in Mexico. The commission, established in March 2001, was composed of 161 academics, activists, government officials from various political parties, and the most prominent gay activists. The group held a series of consultations, regional fora, and meetings with experts and members of civil society at large throughout 2001. After these consultations it produced a final report in which its members presented an antidiscrimination draft bill and recommended the establishment of a national council tasked with two main objectives: ensuring that such a law be implemented and promoting more generally a "culture of tolerance" in the country (Comisión Ciudadana de Estudios contra la Discriminación 2001). The Assembly presented its recommendations to the president in November 2001. Within weeks, Fox sent the bill to Congress with no changes. In April 2003, both chambers of Congress unanimously approved the bill (*El Universal*, April 11, 2003). It was signed into law in June of the same year by the president who also issued a presidential decree to accelerate

---

[8] Interview, Mexico City, July 24, 2007.
[9] The original text included "sexual preferences," but upon the unwavering insistence of social conservative PAN Senator Diego Fernández de Cevallos, "sexual" was dropped when voted in the upper chamber. As part of a significant human rights reform launched in 2010 and completed in 2011, "preferences" was replaced with "sexual preferences."

its implementation (*La Jornada*, June 10, 2003). The new law became Mexico's first national law designed to protect vulnerable groups, and it established the National Anti-Discrimination Council (*Consejo Nacional para Prevenir la Discriminación*, CONAPRED).

The enactment of the law and the creation of the council thus meant that the issue of respect for sexual minorities had not only been placed on the national political agenda but was also followed up by government action. The salience of such human rights during the election campaign, which was largely due to the broader context of Mexican democratization, created a context propitious for the advancement of policies framed around rights. Unlike Argentina, where a national law against discrimination had not yet been passed by mid-2014, the enactment of the antidiscrimination law in Mexico at the national level, the first in the region, rendered any discriminatory legal provisions at the subnational level essentially unenforceable. The numerous municipal and state legal provisions that established penalties for acts against "morality and good customs" in municipal and state laws,[10] which were historically used to harass and detain sexual minorities, were thus rendered inapplicable. The law may be criticized for lacking teeth, as its violators are not subject to criminal penalties,[11] but it has been strategically used by activists to push for subsequent policies, such as the launch of antihomophobia campaigns (Díez 2010) and the claims against the unconstitutional state civil codes that define marriage between a man and a woman (*Notiese*, July 9, 2014).

Moreover, the establishment of CONAPRED, which is tasked with the implementation of the law, has contributed to keeping the issue of antidiscrimination against sexual minorities atop national discussions. Since the passage of the law, by early 2014 eighteen states had introduced similar legislation at the subnational level, out of which thirteen established

---

[10] Large cities, such as Monterrey (the country's second largest) still possessed these provisions by the late 1990s. For a discussion see Roemer 1998.

[11] In addition to mandating public institutions to undertake programs to eliminate discrimination, the law provides CONAPRED with the capacity to investigate discriminatory cases once complaints are submitted. It has the authority to issue public statements denouncing discriminatory actions, when found, as well as to summon perpetrators and victims of discriminatory acts to a conciliation meeting. Over the years public statements issued by the institution have attracted significant media attention, especially when those found having committed discriminatory acts are celebrities or politicians. The institution also has the authority to provide legal advice to victims should they wish to pursue legal action. In a highly publicized case, it supported Roberto Mendoza Ralph's litigation against Coca-Cola, which had allegedly fired him because of his sexual orientation in 2005 (*Reforma*, February 3, 2006).

steep penalties ranging from three to six years in jail for discriminatory acts against sexual minorities.

Civil Unions

The fight for negative freedoms waged by gay and lesbian activists in Mexico unfolded in tandem with a push for same-sex relationship recognition. The devastating effects the HIV/AIDS crisis had on Mexico's gay men in the late 1980s and early 1990s demonstrated to many activists the importance of having the state recognize, and extend benefits to, same-sex couples. As in Argentina, the disease ravaged the lives of numerous gay men. Not having their relationships legally recognized meant that they were unable to access a variety of socioeconomic benefits, such as health care or pensions, and, frequently, their possessions were taken away by their partners' relatives upon death.

Among the various policy objectives activists had set during and after the 1998 forum was the demand for social protection for same-sex partners and the recognition of gay marriages. In the negotiations activists held with the PRD leadership following the forum they were only able to convince legislators to support antidiscrimination provisions. Same-sex recognition did not gain support. However, the push for it intensified shortly after. In a striking similarity with the Argentine experience, 2000 marked the beginning of well-organized efforts to demand the enactment of same-sex civil unions. In the case of Mexico, the alliance formed between Diversa and the PDS prior to the 2000 elections yielded the election of the feminist and openly gay activist Enoé Uranga as deputy in Mexico City and Díaz, perhaps Mexico's most prominent gay activist, as her *suplente* (alternate legislator).

Emboldened by having achieved the enactment of Mexico's first antidiscrimination legislation the year before, and taking advantage of the democratic opening the 2000 elections represented, Uranga and Díaz, as well as activist and intellectual Claudia Hinojosa, decided in the weeks after the election to push for civil unions in the city's Legislative Assembly. Soon after taking up office, they began to coordinate efforts with other activists – among whom were the Director of *Letra S*, Alejandro Brito and lawyer and activist Rodolfo Millán – to work on a strategy. They decided that a central component of their plan was to weave a broad socially based network of citizens to initiate public debate on the proposal through the media, supported by respected individuals attempting to influence public opinion and exert pressure on legislators. For them, gaining the endorsement of other social movements and actors was one of the most effective ways to sway both the public and city deputies.[12] The Citizens Network in the Support of the Cohabitation Law (*Red Ciudadana de Apoyo a la Ley de Sociedades de Convivencia*) was thus created. While the size of the network varies depending on the source, their creators managed to enlist numerous renowned artists, intellectuals, and academics who publicly supported their cause. Some surveys list at least 180 organizations.[13]

With the support of legal experts, Uranga presented a civil-union bill to the Mexico City Legislative Assembly in early 2001. Once the bill was introduced to the council, an important public debate ensued, igniting strong opposition to and support for the legal recognition of same-sex couples. An important part of their strategy was to win the debate in the court of public opinion. Activists thus organized a series of public events in which renowned celebrities and public figures, such as actor Gael García Bernal, publicly endorsed the bill.

Despite the wide support activists managed to obtain from state and nonstate actors, and the pressure their extensive network of allies exerted on city deputies to approve the bill, they, unlike their Argentine counterparts, were unable to obtain the endorsement from the city mayor and his allies in the Legislative Assembly because of the mayor's ideological positioning and broader political calculations. Various members of PRD supported the bill, including, importantly, the party's leader in the Assembly. However, the mayor, Manuel Andrés López Obrador, opposed it. Representing a more traditional and socially conservative wing of the Mexican Left,[14] and given the close relationship he attempted to build with the Catholic Church as he planned to run for the presidency in 2006 (Díez 2010), López Obrador opposed the bill and gave instructions to

---

[12] Interview, Enoé Uranga, Mexico City, July 7, 2008.

[13] These included most gay NGOs; members of *Demysex* (referred to in Chapter 3), academics Daniel Caséz, Careaga, and Amuchástegui; individuals from prestigious academic institutions and professional associations, such as from the prestigious El Colegio de México and the Mexican Psychiatric Association; feminists groups and activists, including Lamas, Lama, and Cristina Pacheco; and legal scholars and jurists, such as Miguel Carbonell and Luis Alcántara Carracá. For one of the most complete lists, see González Pérez 2007, 27–8.

[14] Contrary to what is commonly conveyed by the Mexican media, López Obrador is not an evangelical Christian but rather a Catholic (Grayson 2011, 20). Given that he has not discussed his religious views publicly over the years, little is known. However, he has invariably opposed the expansion of sexual and reproductive rights and is closely associated with the more traditional ideological currents of the Mexican Left. Within the PRD he was associated with the National Democratic Left faction (*Izquierda Democrática Nacional*), before forming his own party in 2014.

city deputies not to support it. Given the tight party discipline that characterizes the Mexican party system, and the perilous consequences that challenging the party line can bring to legislators,[15] opposition from the party that commanded a legislative majority soon crystallized. By the end of that Legislative Assembly's term in August 2003, the bill died as its proponents were unable to win support given the mayor's opposition. Because López Obrador did not change his position, and given that his party continued to have a majority of seats in the Legislative Assembly after the local mid-term elections of 2003, the impossibility to push for the passage of the bill remained. Yet, activists and their allies in the Citizens Coalition continued to operate and to apply pressure on city deputies after 2003 to support the proposal. Indeed, the coalition grew in number and strength, as reflected by the increasing number of activities they carried out. According to several city deputies, the coalition's lobbying efforts after the introduction of the bill were not only crucial in the eventual passage of the legislation, but proved important in obtaining public support, thereby making it easier to induce policy change.

Conditions changed dramatically after the 2006 elections, provoking a realignment of forces with the election of Marcelo Ebrard Casaubón as mayor. Ebrard (a socially progressive individual) had openly supported the civil-union bill. Moreover, the Social Democratic Party (*Partido Social Demócrata*, PSD) performed better electorally in 2006, increasing its presence in the Legislative Assembly. The party was the main architect behind the establishment of a "progressive alliance" among city deputies and responsible for the reintroduction of the bill within a month of the election. The realignment of forces created a window of opportunity that allowed policy proponents to obtain the necessary votes to pass the bill. It was reintroduced to the Assembly soon after the start of the city's legislative period, obtained a majority of votes two months later, and was subsequently promulgated into law by the mayor shortly thereafter. The ability of activists to frame their demand as an issue of human rights, equality, and democratic deepening, in a context in which human rights had become deeply entrenched into Mexico's democratization process, proved critical (Díez 2013).

The parallels between the passage of civil unions in Mexico City and Buenos Aires are indeed striking: in both cases, broad-based coalitions,

---

[15] The Mexican constitution bars the consecutive reelection of legislators and that often means that they depend on party leaders and bosses for jobs once their terms come to an end.

in which women's groups played important roles, were successful in advancing policy proposals that resonated with larger debates and that helped convince legislators to endorse the expansion of a sexual right. Similar to the Argentine experience, the push and eventual attainment of civil unions at the subnational level contributed to the solidification of networks among state and nonstate actors and were important exercises that allowed activists to acquire knowledge regarding effective lobbying strategies and the advancement of well-framed arguments – knowledge that was applied in the pursuit of gay marriage two years later.

The Pursuit of Gay Marriage

Moral Policy Fragmentation

The enactment of same-sex civil unions in Mexico City was the first in a series of moral policy reforms the Ebrard administration undertook that galvanized debates in Mexico and contributed to policy fragmentation across the country. Ebrard's reformist agenda, overtones of which resembled the one articulated by the Kirchner administrations in Argentina, was hinged on a vision that strongly stressed human rights.

Upon taking office in December 2006, Ebrard, in his first speech as mayor of Mexico City, outlined his vision of governance, one that strongly emphasized the need to expand what he called "social rights" to improve the welfare and quality of life for the city's residents. As one of seven "strategic axes," Ebrard called for the need to push for a political reform that would assert the city's autonomy from the federal government and allow for the expansion of "full citizenship rights." As he declared, "to guarantee equality we need to think of the city and make the city for women, to deepen our attention to the disabled, act toward our ethnic communities as well as to our migrants and their families" (*Reforma*, December 6, 2006). Ebrard's administration implemented his vision of rights expansion making Mexico City one of the most socially progressive jurisdictions in Latin America. The policy change that understandably has attracted the most attention is the decriminalization of abortion: less than five months after Ebrard assumed power, the city reformed its criminal code allowing pregnant women to terminate their pregnancies within twelve weeks of conception.[16] Mexico

---

[16] For analyses of that reform, see Sánchez Fuentes, Paine, and Eliott-Buettner 2008; MacDonald and Mills 2010; and Becker and Díaz Olavarrieta 2013.

City became thus the second jurisdiction in Latin America, after Cuba, in which abortion is legal beyond cases of rape, incest, or when a woman's health is at risk.[17] However, the decriminalization of abortion is part of a longer series of moral policy reforms Ebrard's administration introduced, which includes the country's first hate-crime legislation, the legalization of "passive euthanasia"[18] (*Ley de Voluntad Anticipada*), and the simplification of procedures to facilitate the attainment of a divorce, or what has colloquially come to be known in Mexico City as "express divorce" (*divorcio expréss*).[19] These reforms ignited a national debate on moral policy, a reaction shaped by Mexico's type of federalism and its party system, producing policy fragmentation.

In Mexico, contrary to Argentina, family law falls under the jurisdiction of the thirty-two subnational governments. The enactment of same-sex civil unions, and marriage, must therefore be pursued at the subnational level. The same occurs with policy areas regulated by the criminal code. Mexico's legal system possesses two levels of criminal codification: the national code regulates offences committed against the country, such as treason; and the subnational codes (the thirty-one states plus Mexico City) regulate offences committed in their territories. Reform dealing with the criminalization of most activities around moral policy – such as abortion, euthanasia, and hate crimes – must be undertaken at the subnational level. Mexico's federalism therefore offers multiple access points to proponents and opponents of moral policy reform. Such access is, of course, primarily used by political parties and their positions on moral policy. Understanding the country's party system is essential to explain subnational variation and national fragmentation.

Mexico's party system is made up of three main political parties. Mexico's Left has been primarily represented by the PRD, a party made up of various factions with different ideological positions (Mossige 2013).

---

[17] In October 2012 Uruguay became the third jurisdiction, although, controversially, women must explain their decision to terminate their pregnancy before a committee made up of three medical professionals. The committee must provide the petitioner possible alternatives (*La Nación*, October 22, 2012). A push by opponents to call for a referendum failed in June 2013 as they were unable to obtain the necessary signatures.

[18] Passive euthanasia refers to an individual's right to refuse medication that would prolong her life in a manner deemed unnecessary.

[19] Under the previous rules, which are very common across Latin America, the onus was on the spouse to provide evidenced reasons (*causales*) to justify the divorce, and it was up to a judge to authorize the divorce. These were lengthy and frequently expensive processes that made it difficult for women and the poor to undertake. Under the new rules divorces are granted without justification, can be pursued unilaterally by one spouse, and are granted within thirty days of application.

The party's position on moral issues depends largely on which faction's leadership gains power at a given time. The Left is also represented by smaller socially progressive parties, such as the PSD, although mostly at the subnational level, as well as the Workers Party (*Partido del Trabajo*, PT). The Right is represented by Mexico's Christian Democratic party, the National Action Party (*Partido Acción Nacional*, PAN).[20] Founded in 1939, PAN was formed largely as a religious organization by activists and associations, such as the National Sinarquist Association (*Unión Nacional Sinarquista*) and the National Parents' Union (*Unión Nacional de Padres de Familia*), in response to the secularism consolidated in the late 1930s by the administration of Lázaro Cárdenas (1934–40) (Loaeza 1999; Shirk 2005; Whus 2008). Unlike Argentina, which does not have a major confessional party, PAN has functioned as a mechanism of representation of predominantly Catholic interests. Indeed, while the party may not be ideologically coherent in economic issues, an aspect that characterizes its membership is religiosity (Magaloni and Moreno 2003). On moral issues PAN pursues a socially conservative agenda backed by powerful economic interests.[21] Since the 1980s, a network has developed among some members of the PAN leadership, socially conservative philanthropic organizations, and private-sector organizations to push for a restrictive agenda on moral issues in line with the Catholic Church's official positions (González Ruiz 2001, 2002a, 2002b).[22] Conservative positions on moral policy are also represented by Mexico's Green Party (*Partido Verde Ecologista de México*, PVEM). The Green Party is a pragmatic political party that over the years has formed alliances with PAN and PRI (*Partido Revolucionario Institucional*, PRI) but which, contrary to most green parties, takes a firm conservative position on moral policy discussions.

The third main political party is, of course, PRI. Ideologically, as the party was built to carry out the ideals of the revolution (Chapter 2), it has historically discursively been a Social Democratic party. From the early 1980s until its national defeat in the 2000 elections, however,

---

[20] The PAN joined the Christian Democratic International in 1998.

[21] Wealthy Mexican magnates Lorenzo Servitje – founder of Bimbo, the world's second-largest bakery – and José Barroso Chávez have over the years financially contributed to the party as well as to numerous social conservative Catholic organizations.

[22] An important member of this network is the Mexican Confederation of Business Owners (*Confederación Patronal de la República Mexicana*). The organization represents some of the biggest Mexican firms and has been led by individuals who are identified with the far-right Catholic groups, such as the movement *El Yunque* (Delgado 2003, 2004).

foreign-trained technocrats dislodged the several factions (*grupos*) that had rotated power for decades (Teichman 2001, 129–59) and the party assumed an economically liberal ideology (de la Garza Talavera 2003). On moral policy, PRI has had an ambivalent and changing position. The technocratic leadership that dominated it during the 1990s supported family planning programs and ratified several international agreements on women's rights. In terms of homosexuality, it did not take a public position. However, after its 2000 presidential loss the party became deeply divided around moral policies. The electoral loss unleashed internal struggles among the many groups as the technocratic wing lost influence and the established left-leaning factions worked to restore the party's social-democratic foundations.[23] These struggles provoked divisions that became evident regarding the party's positions on moral policy. While the national leadership promoted an ideological discourse based on social-democratic principles, especially after the ascension to its leadership by Beatriz Paredes in 2007, at the subnational level numerous PRI factions took conservative positions as they competed with PAN.

Ebrard's reformist agenda ignited a national debate to which the main political parties reacted by pushing for and against moral policy reform at the subnational level. The decriminalization of abortion in Mexico City in 2007 provoked a strong backlash from conservative forces across the country and PAN led a campaign to prevent the passage of similar legislation. Soon after the reform, Felipe Calderón's PAN administration (2006–12), through its attorney general, challenged the law before the Supreme Court arguing that health law fell under the jurisdiction of the national government and that it violated constitutional provisions guaranteeing the right to life. In an eight-to-three vote, in August 2008 the Court upheld Mexico City's law stating that: "to affirm that there is an absolute constitutional protection of life in gestation would lead to the violation of the fundamental rights of women."[24] As a reaction to this ruling, subnational PAN governments, in an effort to shield their states from adopting similar legislation, began to reform state constitutions introducing clauses protecting life from the moment of conception. Starting with reforms in traditionally PAN-held states, such as Baja California, numerous states reformed their constitutions to that effect and, by the

[23] Interview, Mauricio López Velásquez, Secretary, Political Committee, National Political Council, PRI, Mexico City, August 8, 2008.
[24] For the best analysis of this case see Vela 2011.

end of 2012, seventeen had done so.[25] Ten of these reforms also banned contraception, including the use of intrauterine devices (GIRE 2012).

The positions of the three main political parties in these reforms reflected, in large part, their ideological positions on moral policy. Out of the seventeen states in which reforms were undertaken, PAN was in power in four (traditional stronghold) states. Reflecting the internal divisions within PRI, and the different position some subnational groups took from its national leadership, in three states PRI supported the reforms in an alliance with PAN, and in nine others it took the lead in passing them. At the subnational level some PRI leaderships took strongly conservative positions on abortion that were at variance from the formal positions taken by its national leadership.[26] In regard to PRD, except for Chiapas,[27] none of the governments that it led passed similar reforms. Moreover, in most of the votes held in the state legislatures, PRD voted against these reforms (Lopreite 2014).

Two of these amendments were challenged before the Supreme Court in 2011. In September of the same year the Court ruled, in two seven-to-three votes, that both reforms were unconstitutional (*Reforma*, September 28, 2011). However, given that eight votes were necessary to overturn them, the vote upheld the constitutionality of the measures, thereby settling the issue.

Gay Marriage: The Origins of Policy

It is within this context of high variation at the subnational level on moral policy that the reform on same-sex recognition has taken place in Mexico. Similar to what occurred with the decriminalization of abortion, the push for civil unions sparked a national debate on gay rights. The debate motivated activists in several states to pursue similar reforms. However, such a push has had very limited effects on policy diffusion.

[25] Prior to 2007 Chihuahua (a PAN stronghold) was the only state to have introduced a right-to-life constitutional provision.

[26] The very limited work that has been carried out on the positioning of PRI state governments and legislators shows that "there coexist various political party systems in the state legislatures that are not simply a reflection of the national [tripartite] dynamic" (López Lara 2012, 51). Álvaro López Lara shows that the behavior of PRI state legislators is closely associated with the positions taken by PAN, whereby the voting median tends to shift to the right when PAN is the stronger competitor. This phenomenon explains, and captures, the overall shift to the right at the subnational level several PRI governments have taken since the party's defeat at the national level in 2000.

[27] The state government was led by a former PRI member when the debate over moral policies accelerated, Juan Sabines Guerrero (2006–12), commonly identified with the more conservative factions within the party.

Following the enactment of civil unions in Mexico City in 2006, state legislators in nine states publicly announced their desire to pursue similar reforms. By mid-2014, bills had been introduced in eight states (Coahuila, Guerrero, Guanajuato, Zacatecas, Yucatán, San Luis Potosí, Puebla, and Jalisco), primarily by PRD state legislators.[28]

As in Argentina, most initiatives have not translated into policy change because of the general weakness of gay and lesbian activism outside Mexico City. This has been the case even in states in which propitious conditions were present, such as Zacatecas. In 2004, Amalia García was elected as the first female governor of the state under the PRD. García, a longtime feminist and militant of several leftist parties prior to the foundation of PRD, had maintained close relationships with several groups that advocated the expansion of sexual and reproductive rights since the late 1980s. She was a member of the Campaign for Women's Access to Justice (Chapter 3). As Rafael de la Dehesa details (2010, 152–3), she was in fact the main actor behind the reform of police bylaws in Mexico City in the early 1990s, which included antidiscriminatory provisions, the first in Mexico and, to my knowledge, Latin America. Widely seen as a social progressive who belonged to the more liberal groups within PRD, García's election to the state governorship opened an opportunity for activists to push for civil unions. In reality, they did not. Interviews with several activists in the state reveal that civil unions were not a priority for their movement given its incipient nature.[29] According to Sara Ortiz García, an artist and member of the lesbian organization *Hijas de la Luna*, their efforts were concentrated on starting a social discussion about homosexuality, mainly through artistic activities, as the first phase of their activism.[30] While allies existed in the state legislature, activists did not articulate the demand. According to María Luisa de la Torre, a PRD state deputy: "as a progressive feminist, I communicated to activists [*colectivo*] my desire to advance on the issue . . . I in fact presented a bill to the legislature. But they did not support it [*no me acompañaron*]. With Amalia as governor we could have attempted it, but there was no

---

[28] There have only been two exceptions. A civil-union bill was introduced in Puebla in 2011 by PAN legislators. These state deputies, however, had been elected under the PRD (the party's only three legislators decided to cross the floor and join the PAN in 2011). Another bill was introduced in February 2013 in Guanajuato by a PRI legislator.

[29] Interviews, Sandra de Santiago Félix and María Luisa de la Torre, Zacatecas, July 12, and José Luis Escareño and María Elena Ortega, Zacatecas, July 13, 2010.

[30] Interview, Zacatecas, July 12, 2010. Zacatecas is one of eighteen states that, by late 2012, had introduced legislation prohibiting discrimination based on sexual orientation. It was enacted by García in 2006.

demand [*reclamo*] from them."[31] Asked about the apparent puzzle of why a socially progressive governor did not enact civil unions after Mexico City had, one of her closest advisors replied, at the end of the governor's term: "In the state of Zacatecas the issue of legal unions between individuals of the same sex was not an explicit citizen demand, I do not remember any social organization supporting that request."[32]

The only exception has been in the northern state of Coahuila, which approved civil unions in 2007. The case exhibits certain particularities that have not been present in any of the other states. Policy change in that state was the product of efforts made by a politically savvy state legislator who took it upon herself, because of personal convictions on equality and rights, to push for the enactment of civil unions. As the debate over civil unions resumed in Mexico City in 2006, Julieta López, a PRI state deputy, decided to undertake changes to the civil code and the Civil Registry Law, to allow for the recognition of same-sex unions. López, a self-identified social progressive influenced by Liberation Theology, saw an opportunity to push civil unions given the internal fissures within the PRI on moral policy and the large public presence of the socially progressive bishop of Saltillo, the state's capital city, Raúl Vera López, had.[33] As she recounted:

The debate in Mexico City opened the conversation. It was my reference point. I saw in Coahuila an opening of political space to go for this, a favorable scene [*escenario favorable*]. . . . Having Vera as bishop helped a great deal because I knew he would not be opposed to it. . . . I also knew, given his trajectory, that the governor would be open to it.[34]

The PRI won the state governorship in 2005, electing Humberto Moreira as governor. It also won a majority of the seats in the state legislature. Because, according to López, Moreira was widely seen as socially progressive in the state of Coahuila, she, despite the near absence of gay mobilization in the state, pushed for the bill.[35] Interviews with activists show that the state legislator solicited their support once she decided to

---

[31] Interview, Zacatecas, July 7, 2008.
[32] Interview, governor's advisor, aboard a Zacatecas-Mexico City flight, July 14, 2010.
[33] Prior to his appointment as bishop to Saltillo, Vera, a vocal proponent of Liberation Theology, was bishop of Altamirano, Chiapas, and was, along with Samuel Ruiz García, directly involved with the Zapatista peace process. He was Adjunct Bishop of San Cristóbal de las Casas in 1995.
[34] Interview, Saltillo, July 21, 2008.
[35] The similarities between gay and lesbian activism in Zacatecas and Coahuila are striking as in both cases activists were mostly focused on artistic activities to bring about social awareness and to ignite social debates around homosexuality.

pursue the bill and that it was not a demand that emanated from them.[36] Given the perceived liberal bent of the governor, and the internal disagreements over moral policy within the PRI, López presented her bill, called the Civil Solidarity Pact, *Pacto Civil de Solidaridad*, in 2006 to the state legislature. Predictably her bill was opposed by PAN and the Green Party and some PRI legislators. However, her arguments in favor of the reform resonated with the more liberal wing of the PRI state leadership. According to Horacio del Bosque Dávila, the state legislature's house leader:

> It was not an easy debate, and there were some elements within our parliamentary group that were not in favor. But here in Coahuila we [the PRI] are trying to build a new party, one that embraces third-generation policies, and this initiative is part of our vision. . . . Questions regarding the merits of capitalism and the flows of capital are over, and one way to distinguish ourselves from the PAN, as we try to return to power, is to pursue these policies, third-generation policies.[37]

The bill was introduced to the legislature on November 13, 2006, sparking a heated debate. López's reading of the political conditions proved accurate as, on January 11, 2007, she managed to obtain the support of nineteen out of the twenty PRI legislators, ensuring the passage of the bill.[38] The governor signed it into law shortly thereafter, and it came into effect in February of the same year. Interestingly, and as López had predicted, Bishop Vera did not articulate any opposition to the bill. The enactment of civil unions in Coahuila is then a case in which a state actor decided to pursue policy change within very rare political opportunities. And rare they were: it is the only jurisdiction outside Mexico City in which civil unions were approved by early 2014. Just as in Argentina, the enactment of civil unions in the capital city had limited ramifications in other jurisdictions.

Similar to Argentina, the approval of civil unions in the capital, and in Coahuila, prompted internal discussions among activists regarding their next objectives. Some activists continued to focus their efforts on

---

[36] Interviews, Aida and Miguel Servin, *Asociación Eux arte y sida*, Saltillo, July 7, 2008, and Gerardo Moscoso, activist, Saltillo, July 8, 2008.

[37] Interview, Saltillo, July 23, 2008.

[38] Soon after its passage, the eight PAN state legislators argued before the state's Superior Court (*Tribunal Superior de Justicia*) that the reform was unconstitutional because it discriminated against traditional marriages. In a ruling handed down in November 2011 the Court upheld the law and in fact ordered the state legislature to reform both the state's constitution and the civil code to allow for adoption (*La Jornada*, November 30, 2011). In early 2014, the state Congress complied by reforming it and allowing for adoption (*Notiese*, February 12, 2014).

HIV/AIDS prevention campaigns. For the most visible ones, those associated with the NGO *Letra S*, the documentation of hate crimes continued to be a priority. Many of the discussions held among activists revolved around whether the next site of their struggle should be the national level. Similar to what happened in Argentina, many activists believed that the gains made at the subnational level could be pursued nationally. Using the case of Mexico City as a beachhead, activists such as Brito and Javier Lagunes surmised that the push for additional rights could be taken to the national level, and the 2009 mid-term federal elections represented an opportunity to do so. As such, and continuing with a long tradition of Mexican gay activism, discussions among activists led to the decision to advance the candidacy of Uranga, the main actor behind the push for civil unions in Mexico City (see preceding text), for a seat in Chamber of Deputies on the PRD ticket.

With the support of the numerous activists, Uranga developed a platform that included five main objectives: a constitutional reform establishing Mexico as a secular state; a gender identity law; constitutional reforms that would prohibit discrimination against sexual orientation; reforms to the national antidiscrimination law introducing criminal penalties; and reforms to social security expanding socioeconomic benefits to same-sex couples who had entered a civil union in Mexico City or Coahuila.[39] Because, as mentioned, family law in Mexico is under the jurisdiction of subnational levels of government, for Mexican activists, unlike their Argentine counterparts, the push for civil unions at the national level was not a possibility. Uranga was successful in her candidacy and elected deputy on July 5, 2009.

For other activists, the gains made in Mexico City and the opportunity Ebrard's reformist agenda offered meant that a further expansion of rights in the city was possible. Lol Kin Castañeda was the main proponent of this view. Castañeda had been a staffer in the human rights committee in Mexico City's Legislative Assembly when the first civil-union bill was introduced (2000–3) and subsequently became director of the Gay Pride Committee. Heavily influenced by the tradition of Mexican gay activism to advance gay rights through partisan politics, and similar to what Uranga had done in 2000, she decided to pursue a seat in the city's Assembly for the 2009 mid-term elections on the PSD ticket for the southern district of Tlalpan.[40] In an attempt to appeal to a broader

[39] Interview, Mexico City, July 2, 2010.
[40] She was one of two openly gay candidates who ran for a seat on city council. The other, Jaime López Vela, ran for the same district on the Workers Party ticket.

electorate, Castañeda crafted a platform that included issues beyond sexual and reproductive rights such as the decriminalization of certain drugs and environmental issues. However, central to her platform was the pursuit of gay marriage in the city. Deeply immersed in the historical debates of gay activism in Mexico, Castañeda retrieved the earlier demand to pursue gay marriage and placed it at the center for her campaign platform. While she shared some of the reservations activists had on marriage given that, she thought, it had deeply patriarchal and religious roots, she also believed that it could have a powerful symbolic effect on social ideas regarding social norms on sexuality and equality. Asked where the idea originated, Castañeda stated:

Gay marriage was not a new idea. The movement had first proposed it in the late 1990s . . . the discussion had taken place in Spain, and some activists in South America had started to talk about it [*manejar el tema*]. For me it was an issue of equality, rights, respect and citizenship. I had my reservations . . . I was immersed [*empapada*] in debates in feminism, but I knew it could be transformational . . . with Ebrard we had an opportunity and we could at least begin the debate.[41]

Castañeda lost the election to the PRD candidate, but her policy objective was nonetheless placed on the legislative agenda soon after the elections.

Divisions within the Movement and Placing Gay Marriage on the Agenda

Castañeda's decision to begin pushing for gay marriage in Mexico City, by adopting it as a campaign promise, divided Mexico's gay movement. While in Argentina such division happened between those who supported civil unions and those who preferred gay marriage, in Mexico the division occurred because of the fragmented nature of moral politics in the country. Given the federated regulation of family law in Mexico, changes to civil codes needed to allow for gay marriage have to be undertaken at the subnational level: in Mexico City and state by state. For some activists, such as Uranga, pursuing gay marriage in Mexico City could potentially bring about a backlash similar to what occurred with the decriminalization of abortion. Uranga argued that, should gay marriage be approved in the capital, conservative forces elsewhere would similarly try to shield their states from the adoption of gay marriage by changing state constitutions to define marriage as between a man and a woman, thereby making it more difficult to reform civil codes.[42] For her the pursuit for gay

---

[41] Interview, Mexico City, June 16, 2010.
[42] Interview, Mexico City, July 3, 2010.

marriage at the national level had to take place through the judiciary. In what she called Plan B, her idea was to challenge heteronormative definitions of marriage at the subnational level through the courts and to force the issue up the judiciary, all the way to the Supreme Court. Given that on moral policy issues the Court had ruled favoring the expansion of sexual and reproductive rights (see Madrazo and Vela 2011), Uranga reckoned, it would likely rule favorably should the issue reach the Court's docket. In an extensive interview, Uranga detailed her strategy. While in Mexico, similar to Argentina, court rulings only affect the parties involved (*inter partes*), inducing five writs of *amparos* in three states would be sufficient to force the Court to pronounce itself in a way that would set national precedence. It would then invalidate provisions in subnational civil codes that defined marriage between a man and a woman.[43]

Despite these divisions and her electoral loss, Castañeda was able to place policy reform on Mexico City's legislative agenda. Similar to Argentina, a smaller socially progressive political party, the PSD, was key to the process. As we have seen, PSD was an important player in the passage of civil unions in Mexico City in 2006 (Díez 2013). To its leadership, the inclusion of sexual rights as policy objectives was foundational and an important way to differentiate itself from the PRD as a more socially progressive political party.[44] In preparation for the 2009 mid-term elections for Mexico City's Legislative Assembly, the party's local leader, David Razú Aznar, contributed to the elaboration of an electoral platform that promoted sexual rights. Specifically, it called for the strengthening of antidiscrimination measures. Gay marriage was not part of the party's campaign neither for these local elections nor for mid-term legislative elections at the national level. In those elections, held on July 5, 2009, Razú was the only candidate for city deputy to have been elected on the PSD ticket, as the party only secured 2.5 percent of the vote. At the national level, the party performed even more poorly, obtaining 1 percent of votes cast. Because, according to Mexican electoral rules, a party must obtain at least 2 percent of the votes to maintain its official party status, it lost its registry. On September 9, once results were officially confirmed by the electoral institute, Razú was forced to become an independent deputy. In the weeks following the election, and up until the first sitting

---

43 Interview, Mexico City, July 3, 2010. As we shall see, a Supreme Court judge declared in late 2012 that this would be a possibility.

44 Interview, Jorge Luis Díaz Cuervo, city deputy 2006–8 and party president 2008–9, Mexico City, July 21, 2008.

of the Assembly on September 14, he engaged in discussions with various state and nonstate actors to develop an agenda to push in the Assembly.

It was during these negotiations that gay marriage was placed on his legislative agenda. He entered into discussions with Castañeda after she lost her own bid for election and asked her to contribute to the development of his policy agenda relating to sexual and reproductive rights. Because gay marriage had been one of her policy priorities, Castañeda agreed to work with him so long as he included gay marriage – a demand that he accepted. Razú's acquiescence was, according to him, not difficult given his own ideological positions and theoretical influences. In a lengthy interview, Razú referred to Amartya Sen's conceptualization of personal capabilities and inclusive development and John Rawls's ideas on justice, to explain that, for him, the adoption of gay marriage contributed to a deepening of citizenship and a fuller integration of gays and lesbians into society.[45] For him the expansion of full citizenship is not possible unless the state intervenes to provide basic socioeconomic goods and guarantee people absolute equality and liberty, which includes full control of their conscience and bodies.[46] Gay marriage fit his political vision.

A favorable political context allowed Castañeda and Razú to place policy reform of gay marriage on the Assembly's legislative agenda. Since the first direct elections in the city were held in 1997, the PRD had been able to secure a legislative majority in council. In the 2009 elections, however, it only obtained 25.64 percent of the votes, a drop of almost 12 percent from the previous election. The results yielded the party thirty out of sixty-four seats. The party, and mayor, therefore needed the support of at least four additional deputies to pass legislation. In the days following the confirmation of the electoral results, Razú, having become an independent deputy, began to negotiate policy positions and potential partisan constellations with the PRD in an effort to build what he termed a "left alliance." Gay marriage was placed in the PRD's legislative agenda during these negotiations. Razú entered discussions with progressive PRD deputies and agreed on twenty-seven policy items as part of a "progressive platform." He subsequently met with the local leader of the PRD, Alejandra Barrales. Barrales, who identified with the mayor's faction within the party, also became the leader of the PRD in the Assembly

---

[45] Interview, Mexico City, July 6, 2010.
[46] Ibid. In the interview Razú referred to the importance his graduate studies at the London School of Economics played in the development of these ideas.

and chair of the powerful Governance Standing Committee (*Comisión de Gobierno*).

At that meeting, Razú accepted an offer to sit as a PRD deputy in exchange for an endorsement of his legislative agenda, which included gay marriage, and for being appointed chair of the Assembly's Standing Committee on Human Rights (*Comisión de Derechos Humanos*).[47] As these negotiations unfolded, Razú and Barrales entered discussions with the mayor's office to gauge his support. According to both of them, as well as advisors close to the mayor, the mayor lent his unqualified support to the initiative as it fit within his socially progressive agenda. During these conversations, Razú also managed to secure the support of one of Ebrard's closest advisors: the director of his legal office Leticia Bonifaz. Bonifaz, a longtime feminist, activist, and academic, would prove critical to the adoption of gay marriage in the following months. By the time of the Assembly's first sitting on September 14, PRD had managed to convince three other deputies to join, bringing the number to thirty-four out of sixty-six. Gay marriage had been placed on the agenda and the stage was thus set for its enactment.

The Enactment of Gay Marriage

The process that led to the enactment of gay marriage in Mexico City shared numerous characteristics with the Argentine case, including its speed.[48] A week after the first sitting of Mexico City's Assembly, on September 21, 2009, Deputy Razú unveiled his legislative agenda, the result of negotiations with the PRD, which included "free marriage" (*matrimonio libre*). When he assumed the chairmanship of the Human Rights Commission the following week, he and Castañeda developed several key elements of their reform strategy. The first one was to push for policy change quickly. The passage of civil unions three years before had shown activists and their allies in the mayor's office the importance of pushing for reform in controversial topics soon after an election in order to limit what hesitant deputies could ask in exchange for their votes. The idea was that, as the legislative agendas of individual deputies solidify, their demands in exchange for votes increase. As an advisor to the mayor put it: "we had to go for it before they settled in (*antes de que se acomoden*)."[49] They also thought it was important in order to prevent

---

47 Interviews, Razú and Barrales, Mexico City, July 6 and 7, 2010.
48 This section draws largely from data collected through personal interviews with seventeen city deputies from the three main political parties (PRD, PAN, and PRI) and seven activists, among others, carried out in Mexico City during July and August 2010.
49 Interview, Mayor Ebrard's legal advisor, Mexico City, January 14, 2011.

opposing forces from articulating convincing arguments against gay marriage. According to the same advisor, they needed to take advantage of the fact that the Catholic Church, the most fervent opponent to reforms in moral policy over the previous three years, was in the midst of another sex-abuse scandal and would be ill-positioned to articulate an argument hinged on moral principles.[50] A second element of the strategy was the formation of a social alliance of activists and allies that would help them shape public opinion in favor of gay marriage and to exert influence on the Assembly to approve the reform. The movement's past experiences in policy reform were central to this idea. Castañeda had worked closely with Uranga when she was a staffer and knew the important role the "social networks of support" had played in the push for civil unions.[51] The third element of their strategy became the development of clear arguments in favor of gay marriage that would be based on ideas of equality, nondiscrimination, and democratic citizenship.

They began to implement their strategy soon after its development. Because Razú had managed to secure the chairmanship of the Human Rights Committee in negotiations with the PRD leadership, he was able to exert control over the committee's agenda and decided to place gay marriage among the committee's top priorities. In consultation with the mayor's office he developed a bill intended to reform various provisions of Article 146 of Mexico City's civil code allowing for marriage between two individuals of the same sex. Razú planned to introduce the reform bill to the Committee in early November. The similarities with the Argentine case are clear: as may be recalled, allies in support of gay marriage chaired the legislative committees that introduced the policy changes to the legislature. As gatekeepers, they played a critical role in the placement of reform on the agenda. Razú and Castañeda also began to build a coalition of supporters from across social sectors. In keeping with the long tradition of Mexican gay and lesbian activism of forming ad hoc coalitions and campaigns to advance specific policy demands, on September 27 Castañeda established the "United Society for the Right

---

[50] This one refers to the Marcial Maciel case. Maciel was the founder of the powerful and highly conservative Legion of Christ movement. Accusations that he had abused children had surfaced years before, but in early 2009 *The New York Times* broke that he had led a double life having had an affair with a woman with whom he fathered a child (February 3, 2009). Over the next several months news emerged that he had fathered several other children and in July 2009 three of them began a civil suit. In September the directors of the Legion of Christ order in Canada and the United States offered a public apology asking for forgiveness.

[51] Interview, Mexico City, June 16, 2010.

to Marriage between People of the Same Sex" (*Sociedad Unida por el Derecho al Matrimonio entre Personas del Mismo Sexo*). Castañeda and other activists, such as Jaime López Vela, drew from the extensive relationships the movement had formed over the years with state and non-state actors to build the coalition, which significantly increased in size in a relatively short period of time.

The coalition was made up of activists and allies that belonged to the broad network of individuals involved in sexual and reproductive rights that crystallized in the 1990s (Chapter 3) and which were involved in the passage of civil unions and the decriminalization of abortion in previous years. It included numerous organizations devoted to the promotion of sexual and reproductive rights, such as the national Democracy and Sexuality Network (itself formed by fifty NGOs), the Mexican Association for Sexual Health (*Asociación Mexicana para la Salud Sexual, A.A.*, AMSSAC), and the Mexican Federation for the Study of Sexuality and Sexology (*Federación Mexicana de Educación Sexual y Sexología A.C.*, FEMESS); feminist NGOS such as the highly visible think tank GIRE, Catholic Women for the Right to Decide, and the National Citizens Observatory for Women's Rights; associations and research institutes affiliated with universities;[52] and independent institutions such as the Mexican Institute of Sexology.[53] The coalition began with approximately fifty members and grew to more than three hundred by late November 2009. Similar to the strategy developed for the passage for civil unions, and resembling the one pursued by Argentine activists, the idea was to rely on these individuals to influence public opinion in favor of gay marriage and, more importantly, to apply pressure on legislators to pass the reform. However, unlike the processes that led to the enactment of civil unions three years prior and gay marriage in Argentina, divisions remained within the movement. Strikingly, in the same way in

---

[52] Many of these were connected through the influential publication *Debate Feminista*.

[53] It also included numerous prominent individuals, such as feminists Lamas, Patricia Mercado, Clara Judisman, Paula Rugeiro, Patricia Olamendi, Orfe Castillo, and Ana María Hernández; academics, such as Patricia Galeana, Careaga (who was also the Secretary General of the International Lesbian and Gay Association, ILGA), Héctor Salinas, Rosa Feijoo Andrade, Xavier Lizárraga, Javier Marmolejo, Susana Lerner, and Carlos Echarri Cánovas; the jurists Miguel Carbonell and Alejandro Madrazo Lajous; journalists, such as Carlos Bonfil, Álvaro Cueva, Rosa María Roffiel, Jenáro Villamil, Braulio Peralta, Rafael Cabrera, and the several reporters and writers that worked for *Letra S*, such as Brito and Antonio Medina; as well as several celebrities, artists, actors, and actresses who are prominent in Mexican public life, such as Diano Bracho, Sabina Berman, Regina Orozco, Maina Castañeda, Julia Arnaut, David Rangel, and Horacio Villalobos, among others.

which Deputy Vilma Ibarra attempted to suppress divisions within the Argentine movement prior to launching the push for gay marriage, Razú attempted to mediate differences among Mexican activists, but found it difficult. In the Mexican case it took several weeks before most activists rallied around the cause. For some of the longtime activists, such as Díaz, Brito and Antonio Medina, embracing the cause would have meant taking away the spotlight from Castañeda, who became the public leader behind the struggle. However, once the process accelerated and they saw that real possibilities existed to approve gay marriage, they quickly closed ranks and deployed their resources to pressure the Assembly to approve the bill.[54]

Castañeda also planned to rely on social media to promote gay marriage. She set up a Facebook page on October 31, titled "I Support Gay Marriage" and launched a campaign, also called "I Support," of video clips, posted on YouTube, of publicly recognizable figures who stated their support for gay marriage.

Activists and their allies, led by Razú and Castañeda, decided to unveil the argumentation in favor of gay marriage as the legislative process got underway. On November 9, Razú announced to the media that a bill seeking to reform the civil code and allow for gay marriage was being analyzed by the mayor's legal team for imminent introduction to the Assembly. The day after, on November 10, Razú, Castañeda, and Barrales held a press conference, representing eighty-seven allied NGOs and individuals, at which they began to articulate the need to approve gay marriage in order to guarantee equality and deepen democratic citizenship. At the conference Razú declared that: "this right for couples of the same sex must be expanded, to citizens who have contributed equally to the economic, social and cultural development of the Mexican nation. Not granting this right violates (*vulnera*) the constitutional principles of non-discrimination, liberty and juridical security" (*Notiese*, November 10, 2010). In an interview he held a week later, Razú also declared that "The intention is to recognize the equal rights for all citizens (*ciudadanos y ciudadanas*) . . . as in other areas, such as paying taxes, they are the same, and there should not be different institutions for citizens: before the law they are the same" (*Notiese*, November 18, 2010).

The clearest early articulation of their arguments in favor of gay marriage transpired at a forum held in the Legislative Assembly on November 21. Titled "Forum for Gay Marriage between People of the Same Sex,"

---

[54] Interview, Díaz and Arturo Medina, Mexico City, June 22 and 25, 2010.

the event outlined in detail the guiding arguments to be used in the process. At the event, deputy Razú declared that "we cannot have different institutions for equal citizens . . . the movement must educate the citizenry [on the importance of guaranteeing equality] . . . we need to create full citizenship."[55] Castañeda, in turn, stated that the project was about "the full exercise of citizenship . . . we want equality . . . no one has the right to tell us which rights we have the right to have."[56]

The framing of these arguments had a strategic component. For activists, previous experiences in moral policy reform had demonstrated the need to mount the push for reform around legal and theoretical argumentative lines that could neutralize opposing arguments, which had generally tended to be framed around moral values, and which would resonate with larger debates. Interviews with the main actors reveal a very strategic component to the process. Castañeda, who had been personally involved in the debates around the enactment of civil unions and the decriminalization of abortion, thought that arguments for gay marriage had to be formulated around legal lines, calling for nondiscrimination and the respect for social diversity. These, she thought, were notions that would appeal to society at large. Asked about the strategic dimension, she stated: "of course we thought about the most effective way to elaborate an argument [*crear una argumentación*]. Here in the capital, since the arrival of the PRD in 1997 the public discourse had shifted toward inclusion, respect and diversity . . . we had to make sure our argument stuck [*pegara*] with social debates."[57] For Razú, a clear connection between gay marriage and democratic citizenship had to be established: "gay marriage was about democratic citizenship . . . Mexico City has been at the forefront of democratization in Mexico and we had to convince people, inside and outside, that this was another step."[58] That connection was very clearly made in an op-ed he wrote in one of Mexico's most widely read newspapers:

No society can be considered completely democratic when it does not have the vocation to protect the sovereignty of each of its members over their bodies and consciences. There are many reasons to push for an initiative of this kind . . . but . . . the most important in social terms is: full citizenship. Behind its adoption there exists an important message that the State sends to the citizenry: civil rights cannot be limited on the basis of personal characteristics when these do

[55] http://www.aldf.gob.mx/, accessed May 13, 2013.
[56] Ibid.
[57] Interview, Mexico City, June 16, 2010.
[58] Interview, Mexico City, July 6, 2010.

not violate the rights of a third party; the contrary would amount to the estab-lishment of different classes of citizenship. The right to equal citizenship and to non-discrimination, enshrined in the first article of our constitution, is guaranteed from the recognition of the right to personal difference.[59]

Arguments in favor of gay marriage, for the main actors leading the pro-cess, were clearly connected to broader concepts of equality, citizenship, social diversity, and democracy. These, they believed, would gain traction with society at large and would help them convince legislators to approve the reform.

Reaction from the three main parties in the Assembly to the formal unveiling of plans to introduce reforms to the civil code was swift and, given their positions on moral policy, predictable. On the same day the press conference was held, PAN deputies declared that the proposal was "populist" given that gay couples already enjoyed the same rights as mar-ried couples because of civil unions, and declared that they would make every effort to prevent its passage (*La Jornada*, November 10, 2009). PRI deputies were divided. PRI Deputy Alan Cristian Vargas Sánchez, after meeting with activists, declared that he would work to have his parliamentary group support the bill (*El Universal*, November 14, 2009). However, four out of the eight deputies, led by Emiliano Aguilar Esquivel, were not supportive at this stage.[60] PRD was mostly divided among three main groups, which reflected the three main factions of the party at the national level. The majority of deputies belonging to the factions identi-fied with the mayor and the party's New Left wing were in favor, while those identified with López Obrador were mostly against.[61] However, at this stage of the process, numerous deputies did not think that the ini-tiative would go far given the ambivalence expressed by several PRD deputies.[62] As a result, PAN deputies, who were the most opposed to the reform, did not think it was necessary to spend much time articulating counterarguments.

The issue of adoption became crucial at this stage and marked one of the most intriguing aspects of the process. Proponents of the bill originally planned not to discuss the issue of adoption in order to lessen opposition.

[59] *El Universal*, August 17, 2010. While this opinion piece was published the day after the Supreme Court ruled on gay marriage in August 2010 (explored in the following text), it captures the connection Razú made between gay marriage and democratic citizenship in a more concise manner than the three-hour interview he gave the author.
[60] Interview, Alicia Téllez, PRI deputy, Mexico City, June 23, 2010.
[61] Interview, Barrales, PRD parliamentary leader, Mexico City, July 7, 2010.
[62] Interview, Federico Manzo Sarquis, PAN deputy, Mexico City, July 8, 2010.

However, according to several actors interviewed, PRD and other deputies would only support the bill were it to exclude the right of married gay couples to adopt. Negotiations ensued and a new draft bill included what came to be known as the "lock" (*candado*) on adoption: an explicit provision that excluded adoption from gay marriage. As we will see in the next section, the day gay marriage was voted by the Assembly the ban on adoption was removed, and there appeared to be some confusion in regard to whether the so-called lock on adoption was a tactic deployed by proponents to gain original support for the bill. While accounts vary depending upon the actor interviewed, their triangulation points to a strategic move: once it became clear that the inclusion of adoption may not yield the desired votes, the plan was to exclude it in order to ensure a vote on the Assembly's floor and to discuss adoption as the vote took place. According to a legal advisor to the mayor, the mayor argued that the ban on adoption was discriminatory and would not sustain a vote in the Assembly.[63] Because of the ban, however, it was relatively easy to convince hesitant legislators to allow the bill to proceed to the various committees for analysis and discussion. The reform bill was officially introduced to the Assembly on November 23 with the support of approximately forty deputies and the signatures of three hundred individuals and organizations.

Opposition came expectedly from PAN deputies. However, because they did not think the bill would go far, and given the speed with which proponents had introduced it, they presented a variety of opposing arguments that did not show coherence.[64] Deputy Frenando Rodríguez Doval, for example, declared that his parliamentary group would analyze how to expand rights to the gay and lesbian community instead of supporting gay marriage for it "would bring about dangerous juridical consequences" (*La Jornada*, November 24, 2009). In an official statement, the PAN parliamentary leader, Mariana Gómez del Campo, argued, along heteronorms, that, despite the bill's ban on adoption, it "would destroy the institutions that have been the source and bastion of our society. It tries to modify the current structure of the family and with it the values that have supported it" (*El Economista*, November 24, 2009). Unlike proponents of the bill, who had developed strategic lines of argumentation, PAN deputies did not elaborate one.

---

[63] Interview, Mayor Ebrard's legal advisor, Mexico City, January 14, 2011.
[64] Interviews, Federico Manzo Sarquis and Fernando Rodríguez Doval, PAN deputies, Mexico City, July 8 and 14, 2010.

The submission of the bill to the Assembly sparked a wide social debate, and for proponents of the bill it marked the beginning of a process of relying on their resources and allies to win the argument in the court of public opinion. They thus asked their extensive network of allies to make public pronouncements in the media and organized a series of events to garner support. Women activists played a key role. For example, Lamas, a longtime ally and someone with close personal connections with prominent activists, penned an opinion piece in the widely read weekly *Proceso*, published the day after the bill was introduced to the Assembly, in which she clearly challenged contemporary heteronormative understandings of sexuality, gender, and family and, using the lines of argumentation activists had developed, argued for an expansion of citizenship:

> The LGTB community demands equal citizenship and with it the right to form a family . . . conservative positions cling to their belief that homosexuality is "unnatural" and forget that anthropology and history have proved the natural character [*naturalidad*] of homosexuality in all societies and throughout history . . . they ignore that, in a secular and pluralist democracy . . . it is not valid to impose a single ethical imperative based on religious beliefs that postulate a supposed "natural" order . . . gay marriage is about equal citizenship.[65]

They also organized a series of events, covered by the media, and attended by jurists, academics, and experts to express publicly their support for the bill. For example, on December 3, Eusebio Rubio, Director General of the Mexican Association for Sexual Health (*Asociación Mexicana para la Salud Sexual, A.C.*, AMSAAC), and Luis Perelman, President of FEMESS, were invited to present research suggesting that marriage between people of the same sex improves the mental and physical well-being of gays and lesbians, argued for the need to recognize social diversity in family arrangements, and countered Natural Law–based arguments (*Notiese*, December 3, 2009). Four days later, at a press conference organized by a youth association, sexologists were asked to present information on the diversity of family arrangements that exist in the city and to challenge arguments about the potential harm gay marriage could have on children (*El Universal*, December 9, 2009). On the same day, in a working reunion, Razú, in an effort to demonstrate the legal soundness of the bill, invited several magistrates from the city's Superior Court of Justice, as well as renowned jurists, to declare that the reform was "legally sound" (*La Jornada*, December 8, 2009). The city's Commission of Human

[65] *Proceso*, November 24, 2009.

Rights also made public declarations during this time in support of the bill. For Razú and Castañeda the goal was to have respected individuals and organizations make public declarations in support of the bill. As in the Argentine case, the key to this was the role played by a variety of allied reporters who belonged to the broader network of relationships and who worked at providing large and positive exposure.[66] Opponents of the bill did not organize similar events and public arguments against the reform were for the most part articulated by Catholic Church officials. Episcopal Vicar Jonás Guerrero Carmona lamented the support the city's Human Rights Commission gave the reform bill and announced the Church's opposition based on Natural Law principles: "For us, as the Catholic Church, the issue is clear: . . . marriage is really a union between a man and woman who give life and . . . people of the same sex will never be able to give life" (*El Universal*, November 25, 2009). Cardinal Javier Lozano Barragán, the Vatican's former Health Minister, made mention of the Church's centuries-old understanding of homosexuality as the heinous sin by referring to homosexuals as "impure" people who engage in "infamous passions" who "will never enter the kingdom of heaven" (*Agence France Presse*, December 2, 2009).

Proponents managed to obtain enough support for the bill in the Assembly to have it voted favorably at the committee level on December 11, with ten in favor and four against, despite legislative maneuvers used by PAN deputies to filibuster the bill. By the time the committee vote was held, they had obtained the written support of approximately five hundred individuals and organizations, including Amnesty International, ILGA, AIDS Healthcare, and the European LGTB Inter-Parliamentary Group. Obtaining the required votes did not require strong pressure from proponents given that the ban on adoption was kept in the version of the bill that was voted.[67] Indeed, upon the request of a PRD deputy, the ban on adoption was expanded into a separate paragraph outlining it in more detail. This, she argued, would guarantee a wider social consensus and a positive vote on the floor. The favorable vote at the committee level marked the intensification of the confrontation between actors for and

---

[66] These include reporters from the news agency CIMAC, Christian Rea Tizcareño (*Notiese*), Francisco Iglesias, Braulio Peralta, and Álvaro Cueva (*Milenio*), Rafael Cueva (*Reforma*), Víctor Espíndola (*Anodis*), Horacio Villalobos (*MVS*), Ella Grajeda (*El Universal*), and Rocío González (*La Jornada*).

[67] As stated by five deputies from the PAN and PRI who belonged to the joint-committee session. Three of them also stated that committee members agreed to allow the bill to proceed to the floor so as to not appear obstructionist.

against the bill, both inside and outside the Assembly, a confrontation that soon generated an intense national debate and that attracted social and political forces beyond Mexico City until the vote on the floor on December 21. The passage of the bill through the committee took several PAN deputies by surprise as they did not think it would make it this far. As one PAN deputy put it: *!nos chamaquearon!* (they fooled us).[68] After an attempt to block the vote through procedural maneuvers, they began to articulate a series of arguments against the reform, some of which they decided to select as their guiding ones thereafter. Echoing arguments advanced when civil unions in Mexico City were approved three years later, some PAN deputies argued that Mexico City did not have the jurisdictional power to legislate on the matter given that it would affect social security legislation, which was a federal responsibility.

Others repeated the heteronormative Natural Law–based arguments advanced by Catholic Church officials days earlier and argued that marriage was a natural and millennial institution between people of opposite sexes and that had as its sole purpose the procreation of the species (*La Jornada*, December 12, 2009). However, they also began to argue for the need to submit the reform to a referendum. Suggesting that the process was illegitimate because it had not been discussed amply by society, they claimed that a public consultation was required because the majority of citizens were opposed to the reform. The idea of a referendum became one of the main arguments that opponents of the reform began to deploy. In effect, a few days after the vote, the PAN parliamentary leader, Gómez del Campo, and the party's national leader, César Nava, declared that they would take the necessary measures to prevent that bill from proceeding and submitted a motion to the Assembly requesting that a referendum be held. The motion was defeated by the floor a few days later (*La Jornada*, December 18, 2009).

Nevertheless, it set the tone for the struggle against the passage of the bill two weeks later, a struggle that took on a different veneer from the one that unfolded in the Argentine case. Because, as we saw in Chapter 4, Argentina does not have a confessional party, opposing forces did not have an institutionalized mechanism through which to mount their opposition. Conservative social forces were thus required to mobilize public opposition and to influence legislators individually. In the case of Mexico City, opposition to gay marriage was led by PAN, which amalgamated

---

[68] Interview, PAN deputy, July 12, 2010. The term comes from *chamaco*, a Mexicanism for novice or kid.

most conservative forces, including the Catholic Church. In the days following the vote on holding a referendum, PAN deputies held internal discussions to see how they could prevent a vote on the floor and, if held, to obtain the necessary votes to defeat the bill. They decided to appoint three deputies as the leaders and spokespersons of their efforts, the most socially conservative among PAN deputies in the Assembly.[69] The decision reflected the confessional nature of the party. Some PAN deputies were not completely opposed to the reform, especially because it included a ban on adoption. Some of them were in fact indifferent. For one deputy the relaxed view among some of them was due to the relatively low average age among PAN deputies in the Assembly: "if you look at our parliamentary group, we are much younger than the average legislator at the national level . . . for some of us the discussion was an non-issue."[70] However, given the origins, nature, and ideological position of the party, as well as the important financial backing the party receives from socially conservative business leaders, all of its legislators were directed by the party's national leadership to oppose the bill.[71] As one PAN deputy explained:

As you know, our party has conservative positions on the family. There were some usual tensions [when we discussed our strategies], but we were all on the same page [*ibamos en la misma linea*] . . . the defense of family is in our party's constitution and we have a responsibility to act according to it . . . the party must also respond to business groups and others that have supported us and with which we have engagements . . . Bimbo, Red Familia, etc.[72]

Nevertheless, despite the unity within the PAN legislative group and the leadership deputies took in opposing reform, backed by strong support from conservative forces, their efforts at blocking reform were unsuccessful. They appeared to have been blindsided by the speed with which the bill was put to a vote on the floor: the vote was held on December 21, two days after the vote to hold a referendum was held and a few days after the committee vote. PAN deputies attempted to convince ambivalent deputies to either vote against or abstain, especially those belonging to the PRI as they were divided. Religious and other conservative groups

---

[69] One of them, Fernando Rodríguez Doval, informally known among his colleagues as "the pope," belongs to the ultra-conservative group *El Yunque* (*Proceso*, May 14, 2010) and is closely related to the Mexican politician Carlos Abascal, also a member of the same group (Delgado 2003, 24; 2004, 180–1).

[70] Interview, PAN deputy, Mexico City, July 8, 2010.

[71] Interviews, five PAN deputies.

[72] Interview, Mexico City, July 14, 2010.

also exerted pressure on these legislators and some of them organized public events declaring their opposition.[73] However, the speed with which the vote was held meant that they were unable either to articulate clear arguments against gay marriage or mount effective pressure on a legislature that was controlled by the PRD. Indeed, sensing the imminent loss, Nava declared that they would challenge in court the constitutionality of the reform, thereby conceding that the vote was lost. PAN deputies also made a last-minute attempt at filibustering the bill arguing that the Assembly did not have the constitutional prerogative to legislate on the matter (*El Universal*, December 21, 2009). That initiative also failed.

For activists and their allies conditions were different as momentum built for reform. As the imminence of the vote became clear, especially after the bill was approved at the committee level, most gay and lesbian activists closed ranks and began to deploy resources to push for approval of the bill.[74] These included some activists, such as members of *Letra S*, who had not taken a leadership role at the beginning of the process to allow Castañeda and Razú to mount the campaign. For them, once it became clear that conditions existed to have the bill approved, they deployed all their resources to ensure its passage.[75] Closing ranks allowed proponents of the reform to expand their coalition in support of the bill and to mount a stronger campaign. As the vote came closer, renowned intellectuals and journalists, such as human rights campaigner and academic Sergio Aguayo and journalist Sergio Sarmiento, took clear public positions in favor of the bill. The various journalists with whom activists had close personal relations (noted in the preceding text) played a key role in providing positive and supportive coverage. The president of National Anti-Discrimination Council, Ricardo Bucio Mujíca, also supported the bill publicly, stating that the constitution was clear that no right could be denied on the grounds of any condition (*El Economista*, December 17, 2009).

While the campaign continued apace in the public sphere, especially through the media, it also involved the harvesting of votes in the legislature. In the two weeks leading up to the vote, scheduled for December 21, activists and their allies engaged non-PAN legislators individually to

---

[73] The conservative organizations that lobbied legislators mentioned during interviews were: Defence of the Family and Values (*Defensa de la Familia y de los Valores*), Courage Latino, Provida, and The College of Catholic Lawyers (*Colegio de Abogados Católicos*).

[74] With the notable exception of Uranga, who, advancing the argument of the potential backlash to the reform in other states, publicly campaigned against the reform.

[75] Interview, Medina, Mexico City, June 22, 2009.

convince them of the merits of the reform advancing the same lines of argumentation that Castañeda and Razú had developed at the beginning of the campaign: that gay marriage was an issue of rights, equality, and part of fuller citizenship. Importantly, members of the coalition began to lobby deputies directly through the submission of literature, phone calls, and personal meetings. Similar to the Argentine case, internal lobbying proved crucial. Meetings were held with deputies three to four times a week soliciting their support.[76] Razú and Castañeda put together a dossier with input from jurists and academics containing scientific evidence as well as legal arguments in defense of the reform.[77] In another similarity with the Argentine case, the push for gay marriage increasingly relied on internal lobbying by allied deputies. In this case the push was led by Barrales, chair of the Governance Standing Committee, and Maricela Contreras, a longtime feminist.[78]

On the day of the vote, December 21, and after another attempt by PAN deputies to postpone the vote failed, Contreras and other PRD deputies deployed arguments that had been articulated by proponents of the bill to convince legislators, arguments that made clearer references to broader debates about Mexico's social diversity, the place the city had occupied in Mexico's democratization, equality, and citizenship. After it was presented to the floor, Contreras declared:

Our society is diverse, our society is plural, our society changes every day . . . there exists a multiplicity of family arrangements and we as deputies have the obligation to respond to that reality. . . . Progress in regard to human rights must include the population that forms part of sexual diversity . . . Mexico City is a city of rights. This is a characteristic which marks the democratic governments of Mexico City, it has been achieved due to the making of public policies with a focus on human rights. The main argument in favor of the reform . . . is the principle of non-discrimination of people with diverse sexual orientation and the recognition that they can exercise all the rights.

PRD Deputy Beatriz Rojas Martínez, stated:

The democratic progress that citizens of the Federal District demand requires legislative reforms that recognize and protect all citizens . . . the reforms . . .

---

[76] According to Razú, like a *cuchillito de palo* (small wooden knife), a Mexican expression meaning doing something continuously and fastidiously.

[77] Interview, Razú, Mexico City, July 6, 2010.

[78] Contreras was a cofounder of the United Socialist Party of Mexico (*Partido Socialista Unificado de México*), which, as detailed in Chapter 3, was the first party in Mexico to accept the candidacies of openly gays and lesbians for the 1982 elections. She was subsequently cofounder of the Mexican Socialist Party and eventually of the PRD.

imply, precisely, an advance in the rights that guarantee the freedom of this city's citizens.

PAN deputies deployed some of the arguments they had been advancing in the weeks leading to vote, such as the "natural" character of the traditional family, the need for social consultation through a referendum, and, strikingly similar to the Argentine experience on the day of the vote, the possibility of working toward a nationwide civil union instead of marriage (despite the fact that family law is administered by subnational governments). However, unlike proponents of the bill, they did not articulate their opposition on clear lines of argumentation. Indeed, several deputies interviewed admitted to not having been strategic in the deployment of arguments and mentioned the speed with which the process unfolded as a main reason. After a three-hour discussion the bill that changed the definition of marriage to one "between two persons" was put to a vote and carried with thirty-nine yeas, twenty nays, and five abstentions. After the vote, Deputy Contreras introduced a motion to delete the ban on adoption of the reform to the civil code. Contreras justified her amendment on discriminatory grounds:

It is a contradiction in terms to push for freedoms and to limit them at the same time. It is not only contradictory to pretend to approve the ban on adoption. . . . To do so would be discriminatory. . . . The reforms . . . are about whether we will take a further step in the democratic progress of the country.

According to interviews, Barrales and Contreras engaged deputies to obtain their support by establishing a clear connection between arguments in favor of gay marriage and the *raison d'être* of their party as an agent of democratic change in the country and the standard bearer of human rights expansion. As Barrales recounted: "I told them that they could not refuse to support the extension of a right as members of our party [a party] that has fought for human rights and democracy . . . we had to convert it into a cause for the left . . . it was an issue of equality. They just could not say no . . . that argument helped me convince several of my *compañeros*."[79]

Her amendment was passed, albeit with a smaller majority, with thirty-one votes in favor, twenty-four against, and nine abstentions (including five from the PRD). The votes reflected broader political party dynamics. On both votes all of the PAN and Green Party deputies voted against. On the first vote, all PRD and PT deputies voted in favor of

[79] Interview, Mexico City, January 14, 2011.

the reform. On lifting the ban on adoption, twenty-nine PRD deputies voted in favor, and none against, and five PRD and four PT deputies abstained. The PRI was split on both fronts: on the first vote, five of them abstained, two voted against, and one failed to cast a ballot. On the second vote, six of them voted against, one abstained, and only one voted in favor. The PRI's vote captured the internal party debates on moral policy reform: according to one deputy, the national leader monitored the vote closely and urged them to abstain from voting.

While some work refers to the surprising introduction to lift the ban on adoption on the day of the vote (Ballina 2013), interviews with deputies and advisors to the mayor suggest that those in charge of leading the push for reform had planned that strategy carefully and that it was not a last-minute maneuver. The same interviews point to strong and constant internal lobbying of PRD deputies to support the inclusion of adoption in the weeks leading up to the vote. The effectiveness of those lobbying efforts, driven by the deployment of arguments aimed at resonating with larger social debates, was very tellingly shown by the fact that Deputy Edith Ruíz Mendicuti, the legislator who had asked to make the ban on adoption explicit in a separate paragraph of the reform bill, voted in favor on both ballots. With the two votes Mexico's Legislative Assembly became the first legislature to approve gay marriage in Latin America.[80]

An Unfinished and Fragmented Process

The approval of gay marriage by Mexico City's Legislative Assembly intensified the national debate over gay marriage, drawing into it social and political forces from beyond the city, shifted the struggle to the judiciary, and set in motion a fragmented process of reform.

The Intensification of the Debate

In the days after the vote, reaction against gay marriage was strong and swift. PAN deputies and the party's national leadership demanded that the mayor veto the reforms and threatened to challenge their constitutionality before the Supreme Court. Making their – hitherto unnoticed – intervention into the debate publicly present, leaders of evangelical groups also requested that Ebrard veto the reforms. Predictably, the fiercest reaction

---

[80] The reform also made common-law marriages accessible to same-sex couples. In addition to civil marriage, in Mexico City two individuals can enter into a *concubinato*, which grants the same rights as marriage. This arrangement can be accessed when the couple lives together for two years or when they cohabit with a common child.

came from the Catholic Church leadership. The bishop of the city of Ecatepec declared that the reforms were a "stupidity" and, the deeply conservative Cardinal Norberto Rivera declared, based on clear Natural Law concepts, sprinkled with pedophilic insinuations, that the reforms were "immoral," an "aberration," and an "onslaught by the evil force" (*Maligno*) "against the Church and the family," which "open the door to the perverse possibility that they [gays and lesbians] can adopt innocent children" (*La Jornada*, *El Universal*, December 22, 2009).

These declarations were but the beginning of an intense confrontation between the Catholic Church leadership and the PRD that lasted several months. Catholic Church officials mounted a public campaign condemning the enactment of gay marriage that involved numerous stern pronouncements not only of the reform but also of the performance of the PRD government in the city. In early January it announced a "suspension of dialogue" with the party (*La Jornada*, January 20, 2010). The PRD, for its part, declared that the Church was violating the secular nature of the Mexican state and the constitution by meddling in political affairs and submitted a complaint to the Ministry of the Interior to stop the campaign. The confrontation continued apace, however, and reached a climax when exchanges became personal. Rivera, undaunted, stated that the Church would not back down from its criticisms against the reform and continued to argue that it destroyed the basic unit of society (*El Universal*, April 11, 2010). Public condemnation of the reform was not limited to the Church. A review of media coverage during this time shows constant pronouncements made by conservative state and nonstate actors against the reform, which included national political leaders, members of the national Congress, members of socially conservative NGOs, and several state governors.

Whereas opposition to gay marriage had not been articulated along clear lines of argumentation, once the vote had taken place opponents decided to frame their opposition on the right of children to have a traditional family and the dangers that gay marriage could bring to children. Importantly, it included the leader of the National Confederation of Christian Evangelical Churches (*Confederación Nacional de Iglesias Cristianas Evangélicas*), who declared that gay marriage endangered the well-being of children for it made them vulnerable to stigmatization (*El Universal*, January 26, 2010). For PAN deputies, focusing on the well-being of children was a strategic decision for they knew it would stir the most public opposition. As a result, they commissioned a poll, with the support of socially conservative groups such as The Knights of Columbus, in early 2010, which showed that public support for the reform stood at 47 percent and that 44 percent of respondents did not support adoption by gay couples (*Reforma*, March 26, 2010). Arguing that the reform lacked consensus they called for its reversion. The national debate was, of course, not limited to opponents of the reform. Activists, academics, and several public figures made continued statements in its defense, and the debate raged fiercely through social media. The debate thus conformed to the larger debates over moral policy in Mexico since Ebrard's election to the mayoralty of Mexico City.

The Struggle Shifts to the Judiciary

The national debate over gay marriage unfolded as the struggle for reform shifted to the judiciary. Pressure on the mayor's office to veto the bill failed. It was promulgated into law on December 29, 2009 and came into force on March 4, 2010. On March 11 the first five gay couples – including Castañeda and her partner, Judith Vásquez, as well as activist and academic Javier Marmolejo, and his partner Carlos Ramos – contracted marriage in a carefully choreographed ceremony held in Mexico City's historic municipal building. The first gay weddings in Mexico were celebrated full of symbolism: they took place against a backdrop that had a bust of Benito Juárez – the Liberal Mexican president of the mid-nineteenth century who instituted the separation of Church and state in the country. However, as these developments took place, challenges to gay marriage took on a litigious turn. A few hours after the vote took place, PAN deputies decided to challenge the constitutionally of the reform. According to the Mexican constitution, any subnational government can challenge the constitutionality of a law if 33 percent of its legislators support the challenge. Despite strong efforts to obtain enough votes in the Legislative Assembly, which was technically possible had they convinced PRI deputies to join them, they failed. The focus then shifted to the national level.

Calderón's government decided to challenge the constitutionality of the reforms before the Supreme Court on the grounds that changing the definition of the family violated the constitutional protection of the (assumed heteronormative) family, it affected the rights of children (placing them at a disadvantage with vis-à-vis those living with heterosexual parents), and it infringed on the jurisdictional delineation on social security protection established by federalism (*Milenio*, January 28, 2010). The mayor declared that the challenge violated the city's autonomy to legislate and that it was politically motivated. Calderón responded by denying the claim and arguing that the attorney general was simply complying with his constitutional mandate to ensure that all legislation enacted in the country passed constitutional muster (*El Universal*, February 2, 2010). As some activists highlighted, such neutrality did not seem to apply to other areas: the government did not challenge any of the constitutional amendments passed by eighteen states criminalizing abortion. The constitutional challenge was supported by a variety of opposing social and political forces in an attempt to annul gay marriages in Mexico City and a concerted strategic campaign was devised by the government in close collaboration with the PAN leadership, religious groups, and civil society groups.[81]

Constitutional challenges were not limited to Calderón's government. Six PAN state governments (Morelos, Guanajuato, Sonora, Jalisco, Baja California, and Tlaxcala) challenged before the Court the reform undertaken in Mexico City with the argument that it could potentially have an effect on the legal frameworks of the states, which define marriage as one between a man and a woman. In February 2010 the Court decided to hear only two of these cases (Jalisco and Baja California).

In response to these constitutional challenges, a broad alliance of state and nonstate actors in support of gay marriage assembled and defended the reforms passed in Mexico City before the Court, countering the arguments made by the attorney general's office. In addition to the argument filed by the mayor's Legal Advisory office, which worked closely with academics from prestigious universities,[82] experts, constitutional scholars, and jurists submitted documentation, briefings, affidavits, and *amicus curiae* in defense of gay marriage. These included the renowned scholars Pedro Salazar and Miguel Carbonell and the legal NGOs DHEAS, Litigio Estratégico de Derechos Humanos, and Asistencia Legal por los Derechos Humanos, as well as the legal clinic of the élite university Centro de Estudios y Docencia Económicas. Support also came from the National Anti-Discrimination Council and Mexico City's Human Rights Commission.

---

[81] According to Arturo Faraela, President of the National Confederation of Christian Evangelical Churches, he held several meetings with the president and the attorney general at which strategies were discussed (interview, Mexico City, July 7, 2010). Two PAN deputies interviewed, as well as a national senator, stated that constant conversations among these various actors were held leading up to the submission of the challenge. Collaboration among some of these actors was not secret. See "PAN y obispos, juntos contra las bodas gay," *Excelsior*, January 7, 2010.

[82] From UNAM, CIDE, UAM, Colegio de México, FLACSO, and CIESAS.

The national debate raged on until late in the summer of 2010 as the Court heard arguments from both sides. On August 5 it handed down a rather extensive ruling upholding the reform. In a majority ruling (nine of eleven justices) it ruled that both same-sex marriage and adoption were constitutional. Disagreeing with the jurisdictional argument entirely – stating that subnational governments had autonomy over their own civil codes – it ruled that gay marriage conformed to Article 4 of the constitution, which mandates the legal protection of the family. Importantly, it challenged Thomist ideas on the family arguing that the law mandates the protection of the family as a "social reality" and not as an ideal model. The recognition of same-sex marriage, it further stated, satisfies the right to have one's family protected and makes effective the right to the free development of one's personality. In regard to adoption, it ruled that the best interests of the child should be determined on a case-by-case basis and that entertaining a question on the varied impact conventional and gay marriages can have on children would be discriminatory. On August 10 it handed down another (9–2) ruling stating that, according to Article 121 of the constitution, all states in the federation must recognize gay marriages contracted in the capital. In regard to the challenges argued by the states of Baja California and Jalisco, on January 23, 2012, in a 7-to-4 decision, it rejected their arguments declaring that the states could not constitutionally challenge reforms approved in a different jurisdiction. With these rulings, the struggle for gay marriage in Mexico City waged by activists and their allies had ended and it became indirectly available to all Mexicans outside the capital city.

Policy Fragmentation with an Eye to the Supreme Court

While the Court's rulings would appear to have settled the debate, they were but a stage in a larger process that has resulted in policy fragmentation shaped by Mexican federalism. Since the rulings, conservative actors have attempted to shield states from the approval of gay marriage. While the phenomenon has not been as strong as the one sparked by the decriminalization of abortion, it has occurred. By mid-2014 three PAN-governed states (Queretaro, Jalisco, and Baja California) tried to shield their jurisdictions from changes in the civil code by explicitly establishing marriage as one between a man and a woman in the states' constitutions. Only the one in Queretaro passed. However, emboldened by the success in Mexico City, activists and their allies were also motivated to push for gay marriage in some states: by late 2013, gay marriage bills had been introduced into the state legislatures of Oaxaca and Coahuila.

It has also had further ripple effects through the judiciary. Noticing that the definition of marriage in Quintana Roo's civil code did not specify gender, two same-sex couples were able to contract marriage in late 2011. After an original push back from the state government, it acceded to subsequent requests and gave directives to the Civil Registry to allow for gay marriages across the state (*La Jornada*, May 3, 2012). Moreover, in early 2013, the mayor of the small town of Cuauhtémoc (population 7,513), in the state of Colima officiated a marriage of a gay couple, basing her decision on the state's antidiscrimination law (*La Jornada*, March 12, 2013). Unlike Argentina, then, access to gay marriage, and social security benefits,[83] has not been equal given the type of federalism regarding family law in Mexico.

Nevertheless, the enactment of gay marriage in Mexico City unleashed the judicialization of the issue, which will very likely lead to policy uniformity across the country. Following the Supreme Court rulings, numerous same-sex couples have submitted demands for writs of *amparo* in several states after their applications for marriage were denied by civil registries. By July 2014, twenty states had done so and several had been granted by lower-level judges in five of them. Some of these *amparo* filings have worked their way up the judiciary and reached the Supreme Court. In late 2012, the Court, in response to filings submitted by three couples from the state of Oaxaca, ruled unconstitutional the provisions of the state's civil code that defined marriage between a man and a woman and mandated the state's registry to marry the couples (*Reforma*, December 6, 2012). It conceded a further thirty-nine to couples, also from Oaxaca, in April 2014 (*La Jornada*, April 23, 2014). These rulings have opened the door for the submission of additional *amparos* requests from across the country, including Queretaro (the only "shielded" state). While, according to Mexico's *inter partes* system, rulings on *amparos* only affect the parties involved, the position the bench has taken on the constitutionality

---

[83] Federalism has also resulted in policy fragmentation in the expansion of social security benefits to same-sex couples that have contracted marriage in Mexico City. Numerous couples have been denied benefits from the country's two main social security institutions, which are administered by the federal government (Díez 2013). They have consequently had to seek writs of *amparo* to access the benefits. By mid-2013, only 22 of the 2,362 couples that had contracted marriage had been able to secure benefits (CNN México, April 23, 2013). The same has occurred with couples from other states. By mid-2013, couples in only three states had been able to secure these rights (*Proceso*, June 3, 2010). A reform to federal social security legislation that expands benefits to all same-sex relationships (civil unions, common law, and marriages) was passed in the Chamber of Deputies in April 2012, but it stalled in the Senate.

of gay marriage can potentially produce a ruling that sets jurisprudence. According to the Supreme Court Justice who wrote the majority ruling in the first Oaxaca case: "over the months we could generate jurisprudence" as the Court's position (*tesis*) enters in contradiction with positions taken by a larger number of lower courts.[84] That is, as more cases reach the Court, and as it rules based on the position it has taken on gay marriage (as can only be expected), it is likely to hand down a ruling in the foreseeable future that will not be limited to the specific *amparo* case but that has universal application. The battle that began in Mexico City will have then come full circle.

---

[84] CNN México interview with José Ramón Cosío Díaz, December 5, 2012 (http://mexico.cnn.com/).

6

Chile: A Case of Policy Stasis

Introduction

Unlike Argentina and Mexico gay marriage has not been enacted in Chile. This chapter looks at the Chilean experience, which is the non-case in the cross-national comparison I present in this book. My analysis shows that the lack of policy reform in Chile on gay marriage is due to the inexistence of the three main factors that were identified in Argentina and Mexico behind policy change. Contrary to the first two cases, Chile's gay and lesbian movement has been historically weak, and such weakness has impeded activists from forming strong networks with state and nonstate actors capable of pushing for policy change. In the first two cases, policy change was also the result of the permeability of the political system by these networks. While in Chile activists have established relationships with some state actors, formal and informal features of its institutional design and party system have allowed for a more inordinate access to the policy process by opponents to the expansion of sexual rights than to proponents. The third variable, the ability of activists and their allies to frame arguments that resonate with national debates, has also played a role. From the return of democracy in 1990 until the 2009–10 elections a broad agreement existed among the Chilean political élites on the rules of the game, an agreement that inhibited political contestation that provided limited opportunities for a real questioning of the terms of citizenship. This agreement significantly limited the ability of proponents of gay marriage to advance arguments in support of gay rights expansion framed around ideas of citizenship and democratic deepening. None of the three factors that I have identified in the other two cases has been present in Chile.

Nevertheless, the 2009–10 presidential elections marked a turning point in the politics of gay rights in the country and it appears that the Chilean case has begun to exhibit elements of the three factors behind policy change identified in the other two cases. The extent to which they solidify and coalesce will likely determine the type of policy change that will take place. Sebastián Piñera's (2010–14) election campaign propelled the issue of gay rights to the national agenda, a phenomenon that helped fuel the strengthening of the gay movement and the formation of stronger networks. It also ended Chile's consensual style of policy making, which has allowed for an increased permeability of the state by gay and lesbian activists and their allies. These developments have occurred within a larger context of unprecedented mass mobilization and a broad societal questioning of the posttransitional Chilean model that was maintained under the *Concertación* years.

The Reform of the Civil Code: A Missed Opportunity

As we saw in Chapter 3, Chile's gay movement weakened by the mid-1990s due to internal dynamics. By the late 1990s activists, contrary to their Argentine and Mexican counterparts, had been unable to attain public visibility to force a national debate on homosexuality, or to articulate a discourse linking sexuality with human rights. Nor did they build coalitions with other groups. It is within this context that the Chilean activists missed the first opportunity to push for reform when it appeared: the reform of Chile's civil code.

As we also saw in the same chapter, in 1992 Chilean activists received some international funding to study the situation of homosexuality in Chile and to mount a campaign to derogate provisions in the criminal code that criminalized same-sex relations (Article 365). Several of the most prominent activists focused their attention on this cause. At first the campaign consisted of raising awareness of the existence of these provisions, which included media interviews during which activists underlined the fact that Chile and Ecuador were the only two countries in Latin America in which same-sex relations were a criminal activity.[1] The awareness campaign reached a climax when, during a European tour in

---

[1] Nicaragua criminalized same-sex relations in 1992, but activists did not seem to be aware of this development.

1993 intended to promote support for a free trade agreement between Chile and the European Union, Patricio Aylwin (1990–4) was publicly confronted on the discrimination of homosexuals in Chile. With the help of Chileans living in exile, he was asked at a press conference what the reasons behind the discrimination of homosexuals in Chile were. Aylwin responded that in Chile all citizens were treated equally and said (incorrectly) that the law did not discriminate against homosexuals, but that "Chilean society does not react with sympathy vis-à-vis homosexuality" (*La Tercera*, May 29, 1993). For activists the application of international pressure on the government was key, especially from Europe, given the collaboration agreement Chile had signed with the European Community soon after the resumption of democratic rule. The agreement (*Cooperation Agreement between the European Community and Chile*) was signed in late 1990. Commonly referred to as a "third-generation agreement," it included a "democratic clause" that committed signatory parties to upholding democratic principles and the respect for human rights. Article 44 of the treaty specifically mentioned nondiscrimination. The agreement was signed by Chile as a first step in establishing freer trade relations and an eventual free trade agreement. However, despite the campaign, Aylwin's administration did not take any steps to decriminalize homosexuality.

Based on a proposal elaborated by the National Women's Service (*Servicio Nacional de la Mujer*, SERNAM), a cabinet-level body established in 1991 tasked with decreasing gender inequality, Aylwin introduced a series of reform bills to the Chamber of Deputies in August 1993 to "modernize" several laws that dealt with rape. The bills included proposed reforms to various clauses of the penal code's "sexual crimes" section. But the proposed reform to the penal code did not contemplate the decriminalization of same-sex behavior (through a reform of Article 365). For gay activists it nonetheless represented an opportunity to pressure Congress to derogate those provisions given that the issue of same-sex relationships would be inevitably discussed.[2]

Soon after the submission of the bill to Congress activists met with deputies from various political parties and asked them to derogate the provisions in Article 365 of the code that criminalized same-sex activity as well as the decades-long provisions in Article 373 that penalized those

---

[2] This is because the older penal code did not establish clearly a definition of rape, using vague and antiquated language. The proposed bill explicitly defined *rape* as "carnal access, through a vaginal, anal or oral medium, to a person older than fourteen years of age" (Biblioteca del Congreso Nacional de Chile 1999).

who "in any way offend the modesty (*pudor*) or good customs."³ Activists were involved at the beginning of the process. Similar to the Argentine and Mexican experiences of policy reform in the mid-1990s, the opportunity to reform the penal code in Chile was characterized by the presence of state allies.⁴ In remarkable similarities, especially with the Argentine case, some activists had developed close relationships with some legislators when they had been politically active in leftist political organizations and movements in previous years. Activist Rolando Jiménez, for example, had been an active member of the Communist Party with Fanny Pollarolo, who in the 1993 legislative elections was elected deputy and joined *Concertación*'s parliamentary faction as an independent.⁵ Other allies included *Concertación* deputies María Antonieta Saa, from the leftist Party for Democracy (*Partido por la Democracia*, PPD), and, after the 1997 elections, Antonio Leal, also from the PPD.

In addition to lobbying deputies directly, they organized an international campaign that consisted of having some allies overseas send letters requesting the derogation of Article 365 of the criminal code. Largely coordinated by Chileans living abroad, letters of support were sent by gay activists in Brazil, Argentina, Mexico, Costa Rica, Spain, Sweden, and Germany. It also included missives from international organizations, such as the International Lesbian and Gay Association and the International Gay and Lesbian Human Rights Commission, some U.S.-based medical organizations, and legislators from various countries in the Global North. Some of this correspondence was framed around the need for Chile to adhere to international standards with the objective of pressuring the country as it sought to restore its image after the long dictatorship. For example, a letter written by Canadian Member of Parliament Svend Robinson, Canada's first openly gay Member of Parliament, urged the lower chamber "to bring Chile's law into line with the world's democracies by repealing the sodomy law. Indeed, the Parliamentary Assembly of the Council of Europe requires that all of Europe's democracies rewrite their laws so that they do not discriminate against lesbians and gay men."⁶

---

³ Interview, Carlos Sánchez, activist and participant of committee discussions, Santiago, November 23, 2009.

⁴ These refer to the drafting of the Buenos Aires constitution in 1996 and the enactment of antidiscrimination legislation in Mexico City in 1998, as detailed in Chapters 4 and 5.

⁵ Pollarolo quit the Communist Party in 1993, ran as an independent in those elections, and subsequently joined the Socialist Party (*Partido Socialista*, PS).

⁶ Letters consulted by the author in the archives of the *Movimiento Unificado de Minorías Sexuales* (Unified Movement for Sexual Diversity, MUMS), Santiago, July 23, 2012.

While the original bill, intended to reform rape, did not contemplate a reform to Article 365, a proposal to derogate its provisions on same-sex behavior was introduced by a Socialist Party (*Partido Socialista*, PS) Deputy in late 1994 as the bill proceeded to discussion in the Standing Justice Committee (*Comisión de Constitución, Legislación y Justicia*). No changes to Article 373 were considered. The move ignited a great deal of debate in Congress and deputies from the two main conservative parties, National Renovation (*Renovación Nacional*, RN) and the Independent Democratic Union (*Unión Demócrata Independiente*, UDI), as well as from the Christian Democratic Party (*Partido Demócrata Cristiano*, DC), opposed the changes. Some conservative legislators opposed the reform with the basic argument that homosexuality was immoral and unnatural. For others, the decriminalization of homosexuality, given the lobbying activists had begun to employ, would unleash a reform process that would eventually lead to gay marriage.

Activists continued with their campaign and met with committee deputies to press for the derogation of Articles 365 and 373. The debate raged for several weeks at the committee level and the result was a compromise: a proposal to decriminalize same-sex activities among consenting adults along with the introduction of a new clause that raised the age of consent for homosexuals to eighteen years, and left it at sixteen for the rest. The proposals were submitted to the floor of the lower house and voted favorably on August 2, 1995. The vote reflected the positions of the various political parties. Only one RN deputy among all Alliance for Chile (*Alianza por Chile*) RN and UDI deputies voted for the reform, while all *Concertación* PS, PPD, and Radical Social Democratic Party (*Partido Radical Social Demócrata*, PRSD) deputies voted in favor. DC deputies were split: fourteen voted in favor and eight against.

Once approved, the bill proceeded to the Senate where resistance was expectedly higher. The binomial electoral system bequeathed by the transition (Chapter 2) favors an overrepresentation of conservative forces in the Chilean parliament. When the reform bill advanced to the Senate, the Alliance held twenty-four seats and *Concertación* twenty-three. Opposition to the reforms of Article 365 was therefore likely to be strong because of the Right's majority, but also because of its hardening of positions on moral policy issues since the transition to democracy. As Merike Blofield argues, Chile's political Right promoted an increasingly conservative moral agenda during the 1990s, which was the result of the penetration of the social bases of the élites by conservative religious organizations, such as Opus Dei and Legionaries of Christ (2006, 95–6).

During the 1990s, they "constructed educational institutes, both schools and universities, fostered think tanks, and created fundamentalist civil society organizations to dominate the framing and agenda-setting of family and sexual morality" (2006, 95). Yet, despite the expected opposition from the Right, lobbying from gay activists weakened dramatically as the movement's internal divisions and disagreements reached a crisis. Many of its members shifted focus to the fight against HIV/AIDS and abandoned the fight for civil rights (Chapter 3). This was partly fueled by the availability of funding made by the Ministry of Health to launch a prevention campaign.[7] The funding allowed a weakened movement to have access to some resources, which they employed to acquire some basic infrastructure. According to activist Leonardo Fernández: "without that money we would not exist today."[8] When the bill reached the Senate's Justice Committee (*Comisión de Constitución, Legislación y Justicia*) for discussion, activists had essentially abandoned their direct lobbying efforts. While they continued to ask allies abroad to submit letters of support, they stopped attending the committee hearings. As Jiménez recounts:

Our campaign [to derogate Article 365] went to the ground. There was disunity in the movement. [Deputy] Poyarolo called me to ask me to go to the Senate Committee meetings [as discussions started]. But I was no longer there. Poyarolo told me that the others had not attended. She called me the next week because no one showed up. People that had been involved before were not there anymore. They had thrown out [*botado*] the effort.[9]

Within this context, the proposal to decriminalize homosexuality was defeated by the Senate Committee in early 1997. According to Chilean parliamentary practice, when disagreements on components of a bill exist between the two chambers, a "mixed" bicameral committee (*Comisión Mixta*) made up of deputies and senators is established to resolve them. Such a Committee was established and, after several weeks of debate and negotiations, on November 18, 1998, it voted in favor of the reform. The final draft kept a difference in the age of consent between same-sex and heterosexual relations. The provisions of Article 373 regarding offences against "modesty and good customs" were also kept. Reflecting the strong opposition that remained, arguments for the reform were couched along conservative lines. Deputy Pía Guzmán (RN), who voted in favor,

[7] Interview, Marco Ruiz, activist, Santiago, November 27, 2009.
[8] Interview, Santiago, July 23, 2012.
[9] Interview, Santiago, October 8, 2009.

declared: "it is not true that we have opted to decriminalize [same-sex relations], but rather to maintain its punishment when the victim is less than eighteen years old, precisely to protect him" (Biblioteca Nacional de Chile 2009, 693).

Once the Mixed Committee approved the reforms, they were subsequently voted favorably by both chambers. The bill was promulgated into law by President Eduardo Frei (1994–2000) on July 2, 1999. According to Deputy Saa, an ally of the movement and a member of the bicameral committee, opposition to the reform in the Senate was overcome (and hence the second vote was favorable) by the delegation of discussions to the bicameral committee.[10] That is, once that committee was tasked with dealing with the issue, the floor was unlikely to reject its recommendations. However, according to other legislators, Chile's increased international exposure and its efforts to secure a free trade agreement with the European Union played a role. Senator Hernán Larraín, a prominent UDI political figure, stated that, because Chile was one of the last countries in (continental) Latin America where same-sex relations were still criminalized, it was simply not possible to oppose the reforms once they gathered some international attention: "we could oppose them in the early 1990s, but not by the end of the decade . . . we were cultivating a positive international image, especially with European officials . . ."[11] While there is no evidence of direct influence, such international pressure seems to have played a role. It is certainly a perception shared by some activists.[12] Nevertheless, what most actors agree on is that activists' lobbying efforts decreased as the process unfolded and the extent to which they were ultimately responsible for the repeal of provisions of Article 365 was limited.

The reform of the penal code represented an opportunity for gay activists to engage with the state and launch a policy reform trajectory to push for further rights, but they failed to seize it. The initial impetus they exhibited to repeal Articles 365 and 373, when the reform of the code was placed on the agenda in 1993, petered out over the years as the movement weakened. The penal code was eventually reformed, but the role activists played appears not to have been decisive. Whereas in Argentina and Mexico movements used early reform opportunities to

---

[10] Interview, Santiago, October 22, 2009.

[11] Interview, Santiago, July 23, 2012. The other country, Ecuador, stopped criminalizing same-sex relations in 1997. It happened as a result of a ruling by its Constitutional Court, which struck down the provisions of its penal code. Larraín voted in favor of the bill proposed by the bicameral committee.

[12] As stated by Fernández. Interview, Santiago, December 17, 2009.

build alliances, learn lobbying strategies, and acquire effective discursive tools, in Chile activists were for the most part focused on internal movement dynamics. In the first two cases early experiences in policy reform contributed to the thickening of relationships with state and nonstate actors, which subsequently helped in the establishment of networks. These networks played critical roles in ensuing policy changes. In Chile, however, some of these relationships (e.g., with parliamentarians) were not cultivated, expanded, or deepened. Neither did activists build alliances with other social movements, such as women's. In the case of Chile, alliances with women's groups could have helped gay activists establish a different relationship with the state given that SERNAM offered the women's movement an entry point into the policy process within the Executive (Franceschet 2004).

By the end of the 1990s, gay activists had been unable to force a social debate on homosexuality and to place gay rights on the national agenda. Importantly, unlike Argentina and Mexico, they failed to articulate a discourse that connected sexual rights with human rights. This all occurred within a context of an increased control of Chile's Right over the terms of debate over sexual and reproductive rights. Indeed, the censorship of movies by the state that challenged public morality lasted until 2002. As Óscar Contardo explains, during the 1990s homosexuality continued to be regarded a taboo moral topic in Chilean society at large and especially among the ruling political classes (2011, 390–404). This scenario contrasted sharply with the Argentine and Mexican experiences where, by the turn of the century, gay rights were well placed in public debates and the struggle for sexual rights began to move to the acquisition of positive rights as gay activists adopted civil unions as their main policy objective. Differences in institutional design would, at first sight, appear to have offered varied possibilities for policy change across the three cases in the mid-1990s. The constitutional reforms implemented in 1994 in Argentina and Mexico devolved power to the capital cities and provided activists with important policy avenues for reform. Activists seized these opportunities and pushed for policy change. Chile, by contrast, has a unitary system of government and the decentralization efforts undertaken during the Aylwin administration were very limited in terms of the policy-making authority devolved to municipalities.[13] However,

---

[13] Kent Eaton's work shows that "mayors, municipal councilors, regional executives and regional councilors in Chile have remained subject to a tremendous amount of discretionary control by the central government" (2004, 10).

the reform of Chile's civil code in the 1990s presented activists with an important opportunity to push for reform, but it was not seized given the movement's weakness.

Stalled Policy Reform, 2001–2009

Placing Gay Rights on the Agenda

The decriminalization of same-sex relations opened a new phase in the evolution of Chile's gay movement and its relationship with the state. Following the split of the movement in 1996, several activists began to work closely with the state on HIV/AIDS prevention campaigns. In 1997, after the initial funding some activists received from the Ministry of Health, they established a new organization – MUMS – to design and administer HIV/AIDS prevention programs. Most of the activists who had partaken in mobilization efforts in the early 1990s joined MUMS. Over the next several years, they managed to establish a collaborative relationship with officials from the Ministry as their activities expanded, a relationship that was facilitated after the reforms of the penal code given that they were no longer *de jure* criminals. Activities included the distribution of information regarding the spread of the virus, the training of transgendered sexual workers as "prevention instructors," and the organization of seminars and information sessions. These activities expanded further in 2000 when MUMS received funding from the European Union. In the eyes of one activist, the relationship they established with the Chilean government was possible because of the attitude that a "subsidiary state" took on the fight against HIV/AIDS: an increased reliance on nongovernmental organizations (NGOs) for the administration and execution of government programs.[14] The new collaborative relationship facilitated the provision of some input from activists into the drafting of Chile's first HIV/AIDS law, promulgated in December 2001. The experience activists had accumulated in the execution of government programs and campaigns proved valuable to state actors in the Ministry of Health, which played an important role in the drafting of the bill.[15] Funding was also made available through the Social Organizations Division (*División de Organizaciones Sociales*) within the Ministry General of the Government (*Ministerio Secretaría General de Gobierno*, SEGEGOB) to run education campaigns.

[14] Interview, Fernández, Santiago, July 23, 2012.
[15] Interview, Ruiz, Santiago, November 27, 2009.

The availability of funding breathed new life into the movement. MUMS activists organized a series of events ranging from information sessions, movie festivals, and discussion groups, which culminated with the organization of the first Gay Pride march in 1999 (Robles 2008, 112–17). It was attended by approximately one thousand individuals.[16] These activities managed to obtain some public attention and the subject of homosexuality began to be covered by the media (see, e.g., *El Mercurio*, July 13, 2000).[17] But it also resulted, in the eyes of some activists, in its depoliticization. Because the bulk of the funding available was earmarked for the administration and delivery of HIV/AIDS prevention programs, it contributed to the institutionalization of these groups' activities, or what one activist called the "NGOization" of the movement.[18] According to an activist: "we transformed ourselves into the implementers of state policy on the population affected by HIV[/AIDS]."[19] As a result, activists did not contest the state and, again in the eyes of some of them, became co-opted.[20]

A main consequence of this dynamic was that Chilean activists, unlike their Mexican, and to a lesser extent their Argentine, counterparts, were unable, at this stage of their trajectory, to use their focus on HIV/AIDS prevention programs to expand their demands and articulate demands that went beyond health policy. As may be recalled from Chapter 3, Mexican activists relied on the funding they received to help fight the HIV/AIDS epidemic to expand networks and to articulate a discourse of rights closely associated with civil rights. MUMS activists attempted to push for antidiscrimination legislation in the early 2000s, as we will see in the following text, but these efforts were soon eclipsed by the leading role the Movement for Homosexual Liberation (*Movimiento de Liberación Homosexual*, MOVILH) undertook in the push for civil unions.

Because most activists focused on health policy an opportunity to start pushing for civil rights opened, one that Jiménez quickly seized. In late 1999, Jiménez recovered the name of the gay organization MOVILH and

---

[16] Interview, Carlos Sánchez (MUMS president 2000–2), Santiago, December 17, 2009.
[17] In what some activists consider to be a watershed event, in June 2001 Chile's public television network, *Televisión Nacional de Chile*, aired a nonsensational documentary on Chile's gay movement.
[18] Interview, Ruiz, Santiago, November 27, 2009.
[19] Interview, Fernández, Santiago, November 25, 2009.
[20] Interview, Ruiz, Santiago, November 27, 2009.

registered it for the first time as an official NGO.[21] Jiménez and MOVILH became the public faces of Chile's gay movement for approximately a decade. Up until 2011, when a new gay organization, *Fundación = Iguales* (Equals Foundation) was formed, Jiménez personified the struggle for gay rights in Chile. According to an activist: "the movement [in the late 1990s] did not have a theoretical foundation (*sustento teórico*). There was a kind of deactivation and a space was left, which Jiménez filled."[22] Jiménez's (almost singlehanded) leadership over the cause of gay rights during the 2000s meant that his personal and political views have defined much of the gay rights struggle in Chile until recently.

Several of these are worth noting. The first is his continued belief that the fight against HIV/AIDS is a state responsibility and not of nonstate actors. Since its registration in 1999, MOVILH has therefore dedicated its efforts to the advocacy of civil rights. Secondly, and similar to Argentina's Homosexual Community (*Comunidad Homosexual Argentina*), MOVILH has worked on the pursuit of civil rights through legislative change. Other groups, such as Gay Action (*Acción Gay*), have been engaged in the promotion of social and cultural change through the organization of a wide array of activities in society. MOVILH, by contrast, has almost entirely been focused on legislative reform. This vision is well captured by the change Jiménez made to the organization's name when he registered it in 1999: from "liberation movement" to "liberation *and* integration movement." For him change must be brought about through institutionalized political processes.[23] Finally, unlike most of his counterparts in Argentina and Mexico, Jiménez's long-standing view has been that the struggle for gay rights encompasses certain characteristics that are not shared with the struggle for gender equality. MOVILH's functioning has therefore not been characterized by coalition building with women's groups.

After its official registration in 1999, one of MOVILH's main efforts for the first several years consisted in bringing public attention to the discrimination suffered by gays and lesbians in Chile. Starting in 2001, it began to capture, document, and report discriminatory cases through the release of annual reports. It also launched a sustained campaign to report individual cases with the intention of gaining public exposure. For Jiménez, the best way to place gay rights on the public agenda was to

[21] Given that homosexuality was criminalized before 1999, gay organizations could not be registered officially.
[22] Interview, Ruiz, Santiago, November 27, 2009.
[23] Interviews, Santiago, October 31, 2009 and July 19, 2012.

publicize concrete cases: "these are not cases of discrimination, these are gays, lesbians and transvestites who are victims of violence. They have names. We need people to understand the personal dimension."[24] In a very systematic way, Jiménez, as the organization's main public figure, actively solicited media coverage when cases of discrimination occurred. For example, in 2004 MOVILH denounced the expulsion of two students from high school for having exhibited "homosexual behavior" (*El Nacional*, September 14, 2004). It prompted the Minister of Education to intervene and reinstate the students two weeks later (*El Nacional*, September 22, 2004). While relatively minor, it managed to attract the attention of national dailies.

Numerous such smaller cases occurred alongside several high-profile ones, some of which in fact ignited national debates. For example, in August 2002, MOVILH released a report alleging irregularities in the investigation following the burning down of a gay club, the Divine, on September 4, 1993 in the city of Valparaiso. Chile's gay community had long suspected that homophobic-inspired arson had been at play. Following the release of the report, MOVILH submitted a complaint to the Ministry of Justice alleging irregularities in the investigation and asking the Ministry to reopen the investigation (*El Mercurio*, August 31, 2002). In October of the following year, a Valparaiso judge acceded to the request and opened another investigation. While it did not lead to any new findings, the case became a symbol of the perceived homophobia perpetrated by the state among gay activists in Chile. Vigils are held every year to commemorate the event and September 4 was declared by MOVILH as the "day of sexual minorities." In another case, a judge was suspended in 2003 without pay for four months by the Supreme Court because he had "gravely compromised the decorum" of upper judicial postings for having attended a gay sauna (*La Tercera*, December 13, 2003). In the same year, the Ministry of Health instructed all blood banks in Chile to administer a questionnaire to donors that required the disclosure of their sexual orientation to ensure the prohibition of blood donations by homosexuals (*La Nación*, June 16, 2003). The following year, the Chilean Army released a document, titled "The Armed Forces and Homosexuality," penned by the institution's Secretary General, in which he alerted that Chilean society "was undergoing a situation of moral relativism" and reaffirmed the institution's policy of refusing gay men to enlist for "moral reasons." It declared that: "This prompts us to affirm

[24] Interview, Santiago, July 19, 2012.

that homosexuals cannot join the army . . . [homosexuality] is not natural to men" (*El Mercurio*, September 10, 2004). In all of these cases, MOVILH held news conferences denouncing such discrimination and managed to attract significant media attention.

Its strategy proved successful as gay rights were slowly placed on the public agenda. Whereas homosexuality was not widely discussed in public by the late 1990s, the denunciation campaign began to force a social debate on the issue. The process, however, differed from what occurred in Argentina and Mexico in two important ways. First, in Argentina and Mexico original attempts to bring attention to discrimination against gays and lesbians, which date back to the early 1980s, were over time joined by other groups, such as women's, in overall efforts to frame discrimination as an affront to human rights. In Mexico, for example, *Letra S*'s campaign to document hate crimes was launched by a commission that included prominent feminists. In Chile, however, Jiménez's MOVILH was the only actor involved in the denunciation of discriminatory cases. Collaboration with other groups, which in Argentina and Mexico helped thicken networks, did not take place.

Second, the strategy of placing gay rights on the agenda through public denunciations contributed to the establishment of a confrontational relationship with the state. That is certainly the image of their tactics that was conveyed through the media. For example, in 2003 MOVILH organized a demonstration to denounce declarations made by the Catholic Church hierarchy on a bill being discussed in Congress to legalize divorce. Some protesters burned a Vatican flag. The event was covered extensively in the media the following day. The main newspapers in Chile reported it with the headline: "Homosexual Movement Burns Vatican Flag" (see *El Mercurio*, August 15, 2003; *La Cuarta*, August 16, 2003). The confrontational approach, and the image the movement created, hindered the development of personal relationships with other social movements and state allies and the establishment of strong and close networks. In both Argentina and Mexico earlier phases of mobilization were also characterized by confrontation, but, by the turn of the century, activists had managed to establish collaborative relationships as they began to gain important policy battles.

Initial Efforts at Policy Reform
Increased public attention to discrimination suffered by sexual minorities in Chile occurred alongside the first concrete efforts to demand the enactment of policies and programs by the state to eradicate it. In late 2000, numerous organizations from across Latin America organized

a conference, the Citizens Conference of the Americas (*Conferencia Ciudadana de las Americas*), in Santiago to coincide with a regional preparatory meeting for the 2001 UN World Conference on Discrimination, Racism and Xenophobia, which was held in Durban, South Africa. The regional preparatory meetings, held in Santiago in early December 2000, were attended by delegations of thirty-five countries in Latin America and the Caribbean and had as a main objective the formulation of regional proposals to be presented at the world conference. Civil society organizations held the Citizens Conference in order to present their own proposals and influence these preparatory meetings. The organization of that initiative was led by the well-established Chilean NGO Ideas Foundation (*Fundación Ideas*), which had been championing the adoption of antidiscrimination measures for some time. By the end of the event its participants agreed on a common proposal to be integrated into the official regional position that had, among numerous recommendations, the need to adopt government programs to reduce discriminations based on sexual orientation. Importantly, and to the surprise of many, the proposal was included in the official declaration agreed upon by the thirty-five states.[25] Sexual orientation was discussed at the Durban Conference and the final official declaration did not make any references to discrimination perpetrated against sexual minorities, but the preparatory meetings in Santiago helped bring together several organizations to discuss the issue of discrimination and to include sexual orientation as one of them.

Discussions and collaboration among these organizations were also fostered by the first government initiatives to tackle discrimination. Also in 2000, and following a meeting of "discriminated minorities in Chile" organized by MUMS, the head of the government's Social Organization Division, Carolina Tohá (a prominent figure within the PPD and supporter of gay rights), agreed to work on the development of Chile's first antidiscrimination plan in collaboration with civil society organizations.[26] The initiative, named *Plan Tolerancia y No Discriminación* (Tolerance and Non-Discrimination Plan), was in part influenced by the attention discussions on discrimination had gathered internationally.[27] Tohá established an "intercultural table" (*mesa intercultural*) that invited representatives of numerous discriminated groups, such as migrants, indigenous groups,

[25] Interview, Francisco Estévez, Director *Fundación Ideas* (in 2000), Santiago, November 6, 2009.
[26] Interview, Sánchez, Santiago, December 17, 2009.
[27] Interview, Carolina Tohá, Santiago, November 19, 2009.

sexual workers, the elderly, and sexual minorities. The effort collected numerous proposals from various groups that were included in a document that served as the foundation for the government's first antidiscrimination plan, launched in 2004.

Both events encouraged many organizations to pursue the enactment of antidiscrimination legislation in Chile. For some activists the political context was favorable. After the governments of two Christian Democratic presidents (1990–2000), the election of Ricardo Lagos (2000–6) in 2000 opened a new opportunity to push for legislation in what in Chile is generally known as *temas valóricos* (moral issues). Lagos, an openly atheist person in his second marriage (in a country where divorce did not become legal until 2004), was the first Socialist president since the overthrow of Salvador Allende in 1973 and personified possibilities for policy change on moral policy. However, during his election campaign Lagos had been clear that not much progress should be expected on gay rights if elected. Asked whether Chileans would see any change on that front during an interview he gave while campaigning in 1999, he responded that: "respect to all human beings does not happen through legislative bills" (*El Mercurio*, December 4, 1999). Nevertheless, for gay activists, his government's initiative to collect proposals to develop an antidiscrimination plan, as well as the mounting international pressure to act, meant that a possibility for change existed. The availability of progressive allies in government, such as Tohá, was seen as key.[28]

As a result, in 2001 activists began to organize in order to persuade the government to enact antidiscrimination legislation. Following the citizens' conference of late 2000, several participant organizations, including MOVILH, formed the Social Network for Diversity (*Red Social por la Diversidad*)[29] to coordinate efforts to push for antidiscrimination reform. Emboldened by Chile's official position during the preparatory Durban talks, the network's members decided to demand a constitutional reform to enshrine the right not to be discriminated against. In May 2002 network representatives met with the Minister of the General Presidency (*Secretaría General de la Presidencia*, SEGPRES)[30] to ask that a proposal, drafted by

---

[28] Interview, Sánchez, Santiago, December 1, 2009.

[29] It included an organization representing relatives of individuals with mental illness, the Relatives of Patients with Mental Illness Group (*Agrupación de Familiares de Pacientes Psiquiátricos*, AFAPS), a Mapuche organization (*Agrupación Mapuche Urbana Mahuidache*), and a migrant organization (*Asociación de Inmigrantes por la Integración Lationamericana*, APILA).

[30] SEGPRES is mainly responsible for executive-legislative relations, the drafting of legislation, and the setting of the presidential agenda.

MOVILH and that called for constitutional reform, be adopted as well as an antidiscrimination plan based on the document agreed upon by NGOs and the Social Organization Division. The Minister agreed to study the proposal, and in fact promised the formation of a committee to do so.

In early 2003, MUMS, in collaboration with the Faculty of Law of the Diego Portales University, unveiled an alternative proposal to enact an antidiscrimination law, not a constitutional reform, which included sexual minorities as a group to be protected. In June of the same year, MUMS and other organizations managed to obtain the support of several *Concertación* Members of Congress who have been strong supporters of gay rights: Saa and Leal from the PPD (referred to in the preceding text), Víctor Barrueto and Patricio Hales, also from the PPD, the Socialists (Isabel) María Isabel Allende and Fulvio Rossi, as well as Osvaldo Palma from RN. These parliamentarians agreed, along with activists as well as representatives from SEGPRES, to establish a "tripartite committee" to support the bill in the Chamber of Deputies. It thus marked the very first proposal to enact antidiscrimination legislation to protect sexual minorities that was endorsed by state actors from both the Executive and the Legislature.[31]

The push to enact antidiscrimination legislation occurred around the same time that the first proposal to recognize same-sex relations was submitted to Congress. Inspired by the adoption of same-sex civil unions in Buenos Aires in 2002, on June 2, 2003 MOVILH and Deputy Saa unveiled at a press conference a bill that would legalize same-sex unions in Chile. Unlike Argentina and Mexico, the pursuit of civil unions in Chile has to be undertaken at the national level given its unitary system. For Saa the events in Buenos Aires provided an opportunity to start the conversation in Chile and the formal submission of a bill to Congress was the most effective way of doing so.[32] The bill was submitted to the Chamber of Deputies on June 11 of the same year and received the support of eighteen deputies from the various parties within *Concertación* (including the ones that supported the antidiscrimination initiative), such as Tohá (PPD). Two months later, MOVILH and Deputy Saa met with the SEGPRES Minister soliciting the support of the Executive. The Minister referred the proposal to the Justice Ministry for analysis.

---

[31] According to Francisco Estévez, Director of *Fundación Ideas* at the time, his organization presented the first proposal in 1995 to Chile's Congress, but it did not receive the endorsement of parliamentarians. Interview, Santiago, November 6, 2009.

[32] Interview, Santiago, October 22, 2009.

The submission of these initiatives placed the issue of gay rights solidly on the public agenda and culminated efforts made by gay activists in Chile to force a debate on the issue. There are strong parallels with the early Argentine and Mexican experiences. In all cases, gay mobilization and its collaboration with allied Members of Congress belonging to smaller social progressive parties were responsible for placing the issue of same-sex relationship recognition on the legislative agenda. Nevertheless, the Chilean experience differs in important ways. In Argentina and Mexico the first attempts at policy reform were characterized by the expansion of networks of individuals allied to the cause. Particularly in terms of antidiscrimination policy, gay activists joined extensive coalitions to push for policy reform. In the case of Chile these were a great deal thinner in part because of the movement's weakness and divisions. While MOVILH advocated the inclusion of antidiscrimination provisions in the constitution, MUMS decided to push for a general antidiscrimination law. The two organizations had allies, but they were small in number and the relationships they established with them were not strong. In the case of MUMS, they established a formal working relation with faculty at the Diego Portales University to draft the legislative proposals but it did not last as MUMS began to focus most of its attention on other activities and their lobbying efforts were overtaken by a more visible MOVILH. As MOVILH's Jiménez assumed a leading role in the push for civil rights, other activists disengaged from the cause. MOVILH's collaboration with other groups was also weak.

The push for the antidiscrimination law arose from a collective effort among several organizations, including those that represented migrants, the disabled, and, eventually, Chile's Jewish community. However, interviews with participants do not reveal the development of close, personal relations. Notably absent from this broad coalition were women's groups. While discrimination on gender was included in the law, and women were one of the many groups to be protected by the legislation, the coalition to which MOVILH belonged did not include any women's groups. In part, this is because women's interests were mostly represented through SERNAM, which pressed the government from within to pass the bill, as well as an organization created in 2005: Humans Corporation (*Corporación Humanas*).[33] But it also was the result of Jiménez's long-standing view on the limited collaboration gay activists should

---

[33] The organization's name does not translate well into English as *humans* in Spanish is feminine.

have with women's groups. But more importantly, the relationships that MUMS and MOVILH managed to forge with various groups were not transferred to the push for civil unions and eventually gay marriage.

The second important difference regards the road from the placement of policy on the agenda to policy reform. In the case of Argentina and Mexico, after placing the issues of antidiscrimination legislation and civil unions on the agenda, activists were successful in achieving policy change. In the case of Chile, the placement of these items on the agenda followed a period of stasis. In both Argentina and Mexico, antidiscrimination legislation was enacted with unanimous votes in a relatively speedy manner in the legislatures where they were presented (Buenos Aires 1996, Mexico City 1998, and Mexico's Congress 2002). These accomplishments not only emboldened activists to push the fight for gay rights further, but also it helped them to strengthen and deepen relationships with their (state and nonstate) allies. In Chile, by contrast, antidiscrimination legislation was not enacted until 2012 and under specific conditions, neither civil unions nor gay marriage has transpired. Part of the explanation is found in Chile's institutional features.

Explaining Stalled Policy Reform

Despite the increased public attention gay rights assumed in the early 2000s and the support bill projects obtained from numerous deputies, by the time *Concertación* was defeated by the right-of-center Alliance in the 2010 elections, no antidiscrimination legislation, civil union, or gay marriage was enacted in Chile as bills stalled in Congress.[34] Part of the explanation for policy stasis, which contrasts with the Argentine and Mexican experiences, is found in the specificities of Chile's policy making under *Concertación*. As may be recalled from Chapter 2, the return to democracy in Chile saw the emergence of a political regime characterized by consensual policy making that favored policy stability over change. Chile's policy-making style under *Concertación* made reform on moral policy difficult. The high threshold needed to enact constitutional reforms meant that the Alliance had a veto over policy change to any structural reforms. However, policy veto was also exercised by the Right over regular legislation: the inclusion of the Alliance leadership into the *democracia de los acuerdos* negotiations essentially provided them with a veto

[34] This section draws from interviews held with three (sitting and former) cabinet ministers, two ministerial chiefs of staff, two deputy ministers, two presidential advisors, and three ministerial advisors. Given the sensitivity of the conversations, interviewees are only identified by name when expressly agreed by them.

entry point into the policy process: their consent was needed to advance on policy. According to a former advisor to President Lagos: "The fundamental principle during the Lagos administration, and which has continued during Bachelet's, is that parliamentary majorities are useless. What we need is the support of part of the opposition."[35]

Moral policy change was also rendered difficult because of the weighty role the DC played within *Concertación*. As one of the main coalition members, the confessional DC represents the interests of socially conservative groups, and especially the Catholic Church. Clearly put by a DC Deputy: "our relationship with the Catholic Church is historic and strong. . . . We do represent their interests and have to take their opinions into account. . . . Some of us are in fact [family] related to members of the Church's hierarchy."[36] Such representation provided the Catholic Church direct access into the policy process and amounted to a veto point over socially progressive legislation. Importantly, controversial moral issues were not even discussed and would not even be placed on the negotiating table.[37] However, the interaction between the Catholic Church and the Executive during the *Concertación* years was not limited to its representation through the DC: it also appears to have taken place directly with the president. Describing the setting of the agenda of moral policy reform under the Lagos administration, one of his advisors stated:

At the beginning of the administration, Lagos invited members of the Catholic Church leadership for dinner. He had them at his home. He communicated to them that he wanted to move on some social policy reforms and that included divorce. They of course disagreed, but they agreed to disagree. [On gay rights] he said that they also made him uncomfortable, even if he was a Socialist, and that it was not an issue that he had promised to pursue. He knew he could only pursue one fight.[38]

Coalition and consensual politics in Chile largely explains policy stasis under the *Concertación* years in gay rights and that gay marriage was not enacted. After the submission of the first bill proposals to enact antidiscrimination provisions to Congress, discussions within the Executive were held for a few months. In late 2004, the SEGEGOB

---

[35] Interview, presidential advisor (2000–6), Santiago, November 6, 2009.

[36] Interview, Carolina Goic, Valparaiso, October 28, 2009.

[37] Interview, Francisco Vidal (Deputy Minister of the Interior, 2000–3, 2005–6, Minister SEGEGOB, 2003–5, Defense Minister, 2009–10), Santiago, July 25, 2012.

[38] Interview, presidential advisor (2000–6), Santiago, December 3, 2009. The same advisor intimated that he was personally designated to negotiate with "bishops" the divorce reform.

Minister, Francisco Vidal, announced that, among the various proposals, the government decided to support a constitutional reform to include antidiscriminatory provisions, including sexual orientation (*El Mercurio*, November 16, 2004). A bill, he declared, would be submitted to Congress by the end of the year. Newly elected Deputy Tohá, an ally, along with the Ideas Foundation and MOVILH, held a press conference a few days later. Sensing opposition within the governing coalition, they urged the government to stop dithering and to submit the bill to Congress quickly. However, DC and Alliance leaders opposed such a measure.[39] The Lagos administration as a result decided not to pursue a constitutional reform and instead presented a bill to enact a general antidiscrimination law in March 2005. While some opposition to the bill was expressed by DC leaders within *Concertación* prior to the bill's submission to the Chamber of Deputies, proponents of the bill in cabinet argued that Chile had committed itself at Durban to implement policies to address discrimination, that the passage of the bill through Congress was not guaranteed, and that a discussion should at least be allowed.[40] Moreover, the bill differed from the one that had been elaborated by MUMS: because it did not seek to establish government institutions to fight discrimination, as in Mexico and Argentina, nor did it mandate the government to launch antidiscrimination programs – it established penalties for antidiscriminatory acts.

The introduction of the bill to Congress ignited a debate that soon focused almost entirely on the two provisions of the bill: the protection of individuals based on their gender identity and sexual orientation. Conservative actors announced the launch of a campaign not to include the two categories into the bill with arguments based on Natural Law.[41] For socially conservative religious groups, the bill, if passed, would prevent them from speaking against homosexuality based on their beliefs.[42] They were opposed to the bill despite the fact that it would not apply for statements made by individuals based on religious convictions. The case against the enactment of an antidiscrimination law was bolstered by a Supreme Court opinion released two months after the bill's introduction

---

[39] Interview, Vidal, Santiago, July 25, 2012.
[40] Interview, presidential advisor (2000–6), Santiago, November 6, 2009.
[41] These included the groups Family Action (*Acción Familia*), the Family and Life Network (*Red por la Vida y la Familia*), Hurry-Up Chile (*Muévete Chile*), the Osorno Union of Evangelical Pastors (*Unión de Pastores Evangélicos de Osorno*), and the television and radio station Crusade for Power Evangelical Movement (*Movimiento Evangelístico Cruzada por el Poder*).
[42] Interview, Bishop Hernán Pérez, President, National Council of Evangelical Bishops of Chile (*Consejo Nacional de Obispos Evangélicos de Chile*), Santiago, July 17, 2012.

to Congress. On May 3, 2005, it declared that such legislation was not needed given that: "the right not to be discriminated against is sufficiently addressed, regulated and protected in the current legal system, and there is therefore no need to establish additional and special measures for their protection" (Biblioteca del Congreso Nacional de Chile 2012, 16–8). Supporters of the bill included the various groups that belonged to the Social Network for Diversity, mentioned in the preceding text, which other organizations joined, such as the Jewish Youth of Chile (*Juventud Judía de Chile*). They held several press conferences over several months and met Members of Congress to press them to vote in favor of the bill. Support for the bill also came from the Executive. In addition to the SEGEGOB's Social Organizations Division, SERNAM's Minister lent her ministry's support. According to various interviewees, SERNAM, and especially its legal office (*Departamento de Reformas Legales*), became one of the strongest supporters of the bill and pushed for its enactment from within the Executive.

Despite such institutional support, opposition to the bill from DC and UDI was strong and, following pressure from evangelical groups and Catholic Church leaders,[43] the provisions to protect individuals from discrimination based on their sexual orientation and gender identity were removed from the bill in a committee vote in June (Biblioteca del Congreso Nacional de Chile 2012, 72–125).

Opposition to the bill within *Concertación* weakened as the presidential elections of 2005 heated up and the issue of discrimination made it to campaign debates. During her campaign, presidential candidate Michelle Bachelet (2006–10, 2014–) spoke about the need to protect minorities from discrimination and to respect social diversity. In her proposed electoral platform, unveiled in October 2005, she became the first presidential candidate in Chile to commit herself to fighting discrimination against sexual minorities. In a document, titled "I am with you" (*Estoy contigo*), she outlined five main axes that would guide her government. The third, "We Are all Chile: A New Treatment for Citizens" (*Chile somos todos: Un nuevo trato para los ciudadanos*), explicitly mentioned that the fight against discrimination, including sexual minorities, would be a priority for her government (Bachelet Jeira 2005).

Such context applied pressure on socially conservative *Concertación* deputies, especially because the elections were particularly tight. Taking advantage of this context, *Concertación* parliamentarians that were

[43] As expressed by five deputies interviewed.

supportive of the bill[44] pushed colleagues that were opposed to vote in favor. Such pressure appears to have worked: in a vote held on October 5 sexual orientation and gender identity were reintroduced to the bill and a majority of deputies voted in favor of several of its articles (*El Mercurio*, October 6, 2005).[45]

Nevertheless, the bill's fate was not the same in the Senate where it stalled until the end of Bachelet's administration due to opposition from socially conservative senators. The issue of protection against discrimination was maintained on the agenda during her administration. In her first state of the union address, for example, she reiterated her commitment to the protection of discriminated groups, including sexual minorities, as well as her support of the bill. This was the first time a Chilean president referred to sexual minorities in the annual May speech. Moreover, proponents of the bill within the Executive coalition pushed hard for the bill. In particular SERNAM Minister, Laura Albornoz, and the Director of SEGEGOB's Social Organizations Division under Bachelet, Estévez – who, as may be recalled, was the director of the NGO Ideas Foundation in the early 2000s and a close ally – took a personal interest in the passage of the bill and lobbied within the Executive and in Congress for support. Their legal offices were instructed to shepherd the bill through Congress and to convince opposing or hesitant actors in the Executive and in Congress to support it.[46] Pressure also mounted from nonstate actors, particularly from the newly established and well-funded Humans Corporation.[47] This NGO, staffed by professional individuals, set up a "legislative monitoring program" within a "parliamentary observatory" office (*Observatorio Parlamentario*) that had as its top priority to lobby for the bill's passage.[48] However, their efforts were not sufficient to overcome opposition. In December 2006 members of the Constitutional Committee voted in favor of the bill so that a full debate would take place on the floor, but the vote did not take place.

[44] These included Leal and Saa (PPD, mentioned in the preceding text), Laura Soto (PPD), Juan Bustos (PS), and Tohá (PS). Interview, Antonio Leal, Santiago, July 24, 2012.
[45] However, deputies did not vote in favor of several provisions that were also controversial, such as the requirement that education plans include the teaching of arbitrary discrimination (Biblioteca del Congreso Nacional de Chile 2012, 176–91).
[46] Interviews, Estévez and Marco Rendón, Director, Legal Office, SERNAM, Santiago, November 6, 2009.
[47] The NGO receives significant funding from organizations such as the Ford Foundation, Oxfam, and the European Union.
[48] Interview, Camila Maturana, Parliamentary Observatory, Humans Corporation Santiago, July 17, 2012.

The dynamic changed two years later after Soledad Alvear joined the Constitution Committee. Alvear, an advocate of women's rights, former SERNAM Minister, and the first DC female president, managed to convince two Alliance committee members (Alberto Espina RN and Andrés Chadwick UDI) to abstain from voting so as to allow a debate on the floor.[49] The bill did not obtain enough support to be voted on the floor, however. At the time *Concertación* held a slight majority of seats in the Senate (eighteen compared to the Alliance's seventeen), which meant that it needed all DC votes to get it passed.[50] It did not. According to a DC senator: "we had the support of all our [*Concertación*] senators, except for the DC. There were, I think, three who would not vote. . . . The pressure from the religious groups was too strong."[51] Indeed, according to several senators interviewed, pressure from Catholic Church leaders, as well as some evangelical groups, was constant and focused on the deletion from the bill of protection against discrimination on the basis of sexual orientation and gender identity.[52] The bill did not proceed to a vote as it was in effect vetoed by the direct access conservative religious groups had through DC senators. Opposition was also articulated within the Executive. From early 2009 until the end of the 2009, SEGEGOB gave the bill the lowest level of discussion priority (*urgencia simple*) five times.[53] It let two of them expire and withdrew the other three upon the insistence of DC actors.[54] The bill remained stalled at the committee level until early 2011, as we will see in the following text.

Chile's consensual democracy also partly explains that same-sex relationships were not legally sanctioned by the state during the *Concertación* years. Deputy Saa's introduction of a civil-union bill to parliament in 2003 was intended to provoke a social debate, capitalizing on the regional debate the adoption of civil unions in Buenos Aires had sparked. She did not expect that the proposal would receive support from the Executive.[55]

---

[49] Interview, Santiago, July 27, 2012. The bill was temporarily blocked by Chadwick (UDI), but he decided to abstain from the vote held in May 2008, allowing the legislation to move onto the Constitutional Committee.

[50] The threshold appeared to be higher after the expulsion of DC senator Adolfo Zaldívar in 2007, who opposed the bill. But, according to two senators interviewed, at least one RN would vote in favor.

[51] Interview, Santiago, July 28, 2012.

[52] Senators that opposed the bill belonged to the more conservative wing of DC, colloquially known in Chile as the *guatones* (whereas the more progressive wing is known as the *chascones*).

[53] Figures retrieved by author from the Congressional Library.

[54] Interview, ministerial advisor, SEGEGOB, Santiago, December 9, 2009.

[55] Interview, Santiago, October 22, 2009.

She was correct. Confirming the beliefs President Lagos had expressed previously that the respect for human rights did not "happen through legislative bills" (see preceding text), and the discussions he held with Catholic leaders soon after becoming president, in a television interview in March 2004, he clearly stated his government's position on civil unions declaring that "the country is not ready for this, things should be done in due course . . . we should not push certain things ahead of their time because right now it is not their moment" (*El Mercurio* March 15, 2004). The bill therefore stalled in Congress until the end of his administration. However, its introduction induced the expected public debate in a way that framed it in subsequent years. While the bill proposed the enactment of civil unions, conservative actors began to articulate their opposition by equating it to gay marriage. Shortly after the bill's introduction to the lower house, Jiménez met with UDI deputies to discuss their position. At the meeting they expressed their support for the regulation of inheritance and patrimony rights of same-sex couples, but opposed it in principle because it was too close to gay marriage. The following year, UDI, RN, and DC deputies introduced a proposal to reform the constitution to prohibit explicitly gay marriage (*El Mercurio*, May 14, 2005).

Supporters of the bill made efforts to clarify that they were pursuing civil unions and not gay marriage, but opponents were successful in ensuring that the debate centered on the possibilities of approving gay marriage. The debate was thus framed as one of gay marriage versus a more technical approach to the regulation of socioeconomic benefits of common-law relationships (*parejas de hecho*). The demands of supporters of civil unions, contrary to their counterparts in Argentina and Mexico, were not framed around human rights and an expansion of citizenship rights. The Catholic Church advanced its opposition to the bill by referring explicitly to the perils of gay marriage, contributing further to the solidification of the debate around gay marriage. The President of the Episcopal Conference of Chile, Bishop Alejandro Goic, indicated that the Church was opposed because it risked prompting "what occurred in Spain, which changes the definition of marriage from one between a man and a woman, to call them spouses . . . that changes the natural order of things and it is something that we obviously will not accept" (*La Segunda*, April 26, 2005).

The debate over same-sex relationship recognition intensified in the months leading up to the 2005 presidential election as gay rights made it to the campaign and remained on the agenda after Bachelet's arrival to power. However, divisions within *Concertación* surfaced quickly.

Bachelet's position on gay marriage was made clear as she ran for the candidacy of *Concertación*'s presidential primaries in 2005. In an interview she declared clearly her opposition to gay marriage and began to refer to the "French solution": "I am not in favor [of gay marriage]. Chile's Civil Code establishes marriage as one between a man and a woman. The French position is different for it guarantees the legality of relationships of people of the same sex so that they deal with their daily issues, such as common goods" (*El Mercurio*, April 28, 2005). Meanwhile, asserting a more progressive position vis-à-vis Bachelet's PS, the Coalition's PPD explicitly included gay marriage as part of its agenda: its leader, Guido Girardi, further called for moving ahead toward reforms on moral policy (*El Mercurio*, August 27, 2005). He knew that the DC would block any proposal to legislate on gay marriage, but his party wanted to keep the debate alive within *Concertación*.[56] DC's opposition crystallized soon thereafter. In a document, titled "DC in the Next Election," its leadership explicitly stated its opposition to gay marriage. Its president, Andrés Zaldívar, declared that the party would not accept "any ambiguities" on moral policy and, while they would support Bachelet, they would do so "from our own values and principles" (*El Mercurio*, October 28, 2005).

The so-called French solution won the day in the Coalition's internal negotiations. Bachelet followed up on her support for this type of civil union and committed herself to the enactment of a legal framework to regulate same-sex couples. In the document outlining her campaign promises she stated that her government would "propose to legislate in order to provide basic legal stability to common-law couples (*parejas de hecho*), irrespective of their composition, and to regulate the acquisition of common goods, inheritance rights, insurance benefits, among other civil matters" (Bachelet Jeira 2005, 90).

Despite her promises to run a more inclusive government (a "citizens' government") through the establishment of a new "social dialogue," to forge a new relationship between the state and society, and to advance on gay rights, neither civil unions nor gay marriage was enacted during her administration. For gay activists Bachelet's endorsement of the so-called French solution in her electoral platform meant that an opportunity to push for civil unions opened up. During the first months of 2006, MOVILH, in collaboration with legal scholars from the Diego Portales University and the University of Chile drafted a bill proposal modeled after the French civil union of 1999 (*pacte civil de solidarité*). The

[56] Interview, Santiago, November 6, 2009.

proposal, called Civil Union Pact (*Pacto de Unión Civil*, PUC), was a legal contract between two individuals regardless of gender intended to provide legal security for common goods and benefits without any modifications to the civil code. Because the debate over civil unions had transpired as one about gay marriage, MOVILH's Jiménez believed that a change of strategy was required and that instead of pushing for a legal union that would protect same-sex couples, they should propose a gender-neutral civil union.[57] The proposed bill was officially unveiled in September 2006 and presented publicly to the SEGRPES Minister. She promised to consider the proposal (*El Mercurio*, September 20, 2006). PUC received the endorsement not only of *Concertación* leaders, but also of the RN leadership. In regard to DC, Alvear's assumption of the party's leadership four months earlier facilitated things given that she belonged to the more socially progressive wing of the party. She endorsed the proposal, along with the leaders of the other three Coalition parties. Rather surprisingly, Lily Pérez, RN's Secretary General also announced her party's support for the civil union stating that "we do not support marriage between two people of the same sex, but we are open to the regularization of all patrimonial rights, health and insurance benefits" (*La Tercera*, September 21, 2006). The UDI leadership rejected the proposal.

The unveiling of the new civil union, as well as the various parties' reaction to it, was covered extensively by the media. But while it may have received important support from most parties, the SEGRPRES Minister, sensing the difficulty of advancing on the issue, foreshadowed the prospects of reform declaring that: "there is a commitment [to the same-sex unions] in the President's program . . . we now have to see if there is a consensus to move forward in this area . . . it is not a short-term priority, although it is in the program" (*La Tercera*, September 21, 2006). Following SEGPRES's promise to consider the bill, one of its deputy ministers instructed MOVILH to obtain the support of Members of Congress to begin internal conversations within the Executive in order to launch the legislative process. By early 2007, MOVILH had managed to secure the support of twenty-four *Concertación* and one RN Members of Congress.

Nevertheless, opposition to the proposal within *Concertación* meant that a consensus was not reached and the bill was not introduced until the end of 2009, as the presidential elections changed dramatically the politics of gay rights in Chile. The momentum that built up around gay rights during the election campaign and the months that followed faded

---

[57] Interview, Santiago, October 13, 2009.

as the Bachelet administration was shaken during its first two years by a series of crises. Two months after her inauguration, the country experienced its largest mass mobilization since the return of democracy as high school students organized and mobilized to demand a reform to the market-reliant education system. The so-called Revolution of the Penguins (*Revolución de los pingüinos*) – in reference to the students' white-and-blue uniforms – built up rather quickly and managed to attract an estimated one million demonstrators to a national strike held on May 30, 2006. It paralyzed the country and represented the first mass popular challenge to *Concertación*'s socioeconomic model.[58] The student mobilization was followed by a series of demonstrations and a general strike held by copper contract workers in 2007 and protests held in 2008 as a result of problems associated with the implementation of a major overhaul of the public transportation system in Santiago. For some observers, these mobilizations represented a challenge to the legitimacy of the posttransition economic model (Garretón 2012, 144–6). In more practical terms, it meant that gay rights dropped from the public agenda and that the possibilities of advancing on the enactment of civil unions or gay marriage diminished drastically. Largely as a consequence of social mobilization, Bachelet shuffled her cabinet in 2007. The "new faces" that she had appointed to her cabinet, in an effort to establish a new governing style, were replaced by old-guard *Concertación* figures that were deemed fit to respond to the crises. SEGRPRES Minister, Socialist Paulina Veloso, who had been open to the civil-union proposal and promised to begin negotiations within the governing coalition, was replaced by the more socially conservative figure of José Antonio Viera-Gallo. Veloso's replacement meant that proponents of civil unions lost an ally within the Executive given the critical role SEGRPRES plays in managing the government's agenda.

The new context diminished the possibility of applying pressure on internal *Concertación* agenda negotiations and to move on policy reform on gay rights, including civil unions. According to a close advisor to Viera-Gallo, the crises confronted by the Bachelet administration meant that the policy agenda within the coalition's discussion in the *grupo político* focused primarily on how to resolve them.[59] However, policy reform did not transpire in the second half of the Bachelet administration

---

[58] For an excellent analysis, see Kubal 2010. For a great, textured account, see Domedel and Peña y Lillo 2008.

[59] Interview, Santiago, December 9, 2009.

once the crises were overcome and her popularity increased to record levels. According to two cabinet ministers interviewed, the issue of civil unions and gay marriage were not formally entertained in *La Moneda* agenda discussions until the end of 2009 because it was clear that no progress would be made given opposition from DC leaders. This was the case despite the existence of supporters of gay rights in the Executive, such as longtime allies Estévez, SEGEGOB's Social Organizations Division, and Tohá, who was appointed SEGEGOB's Minister in 2009. Support for the PUC was expressed in writing by twenty-four Members of Congress – which included the ones that had been supportive of gay rights, such as Saa, Girardi, and Leal. However, consensual politics in Chile prevented the issue of same-sex recognition even to make it to a discussion within the Executive.

The Executive's failure to support civil unions, despite Bachelet's endorsement during the election campaign, as well as *Concertación*'s general position on moral policy, provoked an important fissure within the coalition, a fissure that marked profoundly the 2009–10 general elections. In an attempt to apply pressure on the Executive to move on the issue, in early March 2008 PS Deputy and *Concertación* precandidate, Marco Enríquez-Ominami announced, in collaboration with MOVILH, his intention to introduce a revised version of the civil union first introduced to Congress in 2003, as well as a bill proposal that would reform the civil code to allow for gay marriage. Enríquez-Ominami argued that, while *Concertación* governments had performed well since the return of democracy on economic issues, they had not caught up with the times and needed to move on moral policy reform (*The Santiago Times*, March 7, 2008). He further argued that Bachelet had committed herself to the regulation of common law same-sex couples and that her government therefore had the obligation to legislate in that area. In a highly publicized case, two months later Enríquez-Ominami accompanied four same-sex couples to a Civil Registry Office to request to be married. Largely symbolic, the move was intended to demonstrate that the civil code discriminated against same-sex couples and to keep the issue on the agenda. However, contrary to what occurred in Argentina and Mexico when proponents of gay marriage began pushing for reform, Enríquez-Ominami spoke about the discriminatory aspect of the civil code and did not articulate an argument that linked gay marriage with larger debates regarding democratic citizenship. As their applications were rejected, he declared that: "Here we have demonstrated that there is an institution that is discriminatory, and that is supported by everyone's taxes, including those who cannot get married" (*La Nación*, May 6, 2008). The differences with arguments advanced in Mexico and Argentina are clear: Enriquez-Ominami's declaration referred to taxpayers, not citizens. His endorsement of both civil unions and gay marriage provoked an intense debate in the media and an expected reaction from conservative actors. But it also galvanized *Concertación* actors. Ten days after the announcement, the PS membership adopted a resolution at their annual general convention in support of gay marriage (*The Santiago Times*, March 17, 2008). Two days later, Enríquez-Ominami tabled his civil-union and gay marriage bills to the lower house of Congress with the support of various *Concertación* deputies, declaring:

> We have to ask ourselves why we have modified so many other aspects of the Civil Code, but not touched its legal definition of marriage, which is, in fact, very discriminatory . . . the topic of civil unions is something that the current government campaigned for . . . I believe that the Chilean society is ready to discuss homosexual marriages . . . but at the same time, the country's elites are not ready for it.[60]

After two years of inaction by Bachelet's administration on same-sex relationship recognition (and the stalled antidiscrimination bill), Enríquez-Ominami's bills not only reignited the debate on gay rights, but he managed to insert them directly into the 2009 election campaign.[61] Enríquez-Ominami lost his bid to run as the precandidate for *Concertación*'s internal primaries under the PS ticket. In June 2009 he announced his independent candidacy for the presidential elections of October of the same year. He portrayed himself as a social liberal and mounted a campaign that sought to mark a clear distinction with the governing coalition on moral policy. He thus campaigned overtly in favor of gay marriage and abortion.[62]

The introduction of the first gay marriage bill to Chile's Congress in 2008 differed substantially from what occurred in Argentina and Chile. As may be recalled, gay activists in both countries managed to obtain the support of a wide variety of state and nonstate actors in the push for both civil unions and gay marriage. In Chile the situation was different: the push for the enactment of the antidiscrimination law was exerted by a handful of organizations and state actors.

---

[60] *The Santiago Times*, March 19, 2009.
[61] The Standing Committee on the Family discussed the civil-union proposal introduced by Enríquez-Ominami on June 17, 2009 but was voted down. The majority of the committee was composed of UDU, RN, and conservative independent deputies.
[62] For the best account of Enríquez-Ominami's ideological position see Navia 2009.

While individuals belonging to this network worked together in lobbying both Congress and the Executive, they did not seem to have established the same level of close personal relationships that bound similar networks in Argentina and Mexico. Support for the antidiscrimination bill among these actors was as a consequence not transferred to the campaign to push for civil unions. Indeed, out of all of the organizations and individuals that formed the core of the network that pushed for the antidiscrimination bill, only a handful of organizations joined the campaign for civil unions.[63] MOVILH's Jiménez managed to obtain the support of additional organizations after the public presentation of the PUC in 2006, some of which had important social standing among Chile's sociopolitical classes, such as the Chile Foundation (*Fundación Chile*) and the Human Rights Program of the Diego Portales University. However, the number of organizations that joined the push for gay marriage after the bill was introduced was significantly smaller when compared to the campaigns to enact both antidiscrimination legislation and the PUC. In effect, other than the several deputies and Members of Congress that supported the bill, MOVILH only obtained the support of a few other gay organizations.[64] Notably absent in the incipient campaign for gay marriage were women's and feminist groups, groups that played key roles in the networks that Argentine and Mexican activists built to push for reform. In large part this was due to differences in priorities. For some of the main women's organizations, such as Humans Corporation, the priority was the enactment of the antidiscrimination bill.[65] But it was also due to the failure of MOVILH's Jiménez to build a personal relationship with these groups in large part as a result of his long-standing position on the role feminism ought to play in struggles for the expansion of gay rights. For example, asked about the relationship Humans Corporation's Maturana had developed with Jiménez, she responded that it was strictly professional and limited to activities related to lobbying for the antidiscrimination bill.[66] Whereas in Argentina and Mexico extensive networks among

---

[63] These are the organizations representing mentally ill individuals (AFAPS), Migrant Groups (APILA), and the Jewish Youth of Chile (MOVILH 2006, 2007).

[64] These were Afirmative Chile (*Afirmación Chile*), the Chilean Federation for Sexual Diversity (*Federación Chilena de la Diversidad Sexual*), the Calama Group for Sexual Minority Rights (*Agrupación de Derehcos Sexuales de Calama*), and the Puerto Montt Cultural Center for Sexual Minorities (*Centro Cultural de las Minorías Sexuales de Puerto Montt*).

[65] Interview, Maturana, Santiago, July 17, 2012.

[66] Ibid.

state and nonstate actors were built to push for gay marriage, in Chile these were very limited indeed.

The Fall of Consensual Politics

The 2009–2010 Election Campaign: Gay Rights on Center Stage

The 2009–10 elections were marked by elements of continuity and change. In the first round of voting held on December 13, 2009, Enríquez-Ominami managed to obtain 20.14 percent of the vote. It was the first time since the return of democracy that an independent candidate managed to siphon a substantial share of the vote from Chile's left-leaning electorate. Enríquez-Ominami's campaign aimed at challenging the ruling coalition's technocratic and "exclusionary" governing style, and his position on moral issues clearly resonated with many voters. After having received the largest share of the votes (44.06 percent) in the first round, the Alliance's Sebastián Piñera received a majority of votes (51.61 percent) when he faced *Concertación's* (former president, 1994–2000) Eduardo Frei in the runoff election of January 17, 2010. This was the first time in fifty-one years, since the election of Jorge Alessandri in 1958 (Chapter 2) that Chile's Right was elected to power. The election ended twenty years of uninterrupted *Concertación* administrations.

Nevertheless, despite these apparently dramatic changes the general elections were characterized by aspects of continuity. While the candidates' electoral platforms differed on some issues, for the most part they agreed on the basic elements of Chile's posttransition socioeconomic model. Piñera, for example, made clear during his election campaign that, if elected, he would not retrench any of the social programs that had been established since the return of democracy, while Enríquez-Ominami and Jorge Arrate (another former *Concertacionista* and independent candidate) promised not to challenge the country's macroeconomic policy. In keeping with Chile's political tradition, the campaign was thus marked by the idea of change within continuity. Given the general agreement that existed among the main candidates on basic socioeconomic policy – in tune with the country's tradition of consensus – candidates were forced to look at other policy areas to differentiate themselves from one another. One of these areas was moral policy, and in particular gay rights. The 2009–10 elections not only brought gays and lesbians to the political center stage, but they marked a dramatic turn in the politics of gay rights.

Similarly to what occurred during the previous general elections, the debate over gay rights started to heat up when parties and candidates began to engage the issue as the election neared. Enríquez-Ominami launched his independent electoral campaign in mid-2009 with a clear support for moral policy reform while the DC precandidate Frei declared his openness to discuss civil unions as he stated on a television interview that "this is the twentieth-first century and there can't be any taboo subjects" (*The Santiago Times*, March 26, 2009). Unlike Bachelet's electoral platform, Frei's did not include any references to, or promises on, gay rights. However, in a widely unexpected turn of events, gay rights were brought onto the electoral scene by Chile's Right. While Piñera had personally supported civil unions during the last election campaign, they had not received the formal consent of the Alliance. Events played out differently this time around.

A month prior to the first round of elections, on October 11, 2009, Piñera's campaign leadership published a document in Chile's *La Tercera* newspaper, titled "Common-Law Agreement" (*Acuerdo de Vida en Pareja*, AVP).[67] The document declared the Alliance's support for the enactment of a civil union and provided the details of the proposal. Its publication ignited an unprecedented debate on gay rights in Chile, which became central to the campaign. Breaking away from Chile's consensual style of policy making, the decision to embrace fully and so publicly same-sex civil unions was taken by RN campaign strategists, with Piñera's full support, without consulting most UDI leaders. While Senator Chadwick, one of UDI's most prominent political figures, was one of the document's coauthors (along with RN Senator Andrés Allamand), the decision to draft and publish the document did not involve the rest of the party's leadership. Piñera's embrace of civil unions was strategic and was meant to portray an image of a renewed, liberal, and nonthreatening Right. According to one of the Alliance's campaign strategists and close Allamand advisor:

It was a campaign issue. It was a strategy to demonstrate that Chile's Right is a lot more heterogeneous than what people see . . . there is a lot of confusion in the electorate. Within the Right there are people like Allamand that are progressive on social issues, and someone like [UDI's José Antonio] Kast that are completely at the other extreme. Allamand is a lot closer to Girardi than to Kast. It was a strategy meant to have people pay attention. It was an explicit strategy to demonstrate that the Right is open. The purpose was to create a strong reaction in the media to get the electorate's attention. We knew that there was going to be a fight within the coalition, especially with UDI. That was the objective. . . . It was

---

[67] The rather clumsy literal translation is Agreement for a Coupled Life.

a dictatorial decision. The decision was taken by the RN's leadership (*cúpulas del partido*).[68]

The objective to provoke a strong media reaction, and the expectation to have tensions within the Alliance were certainly met. A strong debate raged in the media over the following weeks and a strong backlash from UDI transpired. UDI members, led by Deputy Kast, decried the lack of consultation and argued that it amounted to the recognition of gay marriage through the back door (*legalización encubierta del matrimonio*). Kast even threatened to abandon the campaign.

The Coalition's internal dispute over the common-law proposal burst onto the public sphere. In a full-page spread in *La Tercera*'s widely read Saturday edition Allamand and Kast faced each other. In an article titled: "Should Stable Relationships Be Regulated?" Allamand reinforced the argument that had emerged in favor of civil unions since the introduction of the first bills to parliament: that the AVP would regulate an already existing reality: in "Chile there are more than two million unmarried couples, building, even if some people would not like to recognize it, an undeniable social reality which is not subject to any regulation" (*La Tercera*, October 17, 2009). Kast, for his part, reiterated the arguments that opponents had been advancing since the debate began in 2005: that the recognition of civil unions amounted to the acceptance of gay marriage:

What lies behind the voices that want to regulate common-law relationships is [the objective] to provide homosexual couples the same recognition that marriage has. If we accept the legal union of hetero and homosexual couples, we extinguish the arguments to promote marriage as an institution and it is foreseeable that these unions, over time, will gain all the prerogatives, already scarce, that marriage has. All the more if we see that the dominant discourse sees discrimination everywhere, even when differences are legitimate and are rationally and naturally founded.[69]

Despite the public airing of the disagreement and UDI's strong reaction, Piñera and his campaign managers decided to continue to endorse their civil-union proposal. In the days following the publication of the civil-union proposal in the media, Piñera declared: "this proposal does not intend to weaken marriage nor to establish gay marriage through the back door, but to solve real problems that real people have" (*La Tercera*, October 14, 2009). What is more, a few weeks later Piñera's campaign

[68] Interview, Santiago, November 11, 2009.
[69] *La Tercera*, October 17, 2009.

launched television advertisements with the slogan "the voice without voice" showing Piñera alongside a gay couple and speaking about the importance of creating a more inclusive country and to stop discrimination (*El Mercurio*, November 22, 2009). The debate was further fueled and the topic of gay rights assumed unprecedented prominence in the election campaign to the extent that, in a televised debate among the four precandidates, three questions regarding Piñera's position on homosexuality were asked by the moderator. This was the first time the word *homosexual* was used in a televised presidential debate in Chile.

Piñera's endorsement of civil unions has several important repercussions. While *Concertación*'s candidate, Frei, had earlier declared his support for civil unions, he excluded them from his official electoral platform. As a result of Piñera's support, his campaign was forced to endorse them explicitly before the first round of elections (*La Nación*, November 24, 2009). Second, the manner in which Piñera defended his support for same-sex relationship recognition solidified the framing of the debate as one between a practical technocratic solution to an existing reality and not one of human rights and democratic citizenship. Inasmuch as his support for gay rights seemed to break new ground for Chile's traditionally conservative Right, it conformed to the country's posttransitional approach to technocratic policy making: the civil-union proposal provided a technical solution to an existing problem. Finally, and more immediately, the Coalition's inclusion of civil unions in its platform offered an opportunity for proponents of civil unions within *Concertación* as well as activists to pressure the Executive to pursue the issue before the end of the administration. In the days following the AVC's unveiling, several Members of Congress, led by PS Deputy Fulvio Rossi, introduced the original PUC to the lower chamber for debate (*La Tercera*, October 14, 2009).

The bill formally entered the legislative process as the Constitution Committee debated it on October 27 following the Executive's designation of second-level priority (*suma*). The fact that gay rights had assumed extensive media coverage, and that the Right was being perceived as being more progressive than *Concertación* in what was shaping up to be a close election, provided an ideal opportunity for supportive legislators to have the Executive support the bill.[70] Nevertheless, similarly to what occurred during the last election campaign, it was not sufficient to overcome the veto exerted by DC legislators. Within a few days, the Executive

[70] Interview, Fulvio Rossi, Valparaiso, October 28, 2009.

was forced to withdraw the bill's *urgencia* upon the insistence of DC deputies. According to an advisor to SEGPRES Minister Viera-Gallo:

> We received calls from DC deputies asking us to withdraw the *urgencia* because of the reaction of the churches in their circumscriptions. We are in the middle of an election. We withdraw legislation that is not viable. Deputies asked us to withdraw it after October 15. You can negotiate with deputies, but not on this issue. Sometimes we can offer something in their circumscriptions [in exchange], [such as] projects, but not on this type of legislation.[71]

Both the PUC and the antidiscrimination bills were not enacted by *Concertación* when Piñera assumed power on March 11, 2010.

Gay Rights under Piñera

The politics of gay rights changed in important ways after the arrival of Piñera to the presidency.[72] Unlike four years earlier, public discussion over same-sex relationship recognition remained atop the public agenda after the election. The debate over gay marriage in Argentina, which unfolded at this time, not only encouraged a discussion in the media, but it also represented an opportunity for Members of Congress supportive of gay rights to push for same-sex recognition in parliament. During the first several months of 2010, three civil-union bills and one gay marriage bill were introduced to the lower house. Importantly, these bills were submitted by legislators without much consultation with gay activists.[73] Senator Rossi's gay marriage bill was endorsed by MOVILH, but it did not collaborate in its drafting. The bill was supported by several other legislators, such as Tohá and Girardi. Piñera's endorsement of civil unions clearly created a strong reaction and liberal legislators appear to have rushed to push for the cause. Several RN deputies also introduced a bill that proposed a constitutional reform explicitly banning gay marriage. The introduction of these bills ensured that the public debate on gay marriage continued after the elections. Significantly, Piñera followed up with his campaign commitment and on June 29 Allamand introduced a new version of the AVP, called Common-Law Agreement (*Acuerdo de Vida en Común*, AVC). The new proposal was weaker than the previous version in that it did not include the regulation of patrimonial benefits. The new bill did not receive the support of UDI Senator Chadwick. According to a

[71] Interview, Santiago, December 9, 2009.
[72] This section draws heavily from interviews carried out with twelve deputies and senators from five political parties in July and August of 2012.
[73] Interviews, Rossi (sponsor of the gay marriage bill), and Deputy Gabriel Silber (sponsor of a civil-union bill), Santiago, July 19 and 23, 2012.

RN Senator, the introduction of the bill was motivated by a desire among the RN leadership to ensure that, in light of developments in Argentina, in Chile the debate was restricted to civil unions.[74]

The bill received input from a new player in gay rights in Chile: Luís Larraín Stieb. Larraín Stieb, who belongs to the established Larraín political family in Chile, took a personal interest in the pursuit of gay rights. He was in fact one of the two men featured in one of Piñera's campaign ads. He was appointed as SEGPRES Advisor in March 2010. In a clear departure from the making of policy under *Concertación*, Piñera's administration did not seek a consensus within the governing Alliance in all policy areas. Indeed, strong divisions within the new governing coalition on civil unions continued, divisions that were publicly articulated and covered extensively by the media. Kast declared his continued opposition to civil unions and warned of severe repercussions should the government decide to continue supporting civil unions. Opposition was not limited to Kast and several UDI and RN legislators, as well as cabinet ministers, made public declarations against the initiative.

Consensual politics on moral policy appeared to have come to an end. The UDI president established a committee to study the issue in July of the same year, which included Chadwick. The committee worked for several months and, by early 2010, it submitted to the Executive a "working document" proposing a much weaker civil union. The disagreements were not reconciled and the RN and UDI leaderships decided in January 2011 to forego party discipline and to allow their legislators a free vote in Congress. Public disagreement was also articulated within *Concertación* over Rossi's gay marriage bill. The new PPD President, Tohá, endorsed publicly the initiative, while the DC leader declared publicly his opposition to the bill, stating that the proposal was noteworthy given that "it will clearly not win consensus within *Concertación*" (*La Tercera*, August 2, 2010). Despite the public debate, the AVC stalled in Congress by mid-2011, and Piñera decided not to include a reference in its 2011 state of the union address due to pressure from the UDI and RN leaderships. This decision provoked another significant change in the politics of gay rights in Chile: the establishment of the Equals Foundation. The day after the presidential speech was delivered, Larraín Stieb gave an interview in *La Terecera*'s Sunday edition denouncing the president's failure to include a reference to civil unions and the government's ongoing inertia on the issue (*La Tercera*, May 22, 2011).

---

[74] Interview, Valparaiso, July 18, 2012.

The interview provoked significant discussion in Chile, which culminated with a television interview with the renowned author Pablo Simonetti (the second best-selling author in Chile) during which he openly declared his homosexuality as well as his support for both civil unions and gay marriage. The interview was a watershed moment for gay activism in Chile as, given the public reaction it provoked (it became the number one trending topic on Twitter for two days) it encouraged the formation of the Foundation: Larraín Stieb, Simonetti, and Antonio Bascuñán, Professor of Law at the University of Chile, decided to establish the organization.[75] The result was a dramatic, and swift, change in gay activism in Chile, one that has had several important repercussions. Because the Larraín family is identified with Chile's Right, the fact that Larraín Stieb became one of the visible faces behind the Foundation has provided Chile's gay rights struggle with a much different veneer: demands for gay rights have been associated with an ampler sector of the population.

Moreover, in a country commonly identified with strong classism and elitist politics (Contardo 2008), the adoption of the cause for gay rights by individuals from the country's political and social élite has allowed for an easier delivery of demands to political actors. Indeed, all of the twelve legislators interviewed since the organization's establishment alluded to the fact that legislators have become a great deal more receptive to activists' demands. Importantly, several legislators refer to the less confrontational approach the new organization adopted when interacting with state actors. As one senator explained: "the scene is very different now. It is the 'Simonetti effect.' It is a new chapter since Simonetti came out. Everyone in Chile likes him and his approach is different . . . he is not like Jiménez, who does guerrilla activism . . . people that didn't listen before listen now."[76]

The Foundation has also built a significant network of allied state and nonstate actors in a truly remarkable short period of time. During the weeks following his television interview, Simonetti received calls from a variety of social and political actors (which included Tohá, Alvear, DC Senator Ximena Rincón, and former cabinet minister Andrés Velasco), as well as established entrepreneurs, artists, and journalists who expressed their desire to join the cause and to contribute in different ways.[77] Tohá and Velasco became members of the Foundation's Board of Directors when it was officially registered in 2011. Foundation activists have since

[75] Interview, Pablo Simonetti, Santiago, July 20, 2012.
[76] Interview, Santiago, July 18, 2012.
[77] Interview, Simonetti, Santiago, July 20, 2012.

then built close working and personal relationships with three key legislators: Senators (DC) Alvear, Rincón, and (PS) Allende. Significantly, and in stark contrast to MOVILH's historic approach, the Foundation has actively established and nurtured links with women's organizations and feminists. For example, Verónica Undirraga (a renowned feminist and law professor) and jurist Karen Atala (see Introduction) are also members of the Foundation's Board of Directors.[78] Chilean gay activism appears to have begun exhibiting some of the characteristics its Argentine and Mexican counterparts possess and which have been crucial in the push for policy change. It has acquired a significant social presence in Chile.

The appearance of the Foundation on the political scene gave momentum for policy reform in gay rights. For the founders of the organization, the priorities were the enactment of the antidiscrimination law and civil unions. While gay marriage was also an objective, they believed that the focus should be on the two pieces of legislation that had been the most debated and which had the best chance of being approved.[79] They thus focused their attention on applying pressure so that both would be passed. In early 2011, Senator Alvear, as newly appointed chair of the Senate's Constitution Committee, had managed to place the discussion of the antidiscrimination bill – which, as we know, had reached the Senate in 2008 – on the committee's agenda. However, opposition from conservative cabinet ministers in *La Moneda*, pressured by religious groups, prevented her from triggering a committee vote.[80]

The context changed with the appointment of Senator Chadwick as SEGEGOB Minister on July 18, 2011. While not supportive, Chadwick had previously abstained from voting on the bill and was open to the idea of at least allowing a vote.[81] Within this new context, the "Simonetti effect" appears to have contributed to passage of the bill by the Senate on November 8, 2011. While opposition to the bill's protection of sexual orientation and gender identity continued (*La Nación*, July 5, 2011), especially from evangelical organizations (whose members at one point

---

[78] While Atala built a very extensive coalition of (national and international) actors in support of her case, which produced the historic ruling by the Inter-American Court of Human Rights in 2010, it did not include MOVILH and there has been very limited (personal and professional) interaction between Jiménez and Atala over the years. Interview, Atala, Santiago, July 26, 2012.

[79] Interview, Simonetti, Santiago, July 20, 2012.

[80] Opposition was most forcefully articulated by the SEGEGOB's minister (UDI) Ena Von Baer, who opposed the inclusion of sexual orientation and gender identity in the bill. She therefore established a working group to study the bill in detail.

[81] Interview, SEGEGOB advisor, Santiago, July 23, 2012.

forced the postponement of a vote in the chamber given their drowning of parliamentary debate with shouts), Alvear, in close collaboration with Rincón and Allende, managed to obtain a majority vote at the committee level on June 2 thereby allowing for a vote of the bill on the Senate floor. According to Alvear, the reaction provoked by Simonetti's public coming out provided an opportunity to push for the legislation.[82] What ensued was an intense lobbying effort from supporters and opponents of the bill.

The coalition that had been built in support of the bill engaged in the harvesting of individual votes through the direct lobbying of senators, reminiscent of the lobbying that networks in Argentina and Mexico practiced. According to a (RN) senator, the lobbying carried out by the Foundation and its allies played an important role in obtaining the necessary votes.[83] It also played a role in diminishing opposition within the Executive.[84] After the vote in the Senate, the bill proceeded to the lower chamber for discussion, after a failed attempt by opposing legislators to have the Constitutional Tribunal rule on the unconstitutionality of the bill.

A dramatic turn of events ensured its final enactment. In the early morning of March 3, 2012, Daniel Zamudio, a gay teen, was brutally attacked by Neo-Nazis in central Santiago. A victim of a hate crime, the profound public reaction the incident unleashed forced the Piñera administration to act swiftly and to ensure the passage of the bill. Three days after the attack, the Minister of the Interior declared the government's intention to give the bill priority in Congress. On the same day the Senate passed a motion declaring its solidarity with Zamudio's family. Zamudio died on March 27 as a result of the injuries he sustained from the attack. Piñera's government consequently announced the designation of a higher level of priority to the bill for discussion in Congress, which it applied on April 3. It was voted in favor in the Chamber of Deputies on May 8 and in the Senate the following day with substantial majorities (*La Tercera*, May 9 and 10, 2012). It was promulgated into law on July 12, thereby bringing to an end eight years of discussion in Congress. The impression among all twelve legislators interviewed, as well as a close advisor to SEGPRES Minister Chadwick, is that Zamudio's death simply made it impossible for most deputies and senators to oppose the bill.

---

[82] Interview, Alvear, Santiago, July 27, 2012.
[83] Interview, Valparaiso, July 18, 2012.
[84] Interview, SEGEGOB advisor, Santiago, July 23, 2012.

While Zamudio's death contributed to the final enactment of the bill, the lobbying efforts carried out by numerous activists and allies proved critical in the passage of the bill in the Senate in late 2011. Importantly, the networks that the Foundation has built since its establishment have also been used to push for civil unions, which are likely to be enacted into law in Chile. After intense lobbying with numerous legislators and staffers in *La Moneda*, on August 9, 2011 Piñera announced, in a carefully choreographed ceremony in the presidential palace, the unveiling of a new (and weaker) version of the AVP, which was introduced to Congress shortly thereafter. The lobbying carried out by Foundation activists, and the close contact Larraín Stieb had with *La Moneda* ministers, appears to have played a central role.[85] Piñera's support for the bill since its unveiling continued to create significant frictions within the Alliance, frictions that were aired and covered by the media. In July 2012, UDI Deputy Patricio Melero publicly decried Minister Chadwick's request to the Chair of the Senate's Constitution Committee, Larraín, to place the AVP on the committee's agenda for discussion (*La Tercera*, July 14, 2012). These tensions appear to have stalled the bill: by the time Piñera left office in March 2014, the bill remained at the committee level in the Senate.

The Return of Concertación and the Prospects of Gay Marriage in Chile

The debate over same-sex recognition in Chile has assumed a technical approach. Arguments in favor of civil unions have been framed as a need to regulate already existing relationships in order to provide them legal protection. It is an argument that was taken up by the government during the first Bachelet administration (the "French solution") and that gained currency during Piñera's administration. It conforms to the technocratic style of policy making that has characterized Chile since the return to democracy and the reason why momentum seems to have gathered behind civil unions and not gay marriage: it resonates with society. Based on the Argentine and Mexican experiences, the prospects that gay marriage will be adopted in Chile in the foreseeable future will likely depend on whether the three factors that I have identified in Chapters 4 and 5 emerge and intersect.

It will first depend on the evolution of the gay and lesbian movement and on whether gay activists in Chile adopt gay marriage as a

[85] SEGEGOB advisor, Santiago, July 23, 2012, and RN Senator, Valparaiso, July 18, 2012.

policy priority. While gay marriage is one of their objectives, they have focused on civil unions as a first step to full same-sex relationship recognition. The strengthening of the movement, largely as a result of the Foundation's eruption onto the political scene (and their ability to establish extensive networks with state and nonstate actors), has clearly contributed to some momentum on gay rights reform. Should activists adopt gay marriage as a policy priority, they will be able to deploy their recently acquired strength to apply increased pressure on the state to push for reform.

The likelihood of reform will also depend upon the type of access a stronger movement has to the policy process and on whether socially conservative forces continue to have an informal veto after the end of Piñera's administration. The prospects on this front are uncertain.

Bachelet decided to return to Chilean politics after having led the UN Agency for Gender Equality and the Empowerment of Women. In March 2013 she announced her desire to run for the presidency again in the 2014 elections. Given the immense popularity she enjoyed when she left office in 2010, she faced little opposition in the internal coalition primaries and became *Concertación*'s (renamed New Majority, *Nueva Mayoría*) presidential candidate (winning with 73 percent of the votes). Bachelet campaigned on a promise to meet demands that had crystallized over the last several years in Chile by committing herself to the implementation of profound reforms, ranging from tax and education reforms to a new constitution. They included gay marriage. After having met with gay and lesbian activists during her campaign, she acquiesced to their demand to include gay marriage as part of her reform program (*La Tercera*, September 21, 2013). This is the first time that a major contending presidential candidate adopted gay marriage as an electoral promise in Latin America. After falling short of winning a majority in the first round against the Alliance's Evelyn Matthei in November 2013, she won the second round in December 13 with 62 percent of the votes. Bachelet returned to *La Moneda* in March 2014 amid high expectations for change.

At first blush, the composition of her new governing coalition would appear to allow gay and lesbian activists greater access to the policy process and to have increased the likelihood of gay marriage reform, especially given Bachelet's explicit endorsement. In an effort to respond to calls for profound social and political change, particularly coming from social movements, Bachelet labored to form a broader coalition. As such,

New Majority includes former leaders of the student movement (that rocked the country years earlier) who won seats in Congress on the Communist Party ticket: Camila Vallejo and Carol Kariola, the highly visible student activists who led the demonstrations in previous years. Vallejo and Kariola, furthest on the Left within the coalition, have openly supported gay marriage. New Majority assumed therefore a more leftist veneer and, except for DC, all the major coalition partners have explicitly supported gay marriage. However, despite the coalition's more leftist configuration, DC holds the balance of power. Even though New Majority won a majority of seats in both chambers, DC votes are needed to pass legislation through the Senate. Any effort at pushing for gay marriage through Congress will therefore depend on Bachelet's ability to obtain DC's support.

The crystallization of such support will depend on the internal debates within DC. However, the party is deeply divided on the issue despite having supported Bachelet's candidacy. Bachelet introduced fifty reform proposals during the first one hundred days of her administration, signaling her commitment to bring about profound reform. Less than two weeks after Bachelet assumed office, her Justice Minister, José Antonio Gómez Urrutia, announced that, given her campaign promise, their administration was preparing a bill proposal on gay marriage (*La Segunda*, March 20, 2014). The announcement forced the DC leadership to react. Senator Patricio Walker declared that the party was divided, and that, should the bill be introduced, DC was prepared to allow for a free vote (*El Mercurio*, March 20, 2014). The bill had not been introduced by the end of July 2014. According to some, failure to introduce the bill to Congress was due to the fact that government did not have the necessary votes from DC, which explained why Bachelet's government was pursuing the AVP.[86]

More importantly, however, Bachelet's return to *La Moneda* appears to have marked a return to consensual politics. During the first months of her administration several of her key campaign promises, such as education and tax reform, remained unfulfilled as she sought to obtain the support from all of her various coalition partners. Policy stasis was primarily the result of her inability to reach policy compromise between DC and the new "student contingent" in Congress (Navia 2014a). Given the president's desire to achieve consensus over policy,

---

[86] As expressed by the Deputy Arturo Squella (*La Tercera*, July 30, 2014).

the frictions that policy negotiations appeared to have created, and the fact that support from DC partners was required to move on policy, the likelihood that contentious issues such as gay marriage will be placed on the agenda and approved remained low. DC therefore continues to have an informal veto.

Lastly, it will also depend on the extent to which a master frame that would facilitate the resonance of arguments for gay marriage emerges, on whether political change allows for the advancement of demands that seek to alter the general consensus that has existed around the posttransitional socioeconomic and political model. An opportunity certainly opened up as a result of the mass student mobilizations that took place during the Piñera administration. While mainly seeking a reform of the education system, some sectors within the student movement have articulated a discourse that has challenged some of the basic tenets of Chile's posttransitional model and state-society relations more generally. Indeed, Vallejo's election campaign was hinged on ideas that called for democratic deepening and rights expansion (*El Mercurio*, September 13, 2013). Such discourse can certainly contribute to the emergence of broader demands given the generalized feeling of frustration among many Chileans.[87] However, despite such frustration among the population, and the widely perceived desire for change, 63 percent of Chileans believed, after the return of Bachelet to the presidency, that broad coalitions are necessary to bring about political change. As Patricio Navia has suggested based on these numbers: "Chileans appear to be comfortable with the idea that it is better to proceed more slowly but avoiding polarization and radicalization" (Navia 2014b). The emphasis on consensus by the political class seems to be supported by a majority of Chileans, which would seem to suggest that a more general renegotiation of social and political agreements is unlikely. Chile's politics would thus seem to continue a long tradition of change within continuity. With these conditions, the emergence of a master frame that would facilitate the resonance of demands for gay marriage seems unlikely.

In the meantime, civil unions are the more likely outcome as momentum behind them gathered pace. In early 2014, the Senate approved, with a 28-to-6 vote, a motion to begin the debate on AVP (*La Nación*, January 7, 2014). During discussions at committee level, activists

---

[87] For example, regarding the "political process," in 2011, 48 percent of Chileans expressed being worried, 43 percent angry, and 39 percent incensed (*La Nación*, December 30, 2011).

managed to convince senators to undertake important modifications, such as granting the AVP civil rather than contractual status. After intense pressure from activists, led by Jiménez and Larraín Stieb, on September 5, 2014, the Senate's Justice Committee voted the bill favorably, paving the way for a vote on the Senate floor (*La Tercera*, September 5, 2014).

Conclusion: Gay Marriage in
Latin America and Beyond

Few would have predicted, scarcely fifteen years ago, that gay marriage would become one of the defining social issues of our time. In the United States, gay marriage has become central to national conversations as gay rights have increasingly been discussed in popular culture, sports, and at dinner tables. The push for the expansion of gay marriage has taken on unprecedented import, and it is not a stretch to suggest that it resembles the struggle for women's suffrage that culminated with the passage of the Nineteenth Amendment in 1920, and the one for racial equality that took a historic step forward with the enactment of the Civil Rights Act fifty years ago. In all three cases, arguments for the expansion of new rights met intense resistance from conservative forces until public opinion changed, a tipping point was reached, and a sense of being on the wrong side of history crystallized among political leaders. President Barack Obama's (2008–16) public endorsement of gay marriage in 2012 may well have marked that inflection point on gay rights in the United States. His change of heart, after a personal "evolution," occurred within a context of larger changes that saw, for the first time, a majority of Americans become supportive of gay marriage and momentum build behind the equality movement: by mid-2014, close to 59 percent of Americans approved of gay marriage; the Defense of Marriage Act (DOMA) was struck down by the Supreme Court; gay marriage was legal in twenty-one states; thirteen state bans were ruled unconstitutional; and all the remaining ones were challenged in court. A ruling by the Supreme Court with universal precedent looks increasingly likely.

These changes are, of course, not limited to the United States. In Europe, following the first three pioneers (The Netherlands, Spain, and

Belgium), eight countries extended the right to marry to their gay and lesbian citizens between 2009 and 2014, and bills were introduced to the parliaments of five others. While in some cases resistance has been strong, and even violent (France), support for gay marriage, while varied, continues to increase in most Western European countries (Pew Research Center 2013).

Yet, the adoption of gay marriage in North America and Western Europe has occurred alongside other regional trends characterized by the retrenchment of gay rights elsewhere. Highlighting the divide between Western and Eastern Europe on the issue, in 2013 voters in Croatia approved a constitutional amendment that defines marriage as one between a man and a woman; the Polish parliament rejected three bills that would have allowed for civil unions; and activists were attacked violently in the capitals of Eastern European and Balkan countries as they attempted to participate in pride parades. Elsewhere in the same year, India's Supreme Court overturned a previous ruling by Delhi's High Court that had decriminalized same-sex relations by striking down provisions of its Penal Code. A month later, in January 2014, Nigeria passed legislation banning same-sex marriage and imposed a fourteen-year jail term for same-sex relations, and Uganda, despite strong international opposition, followed suit with the enactment of a similar antigay law a month later.[1] A comparable bill was introduced to Ethiopia's parliament the following month. These developments took place after an escalation to the persecution of gays in several African countries in previous years (*The Washington Post*, February 24, 2014). The legislation that caught most of the attention was, of course, Russia's antigay propaganda law, which placed the issue of gay rights at center stage in the lead up to the 2014 Sochi Winter Olympic Games. Intraregional differences have not only created frictions in international relations, as northern countries publicly reprimand eastern and southern ones for the retrenchment of gay rights (*The New York Times*, March 2, 2014), but they highlight a clear global divide on gay rights.

It is within this global context of crosscurrents, which *The Economist* has labeled the world's "gay divide" (October 11–17, 2014), that Latin America, to the surprise of many, has come to the forefront of the

---

[1] The law was overturned by Uganda's Constitutional Court on August 1, 2014 (*The Globe and Mail*, August 2, 2014). However, the ruling was not based on constitutional grounds but rather on a technicality: lack of quorum in parliament when it was voted. The reintroduction of the bill therefore remains a possibility.

expansion of gay rights. A region often described as "devoutly Catholic" and *machista* has seen, over a relatively short period of time, an unprecedented expansion of sexual rights. Given the region's perceived political culture, Latin America does not appear, at first glance, to be a propitious place in which these changes could transpire. But transpire they have: from the enactment of the world's most advanced gender identity law (Argentina) to the enshrining of constitutional provisions that protect citizens from discrimination based on sexual orientation (Ecuador, Mexico, and Bolivia), several countries in the region have reformed legal frameworks and have extended rights to sexual and gender minorities. One of the areas in the region's "gay-rights revolution" (Encarnación 2011) is gay marriage. In several jurisdictions of the region – following fierce debates that have seen the collision between historically dominant views on the ethics of sexuality and demands for the expansion of sexual rights – the right to marry has been extended to citizens regardless of gender or sexual orientation. These changes have placed Latin America at the forefront of sexual rights in the Global South, and, indeed, the world. Nonetheless, as I highlighted in the introduction to this book, same-sex relationship recognition has varied widely across the region: while some countries have extended marital rights to same-sex couples (Argentina, Uruguay, and Mexico), most have not, and yet others have enacted constitutional reforms that explicitly ban gay marriage (Honduras and the Dominican Republic). In terms of gay rights, then, Latin America is hardly homogeneous.

In this volume I set out to explore these developments in an attempt to explain cross-national variance in gay marriage recognition. The central research question that guided this book is: What explains that gay marriage has been extended in some Latin American countries and not others? To answer it I selected three cases that exhibit variance in gay marriage expansion while sharing important general similarities, such as levels of economic and human development, industrialization, education, and urbanization: Argentina, Chile, and Mexico. In this conclusion I review the main findings of this book and explore their practical and theoretical implications.

Restating the Argument

Based on extensive research, I have argued that three main factors explain policy stasis and change in gay marriage recognition in Argentina, Chile, and Mexico. *The first one is the ability and willingness of activists to form coalitions and networks with a variety of state and nonstate actors in their push for policy change.* Gay and lesbian activism has been central to gay marriage recognition in the countries that have seen policy change. Argentina and Mexico have the region's oldest gay movements, and it is no coincidence that they are the two countries in which gay marriage was first approved. In the two cases, gay and lesbian activists began organizing in the late 1960s and early 1970s to demand a change in the regulation of sexuality. Their early struggles were important in gaining public space, acquiring effective discursive tools, and developing political strategies that allowed activists to achieve concrete early policy objectives. They thus launched policy trajectories on which they subsequently built to pursue further rights. The same has not been the case for Chile. Unlike Argentina and Mexico, Chile experienced some gay mobilization in the early 1990s, but, largely as a result of internal divisions, the movement weakened considerably and activists were unable to force social debates on homosexuality until the early 2000s.

Nevertheless, activism is not, on its own, a factor behind policy change. Policy change has been partly the result of effective pressure applied on policy makers to recognize gay marriage by networks composed of state and nonstate actors. Gay marriage was approved in the two cases in which gay and lesbian activists were able *and* willing to weave coalitions of like-minded state and nonstate actors in the pursuit of their policy objectives. In both Argentina and Mexico activists have formed relationships with multiple actors with whom they share ideological affinities, actors that joined their push for gay marriage. In the case of nonstate actors, alliances with intellectuals and academics, women's organizations and human rights groups appear to have been of particular significance. In both cases, activists built these relations over longer policy trajectories than in Chile. In the last case, partly as a result of the weakness of mobilization, and of the masculinist position adopted by the leading activists, networks have been much smaller, and weaker. State allies have been important members of these networks. Close collaboration between activists and state actors, also over periods of time, contributed to the formation of relationships that helped in the pursuit of policy change. Allied state actors appear to have been central in applying pressure on other policy makers to support policy change. The analysis of the Argentine and Mexican experiences shows that these state allies were, for the most part, women. They are the unsung heroines of the story.

The second factor is the access to the policy-making process these networks had, which was conditioned by a country's institutional features. State institutions are also important to explain policy variance in gay marriage recognition across the three cases analyzed in this book. Activism must be placed within its structural context. Institutions matter. The evidence I present in this book suggests that a country's institutional features condition the type of access to the policy process that proponents and opponents of gay and lesbian rights have. Policy change has transpired in the two countries in which political institutions allow access to proponents of gay and lesbian rights and in which opponents do not have formal or informal veto power to block activists' demands. The regulation of family law and institutional design determine the arena on which activists and their allies concentrate their efforts to bring about policy change. In Argentina and Chile, civil codes, which regulate marriage, are administered by national governments, while in Mexico marriages are regulated by the states. In the first two cases, activists and their allies have had to pursue policy change on gay marriage at the national level whereas in Mexico they have had to do so at the subnational level. When the regulation of marriages is decentralized and administered by subnational governments, it offers activists multiple policy venues to push for change. As we saw, however, given that gay activism has been concentrated in Mexico City, the push for change has mostly been pursued in the capital. More important than the type of institutional design, unitary versus federal system, is the *type* of federalism that characterizes a country that shapes policy venues. While Argentina also possesses a federal system, policy reform has had to be undertaken at the national level.

While institutional design determines the policy venues activists and their allies must enter to demand policy change, access to the policy process is shaped by an additional institutional feature: political party systems. Political parties condition the access that proponents and opponents have to the policy process. Policy change has occurred in countries in which the political party system allows for the representation of the interests of pro-gay marriage networks into the policy-making process. The peculiarities of the Chilean posttransition political system provide an overrepresentation of socially conservative parties in both the executive and the legislative branches. Center-left parties, and smaller socially progressive ones, have been forced to govern in a coalition with the socially conservative Christian Democrats (*Partido Demócrata Cristiano*, DC). Given the close links members of the Christian Democratic Party have with the Catholic Church hierarchy, opposition to the advancement of gay and lesbian rights has had a direct entry point into the policy-making process, which amounts to an informal veto. Support for policy reform on gay and lesbian rights from socially liberal members from other parties within the coalition has been suppressed and attempts at recognizing gay marriage blocked. Access to the policy process is conditioned differently in Argentina and Mexico. In Argentina, where there does not exist a confessional party, access by both proponents and opponents of gay marriage was undertaken through various political parties and individual legislators. The absence of a confessional party means that socially conservative actors do not count on a direct channel into the policy process. In Mexico, opposition to gay marriage is articulated through the confessional National Action Party (PAN), which represents the interests of socially conservative groups, especially the Catholic Church. However, because gay marriage reform has to be undertaken at the subnational level given the country's type of federalism, PAN can only block reform when it forms government at the state level, or when it forms an alliance with socially conservative party members from the Institutional Revolutionary Party.

The third factor is the alignment of collective action frames with master frames that facilitated the advancement of demands for gay marriage expansion. It refers to the ability of activists and their allies to frame their demands in a manner that resonates with larger social debates. Frame alignment played a role in policy change. In the two cases in which gay marriage was approved, network members strategically framed their demands as an issue of human rights and equality and as part of much broader discussions over citizenship and democracy. The collective action frames were intended to resonate with national debates regarding the country's democratization process, which had developed master frames that contained human rights as important parts of democracy. In the two cases in which gay marriage was approved, Argentina and Mexico City, the governments of Cristina Fernández de Kirchner and Marcelo Ebrard deepened the importance of these frames by emphasizing human rights as part of their political priorities. The similarities are rather salient. The development of these master frames is linked to the type of transition to democracy that has taken place in both countries. In both Argentina and Mexico, democratization has been characterized by higher social mobilization and by a greater and more sustained political contestation.

The same has not been the case in Chile. The type of transition to democracy the country underwent conditioned political debates. The return to civilian rule in 1990 saw a significant decline of social mobilization and the emergence of a consensual type of politics that limited significantly discussions on the terms of citizenship and democracy. In Chile a master frame that would facilitate demands for a deepening of democratic citizenship did not appear to begin to emerge until the early 2010s.

Implications

Public Policy, Social Movements, and Networks

These findings contribute to debates in a number of literatures in public policy, comparative politics, and social movements. In terms of public policy, my analysis underscores the importance of taking a historical approach in the study of policy making. Frequently, policy scholars tend to take snapshots of policy processes that can mask the complexities that are at play among the various policy actors involved. Comparativists looking at public policy at times isolate elements in ways that do not take into account the complex histories of the various countries compared. This appears to be especially important when the policy under study is likely to be influenced by nonstate actors, such as moral policy reform. Internal group dynamics, the relationship nonstate actors develop with state actors, and the articulation of the strategies and tactics that activists and their allies deploy to influence policy take shape over time. As I have shown, the fight for same-sex relation recognition in Argentina and Mexico is not new: it is but one policy objective along a much longer policy trajectory that has characterized the push for the expansion of gay rights in both countries. An appreciation of such policy trajectories appears to be crucial to understanding the manner in which nonstate actors interact among themselves and vis-à-vis the state in the pursuit of consequent policy goals.

The findings also have implications for debates regarding the relationship between public policy and policy networks. Work on public policy has long identified the role policy networks play in the policy process, but much less attention has been paid to the role that social movements play in the formation of these networks and in the shaping of policy more generally. Indeed, the link between social movements and public policy making has historically been ignored by political scientists beyond their ability to place certain issues on the policy agenda (Meyer 2005). It has been argued that, while they may matter, the measure of their impact is too abstract to be captured (Johnson 2008). It has also been argued, specifically on gay marriage reform, that it is difficult to disentangle the effects of social mobilization in light of other mitigating factors (Pettinicchio 2012), such as the impact of religious communities (Kollman 2007). These apparent obstacles can be overcome, as I have demonstrated, by opening the black box of the policy process and retrieving data directly from policy makers on the factors behind policy change. Such data collection is evidently challenging for it requires the painstaking work necessary to carry out numerous in-depth personal interviews with policy actors. But it is not impossible. It requires a careful study of the various attempts at bringing about legislative reform, the identification of the main actors behind policy change, and the collection of data on the process from them.

The availability of sympathetic state actors is crucial for the formation of the networks I have identified in this study. As the cases of Argentina and Mexico demonstrate, close working relationships between activists and their allies within the state, both in the executive and legislative branches of government, are key in bringing about policy change. Such finding conforms with a growing body of literature that points to the central role state allies play in the expansion of gay and lesbian rights (Andersen 2005; Marsiaj 2012; Pettinicchio 2012; Rayside 2008; Tremblay, Paternotte, and Johnson 2011). Links between activists and state allies appear in turn to have transformed broader relationships between movements and the state from confrontation to collaboration, a phenomenon that has also been identified in work that has explored the relationship between gay and lesbian movements and the state in several countries, both industrialized and developing (Tremblay, Paternotte, and Johnson 2011).

Finally, this book underscores the importance of agency and social movements in policy reform. According to David Pettenicchio, in a recent review of the research on same-sex policies, it is difficult to argue that the presence of "gay communities" and social movements explains variation in Western countries "because, by and large, all countries in the West saw the rise of 'new social movements' and the growth of identity politics" (2012, 540–1). It is true that the mere presence of gay activism is not enough to explain policy change: as we have seen, Chile has had gay activism for a while, yet no change has occurred. Presence is not enough, however. Rather, it is about the type of activism. As this book shows, policy reform is the result of the ability and *willingness* of activists to form coalitions with other groups, and establish relationships with state actors to push for policy change. The type of activism; the ability and willingness of activists to work with other state and nonstate actors; and the development of efficient strategies and discursive tools are more important than mere presence.

Institutions

My analysis also has implications for several debates on institutions in comparative politics. The first one regards the extent to which institutional design influences variance in policy outcomes. Work on federalism and moral policy reform has shown that decentralized, federal systems provide activists with a "federalism advantage," which allows for "venue shopping" to pursue policy goals (Bashevkin 1998; Chappell 2002). Some of this work has begun to show that federal systems may be more open to policy change that trickles up to the national level. These phenomena have also been identified in gay rights reform: some scholars have found that federalism is more favorable to social movement demands as it offers a number of different access points (Paternotte 2008; Smith 2008). This contrasts with unitary systems that offer few access points to civil society groups (Kollman and Waites 2012). However, research has also found that federal systems offer multiple veto points to block progressive reform, both in gender policy (Immergut 1992) and gay rights policy (Bernstein 2012). Other work suggests that too many policy sites can overwhelm social movements, weakening their reform capacity (Haussman 2005).

The comparison among Argentina, Mexico, and Chile suggests that federalism can have an effect on social movement behavior. There is no question that the decentralization in both Argentina and Mexico during the 1990s, which devolved significant policy-making authority to Mexico City and Buenos Aires, offered activists important policy windows to push for reform. Their interaction with municipal policy makers provided them with a great practice ground to hone strategies and policy frames, on which they subsequently relied to push for gay marriage. However, as I have shown, there must first be activism in order for these policy windows to be used. Chile's gay and lesbian movement did not strengthen until the mid-2000s, and, as it did, activists began to push for policy reform in areas such as antidiscrimination policy at the local level. There is then more than a difference between federal and unitary systems. The point here is that federalism can offer multiple policy windows, but there must first be activists willing to attempt to jump through them.

The extent to which federalism shapes policy making is necessarily linked to the jurisdictional delineation of policy prerogatives, which is frequently policy specific. While, for example, municipalities in both unitary and federal systems generally have the authority to pursue some kind of antidiscrimination initiative, the same does not apply for other areas, such as family law, which includes gay marriage. The role federalism plays in gay marriage reform depends on what level of government is legally in charge of the administration of marriage. The most obvious comparison here is the United States and Canada. As Miriam Smith suggests (2008), differences in the type of federalism between the two countries largely explain the fact that in Canada gay marriage has been approved nationally while in the United States struggles have unfolded at the state level. The difference between the Argentine and Mexican cases speaks directly to Smith's findings: in all four cases, policy reform has been shaped by the type of federalism.

Nevertheless, federalism must not be overstated as it interacts with other institutional factors. Indeed, work on moral policy reform has found that the vertical distribution of powers does not on its own explain variance in policy outcomes. For example, Susan Franceschet and Jennifer Piscopo find, by looking at women's reproductive rights, that decentralization has devolved policy-making power in both unitary and federal systems (Argentina and Chile) allowing for certain policy-making autonomy, but, while they also find that federalism explains subnational variation in policy outcomes, such variation is related to political party dynamics, and specifically to the centralization of political parties (2013). Debora Lopreite also identifies the interplay between institutional design and party politics. Comparing policy variance on reproductive rights in Argentina and Mexico, Lopreite's research shows that, while federal arrangements define the arenas in which advocates challenge governments, the content and variation of outcomes are related to women's positions on abortion and contraception, which are in turn shaped by party affiliation and ideology (2014).

Party politics also matter for gay marriage reform: the analysis and data I have presented in this book suggest that, in addition to federalism, the party system is an institutional feature that explains policy variance across the cases for it conditions the type of access policy actors have to the process. These findings have implications for debates over the role leftist parties play in promoting moral policy reform (Kittleson 2006; Manzur 2002). In the case of Latin America, Mala Htun and Timothy Power have found, for example, that leftist parties are more likely to promote women's rights, even more so than female legislators (2006). The role of leftist parties in moral policy reform is of particular importance in Latin American given the region's move to the Left over the last fifteen years, the so-called pink tide (Cameron and Hershberg 2009; Weyland, Madrid, and Hunter 2010). Nonetheless, while the presence of social democratic parties is important for gay marriage recognition, it is not sufficient. As Shawn Schulenberg demonstrates (2012), the positions of leftist parties on gay marriage vary significantly across Latin America, and while some have supported some negative sexual rights, most have not supported gay marriage. To my knowledge, the only major leftist party that has openly supported gay marriage in Latin America has been Michelle Bachelet's Socialist Party during the 2014 presidential election. And it remains to be seen, given the particularities of Chile's consensual politics (which appear to have been restored during Bachelet's second term), whether that will be enough to allow for policy reform. Leftist parties seem to be more sympathetic to the advancement of gay rights. As David Paternotte, Manon Tremblay, and Carol Johnson suggest, leftist parties are more inclined to support lesbian and gay demands, but that support is not automatic: it is "rather the result of talks between activists and party officials" (2012, 220). The implications are twofold. First, sympathy for the advancement of negative rights does not always translate into open support for gay marriage; and, second, pressure from actors belonging to networks is crucial. In both Argentina and Mexico, Fernández de Kirchner's and Ebrard's sympathy had to be turned into action by activists and allies.

Another implication for debates on institutions regards executive-legislative relations and, in particular, the role the legislative plays in policy making. A generation of political scientists was influenced by the idea that posttransition Latin American legislatures matter little because they essentially function as rubber-stamping institutions that acquiesce willingly to the policy will of executives. That notion was best captured by the concept of "delegative democracy" elaborated by Guillermo O'Donnell in the early 1990s (1991). We now know that, in some cases, it simply is not true. While presidents are undoubtedly the most important policy actors in many countries of the region, especially in some policy areas, such as security (Díez 2012), we also know that parliaments are important in many others. As mentioned in Chapter 4, Ernesto Calvo, in the most exhaustive work on the Argentine Congress (the very institution from which O'Donnell drew inspiration to develop that idea), debunks the long-established myth that Argentina's Congress is weak by showing that, from 1983 to 2007: Congress rejected 41 percent of bills submitted by the Executive; it modified a third of all bills submitted; and

58 percent of the bills approved by Congress emanated from the legislature (2014). Even in systems in which the Executive has strong *de jure* powers, legislatures play important roles. In posttransitional Chile – often claimed as having the strongest presidentialist system in the democratic world – posttransition presidents have consistently consulted and negotiated with legislators in the making of policy, including the all-important budget (Siavelis 2014). Legislatures matter and the comparison I present in this book confirms that, at least in the gay rights area, they particularly do so: in all three cases legislative bodies were the primary sites of struggle in the push for the expansion of rights. Activists and their allies have also applied pressure on executives and judiciaries to bring about policy reform, but their main targets were legislators. How they matter depends on other institutional dynamics, and in some cases they do so in different ways. In both Argentina and Mexico, activists used legislatures to build support for policy change, and subsequently forced the Executive to follow suit. In the case of Chile, given its consensual style of policy making, which involves constant negotiation with Congress, activists have been unable to push for reform given opposition in the legislature. Indeed, while Michelle Bachelet included gay marriage in her 2013 electoral program, and regardless of the sincerity of her commitment to it, dynamics in Congress, and particularly the ability of activists and allies to build support, will likely determine whether gay marriage will be achieved. Because moral policy reform rarely figures as a priority for governments, legislatures seem to play a particularly important role. It is perhaps time to discard the stylized notion that Latin American parliaments are weak and provide some nuance to the discussion by making it policy specific.

The findings I have presented also have implications for debates regarding the judiciary and the rule of law. Students of Latin America have also been influenced by the idea that, in the region of the "unrule of law" (O'Donnell 1998), and with the usual exceptions of Uruguay, Chile, and Costa Rica, legal and justice systems are weak, ineffectual, corrupt, and systematically responsible for grave injustices. That courts have not been able to reverse the region's history of injustice and gross inequalities is true, as is the fact that, compared to established democracies, Latin American courts are weak. However, courts have become more effective and consequential, and laws matter more now. Indeed, the region has begun a process of judicialization of politics in general, and policy making in particular, which "has provided actors with an efficient instrument to advance and protect particularistic demands" and that is characterized by court decisions that are having "an effect on specific public policies by changing the distribution of goods and forcing the consideration of new topics, such as health, gender and the environment" (Smulovitz 2012, 106). Judicialization has increased rights' consciousness, and that has allowed for new understandings of citizenship and constitutions (Seider, Schjolden, and Angell 2005). These changes have included the struggle for gay rights. As we have seen, gay and lesbian activists have relied on courts to push for reform.

Courts matter, although the manner in which they do varies. While legislatures are the main site of struggle, judiciaries have played important, supportive roles. In the case of Argentina, the judicialization of gay rights can be traced back decades, as activists have relied on casework to advance a variety of claims. In the case of gay marriage, activists' challenges based on the unconstitutionality of the country's civil code contributed to the placement of their policy objective on the legislative agenda. In the case of Mexico, the challenge to the constitutionality of the gay marriage reform approved by Mexico City had the effect of extending the right to marriage to the entire territory: as may be recalled, the Supreme Court ruled that marriages contracted in Mexico City must be recognized in all other states. Moreover, painstaking casework, based on the logic of that ruling, has allowed for an expansion of gay marriage to couples in other states and, similarly to what has occurred in the United States, the likelihood of having the Supreme Court hand down a ruling with universal precedent has increased. Chile, again, seems to be the exception: given the generalized (and justified) perception among gay activists that Chile's judiciary is socially conservative (King 2013), judicialization has not taken place.

Finally, my analysis underlines the importance of informal institutions. Scholars of Latin America, and the Global South more broadly, have increasingly paid attention to the role institutions play in politics and policy making in a more systematic way (Franceschet and Díez 2012; Helmke and Gretchen 2005; MacLean 2010). It is simply impossible to understand policy stasis in Chile in the comparison of the three cases I have presented without looking at the informal discussions and negotiations that take place within the governing coalition, between the Executive and the legislative, and between state actors and powerful social groups in the making of policy. These negotiations are undergirded by a variety of informal institutions. While work on Chile has identified some of them, such as the *cuoteo* (Siavelis 2014), my analysis has identified others, such as the *grupo político*. The country's consensual style of making policy is of particular relevance in the area of moral policy reform given the opposition that exists among socially conservative actors who have a de facto veto point: consensual dynamics forestall the discussion of contentious social issues. Indeed, consensus is one of the reasons why gay marriage has not been enacted in Chile and will likely not be in the foreseeable future should consensual politics continue to shape policy making, as seems to be the case under Bachelet's second administration.

Framing

This book also contributes to numerous studies that have underlined the importance of the development of collective action frames by gay and lesbian activists to achieve their policy objectives (Andersen 2005; Díez 2011, 2013; Mucciaroni 2008), whether they be legal, cultural, or scientific in nature. They also underline the potential opportunities that processes of democratization can offer for the advancement of gay and lesbian rights. The Argentine and Mexican cases are similar to the South African experience, in which democratization was also characterized by the emergence of a master frame of equality and nondiscrimination that was seized by gay activists to press for reform. Demands for human rights could simply not be denied (Croucher 2011). That largely explains why South Africa's 1994 constitution was the first in the world to prohibit discrimination on sexual orientation, and that the country became the first in the Global South to recognize gay marriage. Political transitions can provide opportunities. But frames are obviously context specific. In the United States, for example, Jo Becker's detailed account of the strategies used by activists in the Equality Movement in the challenges to the constitutionality of California's Proposition 8 and subsequently to DOMA shows the importance of frames in convincing policy actors (2014). In the U.S. case, activists and allies relied on frames that they knew would resonate, frames based on ideas of family, love, and equality. Understanding the broader politics and debates must be taken into account.

Beyond the Three Cases

A question this book may expect to generate regards the applicability of the factors that I have identified here to other cases in Latin America. Because policy change in gay marriage is primarily induced by activists and their allies, the transferability of the model I have developed necessarily depends on whether a country possesses a strong gay and lesbian movement and on the ability and willingness of activists to forge the necessary networks to bring about reform. The two logical cases would be Brazil and Colombia, cases that have exhibited visible gay and lesbian mobilization.

While Brazil has one of the oldest gay movements in the Americas, gay activism has not adopted gay marriage as a policy priority. Brazilian gay activism has focused primarily on combating violence perpetrated against sexual minorities and not gay marriage, and even though they have sought same-sex relationship recognition, they have favored civil unions (Schulenberg 2010). At the risk of stating the obvious, activists would first need to decide to adopt gay marriage as a priority and devote the necessary resources in the pursuit of reform in order for it to transpire. If one lesson is to be drawn from this book it is that rights are conquered, not willingly extended. Brazil is also a federal state, but unlike Mexico, and like Argentina, marriage is administered by federal law, which means that the pursuit for reform on gay marriage must be attempted federally. The Mexican experience is therefore not replicable, and the Argentine one is unlikely: in contrast to Argentina, the Brazilian Congress presents formidable obstacles for civil society actors to advance legislation that is not part of the Executive's priorities, which of course includes moral policy. Given the fractured nature of its party system, the Executive requires the support of a variety of smaller parties and factions to push legislation through the legislature. Conservative groupings representing Brazil's large socially conservative Evangelical community are as a result able to wield significant influence, which amounts to a veto power over moral policy reform. The Brazilian case thus resembles the Chilean one on some level. Nothing illustrates this better than President Dilma Rousseff's (2011–) need to meet with religious leaders during the runoff to her presidential election in late 2010. After that meeting she was forced to sign an open letter in which she promised to respect the family and committed herself not to pursue reform in the moral policy area (Marsiaj 2013).

Because the federal legislature presents formidable obstacles, Brazilian activists have fought for same-sex relationship recognition (civil unions) and the expansion of benefits at the subnational level and through the judiciary. Their efforts culminated in two historic rulings: in May 2011, the country's Supreme Federal Court ruled that all civil unions must be recognized throughout the country; and on May 2013 the National Council of Justice ordered all notary publics to register same-sex civil unions as marriages upon request. The benefits of gay marriage were therefore expanded universally. Given that Brazilian activists have preferred civil unions over marriage, and that the ruling essentially extends gay marriage rights to same-sex couples, the likelihood of gay marriage transpiring in Brazil, through a reform of the civil code, is rather low.

The factors that I have identified do not seem to apply to Colombia either. While Colombian gay activism does not possess the historical strength that it does in Argentina or Brazil, it has assumed increased public visibility over the last ten years (Serrano 2011). *Colombia Diversa* (Diverse Colombia) is the leading gay rights organization fighting for the expansion of gay rights. Within a larger context of the judicialization of minority and cultural rights, facilitated by the adoption of a new Constitution promulgated in 1991 (colloquially known as the Human Rights Constitution), and as a result of their inability to promote reform through the Colombian Congress,[2] *Diversa* opted early on to pursue the expansion of rights through litigation. Soon after its formation, it launched numerous challenges before the Constitutional Court that sought to wrest a variety of socioeconomic rights for same-sex couples, many of which have been successful (Azuero and Albarracín 2009). The pursuit of gay marriage has unfolded along this judicial route. *Diversa* presented a constitutional challenge to the civil code's definition of marriage before the Court in 2010. The Court ruled that same-sex couples constituted a family. It also mandated Congress to legislate on the matter within two years (by June 2013). Two gay marriage bills and two civil-union bills were introduced over the next several months, but stalled at the committee level. Under the leadership of Senator Armando Benedetti (Social Party of National Unity), a bill proposing the legalization of gay marriage, through a change to the civil code, was introduced in October 2012. After a favorable vote at the committee level in late 2012, the bill made it to the Senate floor and was voted on in April 2013. However, without the support from President Juan Manuel Santos (2010–) and with strong opposition from the Catholic Church, the bill was defeated on the floor fifty-one votes to seventeen (*El Tiempo*, August 24, 2013). Asked what led to the defeat, Benedetti responded:

I go by the words from Interior Minister Fernando Carrillo, in which he explicitly and tactically said that they do not want to lose the Church's support or to

---

[2] The first gay marriage bill was introduced in 2001 by Senator Piedad Córdoba, but upon a favorable vote at the committee level, the backlash from Conservative senators and the Catholic Church hierarchy was fast and furious, which killed the bill (*El Tiempo*, November 12, 2002). Subsequent attempts were made as progressive legislators reintroduced other versions of the bill. However, lack of support from President Alvaro Uribe (2002–10) and pressure from the Catholic Church hierarchy stalled those efforts (Lemaître 2009).

upset it. The attitude is such that he did not even go to Congress on Wednesday or today [day of the vote]. It is not a priority.[3]

The Colombian Congress's failure to legislate on the matter has left the legal status of gay marriage in Colombia in a state of uncertainty. Two years after the Court's ruling, civil registries began to recognize civil unions, even in light of a backlash from the attorney general who applied pressure to stall them. However, given the legal uncertainty of these relationships, *Diversa* and other activists, academics, and lawyers decided to continue to push for the legal, and a literal, recognition of gay marriage. Their strategies proved fruitful: starting on September 20, 2013, several lower-level judges began to rule in favor of recognizing marriages performed for same-sex couples (see *El Espectador*, September 28, 2013, November 27, 2013). Some of these rulings have been overturned by other courts, however.

These developments are likely to push the issue back up to the Constitutional Court, which, given both its previous recognition that same-sex couples form a family and Congress's failure to legislate on the matter, could hand down a ruling with universal precedent. The case of Colombia is then one of a comparatively weaker movement that has confronted similar obstacles to bring about reform in Congress (as Brazil and Chile), and in which, as a result, activists have been forced to pursue the judicial road (Brazil) given that it offers possibilities (unlike Chile). The result has thus far been one of legal uncertainty.

The last case that warrants mention is Uruguay.[4] It is the first country in Latin American to have approved civil unions at the national level, and it legalized gay marriage in 2013 after a strong push by activists led by the leading gay rights organization, *Ovejas Negras* (Black Sheep). Because in this case the country has approved gay marriage, the reader is logically expected to question the extent to which the factors that I have identified in Argentina and Mexico were at play in Uruguay. Based on the civil union experience and interviews with the leading actors (admittedly prior to the enactment of gay marriage), it would appear that elements of the identified factors could have been at play. First, the Uruguayan gay and lesbian movement has not had the historic public visibility of its Argentine and Mexican counterparts. However, since its foundation in 2004 *Ovejas Negras* has assumed a very important public presence and has forced

[3] *Semana*, April 14, 2013.
[4] The discussion of Uruguay draws from personal interviews held in Montevideo from October 19 to November 10, 2010, with five activists and seven legislators.

national discussions on gay rights. According to Deputy Washington Abdala, the founding of the organization marked a watershed moment in the discussions of gay rights (*un antes y un después*) in society and especially within the political class.[5] But beyond their public presence, they played an important role in bringing about civil unions and in the passing of a gender identity law in 2009. According to Senator Margarita Percovich, the main legislator behind civil-union reform: "People usually identify me with the process [to bring about reform], but the organization [*colectivo*] *Ovejas Negras* was instrumental in bringing it about, and especially in pushing society and politicians forward."[6] Activism played a role in that reform, and it appears that it was crucial to the enactment of gay marriage (*The Guardian*, August 1, 2014).

Uruguayan activists appear to have acquired numerous allies in a remarkably short period of time. Part of the reason relates to the many relationships activists seem to have with multiple social actors given that they joined the cause of gay rights after having been militants in other movements, such as women's and labor. According to Valeria Rubino (an *Ovejas Negras* activist and Member of Congress during the passage of gay marriage), multiple militancy was important in gaining allies behind the push for civil unions.[7] Networks appear to have formed.[8] According to Diego Sempol, an academic and leading member of *Ovejas Negras*, alliance formation has been important to the success in the expansion of gay rights in Uruguay (2014). Nonetheless, both the strength that gay and lesbian activism has acquired over a short period of time and the extent and strength of networks they have formed requires further investigation.

Institutional access to the policy process by activists was available during the approval of civil unions and appears to have continued. In large part it has been the result of the assumption of power by the Broad Front (*Frente Amplio*) in the 2004 elections, which dislodged the historic rotation between the two main parties of Uruguayan politics: the National and Red parties. The Broad Front has held the presidency since then as well as a majority of seats in both chambers. The Broad Front, founded in the early 1970s, is a coalition of leftist parties that has strong links with grassroots social movements. Access to the policy process in

---

[5] Interview, Montevideo, October 29, 2010.
[6] Interview, Montevideo, October 25, 2010.
[7] Interview, Montevideo, October 22, 2010.
[8] Tellingly, the various activists interviewed frequently offered to share the personal phone numbers of Members of Congress and other state actors.

Congress (Uruguay has a unitary system) for gay and lesbian activists was greatly facilitated by the election of a political coalition that has been sustained by progressive social movements.[9] Moreover, such access has not been obstructed by conservative social forces. In Uruguay, widely considered the most secular country in the Americas, the political representation of religious groups in Congress is minimal. Indeed, even within the main conservative party, the National Party, Members of Congress do not expect to obtain support by appealing to religious arguments and in fact fear that, given the country's deeply entrenched secularism, attempts at doing so may backfire.[10] The little opposition the gay marriage bill had in Congress is best illustrated by the final tally of yeas and nays: the Chamber of Deputies voted 81–6 in favor of the bill, and the Senate 23–8.

Finally, similar to their Argentine counterparts, Uruguayan activists have attempted to frame the push for gay rights in a manner resonant of broader social discussions. They in fact emulated the same arguments advanced by Argentine activists by referring to "equal marriage," using the slogan "the same names, with the same rights," and by arguing that it was a question of the deepening of democratic citizenship. Strategic framing was certainly in activists' minds: as Sempol stated, seven days after the Senate approved the gay marriage bill, "discourses framed around equality gain great traction in a secular society with a long tradition of civil rights expansion" (*El País*, April 9, 2013). However, the extent to which these arguments played a role in convincing policy makers to approve gay marriage needs further investigation, as does the role played by the other factors I have identified.

Gay Marriage and Citizenship: Closing the Circle

Gay and lesbian activists, the protagonists in this book, have pushed the boundaries of citizenship. They have advanced demands for the expansion of a variety of rights by forcing a redefinition of citizenship and a deepening of democratic governance. They have contributed to challenging the divide between the private and the public (first started by feminist theories and women's movements), challenged historically dominant heteronormative understandings of Latin American societies, and helped to expose the naturalness of sexual diversity in their demands for rights. In short, they have sexualized Latin American citizenship. Their struggles

[9] Interview, Mónica Xavier, Broad Front Senator 2005–10, Montevideo, October 29, 2010.
[10] Interview, Alvaro Lorenzo, National Party Deputy, Montevideo, November 3, 2010.

form part of a well-established lineage of attempts at redefining citizenship in the region after the return to democratic rule. Women's movements have gendered citizenship by exposing its patriarchal foundations and indigenous groups have challenged homogenizing propositions of Liberal understandings of citizenship by calling for pluriethnic and multicultural states. Latin Americans therefore appear to be at the forefront of pushing the boundaries of what citizenship means.

The sexualization of citizenship through the push for gay marriage in Latin America invites final reflections. Debates over the contents of citizenship are not confined to theory. Gay and lesbian activism in some Latin American countries is characterized by a very close relationship among activists, academics, and intellectuals. Conversations of what citizenship entails has been informed by theoretical debates and their implementation on the ground. But theorists' work has also been informed by activism. Theory has informed agency, and agency theorization. Gay and lesbian activists have benefited from the direct contribution Latin American theorists have made to the movement, and the theorization of Latin American intellectuals has been nurtured by praxis.

The criticisms leveled against gay marriage have been numerous, especially by Queer theorists. A dominant one, in Latin America and beyond, regards the desirability of setting gay marriage as a policy priority. Such debates can be informed by the stories I have presented in this book. To many activists and academics in Latin America, the push for gay marriage is not restricted to the particularistic socioeconomic benefits that marriage confers to same-sex couples: the struggle on its own is instrumental in forcing national discussions on homosexuality and has a pedagogical component. Fighting for gay marriage serves to debunk misconceptions, stereotypes, and falsehoods about homosexuality and parenting, and that process, in and of itself, builds citizenship. For many in Latin America the fight for gay marriage has been about the making of the subjects of rights.

It is also important to acknowledge that, at least in some Latin America countries, the push for gay marriage is but part of a gamut of demands being pursued. In Argentina, Chile, and Mexico, gay and lesbian organizations have pushed for gay marriage while pursuing negative rights. They have continued to push for more and stronger discrimination provisions, document the perpetration of hate crimes, and fight homophobia. The push for gay rights has not been confined to gay marriage. To some activists and intellectuals in Latin America, there does not exist a hierarchy of rights: all rights are worth pursuing and which ones a movement decides to prioritize at times depends on political junctures – it is often a strategic discussion. The case of Argentina is rather instructive. The struggle for gay marriage was joined by members of the larger sexual minority community who have adopted a larger approach to the push for rights. It explains why transgendered activists in Argentina joined the fight for gay marriage, and why gays and lesbians in turn joined the fight for gender identity two years later, which resulted in the enactment of the most advanced gender identity law in the world.[11]

The definition of democracy and citizenship has been contentious for millennia. In Latin America, gay and lesbian activists have contributed to the debate, challenging the terms of citizenship by sexualizing it through the fight for gay marriage. They have contributed to the practical and theoretical evolution of what citizenship and democracy in Latin American mean.

---

[11] Most advanced because it is the only one that completely demedicalizes and depathologizes transgenderism. The acquisition of a new gender has been reduced to a simple administrative procedure that does not require a legal or medical opinion. An estimated six thousand Argentines had accessed one of the most basic of rights by early 2014: the right to an identity.

Bibliography

Adam, Barry D. 2003. "The Defense of Marriage Act and American Exceptionalism: The 'Gay Marriage' Panic in the United States." *Journal of the History of Sexuality* 12: 259–76.

Aguayo Quezada, Sergio. 2010. *Vuelta en U: Guía para entender y activar la democracia estancada*. México, DF: Taurus.

Alberro, Solange. 1992. *Del gachupín al criollo: O cómo los españoles de México dejaron de serlo*. Mexico City: El Colegio de México.

Alonso, Paula. 2000. *Between Revolution and the Ballot Box: The Origins of the Argentine Radical Party in the 1890s*. Cambridge: Cambridge University Press.

Álvarez, Sonia. 1999. "Advocating Feminism: The Latin American Feminist Boom." *International Feminist Journal of Politics* 1, no. 2: 181–209.

Anaya Muñoz, Alejandro. 2009. "Transnational and Domestic Processes in the Definition of Human Rights Policies in Mexico." *Human Rights Quarterly* 31, no. 1: 35–58.

Andersen, Ellen Ann. 2005. *Out of the Closets and into the Courts: Legal Opportunity Structures and Gay Rights Litigation*. Ann Arbor: University of Michigan Press.

Andía, María G. 2013. "Legal Mobilization and the Road to Same-Sex Marriage in Argentina." In *Same-Sex Marriage in Latin America: Promise and Resistance*, ed. Jason Pierceson, Adriana Piatti-Crocker, and Shawn Schulenberg. Lanham, MD: Lexington Books, 131–50.

Angell, Alan. 1972. *Politics and the Labor Movement in Chile*. London: Oxford University Press.

Arditti, Rita. 1999. *Searching for Life*. Berkeley: University of California Press.

Arendt, Hannah. 1998. *The Human Condition*. Chicago: University of Chicago Press.

Azuero, Alejandra, and Mauricio Albarracín. 2009. *Activismo judicial y derechos de los LGBT en Colombia: sentencias emblemáticas*. Bogotá, D.C.: Instituto Lationamericano de Servicios Legales Alternativos.

Bachelet Jeria, Michelle. 2005. *Programa de gobierno 2006–2010, Michelle Bachelet, Estoy Contigo*. Santiago, Chile: Concertación de Partidos por la Democracia.

Ballina, Santiago. 2013. "The Sombrero Comes Out of the Closet: Gay Marriage in Mexico City and a Nation's Struggle for Identity." In *The Unacceptable*, ed. John Potts and John Scannell. Basingstoke, UK: Palgrave Macmillan, 80–102.

Bamforth, Nicholas. 1997. *Sexuality, Morals and Justice: A Theory of Lesbian and Gay Rights Law*. London: Cassell.

Banaszak, Lee A., Karen Beckwith, and Dieter Rucht, eds. 2003. *Women's Movements Facing the Reconfigured States*. Cambridge: Cambridge University Press.

Bao, Daniel. 1993. "Invertidos sexuales, tortilleras and maricas machos: The Construction of Homosexuality in Buenos Aires, Argentina, 1990–1950." *Journal of Homosexuality* 24, nos. 3–4: 183–219.

Bashevkin, Sylvia. 1998. *Women on the Defensive*. Chicago: University of Chicago Press.

Bazán, Osvaldo. 2010. *Historia de la homosexualidad en la Argentina*. Buenos Aires: Editorial Marea.

Becker, David, and Claudia Díaz Olavarrieta. 2013. "Decriminalization of Abortion in Mexico City: The Effects on Women's Reproductive Rights." *American Journal of Public Health* 103, no. 4: 585–9.

Becker, Jo. 2014. *Forcing the Spring: Inside the Fight for Marriage Equality*. New York: Penguin.

Beiner, Ronald. 1995. "Why Citizenship Constitutes a Theoretical Problem in the Last Decade of the Twentieth Century." In *Theorizing Citizenship*, ed. Ronald Beiner. Albany: State University of New York Press, 1–27.

Béland, Daniel. 2005. "Ideas and Social Policy: An Institutionalist Perspective." *Social Policy and Administration* 39, no. 1: 1–18.

Béland, Daniel, and Robert Henry Cox, eds. 2011. *Ideas and Politics in Social Science Research*. New York: Oxford University Press.

Bell, David, and Jon Binnie. 2000. *The Sexual Citizen: Queer Politics and Beyond*. Cambridge: Polity Press.

Bellucci, Maribel. 2010. *Orgullo: Carlos Jáuregui, Una Biografía Política*. Buenos Aires: Emecé.

Ben, Pablo. 2010. "Male Same-Sex Sexuality and the Argentine State, 1880–1930." In *The Politics of Sexuality in Latin America: A Reader on Lesbian, Gay, Bisexual and Transgender Rights*, ed. Javier Corrales and Mario Pecheny. Pittsburgh: University of Pittsburgh Press, 33–43.

Benhabib, Seyla. 1996. "Toward a Deliberative Model of Democratic Legitimacy." In *Democracy and Difference*, ed. Seyla Benhabib. Princeton, NJ: Princeton University Press, 67–94.

Bennassar, Bartolomé. 1979. *Le modèle sexuel: L'inquisition espagnole XVe–XIXe siècle*. Paris: Hachette.

Berlant, Lauren, and Michael Warner. 1998. "Sex in Public." *Critical Inquiry* 4, no. 2: 547–66.

Berlin, Isaiah. 1969. *Four Essays on Liberty*. Oxford: Oxford University Press.

Biblioteca del Congreso Nacional de Chile. 1999. *Historia de la ley No. 19.617.* Santiago, Chile: Congreso Nacional de Chile.

2012. *Historia de la Ley 20.609.* Santiago, Chile: Congreso Nacional de Chile.

Bimbi, Bruno. 2010. *Matrimonio igualitario. Intrigas, tensiones y secretos en el camino hacia la ley.* Buenos Aires: Planeta.

Bizberg, Ilán. 2010. "Una democracia vacía: Sociedad civil, movimientos sociales y democracia." In *Movimientos Sociales, Vol. VI, Los grandes problemas de México,* ed. Ilán Bizberg and Francisco Zapata. México, DF: El Colegio de México, 21–60.

Blancarte, Roberto. 2001. "Laicidad y secularización." *Estudios sociológicos* 19, no. 3: 843–55.

Blanco, José Joaquín. 1979. "Ojos que da pánico soñar." *Sábado,* March 17.

Blasius, Mark, ed. 2001. *Sexual Identities, Queer Politics.* Princeton, NJ: Princeton University Press.

Blofield, Merike. 2006. *The Politics of Moral Sin: Abortion and Divorce in Spain, Chile and Argentina.* New York: Routledge.

Boesten, Jelke. 2006. "Pushing Back the Boundaries: Social Policy, Domestic Violence and Women's Organizations in Peru." *Journal of Latin American Studies* 38, no. 2: 355–78.

Bonner, Michelle. 2007. *Sustaining Human Rights: Women and Argentine Human Rights Organizations.* University Park: Pennsylvania State University Press.

Borland, Elizabeth, and Barbara Sutton. 2007. "Quotidian Disruption and Women's Activism in Times of Crisis, Argentina 2002–2003." *Gender and Society* 21, no. 5: 700–22.

Boyer, Richard. 1995. *Lives of the Bigamists: Marriage, Family and Community in Colonial Mexico.* Albuquerque: University of New Mexico Press.

Bracamonte Allaín, Jorge. 1998. "Los nefandos placeres de la carne. La iglesia y el estado frente a la sodomía en la Nueva España 1721–1820." *Debate Feminista* 18 (October): 393–415.

Briones, Claudia, and Marcela Mendoza. 2003. "Urban Middle-Class Women's Responses to Political Crisis in Buenos Aires." The University of Memphis Center for Research on Women. Unpublished Manuscript.

Brown, Stephen. 2002. "'Con discriminación y represión no hay democracia': The lesbian and gay movement in Argentina." *Latin American Perspectives* 29, no. 2, 119–38.

Brown, Wendy. 1995. *States of Inquiry: Power and Freedom in Late Modernity.* Princeton, NJ: Princeton University Press.

Buckhart, Louise. 1997. "Mexica Women on the Home Front: Housework and Religion in Aztec Mexico." In *Indian Women of Early Mexico,* ed. Susan Schroeder, Stephanie Wood, and Robert Kaskett. Norman: University of Oklahoma Press, 25–43.

Calhoun, Cheshire. 2000. *Feminism, the Family and the Politics of the Closet: Lesbian and Gay Displacement.* Oxford: Oxford University Press.

Calvert, Susan, and Peter Calvert. 1989. *Argentina: Political Culture and Instability.* Pittsburgh: University of Pittsburgh Press.

Calvo, Ernesto. 2014. *Legislator Success in Fragmented Congresses in Argentina: Plurality Cartels, Minority Presidents, and Lawmaking.* New York: Cambridge University Press.

Calvo, Kerman. 2007. "Sacrifices That Pay: Polity Membership, Political Opportunities and the Recognition of Same-Sex Marriage in Spain." *South European Society and Politics* 12, no. 3: 295–314.

Cameron, Maxwell A., and Eric Hershberg, eds. 2010. *Latin America's Left Turns: Politics, Policies and Trajectories of Change.* Boulder, CO: Lynne Rienner as subseq.

Cardín, Alberto. 1989. *Guerreros, chamanes y trasvestis. Indicios de la homosexualidad en los exóticos.* Barcelona: Tusquets.

Carey, John. 2002. "Parties, Coalitions and the Chilean Congress in the 1990s." In *Legislative Politics in Latin America*, ed. Scott Morgenstern and Benito Nacif. New York: Cambridge University Press, 222–53.

Carey, John, and Matthew Shugart, eds. 1998. *Executive Decree Authority.* Cambridge: Cambridge University Press.

Carrasco, Rafael. 1985. *Inquisición y represión sexual en Valencia: Historia de los sodomitas, 1565–1785.* Barcelona: Laertes.

Carrier, Joseph M. 1995. *De los Otros: Intimacy and Homosexuality among Mexican Men.* New York: Columbia University Press.

Cavarozzi, Marcelo. 1992. "Patterns of Elite Negotiation and Confrontation in Argentina and Chile." In *Elites and Democratic Consolidation in Latin America and Southern Europe*, ed. John Higley and Richard Gunther. Cambridge: Cambridge University Press, 208–36.

Centeno, Miguel A., and Patricio Silva, eds. 1998. *The Politics of Expertise in Latin America.* New York: St. Martin's Press.

Chand, Vikram K. 2001. *Mexico's Political Awakening.* Notre Dame: University of Notre Dame Press.

Chappell, Louise. 2002. *Gendering Government.* Vancouver: University of British Columbia Press.

Clérico, Laura, and Martín Aldao. 2010. *Matrimonio Igualitario: Perspectivas sociales, políticas y jurídicas.* Buenos Aires: Eudeba.

Collins, Cath. 2009. "Human Rights Trials in Chile during and after the 'Pinochet Years.'" *The International Journal of Transitional Justice* 4, no. 1: 67–86.

Comunidad Homosexual Argentina (CHA). 1998. *Informe Anual Sobre Violaciones a los Derechos Humanos y Civiles en la Republica Argentina Basadas en la Orientación Sexual de las Personas y de las Personas que viven con VIH/SIDA.* Buenos Aires: Comunidad Homosexual Argentina.

2002. *Informe Anual 2002. Legislación – Represión Policial – Asesinatos – Denuncias y otros hechos relacionados con la Discriminación por Orientación Sexual e Identidad de Género.* Buenos Aires: Comunidad Homosexual Argentina.

Conrad, Ryan, ed. 2010. *Against Equality: Queer Critiques of Gay Marriage.* Oakland, CA: AK Press.

Contardo, Óscar. 2008. *Siútico: Arribismo, abajismo y vida social en Chile.* Santiago: Vergara.

2011. *Raro: Una historia gay de Chile.* Santiago: Planeta.

Corrales, Javier, and Mario Pecheny. 2010a. "Six Reasons Why Argentina Legalized Gay Marriage First." *Americas Quarterly.* http://www.americasquarterly .org/node/1753.

——— 2010b. "The Comparative Politics of Sexuality in Latin America." In *The Politics of Sexuality in Latin America: A Reader on Lesbian, Gay, Bisexual and Transgender Rights*, ed. Javier Corrales and Mario Pecheny. Pittsburgh: University of Pittsburgh Press, 1–30.

Corvino, John. 2005. "Homosexuality and the PIB Argument." *Ethics* 115: 501–34.

Cossman, Brenda. 2007. *Sexual Citizens: The Legal and Cultural Regulation of Sex and Belonging.* Stanford, CA: Stanford University Press.

Croucher, Sheila. 2011. "South Africa: Opportunities Seized in the Post-Apartheid Era." In *The Lesbian and Gay Movement and the State: Comparative Insights into a Transformed Relationship*, ed. Manon Tremblay, David Paternotte, and Carol Johnson. Surrey, UK: Ashgate, 153–66.

Dagnino, Evelina. 2003. "Citizenship in Latin America: An Introduction." *Latin American Perspectives* 30, no. 2: 211–25.

de la Dehesa, Rafael. 2010. *Queering the Public Sphere in Mexico and Brazil: Sexual Rights Movements in Emerging Democracies.* Durham, NC: Duke University Press.

De la Garza Talavera, Rafael. 2003. "Del nacionalismo al liberalismo: la transformación ideológica del Partido de la Revolución." In *Partido Revolucionario Institucional: Crisis y refundación*, ed. Francisco Reveles Vázquez. México, DF: Gernika, 315–46.

Delgado, Álvaro. 2003. *El Yunque: La ultraderecha en el poder.* México, DF: Plaza y Janés.

——— 2004. *El ejército de Dios: Nuevas revelaciones sobre la extrema derecha en México.* México, DF: Plaza y Janés.

Della Porta, Donatella, and Sidney Tarrow, eds. 2005. *Transnational Protest and Global Activism: People, Passions, and Power.* Lanham, MD, and Oxford: Rowman and Littlefield.

De Vylder, Stefan. *Allende's Chile: The Political Economy of the Rise and Fall of the Unidad Popular.* Cambridge: Cambridge University Press.

Díez, Jordi. 2006. *Political Change and Environmental Policymaking in Mexico.* New York: Routledge.

——— 2008a. "Conclusion." In *Global Environmental Challenges: Perspectives from the South*, ed. Jordi Díez and O. P. Dwivedi. Toronto: University of Toronto Press, 301–8.

——— 2008b. "Globalization and Environmental Challenges Confronting the South." In *Global Environmental Challenges: Perspectives from the South*, ed. Jordi Díez and O. P. Dwivedi. Toronto: University of Toronto Press, 11–42.

——— 2010. "The Importance of Policy Frames in Contentious Politics: Mexico's 2005 Anti-Homophobia Campaign." *Latin American Research Review* 41, no. 1: 33–54.

——— 2011a. "Argentina: A Queer Tango between the LG Movement and the State." In *The Lesbian and Gay Movement and the State: Comparative Insights into a Transformed Relationship*, ed. Carol Johnson, David Paternotte, and Manon Trembaly. Surrey, UK: Ashgate, 13–25.

2011b. "La trayectoria política del movimiento lésbico-gay en México." *Estudios Sociológicos* 29, no. 86: 687–712.

2012. "Presidentialism and Policy-making in Latin America: The Case of Mexico." In *Comparative Public Policy in Latin America*, eds. Jordi Díez and Susan Franceschet. Toronto: The University of Toronto Press, 34–53.

2013. "Explaining Policy Outcomes: The Adoption of Same-Sex Unions in Buenos Aires and Mexico City." *Comparative Political Studies* 46, no. 2: 212–35.

Díez, Jordi, and Susan Franceschet. 2012. *Comparative Public Policy in Latin America*. Toronto: University of Toronto Press.

Domedel, Andrea, and Macarena Peña y Lillo. 2008. *El mayo de los pingüinos*. Santiago: Ediciones Radio Universidad de Chile.

Eaton, Kent. 2004. "Risky Business: Decentralization from above in Chile and Uruguay." *Comparative Politics* 37 no. 1: 1–22.

Eltantawy, Nahed. 2008. "Pots, Pans, and Protests: Women's Strategies for Resisting Globalization in Argentina." *Communication and Critical/Cultural Studies* 5, no. 1: 46–63.

Encarnación, Omar. 2011. "Latin America's Gay-Rights Revolution." *Journal of Democracy* 22 no. 2: 104–18.

2013. "International Influence, Domestic Activism, and Gay Rights in Argentina." *Political Science Quarterly* 128, no. 4: 687–716.

Engeli, Isabelle, Christoffer Green-Pedersen, and Lars Thorup Larsen, eds. 2012. *Morality Politics in Western Europe: Parties, Agendas and Policy Choices*. New York: Palgrave Macmillan.

Epstein, Edward. 2003. "The Piquetero Movement of Greater Buenos Aires: Working Class Protest during the Current Argentine Crisis." *Canadian Journal of Latin American and Caribbean Studies* 28, nos. 55–56: 11–36.

Eribon, Didier. 1999. *Réflexions sur la question gay*. Paris: Fayard.

Eskridge, William. 1996. *The Case for Same-Sex Marriage*. New York: Free Press.

Ettelbrick, Paula. 1993. "Since When Is Marriage the Path to Liberation?" In *Lesbians, Gay Men, and the Law*, ed. William B. Rubenstein. New York: New Press, 401–6.

Falleti, Tulia G. 2010. *Decentralization and Subnational Politics in Argentina*. New York: Cambridge University Press.

Fassin, Éric. 2008. *L'inversion de la question homosexuelle*. Paris: Amsterdam.

Figari, Carlos. 2010. "Per scientiam ad justitiam! Matrimonio igualitario en Argentina." *Mediações* 15, no. 1: 125–45.

Foucault, Michel. 1978. *The History of Sexuality: An Introduction*, Vol. 1. New York: Vintage.

Foweraker, Joe. 1990. "Popular Movements and Political Change in Mexico." In *Popular Movements and Political Change in Mexico*, ed. Joe Foweraker and Ann L. Craig. Boulder, CO, and London: Lynne Rienner, 3–20.

Franceschet, Susan. 2004. "Explaining Social Movement Outcomes: Collective Action Frames and Strategic Choices in First- and Second-Wave Feminism in Chile." *Comparative Political Studies* 37, no. 5: 499–530.

2005. *Women and Politics in Chile*. Boulder, CO: Lynne Rienner.

Franceschet, Susan, and Jordi Díez. 2012. "Thinking about Politics and Policymaking in Contemporary Latin America." In *Comparative Public Policy in Latin America*, ed. Jordi Díez and Susan Franceschet. Toronto: University of Toronto Press, 3–33.

Franceschet, Susan, and Jennifer Piscopo. 2013. "Federalism, Decentralization and Reproductive Rights in Argentina and Chile." *Publius* 43, no. 1: 129–50.

Frank, David John, and Elizabeth H. McEneaney. 1999. "The Individualization of Society and the Liberalization of State Policies on Same-Sex Sexual Relations, 1984–1995." *Social Forces* 77: 911–43.

Friedman, Edward. 1999. "The Painful Gradualness of Democratization: Proceduralism as a Necessarily Discontinuous Revolution." In *Democracy and Its Limits: Lessons from Asia, Latin America and the Middle East*, ed. Howard Handleman and Mark Tessler. Notre Dame: University of Notre Dame Press, 321–340.

Friedman, Elisabeth J. 2009a. "Re(gion)alizing Women's Human Rights in Latin America." *Politics and Gender* 5, no. 3: 349–75.

2009b. "Progressive Colonization? The Diffusion of Sexual Rights in Ibero-America." Paper presented at the 2009 Meetings of the Latin American Studies Association, Rio de Janeiro, June 11–14.

2012. "Constructing 'The Same Rights with the Same Names': The Impact of Spanish Norm Diffusion on Marriage Equality in Argentina." *Latin American Politics and Society* 54, no. 4: 29–59.

Fuentes, Claudio. 2012. *El pacto: Poder, constitución y políticas públicas en Chile (1990–2010)*. Santiago: Ediciones Universidad Diego Portales.

Gallegos Montes, Gabriel. 2007. *Patrones de iniciación sexual y trayectorias de emparejamiento entre varones en la Ciudad de México: una mirada biográfica-interaccional en el estudio de la sexualidad*. Doctoral thesis, Centro de Estudios Demográficos y Urbanos, Colegio de México.

Galván Díaz, Francisco. 1988. *El sida en México: los efectos sociales*. México, DF: Universidad Autónoma Metropolitana.

Garay, Candelaria. 2007. "Social Policy and Collective Action: Unemployed Workers, Community Associations and Protest in Argentina." *Politics and Society* 35, no. 2: 301–28.

Gargarella, Roberto. 2010. "Democracia y derechos humanos en los años de Raúl Alfonsín." In *Discutir Alfonsín*, ed. R. Gargarella, M. V. Murillo, and M. Pecheny. Buenos Aires: Siglo Veintiuno, 23–40.

Garretón, Manuel Antonio. 2012. *Neoliberalismo corregido y progresismo limitado: los gobiernos de concertación en Chile 1990–2010*. Santiago: Editorial Arcis.

Garza Carvajal, Federico. 2000. *Vir: Conceptions of Manliness in Andalucía and México, 1561–1699*. Amsterdam: Amsterdamse Historische Reeks.

Giddens, Anthony. 1992. *The Transformation of Intimacy: Sexuality, Love and Eroticism in Modern Societies*. Stanford, CA: Stanford University Press.

González, Francisco. 2008. *Dual Transitions from Authoritarian Rule: Institutionalized Regimes in Chile and Mexico, 1970–2000*. Baltimore, MD: Johns Hopkins University Press.

González Pérez, César Octavio. 2001. "La identidad Gay: Una identidad en tensión." *Desacatos*, Spring–Summer.

González Pérez, María de Jesús. 2007. "La representación de las familias diversas: ley de sociedades de convivencia." *El Cotidiano* 22, no. 146: 21–31.

González Ruiz, Edgar. 2001. *La última cruzada: de los cristeros a Fox.* México, DF: Grijalbo.

——— 2002a. *La sexualidad prohibida: Intolerancia, sexismo y represión.* México, DF: Plaza Janés.

——— 2002b. *Los Abascal: Conservadores a ultranza.* México, DF: Grijalbo.

Grayson, George W. 2011. *Mexican Messiah: Andrés Manuel López Obrador.* University Park: Pennsylvania State University Press.

Green, Adam I. 2002. "Gay but Not Queer: Toward a Post-Queer Study of Sexuality." *Theory and Sexuality* 31, no. 4: 521–45.

Green, James. 1994. "Feathers and Fists: A Comparative Analysis of the Argentine and Brazilian Gay Rights Movements of the 1970s." Paper presented at the Latin American Studies Association, Atlanta, Georgia, March 10.

——— 1999. *Beyond Carnival: Male Homosexuality in Twentieth-Century Brazil.* Chicago: University of Chicago Press.

Greenberg, David F. 1988. *The Construction of Homosexuality.* Chicago: University of Chicago Press.

Grupo de Información en Reproducción Elegida (GIRE). 2012. *Derechos humanos de las mujeres y la protección de la vida prenatal en México.* México, DF: Grupo de Información en Reproducción Elegida, A.C.

Gruzinski, Serge. 1993. *The Conquest of Mexico: The Incorporation of Indian Societies into the Western World, 16th–18th Century.* Cambridge: Cambridge University Press.

Guzmán Bouvard, Marguerite. 1994. *Revolutionizing Motherhood: The Mothers of the Plaza de Mayo.* Oxford: SR Books.

Hagopian, Frances. 2007. "Latin American Citizenship and Democratic Theory." In *Citizenship in Latin America*, ed. Joseph S. Tulchin and Meg Ruthenburg. Boulder, CO: Lynne Rienner, 11–56.

Halley, Janet. 1989. "The Politics of the Closet: Towards Equal Protection for Gay, Lesbian, and Bisexual Identity." *UCLA Law Review* 36: 915–76.

Hass, Liesl. 1999. "The Catholic Church in Chile: New Political Alliances." In *Radical Women in Latin America: Right and Left*, ed. Christian Smith and Joshua Pokopy. University Park: Pennsylvania State University Press, 43–66.

Haussman, Melissa. 2005. *Abortion Politics in North America.* Boulder, CO: Lynne Rienner.

Heclo, Hugh. 1978. "Issue Networks and the Executive Establishment." In *The New American Political System*, ed. Anthony King. Washington, DC: American Enterprise Institute, 87–144.

Hiller, Renata. 2008. "Lazos en torno a la Unión Civil: Notas sobre el discurso opositor." In *Todo sexo es político: Estudios sobre sexualidades en Argentina*, ed. M. Pecheny, C. Figari, and D. Jones. Buenos Aires: Libros del Zorral, 149–67.

——— 2010. "Reflexiones en torno a la Ley de Matrimonio Igualitario." In *Matrimonio Igualitario: Perspectivas sociales, políticas y jurídicas*, ed. Renata Hiller, Rafael de la Dehesa, Ernesto Meccia, and Mario Pecheny. Buenos Aires: Eudeba, 85–130.

2011. "Parlamentos: Tensiones en torno a la representación en el debate sobre el matrimonio gay-lésbico." In *Voces polifónicas: Itinerarios de los géneros y las sexualidades*, ed. M. A. Gutiérrez. Buenos Aires: Ediciones Godot, 167–200.

Hiller, Renata, Aluminé Moreno, and Ana Mallimaci. 2007. "Enlazadas." In *Cumbia, Copeteo y Lágrimas: informe nacional sobre la situación de las travestis, transexuales y transgéneros*, ed. Lohana Berkins. Buenos Aires: Asociación de Lucha por la Identidad Travesti-Transexual, 87–99.

Hipsher, Patricia. 1996. "Democratization and the Decline of Urban Social Movements in Chile and Spain." *Comparative Politics* 28, no. 3: 273–97.

Hochstetler, Kathryn, and Margaret E. Keck. 2007. *Greening Brazil: Environmental Activism in State and Society*. Durham, NC: Duke University Press.

Htun, Mala. 2003a. "Women and Democracy." In *Constructing Democratic Governance in Latin America*, ed. Jorge I. Domínguez and Michael Shifter. Baltimore, MD: Johns Hopkins University Press, 118–36.

2003b. *Sex and the State: Abortion, Divorce and the Family under Latin American Dictatorships and Democracies*. New York: Cambridge University Press.

Htun, Mala, and Timothy Power. 2006. "Gender, Parties and Support for Equal Rights." *Latin American Politics and Society* 48, no. 4: 83–104.

Htun, Mala, and Laurel Weldon. 2012. "The Civic Origins of Progressive Policy Change: Combating Violence against Women in Global Perspective, 1975–2005." *American Political Science Review* 106, no. 3: 548–69.

Inglehart, Ronald. 1988. "The Renaissance of Political Culture." *The American Political Science Review* 82, no. 4: 1203–30.

Inglehart, Ronald, and Christian Welzel. 2005. *Modernization, Cultural Change and Democracy: The Human Development Sequence*. New York: Cambridge University Press.

Insausti, Joaquín. 2014. "La reconstrucción memorial de la persecución estatal de los homosexuales." Paper presented at the XI Argentine Congress of Social Anthropology, Rosario, Argentina, July 23–26.

Jackson, Peter A. 2009. "Capitalism and Global Queering National Markets, Parallels among Sexual Cultures, and Multiple Queer Modernities." *GLQ: A Journal of Lesbian and Gay Studies* 15, no. 3: 357–95.

James, Daniel. 1988. *Resistance and Integration: Peronism and the Argentine Working Class 1946–1976*. Cambridge: Cambridge University Press.

Jamieson, Lynn. 1998. *Intimacy: Personal Relationships in Modern Society*. Cambridge: Polity.

Jáuregui, Carlos. *La homosexualidad en la Argentina*. Buenos Aires: Terso.

Johnson, Diane E. 2001. "Argentina: Parties and Interests Operating Separately by Design and Practice." In *Political Parties and Interest Groups: Shaping Democratic Governance*, ed. Clive S. Thomas. Boulder, CO: Lynne Rienner, 229–46.

Johnson, Erik W. 2008. "Social Movement Size, Organizational Diversity and the Making of Federal Law." *Social Forces* 86, no. 3: 967–93.

Johnson, Erik W., Jon Agnone, and John D. McCarthy. 2010. "Movement Organizations, Synergistic Tactics and Environmental Public Policy." *Social Forces* 88, no. 5: 2267–92.

Johnson, Lyman, and Sonya Lipsett-Rovera, eds. 1998. *The Faces of Honor: Sex, Shame and Violence in Colonial America*. Albuquerque: University of New Mexico Press.

Joignant, Alfredo. 2012. "La raison d'état. Usages politiques du savoir et gouvernement « scientifique » des technopols au Chili (1990–1994)." *Revue Internationale de politique comparée* 19, no. 3: 89–125.

Jones, Mark. 2002. "Explaining the High Level of Party Discipline in the Argentine Congress." In *Legislative Politics in Latin America*, ed. Scott Morgenstern and Benito Nacif. New York: Cambridge University Press, 147–84.

Jones, Mark, and Wonjae Hwang. 2005. "Provincial Party Bosses: Keystone of the Argentine Congress." In *Argentine Democracy: The Politics of Institutional Weakness*, ed. Steven Levitsky and Victoria Murillo. University Park: Pennsylvania State University Press, 115–28.

Kaplan, Morris. 1997. *Sexual Justice: Democratic Citizenship and the Politics of Desire*. New York: Routledge.

Kaplan, Temma. 2006. "Final Reflections: Gender, Chaos and Authority in Revolutionary Times." In *Sex in Revolution: Gender, Politics and Power in Mexico*, ed. Jocelyn Olcott and Mary Kay Vaughn. Durham, NC: Duke University Press, 261–76.

Karl, Terry Lynn. 1990. "Dilemmas of Democratization in Latin America." *Comparative Politics* 23, no. 1: 1–21.

Karst, Kenneth. 1989. *Belonging to America: Equal Citizenship and the Constitution*. New Haven, CT: Yale University Press.

Kaufman, Robert. 1972. *The Politics of Land Reform in Chile, 1950–1970*. Cambridge, MA: Harvard University Press.

Keck, Margaret, and Kathryn Sikkink. 1998. *Activists beyond Borders: Advocacy Networks in International Politics*. Ithaca, NY: Cornell University Press.

Kenny, Meryl. 2007. "Gender, Institutions and Power: A Critical Review." *Politics* 27, no. 2: 97–100.

King, M. Dawn. 2013. "The Role of Societal Attitudes and Activists' Perceptions on Effective Judicial Access for the LGTB Movement in Chile." *Interface* 5, no. 1 (May): 183–203.

Kittilson, Miki Caul. 2006. *Challenging Parties, Changing Parliaments: Women and Elected Office in Contemporary Western Europe*. Columbus: Ohio State University Press.

Kollman, Kelly. 2007. "Same-Sex Unions: The Globalization of an Idea." *International Studies Quarterly* 51: 329–57.

———. 2013. *The Same-Sex Unions Revolution in Western Democracies: International Norms and Domestic Policy Change*. Manchester, UK: Manchester University Press.

Kollman, Kelly, and Matthew Waites. 2012. "United Kingdom: Changing Political Opportunity Structures, Policy Success and Continuing Challenges for Lesbian, Gay and Bisexual Movements." In *The Lesbian and Gay Movement and the State: Comparative Insights into a Transformed Relationship*, ed. Monon Tremblay, David Paternotte, and Carol Johnson. Surrey, UK: Ashgate, 181–95.

Koppleman, Andrew. 1994. "Why Discrimination Against Lesbians and Gay Men Is Sex Discrimination." *New York University Law Review* 69: 197–287.

1996. *Antidiscrimination Law and Social Equality.* New Haven, CT: Yale University Press.

1997. "Sex, Law, and Equality: Three Arguments for Gay Rights." *Michigan Law Review* 95: 1636–67.

Kubal, Mary Rose. 2010. "Challenging Consensus: The Politics of Protest and Policy Reform of Chile's Education System." In *The Bachelet Government: Conflicts and Consensus in Post-Pinochet Chile,* ed. Silvia Borzutzky and Gregory B. Weeks. Gainesville: University of Florida Press, 117–57.

2012. "Transnational Policy Networks and Public Security Policy in Argentina and Chile." In *Comparative Public Policy in Latin America,* ed. Jordi Díez and Susan Franceschet. Toronto: University of Toronto Press, 176–204.

Laguarda, Rodrigo. 2009. *Ser gay en la ciudad de México: Lucha de representaciones y apropiación de una identidad, 1968–1982.* Mexico City: CIESAS.

Lamas, Marta. 2001. "De la autoexclusión al radicalismo participativo. Escenas de un proceso feminista." *Debate Feminista* 23 (April): 97–127.

Larocque, Sylvain. 2006. *Gay Marriage: The Story of a Canadian Social Revolution.* Toronto: James Lorimer and Co.

Lawson, Chappell H. 2002. *Building the Fourth State: Democratization and the Rise of the Free Press in Mexico.* Berkeley: University of California Press.

Lax, Jeffrey R., and Justin H. Phillips. 2009. "Gay Rights in the States: Public Opinion and Policy Responsiveness." *American Political Science Review* 103, no. 3: 367–86.

Lee, Patrick, and Robert George. 1997. "What Sex Can Be: Self-Alienation, Illusion, or One- Flesh?" *American Journal of Jurisprudence* 42: 135–57.

Lemaître, Julieta. 2009. *El derecho como conjuro: fetichismo legal, violencia y movimientos legales.* Bogotá: Siglo del Hombre.

Lewis, Paul. 1990. *The Crisis of Argentine Capitalism.* Chapel Hill: University of North Carolina Press.

Lijphart, Arend. 1968. *The Politics of Accommodation: Pluralism and Democracy in the Netherlands.* Berkeley: University of California Press.

Linz, Juan. 1990. "The Perils of Democracy." *Journal of Democracy* (Winter): 51–69.

Lizárraga, Xabier. 2003. *Una historia socio-cultural de la homosexualidad: Notas sobre un devenir silenciado.* México, DF: Paidós.

Loaeza, Soledad. 1999. *El Partido Acción Nacional: La larga marcha, 1939–1994: Oposición leal y partido de protesta.* México, DF: Fondo de Cultura Económica.

López Lara, Álvaro. 2012. "Comparando el mapa espacial de las legislaturas estatales de México." *Cuadernos da Escola do Legislativo* 13, no. 21: 10–56.

Lopreite, Debora. 2014. "Explaining Policy Outcomes in Federal Contexts: The Politics of Reproductive Rights in Argentina and Mexico." *Bulletin of Latin American Research* 33, no. 4: 389–404.

Loveman, Brian. 1980. *Chile: The Legacy of Hispanic Capitalism.* Oxford: Oxford University Press.

Lozano, Genaro. 2013. "The Battle for Marriage Equality in Mexico, 2000–2011." In *Same-Sex Marriage in Latin America: Promise and Resistance,* ed. Jason

Pierceson, Adriana Piatti-Crocker, and Shawn Schulenberg. Plymouth, UK: Lexington Books, 151–66.

Lumsden, Ian. 1991. *Homosexualidad. Sociedad y Estado en México.* México: Solediciones/Canadian Gay Archives.

Lupien, Pascal. 2011. "The Incorporation of Indigenous Concepts of Plurinationality into the New Constitutions of Ecuador and Bolivia." *Democratization* 18, no. 3: 774–96.

Macdonald, Laura, and Lisa Mills. 2010. "Gender, Democracy and Federalism in Mexico: Implications for Reproductive Rights and Social Policy." In *Federalism, Feminism and Multilevel Governance*, ed. Melissa Haussman, Marian Sawer, and Jill Vickers. Surrey, UK: Ashgate, 187–98.

Macedo, Stephen. 1996. "Against the Old Sexual Morality and the New Natural Law." In *Natural Law, Liberalism, and Morality*, ed. Robert P. George. Oxford: Oxford University Press, 27–48

MacLean, Lauren M. 2010. *Informal Institutions and Citizenship in Africa: Risk and Reciprocity in Ghana and Côte d'Ivoire.* New York: Cambridge University Press.

Madrazo, Alejandro, and Estefanía Vela. 2011. "The Mexican Supreme Court's (Sexual) Revolution?" *Texas Law Review* 89, no. 7: 1867–93.

Maffre, Juliette. 2014. *La légalisation du mariage homosexuel en Argentine.* Paris: L'Harmattan.

Magaloni, Beatriz, and Alejandro Moreno. 2003. "Catching All Souls: The Partido Acción Nacional and the Politics of Religion in Mexico." In *Christian Democracy in Latin America: Electoral Competition and Regime Conflicts*, ed. Scott Mainwaring and Timothy R. Scully. Stanford, CA: Stanford University Press, 247–72.

Magis, Carlos. 2000. "Enlace entre políticas e investigación. El caso del sida." In *De la investigación en salud a la política: La difícil traducción*, ed. Mario Bronfman, Ana Langer Glass, and James Trostle. México: Editorial El Manual Moderno, 91–118.

Mainwaring, Scott and Matthew Soberg Shugart, eds. 1997. *Presidentialism and Democracy in Latin America.* New York: Cambridge University Press.

Mainwaring, Scott, Guillermo O'Donnell, and Samuel Valenzuela, eds. 1992. *Issues in Democratic Consolidation: The New South American Democracies in Comparative Perspective.* Notre Dame: University of Notre Dame Press.

Mainwaring, Scott, Guillermo O'Donnell, Samuel Valenzuela, and Christopher Welna, eds. 2003. *Democratic Accountability in Latin America.* Oxford: Oxford University Press.

Mallimaci, Fortunato. 2000. "Catolicismo y liberalismo: las etapas del enfrentamiento por la definición de la modernidad religiosa en América Latina." *Sociedad y Religión* nos. 20–21: 22–56.

Mamalakis, Markos. 1976. *Growth and Structure of the Chilean Economy: From Independence to Allende.* New Haven, CT: Yale University Press.

Marshall, Thomas H. 1950. *Citizenship and Social Class, and Other Essays.* Cambridge: Cambridge University Press.

Marsiaj, Juan P. 2006. Social Movements and Political Parties: Gays, Lesbians and *Travestis* and the Struggle for Inclusion in Brazil. *Canadian Journal of Latin American and Caribbean Studies* 31, no. 62: 167–96.

2012. "Federalism, Advocacy Networks, and Sexual Diversity Politics in Brazil." In *Comparative Public Policy in Latin America*, ed. Jordi Díez and Susan Franceschet. Toronto: University of Toronto Press, 126–49.

2013. "Neoliberal Incorporation and Sexual Diversity Politics under the PT in Brazil." Paper presented at the 2013 Meeting of the Latin American Studies Association, Washington, DC, May 29–June 1.

Matthews, J. Scott. 2005. "The Political Foundations of Support for Same-Sex Marriage in Canada." *Canadian Journal of Political Science* 38, no. 4: 841–66.

Mattiace, Shannan. 2012. "Social and Indigenous Movements in Mexico's Transition to Democracy." In *The Oxford Handbook of Mexican Politics*, ed. Roderic Ai Camp. New York: Oxford University Press, 398–422.

Mead, Lawrence. 1986. *Beyond: Entitlement: The Social Obligations of Citizenship*. New York: Free Press.

Meier, Kenneth J. 1994. *The Politics of Sin: Drugs, Alcohol and Public Policy*. Armonk, NY: M. E. Sharpe.

1999. "Drugs, Sex, Rock and Roll: A Theory of Morality Politics." *Policy Studies Journal* 27, no. 4: 681–95.

Meyer, David S. 2005. "Social Movements and Public Policy: Eggs, Chicken and Theory." In *Routing the Opposition: Social Movements, Public Policy and Democracy*, ed. David S. Meyer, Valerie Jenness, and Helen Ingram. Minneapolis: University of Minnesota Press, 1–26.

Middlebrook, Kevin J., and Eduardo Zepeda. 2003. "On the Political Economy of Mexican Development Policy." In *Confronting Development: Assessing Mexico's Economic and Social Policy Challenges*, ed. Kevin J. Middlebrook and Eduardo Zepeda. Stanford, CA: Stanford University Press, 3–52.

Mill, John Stuart. 1974. *A System of Logic, Ratiocinative and Inductive: Being a Connected View of the Principles of Evidence and the Methods of Scientific Investigation*. Toronto: University of Toronto Press.

Mogrovejo, Norma. 1999. "Sexual Preference, the Ugly Duckling of Feminist Demands: The Lesbian Movement in Mexico." In *Same-Sex Relations and Female Desires: Transgender Practices across Cultures*, ed. Evelyn Blackwood and Saskia E. Wieringa. New York: Columbia University Press, 308–35.

Mohr, Richard. 1990. *Gays/Justice*. New York: Columbia University Press.

Molyneux, Maxine. 2008. "The 'Neo-Liberal Turn' and the New Social Policy in Latin America: How Neo-Liberal, How New?" *Development and Change* 39, no. 5: 775–97.

Monsiváis, Carlos. 1987. *Entrada libre: crónicas de la sociedad que se organiza*. México: Ediciones Era.

2001. "Los iguales, los semejantes, los (hasta hace un minuto) perfectos desconocidos (A cien años de la redada de los 41)." *Debate Feminista* 12, no. 24 (October): 301–27.

2004. "La emergencia de la Diversidad: las comunidades marginales y sus batallas por la visibilidad." *Debate Feminista* 15, no. 29: 187–205.

Monter, William. 1990. *Frontiers of Heresy: The Inquisition from the Basque Lands to Sicily*. Cambridge: Cambridge University Press.

Mooney, Christopher. 1999. "The Politics of Morality Policy: Symposium Editor's Introduction." *Policy Studies Journal* 27, no. 4: 675–80.

Morgenstern, Scott, and Benito Nacif, eds. 2002. *Legislative Politics in Latin America*. Cambridge: Cambridge University Press.

Mossige, Dag. 2013. *Mexico's Left: The Paradox of the PRD*. Boulder, CO: Lynne Rienner.

Mucciaroni, Gary. 2008. *Same Sex, Different Politics: Success and Failure in the Struggles over Gay Rights*. Chicago: University of Chicago Press.

Nardi, Peter. 1998. "The Globalization of the Gay and Lesbian Socio-Political Movement: Some Observations about Europe with a Focus on Italy." *Sociological Perspectives* 41, no. 3: 567–86.

Narveson, Jan. 2001. *The Libertarian Idea*. Peterborough, ON: Broadview.

Navia, Patricio. 2010. *El díscolo: Conversaciones con Marco Enríquez-Ominami*. Santiago: Debate.

———. 2014a. "Los ayatolas de Michelle Bachelet." Infotalam.com, July 10.

———. 2014b. "Los chilenos prefieren el consenso." Infotalam.com, August 20.

Negretto, Gabriel. 2001. "Procesos constituyentes y distribución de poder: la reforma del presidencialismo en Argentina." *Política y Gobierno* 8, no. 1: 117–66.

Nesvig, Martin. 2001. "The Complicated Terrain of Latin American Homosexuality." *Hispanic American Historical Review* 81: 3–4.

Núñez Noriega, Guillermo. 2000. *Sexo entre Varones: poder y resistencia en el campo sexual*. México: Universidad Nacional Autónoma de México.

———. 2007. *Masculinidades e identidad: identidad, sexualidad y sida*. México: Porrúa.

O'Donnell, Guillermo. 1991. 'Democracia Delegativa.' *Novos Estudos* 31: 25–40.

———. 1998. "Polyarchies and the (Un)Rule of Law in Latin America." Paper presented at the 1998 Meeting of the Latin American Studies Association, Chicago, September 24–26.

Okin, Susan Moller. 1989. *Gender, Justice, and the Family*. New York: Basic Books.

Oppenheim, Lois Hecht. 1993. *Politics in Chile: Democracy, Authoritarianism and the Struggle for Democracy in Chile*. Boulder, CO: Westview Press.

Oxhorn, Philip. 1994. "Where Did All the Protesters Go? Popular Mobilization and the Transition to Democracy in Chile." *Latin American Perspectives* 21, no. 3: 49–68.

———. 1995. *Organizing Civil Society: The Popular Sectors and the Struggle for Democracy in Chile*. Philadelphia: Pennsylvania State University Press.

Pal, Leslie. 2006. *Beyond Policy Analysis: Public Issue Management in Turbulent Times*. Toronto: Nelson.

Pascoe, Peggy. 2000. "Sex, Gender and Same-Sex Marriage." In *Is Academic Feminism Dead? Theory and Practice*, ed. Social Justice Group at the Center for Advanced Feminist Studies. New York: New York University Press, 86–129.

Paternotte, David. 2011. *Revendiquer le mariage gay: Belgique, France, Espagne*. Brussels: University of Brussels.

Paternotte, David, and Kelly Kollman. 2013. "Transnational Networks and the Expansion of LGBT Rights in Europe." In *Global Rights, Global Movements*, ed. Ronald Holzhacker and Kathleen Lahey. New York: New York University Press, 86–129.

Pecheny, Mario, and Rafael de la Dehesa. 2010. "Sexualidades y políticas en América Latina: un esbozo para la discusión." In *Sexualidade e política na América Latina: histórias, interseções e paradoxos*, ed. Sonia Corrêa and Richard Parker. Rio de Janeiro: Sexuality Policy Watch, 31–79.

Pecheny, Mario, Carlos Figari, and Daniel Jones, eds. 2008. *Todo sexo es político: Estudios sobre sexualidades en Argentina*. Buenos Aires: Libros del Zorral.

Perlongher, Néstor. 1985. "Una historia del FLH." In *Homosexualidad: Hacia la Destrucción de los mitos*, ed. Zelmar Acevedo. Buenos Aires: Ediciones del Sur, 272–8.

Peruzzotti, Enrique. 2005. "Demanding Accountable Government: Citizens, Politicians, and the Perils of Representative Democracy in Argentina." In *Argentine Democracy: The Politics of Institutional Weakness*, ed. Steven Levitsky and María Victoria Murillo. University Park: Pennsylvania State University Press, 229–49.

Pettinicchio, David. 2012. "Current Explanations for the Variation in Same-Sex Marriage Policies in Western Countries." *Comparative Sociology* 11: 526–57.

Pew Research Center. 2013. *The Global Divide on Homosexuality: Greater Acceptance in More Secular and Affluent Countries*. Washington, DC: Pew Research Center.

Phelan, Shane. 2001. *Sexual Strangers: Gays, Lesbians and the Dilemmas of Citizenship*. Philadelphia: Temple University Press.

Pierceson, Jason, Adriana Piatti-Crocker, and Shawn Schulenberg. 2010. *Same-Sex Marriage in the Americas: Policy Innovation for Same-Sex Relationships*. Plymouth, UK: Lexington Books.

Pierson, Paul. 1994. *Dismantling the Welfare State: Reagan, Thatcher, and the Politics of Retrenchment*. Cambridge: Cambridge University Press.

Plummer, Ken. 1980. *The Making of the Modern Homosexual*. London: Hutchinson.

2003. *Intimate Citizenship: Private Decisions and Public Dialogues*. Montreal and Kingston: McGill-Queen's University Press.

Polikoff, Nancy. 1993. "We Will Get What We Ask For? Why Legalizing Gay and Lesbian Marriage Will Not 'Dismantle the Legal Structure of Gender in Every Marriage.'" *Virginia Law Review* 79, no. 7: 1535–50.

Politzer, Patricia. 2001. *Fear in Chile: Lives under Pinochet*. New York: Free Press.

Posner, Paul. 2008. *State, Market and Democracy in Chile*. New York: Palgrave Macmillan.

Posner, Richard. 1992. *Sex and Reason*. Cambridge: Cambridge University Press.

Potash, Robert. 1969. *The Army and Politics in Argentina, 1928–1945: Yrigoyen to Perón*. Stanford, CA: Stanford University Press.

1980. *Army and Politics in Argentina, 1945–1962: Perón to Frondizi*. Stanford, CA: Stanford University Press.

Purcell Kaufman, Susan. 1975. *The Mexican Profit Sharing Decision*. Berkeley: University of California Press.

Pye, Lucian W. 1991. "Political Culture Revisited." *Political Psychology* 12: 487–508.

Ranis, Peter. 2006. "Factories without Bosses: Argentina's Experiences with Worker-Run Enterprises." *Labor: Studies in Working-Class History of the Americas* 3, no. 1: 11–23.

Rapisardi, Flavio, and Alejandro Modarelli. 2001. *Fiestas, baños y exilio en la última dictadura.* Buenos Aires: Sudamericana.

Rayside, David. 2008. *Queer Inclusions, Continental Divisions: Public Recognition of Sexual Diversity in Canada and the United States.* Toronto: University of Toronto Press.

——— 2010. "The Distinctive Centrality of Marriage in the United States." In *Same-Sex Marriage in the Americas,* ed. Jason Piercson, Adriana Patti-Crocker, and Shawn Schulenberg. Lanham, MD: Lexington, 203–26.

Rich, Adrienne. 1980. "Compulsory Heterosexuality and the Lesbian Experience." *Signs: Journal of Women in Culture and Society* 5, no. 4 (Summer): 631–60.

Roberts, Kenneth. 1998. *Deepening Democracy? The Modern Left and Social Movements in Chile and Peru.* Stanford, CA: Stanford University Press.

Robles, Victor Hugo. 1998. "History in the Making: The Homosexual Liberation Movement in Chile." *NACLA Report on the Americas* 31, no. 4: 36–44.

——— 2008. *Bandera hueca: Historia del movimiento homosexual de Chile.* Santiago: Cuarto Propio.

Rock, David. 1975. *Politics in Argentina, 1890–1930. The Rise and Fall of Radicalism.* Cambridge: Cambridge University Press.

——— 1987. *Argentina 1516–1987: From Spanish Colonization to Alfonsín.* Berkeley and Los Angeles: University of California Press.

Rodríguez Collao, Luis. 2004. *Delitos Sexuales.* Santiago: Editorial Jurídica de Chile.

Roemer, Andrés. 1998. *Sexualidad, derecho y política pública.* México, DF: Porrúa.

Ross, Marc H. 2009. "Culture and Identity in Comparative Political Analysis." In *Comparative Politics: Rationality, Culture and Structure,* ed. Mark I. Lichbach and Alan S. Zuckerman. New York: Cambridge University Press, 42–80.

Russo, Sandra. 2011. *La presidenta: Historia de una vida.* Buenos Aires: Editorial Sudamericana.

Salessi, Jorge. 1995. *Médicos, maleantes y maricas.* Rosario: Beatriz Viterbo.

Sánchez Fuentes, María Luisa, Jennifer Paine, and Brook Elliott-Buettner. 2008. "The Decriminalisation of Abortion in Mexico City: How Did Abortion Rights Become a Political Priority?" *Gender and Development* 16, no. 2: 345–60.

Schmidt, Samuel. 1991. *The Deterioration of the Mexican Presidency: The Years of Luis Echeverría.* Tucson: University of Arizona Press.

Schulenberg, Shawn. 2010. "Policy Stability without Policy: The Battle for Same-Sex Partnership Recognition in Brazil." In *Same-Sex Marriage in the Americas: Policy Innovation for Same-Sex Relationships,* ed. Jason Piercson, Adriana Piatti-Crocker, and Shawn Schulenberg. Lanham, MD: Lexington, 93–127.

2012. "The Construction and Enactment of Same-Sex Marriage in Argentina." *Journal of Human Rights* 11, no. 1: 106–25.

2013. "The Lavander Tide? LGTB Rights and the Latin American Left Today." In *Same-Sex Marriage in Latin America: Promise and Resistance*, ed. Jason Piercson, Adriana Piatti-Crocker, and Shawn Schulenberg. Lanham, MD: Lexington, 23–39.

Schwaller, John F. 2011. *The History of the Catholic Church in Latin America: From Conquest to Revolution and Beyond*. New York: New York University Press.

Sebreli, Juan José. 1997. *Escritos sobre escritos, ciudades bajo ciudades*. Buenos Aires: Sudamericana.

Sempol, Diego. 2013. "Violence and the Emergence of Gay and Lesbian Activism in Argentina, 1983–90." In *The Sexual History of the Global South: Sexual Politics in Africa, Asia and Latin America*, ed. Saskia Wieringa and Horacio Sívori. New York: Zed, 99–120.

2014. "The Politicization of Sexuality: The LGTBTTBQI Movement and State Regulations in Uruguay (1980–2013)." Paper presented at the 2014 World Pride Human Rights Conference, Toronto, June 25–27.

Serrano, José Fernando. 2011. "Articulación entre la academia, arte, movimientos socials y políticas públicas: diez años de Ciclo Rosa en Colombia." In *Cartografías queer: sexualidades y activismo LGBT en América Latina*, ed. Daniel Balderston and Arturo matute Castro. Pittsburgh: Instituto Internacional de Literatura Iberoamericana, 259–88.

Shirk, David. 2005. *Mexico's New Politics: The PAN and Democratic Change*. Boulder, CO: Lynne Rienner.

Siavelis, Peter. 2014. "From a Necessary to a Permanent Coalition." In *Democratic Chile: The Politics and Policies of a Historic Coalition, 1990–2010*, ed. Kirsten Sehnbruch and Peter M. Siavelis. Boulder, CO: Lynne Rienner, 15–41.

Siavelis, Peter, and Arturo Valenzuela. 1996. "Electoral Engineering and Democratic Stability: The Legacy of Authoritarian Rule in Chile." In *Institutional Design in New Democracies: Eastern Europe and Latin America*, ed. Arend Lijphart and Carlos H. Waisman. Boulder, CO: Westview Press, 77–99.

Sieder, Rachel, Line Schjolden and Alan Angell, eds. 2011. *The Judicialization of Politics in Latin America*. New York: Palgrave Macmillan.

Sigal, Pete. 1997. "The Politicization of Pederasty among the Colonial Yucatecan Maya." *Journal of the History of Sexuality* 8, no. 1: 1–24.

Sigmund, Paul. 1977. *The Overthrow of Allende and the Politics of Chile, 1964–1976*. Pittsburgh: University of Pittsburgh Press.

Silva, Eduardo. 1996. *The State and Capital in Chile: Business Elites, Technocrats, and Market Economics*. Boulder, CO: Westview Press.

Sívori, Horacio Federico. 2004. *Locas, chongos y gays: Sociabilidad homosexual masculina durante la década de 1990*. Buenos Aires: Editorial Antropofagia.

Skocpol, Theda. 2003. "Doubly Engaged Social Science." In *Comparative Historical Analysis in the Social Sciences*, ed. James Mahoney and Dietrich Rueschemeyer. New York: Cambridge University Press, 407–28.

Smith, Anne Marie. 2007. *Welfare Reform and Sexual Regulation*. Cambridge: Cambridge University Press.

Smith, Miriam. 2008. *Political Institutions and Lesbian and Gay Rights in the United States and Canada.* New York: Routledge.

Smith, William. 1989. *Authoritarianism and the Crisis of Argentina's Political Economy.* Stanford, CA: Stanford University Press.

Smulovitz, Catalina. 2012. "Public Policy by Other Means: Playing the Judicial Arena." In *Comparative Public Policy in Latin America*, eds. Jordi Díez and Susan Franceschet. Toronto: The University of Toronto Press, 105–25.

Snow, David A., and Robert D. Benford. 1992. "Master Frames and Cycles of Protest." In *Frontiers in Social Movement Theory*, ed. Aldon D. Morris and Carol McClurg Mueller. New Haven, CT: Yale University Press, 133–55.

Sousa, Lisa Mary. 1997. "Women and Crime in Colonial Oaxaca: Evidence of Complementary Gender Roles in Mixtec and Zapotec Soceties." In *Indian Women of Early Mexico*, ed. Susan Schroeder, Stephanie Wood, and Robert Haskett. Norman: University of Oklahoma Press, 199–214.

Stallings, Barbara. 1978. *Class Conflict and Development in Chile.* Stanford, CA: Stanford University Press.

Stepan, Alfred. 1988. *Rethinking Military Politics: Brazil and the Southern Cone.* Princeton, NJ: Princeton University Press.

Stephen, Lynn. 2002. "Sexualities and Genders in Zapotec Oaxaca." *Latin American Perspectives* 29, no. 2: 41–59.

Stone, Deborah. 2001. *Policy Paradox: The Art of Political Decision Making.* New York: W. W. Norton and Company.

Sutherland, Juan Pablo. 2001. *A corazón abierto. Geografía literaria de la homosexualidad en Chile.* Santiago: Editorial Sudamericana.

Sutter, Anne. 2008. "Movimiento feminista y política partidista en México: la experiencia de Diversa." In *Mujeres y escenarios ciudadanos*, ed. Mercedes Prieto. Quito: FLACSO, 237–55.

Sutton, Barbara. 2007. "Poner el Cuerpo: Women's Embodiment and Political Resistance in Argentina." *Latin American Politics and Society* 49, no. 3: 129–62.

Tamayo, Jaime. 1990. "Neoliberalism Encounters Neocardenismo." In *Popular Movements and Political Change in Mexico*, ed. Joe Foweraker and Ann L. Craig. London and Boulder, CO: Lynne Rienner, 121–36.

Teichman, Judith A. 2001. *The Politics of Freeing Markets in Latin America: Chile, Argentina, and Mexico.* Chapel Hill: University of North Carolina Press.

  2012. "The New Institutionalism and Policy-making in Chile." In *Comparative Public Policy in Latin America*, ed. Jordi Díez and Susan Franceschet. Toronto: University of Toronto Press, 54–77.

Thelen, Kathleen, and Sven Steinmo. 1992. "Historical Institutionalism in Comparative Politics." In *Structuring Politics: Historical Institutionalism in Comparative Analysis*, ed. Sven Steinmo, Kathleen Thelen, and Frank Longstreth. Cambridge: Cambridge University Press, 1–32.

Tomás y Valiente, Francisco. 1990. *Sexo barroco y otras transgresiones premodernas.* Madrid: Alianza.

Torres-Ruiz, Antonio. 2011. "HIV/AIDS and Sexual Minorities in Mexico: A Globalized Struggle for the Protection of Human Rights." *Latin American Research Review* 46, no. 1: 30–54.

Tremblay, Manon, David Paternotte, and Carol Johnson. 2011. *The Lesbian and Gay Movement and the State*. Surrey, UK: Ashgate.

United Nations Development Program (UNDP). 2010. *Human Development Report*. New York: Oxford University Press.

Vaggione, Juan Marco. 2011. "Sexual Rights and Religion: Same-Sex Marriage and Lawmakers' Catholic Identity in Argentina." *University of Miami Law Review* 65, no. 3: 935–54.

Van Cott, Donna Lee. 2007. "Latin American Indigenous Peoples." *Journal of Democracy* 18, no. 4: 127–42.

Vargas Paredes, M. Saúl. 2010. *Entre bosques y reformas de gobierno*. México, DF: Porrúa.

Vela, Stefanía. 2011. "La Suprema Corte y el matrimonio: una relación de amor." Unpublished BA thesis, Faculty of Law, Instituto Tecnológico Autónomo de México, Mexico.

Verdugo, Patricia. 2001. *Chile, Pinochet, and the Caravan of Death*. Coral Gables, FL: North-South Center Press.

Villafuerte García, Lourdes. 2005. "Los estudios del Seminario de Historia de las Mentalidades sobre sexualidad." In *Sexualidades en México: algunas aproximaciones desde la perspectiva de las ciencias sociales*, 2nd ed., ed. Yvonne Szasz and Susana Lerner. Mexico City: El Colegio de México, 251–65.

Villalpando, Waldo, Daniel Feierstein, and Mirando Cassino. 2006. *La discriminación en Argentina: Diagnóstico y propuestas*. Buenos Aires: Eudeba.

Waites, Matthew. 1996. "Lesbian and Gay Theory, Sexuality and Citizenship." *Contemporary Politics* 2, no. 3: 139–49.

Walzer, Michael. 1989. "Citizenship." In *Political Innovation and Conceptual Change*, eds. T. Ball, J. Farr, R. L. Hanson, Cambridge: Cambridge University Press, 211–220.

Wardle, Lynn. 1996. "A Critical Analysis of Constitutional Claims for Same-Sex Marriage." *Brigham Young University Law Review* 1: 1–101

Warner, Michael. 2000. *The Trouble with Normal: Sex, Politics and the Ethics of Queer Life*. Cambridge, MA: Harvard University Press.

Weeks, Jeffrey. 1998. "The Sexual Citizen." *Theory, Culture and Society* 15, no. 3: 35–53.

Weeks, Jeffrey, Brian Heaphy, and Catherine Donovan. 2001. *Same-Sex Intimacies: Families of Choice and Other Life Experiments*. London: Routledge.

Weldon, Laurel. 2012. *When Protest Makes Policy: How Social Movements Represent Disadvantaged Groups*. Ann Arbor: University of Michigan Press.

Weyland, Kurt, Raúl L. Madrid, and Wendy Hunter, eds. *Leftist Governments in Latin America: Successes and Shortcomings*. New York: Cambridge University Press.

Whus, Steven. 2008. *Savage Democracy: Institutional Change and Party Development in Mexico*. University Park: Pennsylvania State University Press.

Wilde, Alexander. 1999. "Irruptions of Memory: Expressive Politics in Chile's Transition to Democracy." *Journal of Latin American Politics* 31, no. 2: 473–500.

Williams, Walter. 1986. *The Spirit and the Flesh: Sexual Diversity in American Indian Culture*. Boston: Beacon Press.

Wintermute, Robert. 1995. *Sexual Orientation and Human Rights.* New York: Oxford University Press.

Yashar, Deborah J. 2005. *Contesting Citizenship in Latin America: The Rise of Indigenous Movements and the Post-Liberal Challenge.* Cambridge: Cambridge University Press.

Young, Iris Marion. 1990. "The Politics of Difference: A Critique of the Ideal of Universal Citizenship." *Ethics* 99: 250–74.

Index

CPSIA information can be obtained
at www.ICGtesting.com
Printed in the USA
LVHW051731240720
661455LV00002B/99

9 781107 491854